THE STATE OR THE MARKET

THE STATE OR THE MARKET

Politics and Welfare in Contemporary Britain

2nd edition

edited by
**Martin Loney, Robert Bocock, John Clarke,
Allan Cochrane, Peggotty Graham and
Michael Wilson**

(S) Sage Publications
London · Newbury Park · New Delhi
in association with The Open University

Chapter One © Tom Hulley and John Clarke, 1991.
Chapter Seven © Mary MacLeod and Esther Saraga, 1988.
First published in *Feminist Review* (28): 16–55.
Chapter Eight © Felicity Edholm, 1982. First published in
E. Whitelegg *et al.* (eds) *The Changing Experience of
Women.* Oxford: Martin Robertson. Reprinted by kind
permission.
Chapter Eleven ©Yvette Rocheron and *Critical Social
Policy*, 1988. First published in *Critical Social Policy* (22):
5–23. Reprinted by kind permission.
Chapter Eighteen © Fiona Williams, 1989. First published in
F. Williams, *Social Policy: A Critical introduction.*
Cambridge: Polity Press. Reprinted by kind permission.

SAGE Publications Ltd
6 Bonhill Street
London EC2A 4PU

SAGE Publications Inc
2455 Teller Road
Newbury Park, California 91320

SAGE Publications India Pvt Ltd
32, M-Block Market
Greater Kailash – 1
New Delhi 110 048

British Library Cataloguing in Publication Data
The state of the market: Politics and welfare in
contemporary Britain. – 2nd ed.
I. Loney, Martin   II. Bocock, Robert
III. Clarke, John
361.60941085

ISBN 0–8039–8641–6
ISBN 0–8039–8642–4 pbk

Library of Congress catalog card number 91 050667

Typeset by Photoprint, Torquay, Devon
Printed and bound in Great Britain by
Biddles Ltd, Guildford and King's Lynn

Contents

Preface and acknowledgements

This Reader is published in conjunction with the Open University second-level course D211: *Social Problems and Social Welfare*. Its second edition has been prepared to coincide with revisions made to the course, and it has been expanded by the inclusion of new material. The chapters it contains are a mix of material specially commissioned by the course team and material reprinted from elsewhere. *Social Problems and Social Welfare* is a course which ranges widely over British society from the individual and the family to conflicts over economic and social policy; from birth to old age; from the public to the private and the shifting boundaries between them. Like other Open University Social Sciences courses, it does not aim to teach a discrete body of facts nor to communicate a set of received wisdoms; rather it seeks to provide students with a solid grounding in the social sciences and a critical awareness of the competing perspectives which offer to explain, inform and change our world.

The production of this book has been made easier by the efforts of a number of people. In particular, we want to acknowledge our debt to the Social Sciences Faculty secretaries who have worked on this book, especially Ann Boomer and Deborah Scotney, and the creative and diligent editing services provided by Melanie Bayley. Hilary Canneaux, Pat Coombes and Varrie Scott provided valuable help in organizing the contributions and facilitating the many meetings which are an inevitable part of the Open University's work.

John Clarke
Allan Cochrane
Peggotty Graham
Michael Wilson

Introduction

'The State or the Market?' is a title which reflects the political conflict over the provision of social welfare in the 1980s. The foundations of this conflict lie in the 'post-war settlement' which created a mixed economy with government intervention in economic policy supported by an expanding system of state welfare. Although the state was never the sole provider of social welfare, the post-war political consensus certainly involved the assumption that it would be the primary provider. Other agencies, such as private health and education or voluntary organizations, had supporting rather than central roles.

The emergence of the question 'The State or the Market?' arises from the break-up of these post-war conditions. The 'settlement' of the mixed economy and expanding state welfare was broken by the impact of a deepening economic crisis during the 1970s, such that the British economy could no longer deliver on its social promises. In particular, it was claimed, the continuing expansion of state-provided welfare could not be funded. Subsequently, the political 'consensus' which had supported that settlement was also broken by the emergence of the 'new conservatism' under the leadership of Margaret Thatcher. Although this new conservatism was made up of many ideological and political strands (see Part III), one central feature was its hostility to the conditions of the post-war settlement, and to the expanded role of state welfare, in particular. It expressed this hostility in commitments to roll back the state, give pre-eminence to market forces, free welfare consumers from the bureaucratic monopolies of state welfare and allow individuals to take responsibility for their own lives.

Both the collapse of the post-war settlement and the rise to power of a new 'ideological politics' in the Conservative governments of the 1980s had profound effects on the other actors in British politics. Labour's failure in government to significantly affect the distribution of wealth and income in Britain or to reverse Britain's long post-war economic decline provided a platform for those who sought more radical solutions. One effect was the creation of the Social Democratic Party by Labour defectors. During the decade of Conservative electoral dominance, the 'centre ground' of British politics has seen a complex series of alliances and realignments following this initial breakaway. The Labour Party itself increasingly sought to lay claim to this centre ground, eschewing the possibility of presenting a radical left-wing opposition to the radicalism of the Right. Latterly, the replacement of Margaret Thatcher by John Major as leader of the Conservative Party threatens to make the political centre even more crowded, since his leadership appears to mark, if not the end of 'ideological politics', then certainly the end of the confrontational style of 'conviction politics' which dominated the 1980s.

Although, like others, we have talked of the 'centre ground' of politics, it is important to remember that this centre is not a permanently fixed point, but a moving target whose place is defined in relation to the other political ideologies around at the time. The result of the 1980s is that the political centre is now placed considerably further to the Right than could ever have been imagined in the 1960s or 1970s. This shift of the centre marks the success of both the ideological onslaught of the new conservatism and the changes in the social, economic and political shape of British society which successive Conservative governments have helped to bring about. The widening gap between rich and poor, the widened role of the market as against the state and the restructuring of the welfare state all represent new starting points for the other political parties.

Social welfare has been in the forefront of the changes during the 1980s. It was a focal point for new Conservative attacks on the errors of the post-war consensus. The welfare state was costly, wasteful, bureaucratic and held the position of a monopoly supplier of services, inhibiting the exercise of consumer choice. Worse still, the welfare state embodied many of the errors of the liberal and permissive political culture of the 1960s. The provision of benefits and services was seen as promoting a 'dependency culture' undermining the individual's intrinsic self-reliance and independence. In other ways, the welfare state undermined sources of traditional authority, particularly those of the family, by taking too much responsibility to itself and its band of experts.

With these criticisms levelled against it, it is not surprising that the welfare state has experienced considerable changes during the 1980s. Indeed, what may be more surprising is the level of continuity in welfare provision in Britain, rather than the pace of change. Levels of social spending have remained stable and even increased in relation to some services and much of the basic infrastructure of welfare provision has not been subjected to any radical degree of reconstruction. Three processes may account for the failure of the expected assault on the welfare state to appear during the 1980s. The first is the continuing, and in some forms, increased demand for welfare provision as a consequence of both demographic and social changes. The increasing numbers of elderly people, rising levels of unemployment, family poverty and home-lessness have all added to pressures on welfare services, as have the discovery of 'new' social problems such as child abuse, and sexual abuse in particular. The other two pressures are more directly political. One concerns the degree to which the constituency of Conservative supporters and voters have direct interests in the continuation of particular benefits from public spending (in such areas as education and mortgage tax relief, for example), such that party electoral calculations limited the room for government action. The other is that the welfare state, or at least particular aspects of the state's welfare function, retained a very high level of public support throughout the 1980s. This was most visible in relation to the National Health Service, as measured in public opinion surveys; in the ability of NHS workers to be able to call on public support in resisting proposed changes, and in the way in which successive Conservative governments have felt obliged to reassure the public that 'the NHS is safe with us'.

The result of these social and political processes is that the wholesale dismantling of the welfare state which many anticipated never took place. That does not mean that there have been no changes. On the contrary, there has been a major reconstruction of welfare provision in Britain, but it has taken more complex and less visible forms than the promise to 'roll back the state' implied. Here we want to draw attention to three main aspects of those changes. The first concerns the shift in the 'mixed economy of welfare', which has seen a shrinking role for state provision and an expanded role for non-state agencies. By non-state agencies we refer to the range of groups increasingly active in the provision of welfare from private enterprise (especially in health care and education) through the voluntary sector (especially in social services and housing) to the family and personal patterns of support. The second concerns the internal reorganization of state services to create new patterns of control of the way welfare works and is delivered. In some cases, there has been increasing direct central government control (for example, over the curriculum in education). In others, there has been the introduction of market forces through greater competition, for example in much of the work of local authorities and latterly in the NHS. Elsewhere, there have been moves to allow and encour-age institutions, ranging from hospitals to schools to housing groups, to 'opt out' of state control.

Finally, the decade of the 1980s was marked by a whole series of moves to tip the public balance between state and private welfare provision. Put simply, this means a sustained effort to make state provision less attractive than its new competitors, such that state services come to feel like a point of last rather than first resort for welfare users. In some cases public funds have been used to support the development of non-state alternatives, as in tax benefits for switching to non-state pension plans or extra funding for schools opting out of local authority control. In others, state services are themselves suffering reduced access or more punitive conditions, which make them less attractive (long NHS waiting lists, residual public sector housing and so on).

In all these ways (and more), the welfare state is changing its character, becoming more 'residual' – the choice of those who have no other choice. It means that the ground of any future politics of welfare has changed considerably: new arrangements, structures and patterns of use have been created which present new starting points for welfare planning. We cannot know what future historians will make of these processes and their effects on the development of welfare in Britain. The purpose of this Reader is to help understand how we got here – to the present mixture of social problems and social welfare that marks contemporary Britain.

The chapters in this Reader trace some of the shape of this web of politics, policy and problems. Some deal with the long-running significance of social problems whose hold on welfare politics is a powerful one, such as poverty and old age. Others deal with ideas and ideologies about the family and their effects on shaping of views about social problems and how they can be responded to. Some are more directly focused on the political arguments of the 1980s and how they shaped the prevailing conflicts over the development of welfare. In that sense, they are already 'historical' pieces, representing the state of argument at a particular time. But from that history, we may learn something of how we got to where we are now.

As editors, we have deliberately sought to include material from a wide range of both social science and political perspectives. The collapse of the post-war consensus means that neither the politics of welfare nor the study of welfare can proceed in a 'neutral' or 'value-free' climate of discussion as social scientists once believed. We are committed to the view that one of the purposes of the social sciences is to provide the means of understanding the diversity of arguments and the means of assessing their consequences. We believe this Reader makes a modest contribution to that process.

I
PRIVATE GRIEFS AND PUBLIC SORROWS

The introduction has indicated the arrival of a new 'welfare order', and emphasizes that with it has come also a whole new set of starting points for welfare planning. At the same time, and as many of the early assumptions about the nature of social problems and social welfare have been superseded by the new ideas, there have been new controversies around the definition of social problems, about who decides whether problems get on the social agenda for action, about what constitute appropriate forms of intervention, and about what, in the increasing 'residualism' of the welfare state of the Thatcher years, is appropriate for intervention by the welfare state at all.

The chapters in this section are all in their different ways concerned with illustrating just how much has been opened up by these new ideas and political conflicts, even if they also illustrate that there are some profound continuities, as John Ditch in his chapter on the deserving/undeserving poor reminds us only too clearly. The section starts with the new questions surrounding social problem definition. These are the subjects of the chapter by Tom Hulley and John Clarke, which offers an analysis of how social problems are defined, of who has the power to make such definitions, and of the interrelationship of that power with prevailing ideologies and discourses. They take an historical look at how past notions of 'deviancy' grounded in individual pathology models of causation continue powerfully to underpin the contemporary tendency to blame the individual for his or her own misfortunes. They contrast this with the social constructionist process of social definition, highlighting the key role played in this by particular social ideas, institutions and ideologies in defining our understanding of the 'normal'. This is linked with the argument that there are certain powerful ideologies and discourses which then provide us with the sets of structural global and local maps that enable us to place ourselves and others within (or without) particular social and ideological norms. It is this placing and the power to place which then define certain individuals and/or groups as 'normal' or 'deviant' and in the case of the latter as a 'social problem'. An important emphasis of this chapter in terms of concerns for welfare is its argument that such ideological definitions, which may themselves shift (witness what has happened over the 1980s), have real consequences for the people involved. That this is likely to be of particular concern where such shifts result also in major changes in what is seen as the legitimate boundary for intervention is itself illustrated by the arguments about individual responsibility (and the difficulties then faced by those struggling to live on reduced social security) which have accompanied the 'rolling back' of the state.

In the second chapter, John Ditch's investigation into how the distinction between the 'deserving' and 'undeserving' poor has been a recurrent theme in the definition of poverty over the ages is a reminder that while much may have changed, and while we may in principle be better at analysing social problems within a wider social context, a great deal stays the same. As Ditch shows, the idea that at least some of the poor are poor because of their own faults and failings (the 'undeserving') has played a significant role in the creation of policies directed at poverty from the nineteenth century right through to the 1990s. Indeed, while Mrs Thatcher may be said to have presided over a new era of 'blaming the victim' she did no more than reassert a set of definitions about the nature of poverty and its causes which have proved highly resistant to change. As a result, the policies which were pursued in the 1980s have, in Britain, left the poor relatively even poorer, and consequently with little power to effect new definitions of their own state or to exercise the control over their own lives promised by the rhetoric of individual responsibility.

The elderly probably continue to count as one of the most obviously 'deserving' groups of the poor. And even though today some 'young pensioners' (with access to private pension schemes and housing capital) may be less relatively poor than in the past, there is little dispute that the very elderly (over-85s) tend to be amongst the poorest of all. Here again, the issue of the links between definitions of problems and social policy remain significant. Thus, as Alan Walker puts it, any 'consideration of the relationship between ageing and social policy must take as its starting point the dominant values of the society in which those policies are framed'. In this case Walker sees one central definition as having been pre-eminent in shaping and dominating the making of social policy about old age in Britain – that the elderly are a dependent and non-productive social group. And he argues that not only have social policies reflected this assumption of dependence, but that in reflecting it, they have also reinforced a dependent status for the elderly, and with it a lack of power for elderly people to define their own problems.

The next three chapters in this section, by Joan Cooper, Patrick Minford and Ann Davis, take a different angle on its central concerns and explore the way in which political conflict over welfare has developed in relation to the future role of just one particular aspect of the welfare state – social work. The focus is on social work in part because as a state service its main development took place alongside the expansion of the welfare state in the period of the post-war consensus; in part because it has come to occupy a central place as the main provider of personal social services for a whole variety of client groups; and in part because it has proved to be one of the most controversial areas of state welfare provision, especially since the late 1970s. The three chapters represent different facets of that controversy. Although written in the middle 1980s and thus not addressing some of the most recent changes in social work, they nevertheless capture some of the most important arguments and pressures which have surrounded social work in recent years. One strand in this controversy has been the argument of the New Right in the 1980s that welfare should be a private rather than a public matter, that the state should be 'rolled back' and that welfare provision should be confined to the provision of a safety net. This view is developed in Patrick Minford's contribution, in which he argues that the state should provide only minimal support, allowing individuals to take greater responsibility for, and to exercise greater choice over, their own welfare. Within such a changed balance of public and private provision, the role for state social work would be much reduced, and focused around a set of residual responsibilities. This argument has found considerable support in Conservative policy-making about welfare, and the promotion of 'consumer choice' has been a central part of their welfare politics throughout the 1980s. This has not, however, resulted in any lessening in the demand for social workers as the providers of services of last resort.

This would not be at all surprising to Joan Cooper, whose argument is that there will always be a continuing demand for social work to continue much as it is. She suggests that there remains a whole series of social problems – of personal crises, needs and deprivation – with which neither private solutions nor other forms of state provision can cope. While these problems persist, so will the need for a service which can respond flexibly to provide personalized care and assistance in moments of crisis. Cooper is relatively sanguine about the ability of the professionals to define the problems and deliver welfare appropriately and sees current models of social work aimed primarily at the individual as appropriate and capable of doing this job. Ann Davis would not agree with this last point, since she is not convinced that the current way of providing social work is adequate. However, she does agree that social work has always been a service for the poor and that the persistence of poverty and its devastating personal consequences mean there continues to be a need for a social work service. Like others on the Left, she argues that the future of social work depends on confronting the issues of political and professional power in which the service is enmeshed, and which define the boundaries of intervention. Thus, in Davis' view it is only by opening up control and accountability to the clients of social work and the communities that social workers aim to serve, and by opening out the power to define what the problem is (or is not) that social work can move forward. The services which social work can provide are still needed, but they need to be delivered through different arrangements of political and professional power.

The final chapter of this section, by Mary Macleod and Esther Saraga, confronts the issue which has come to dominate the world of social work during the late 1980s and early 1990s – the sexual abuse of children. From Cleveland to Rochdale and the Orkneys, social workers have found themselves enmeshed in major public controversies about how to respond to the discovery of sexual abuse. Where in the physical abuse cases of earlier years they came under attack for doing too little, too late, in the sexual abuse cases they have been accused of doing too much, too soon. In part, this is because the sexual abuse of children raises uncomfortable anxieties about the private world of the family and sexuality within it, and disbelief that 'normal' men (for sexual abuse is an almost exclusively male activity) can behave in this way. Although research and survey evidence suggests that sexual abuse within families is widespread, discovery and action by social workers attracts enormous hostility and has created a backlash from individuals and institutions defending the rights of the parent. Macleod and Saraga's chapter explores the silence over the nature of sexual abuse, as opposed to the intense public debate about what social workers should or should not do. They then consider some of the assumptions about family relationships which have influenced patterns of intervention. Sexual abuse has become the dominant frame for the politics of social work at present, but it intersects with, rather than displaces, the other concerns about what sort of social work service is to be provided and under what political and professional conditions. What Macleod and Saraga insist needs to be added to these considerations is an understanding of the intersection between social work and the social relations of age and gender within the family.

In their different ways each of these chapters illustrates how significant the break-up of the welfare consensus has been and just how many welfare issues are now opened up to political and ideological conflict. By focusing on one aspect of the welfare state, social work, which works on the intersection of the public and private worlds, it is also possible to see just how many of the prevailing assumptions of the 1960s and 1970s have been dismantled or called into question. These chapters also illustrate how the ending of consensus brought with it a series of questions. Who has the power to define social problems? Whose definitions of problems prevail? What sort of responses and interventions follow from those definitions and will be made to those problems?

Such questions will remain as significant for understanding the creation of any new political consensus as they are for tracing the break-up of the post-war variety.

1
Social problems: social construction and social causation

Tom Hulley and John Clarke

There is a simple, but valuable, distinction between two ways of approaching the explanation of social problems. On the one hand, there are claims that problems arise from the defects of particular individuals. On the other, they are seen as the result of particular patterns of social organization. There are, of course, intermediate explanations which try to merge these individual and structural approaches in differing combinations. We shall return to these later but this basic distinction between individual and structural approaches provides the most useful starting point.

One very familiar example of a social problem – poverty – illustrates the significance of this basic distinction. We can see that some people are visibly badly dressed, poorly housed, under-nourished, short of money and generally worse off than others. We can add to this figures detailing the different sources and levels of income which enable us to define who the poorest members of our society are. But identifying poverty is not the same as explaining it. 'Why', we may innocently enquire, 'do some people have less money?'

Structural explanations of this condition would focus on the social patterns involved in the distribution of wealth and income. The inequalities in this distribution would be explained by reference to the way in which society, and particularly, the economy, is organized. The individual character or behaviour of poor people would not be a feature of this analysis. By contrast, individualist explanations would focus on the shortcomings of those individuals who fail to do as well as others. They point to defects in the character, personality or behaviour of individuals which have impaired their chances to progress in life.

Although we have distinguished these two approaches to the explanation of social problems, it is important to note that one of them – the individualist approach – is both more familiar and more popular. Whatever social problem is being discussed, there is a strong likelihood that the explanations which first spring to mind will be ones which start from the defects of individuals. This predominance of individualist explanations is true both in the social sciences and in what we might call 'everyday' accounts of social problems: what 'everybody knows' about poverty, unemployment, crime, and so on. This leaning towards individualism produces two problems for the study of social problems within the social sciences. The first is that introducing structural explanations of social problems runs 'against the grain' of what is commonly understood or taken for granted. This mismatch between structural explanations and the individualist tendency of everyday accounts of social problems is what underpins the criticism that 'social scientists make excuses for' whoever is seen as the problem. Individualist explanations keep a tidy fit between the cause of a social problem (individual defects) and the pressure to identify someone as responsible/guilty/at fault. The second problem which the predominance of individualist explanations raises is that of how to account for this dominance and to explore its consequences for social problems. These questions are also associated with criticisms levelled at social scientists; that they are disruptive, radical or critics of the status quo by asking difficult questions about what is 'taken for granted' by members of a society.[1]

Leaving such criticisms aside for the moment, let us look further at the individualist or defect explanations of social problems. We said earlier that such explanations were more popular in the social sciences themselves as well as in everyday accounts. Indeed, whole branches of sociology, psychology and criminology have devoted themselves to the search for the defects which cause social problems. We might define this as the attempt to discover the 'X' factor; the thing which distinguishes 'normal' people from those (the 'deviant') who are the cause of social problems: what is it that makes some people become poor/commit crimes/use drugs/get divorced when most people do not? Even if we just take one of those problems – why do some people commit crimes? – the list of possible candidates for the 'X' factor is enormous. There is something different about their upbringing, their mental processes, their relationship with their parents, their absorption of morality, the area in which they live or their biology. The earliest criminologists placed considerable emphasis on biology as the factor which distinguished the 'criminal type' from the normal citizen. Cesare Lombroso, for example, described his discovery of the 'secret' of criminality while examining the skull of the famous brigand Vihella:

> This was not merely an idea but a flash of inspiration. At the sight of that skull, I seemed to see all of a sudden, lighted up as a vast plain under a flaming sky, the problem of the nature of the criminal – an atavistic being who reproduces in his person the ferocious instincts of primitive

humanity and the inferior animals. Thus were explained anatomically the enormous jaws, high cheek bones, prominent superciliary arches, solitary lines in the palms, extreme size of the orbits, handle-shaped or sensile ears found in criminals, savages and apes, insensitivity to pain, extremely acute sight, tattooing, excessive idleness, love of orgies and the irresistible craving for evil for its own sake, the desire not only to extinguish life in the victim but to mutilate the corpse, tear its flesh and drink its blood. [Lombroso, 1911: xiv]

Eighty years later, Lombroso's description looks somewhat ridiculous but it shares the same organizing principle with more recent and more reasonable-sounding approaches. The search for the 'X' factor has continued, embracing such diverse issues as poor parenting, bad schooling, rates of hormonal activity and chromosomal structure. Just as in Lombroso's comparison of the skulls of criminals with the skulls of the law-abiding, the search for the 'X' factor has been based on comparisons between two 'populations': the deviant and the normal. If one could find the factor which separated these two populations, one might be in a position to stop people being deviant or at least know whom to watch carefully. In the early 1960s, however, an American sociologist raised a fundamental challenge to this view of how to go about explaining deviance. In *Outsiders* (1963), Howard Becker argued that rather than deviance being the property of an act, it was in fact a 'label' – a social definition – attached to the act by others:

> Social groups create deviance by making the rules whose infraction constitutes deviance and by applying those rules to particular people and labelling them as outsiders. From this point of view, deviance is *not* a quality of the act the person commits but rather a consequence of the application by others of rules or sanctions to an 'offender'. The deviant is one to whom that label has successfully been applied; deviant behaviour is behaviour that people so label. [Becker, 1963: 9]

This brief observation revolutionized the study of social problems. It has two consequences to which we want to draw particular attention. In relation to the search for the 'X' factor, it questions the assumption that we can separate out 'deviants' and 'normals' in order to compare them, because the separation itself is a social process. Some people are caught, tried and as a result labelled as 'criminals' – but we cannot be sure that all law-breakers have been caught and found guilty, nor can we be sure that all those found guilty have in fact broken the law. Miscarriages of justice are not unknown. The result is that the 'deviant' population may contain 'normals', while the 'normal' population will contain undiscovered 'deviants'. As a result, comparison between them as if they were 'pure' populations will be flawed. Let us take a hypothetical example. If we suggest that people of low intelligence are more likely to break the law, and discover that the average intelligence of the prison population is lower than the average intelligence of those not in prison, we can draw up the following grid:

Below Average Intelligence	Above Average Intelligence
+ (commit criminal acts)	− (do not commit criminal acts)

Figure 1

But we must also take account of the fact that our populations may not be pure: that is, they may include both 'false positives' (people of low intelligence who have not broken the law) and 'false negatives' (people of average to high intelligence who have broken the law but got away with it):

Below Average Intelligence	Above Average Intelligence
+ (commit criminal acts)	− (do not commit criminal acts)
− (falsely accused of committing criminal acts)	+ (commit criminal acts but are not discovered)

Figure 2

This picture may be further complicated by the way the factor itself can affect the process of 'labelling'. In this example, it is possible that law-breakers of average to high intelligence are more successful at evading discovery. Using such factor analysis to predict who is or will be deviant always carries with it the problems of false negatives and false positives. We may as a result be concentrating on the wrong people. The only thing that we can be sure that the 'known deviants' have in common is that they have been subject to the labelling process itself. They have been socially defined as deviant.

It is this process of social definition or social construction which is Becker's major contribution to the study of social problems. It opens up a series of questions for the social sciences to consider:

1   What conditions come to be defined as social problems? (For example, the maltreatment of children took place long before *child abuse* was defined as a social problem.)
2   Who defines them? Which individuals or groups have the power or authority to identify conditions as social problems?
3   How are they defined? What are the causes or explanations advanced for the problem being defined?
4   What are the social consequences of these definitions? Responses to a social problem are shaped by definitions of its cause; for example, explanations which put low intelligence as a cause of criminality led to arguments that the breeding of future generations of people with low intelligence should be restricted.

These questions concern the social *construction* of social problems, rather than their social *causation*. In British society, the process of constructing social problems tends to have a number of common features. First, social problems are identified with deviant or abnormal *minorities*, who are contrasted with an assumed normal majority. Attempts to define social problems in ways which challenge this abnormal minority/normal majority construction of problems are likely to be resisted very strongly. For example, in the social construction of drug-taking as a social problem, definitions of drug-taking which argued that most British adults were drug users (including use of alcohol, tobacco, tranquillizers, sleeping pills, and so on) were marginalized in favour of definitions of the drug problem as confined to a deviant minority who took 'illegal' drugs.

Secondly, the distinction between normal and deviant tends to fit with individualist 'defect' explanations of the problem: deviants have the 'X' factor which separates them from the normal majority. In this process, our view of the 'normal' is as important as the explanation for why some are deviant. What is identified as normal is a whole bundle of expectations about how people will live their lives in our society. 'We' grow up in families, go to school, get qualifications, get jobs, fall in love, get married, buy a house, have children, look after them, send them to school, and so on. Although many people's lives do not, in fact, fit these expectations, they nevertheless persist as an ideal of what normal life is like, against which we measure 'deviants'.

Thirdly, these expectations – these 'norms' – are social. That is, they are specific to a particular society (Britain) at a particular point in its history (the late twentieth century). Other societies have different patterns of expectations – about families, gender roles within families and the nature of work. Our own society has had different expectations at other points in its history. For example, the expectation that it is normal to buy a house is relatively recent. For earlier generations it was a privilege restricted to the comparatively wealthy. Equally, think how norms about bringing up children have changed since the Victorian expectation that 'children should be seen and not heard'. In spite of norms being socially and historically specific, the particular pattern of norms is equated in most societies with the 'natural' way of doing things. The dominant view of normal life often assumes that it fits with a natural (or God-given) order. This view denies that norms are *chosen* and also ignores important variations between cultures and through time.

In Britain ideas of family life play a central role in this cluster of normal/natural ideas about social behaviour and social problems. Indeed, the idea of the family provides a point at which our views of what is normal and what is natural meet. The family is seen as the natural institution through which people grow and develop, where they learn social identities, acquire values and learn how to behave properly. These ideas of family life interlock with other patterns of social expectations about what is normal and natural – in particular, expectations about gender and age. At its simplest, this network of ideas assumes that women will care for children and make a home while men take responsibility for earning the material necessities, making essential decisions and offering protection to the other members of the family. Families begin with a heterosexual couple who provide the stable base from which to produce and bring up children. Children remain in the household until they reach adulthood, moving from a state of dependence towards increasing independence. These elements form the core of what has been called 'familial ideology' and are also the basis of 'traditional morality' in Britain.

The links between these patterns of ideas and the processes of defining social problems are sketched in Figure 3, showing how familial ideology connects to the identification of differences between the normal and deviant, and how deviance is likely to be identified as the result of a 'defect' (that is, those causing social problems lack something which makes the rest of 'us' normal).

Societies are not static, and the precise pattern of prevailing or dominant social norms is liable to change. For example, the rising numbers of divorces and remarriages may come to be accepted as

Figure 3   *The social construction of social problems*

part of 'normal' family life (rather than the presumption of lifelong partnerships). But their acceptance is not just a matter of whether they are 'statistically normal' (whether the majority of marriages end in separation or divorce) but it is also a matter of ideological conflict about what should be treated as normal. This process of determining what is commonly accepted as normal shows that norms are chosen rather than natural. During the 1980s in Britain, for example, proponents of traditional morality have been trying to promote a return to the 'old certainties' (the security of proper family life, in particular) in the face of what they see as a 'liberalization' of moral values (easier divorces, more single-parent families, and so on). Ideological conflict tends to be important in affecting where the line between 'normal' and 'deviant' is drawn but the fundamental principle of distinguishing between the two remains central to the processes of constructing social problems and still tends to produce a view of deviance as the result of an individual defect.

Figure 4 traces this line of connection between deviance and defect, as well as adding two new elements to the original Figure 3: ideology/discourse and intervention. Our views of the distinction between normal and deviant are underpinned by the prevailing ideologies and discourses which produce definitions of the normal and acceptable and which present explanations of the abnormal and deviant. By ideologies and discourses, we refer to sets of interlinked beliefs which provide ways of mapping and defining reality. As 'social maps' they lead to particular courses of action by providing ways of orienting ourselves to the world in which we live – like maps they identify the best routes to take and which behaviours are not allowed: the 'no entry' signs for disapproved behaviour. Although there are more complex arguments, for us the most important distinction between ideologies and discourses lies in their 'global' and 'local' qualities. By ideologies we tend to refer to wide-ranging systems of ideas which link individuals, social institutions like the family, gender roles, politics and the shape of the overall society

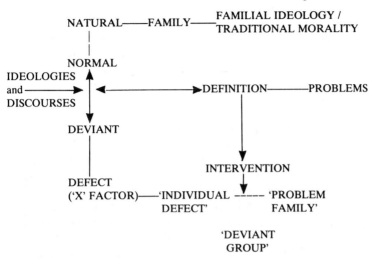

Figure 4 *Social construction and social intervention*

and its place in the world. To follow the map analogy, ideologies are maps of the overall structure which allow us to place ourselves and discern the main lines of connection to everywhere else. Discourses are more 'local' – the detailed maps of a particular aspect of the society. They are associated with specialized knowledge or expertise and tend to be the province of 'experts'. The rest of us know such maps are there and the experts (doctors, lawyers, social workers and so on) can be consulted if needed. Although such 'maps' are more local, they have important consequences for the wider social ideologies because of the authority that accompanies 'expertise'. Wider social ideologies draw on such specific discourses in framing the images of the society (for example in our notions of the rule of law, health, mental health and the like). At the same time, discourses tend to embody the main dimensions of dominant social ideologies and then work them out in more complex detail (for example, the medical profession's production of knowledge about 'normal' and 'abnormal' sexuality).

Two other things need to be said about ideology and discourse. Both are not stable or fixed. In most societies a dominant ideology can be identified as well as resistances to it from other ideological positions. In modern British society, the dominant ideology is a *hybrid* created out of the acceptance of patriarchal and capitalist relations; liberal-democratic government; and a particular set of values derived mainly from Judaeo-Christian tradition. Extending this 'hybrid' analogy, the ideology changes over time but different 'strains' retain the same key elements. It is challenged by sub-ordinate ideologies, which may be non-patriarchal, non-capitalist and alternative in other ways. Often these challenges are partial, so Marxist ideology may be seen to resist capitalist and religious ideas, but not patriarchal ones. Discourses, at a 'local' level, can work as forms of resistance to parts of the dominant ideology and thus may influence partial change. More often, discourses serve to contain resistance within a limited area. For example, feminist discourses on health, the family and education may have successfully amended parts of the dominant ideology without replacing any key elements.

The most consistent area of resistance to dominant ideology concerns the definition of what is seen as normal. For example, violence against women in the home was until recently not identi-fied publicly as a social problem. It was viewed, perversely enough, as a 'private' matter – taking place and to be settled 'behind closed doors'. This definition dominated both in general ideology and in the relevant discourse – the law – embodied in the workings of the police and the courts, who were reluctant to 'interfere in private matters'. This definition has been challenged by women's groups, who argue that the exercise of male power through violence is an issue of public concern no matter where it takes place. Such challenges have affected general social ideologies (to some extent) and the expert discourses of the law (to some extent). What emerges, though, is the avoidance or suppression of challenges which claim that this problem has its roots in structural conditions (male power) rather than in defective individuals. Thus, domestic violence, while accepted as a social problem, is linked back to 'defect' theory, identifying the defect in the aggressor (a few bad apples who cannot control themselves) or, more perniciously, finding defects in the victims (women who 'invite' violence).

This leads to the second feature of dominant ideologies and discourses, which is the way in which they are organized around the opposition of normal and deviant. This distinction is a major principle around which the maps are drawn and even though what counts as a problem may shift, the attempt is made to map all problems around this opposition, resulting in the identification of deviance with defect. The effect of this mapping of the social world might be summarized as 'in spite of a few bad apples, the vast majority of people are normal, thank goodness'. This process can effectively marginalize or discredit resistance. So even at a personal level, people who do not or cannot fulfil normal expectations may accept blame and feel guilty. This has been well expressed by women who have taken the exceptional and 'abnormal' step of leaving the family. They felt that staying would have been more damaging to their families and themselves. They suffered greatly because of normal expectations but showed how their 'deviancy' helped create better family relations (Parkin, 1990). By contrast, respectable, law-abiding men who have killed their partners, demonstrate how 'normality' can be a cause of destructive interpersonal actions (Smith, 1989). Normality imposes a personal surrender to intolerable pressures while resistance is perceived as deviance. The imposition of normality can be seen to cause violence and breakdown. This might explain, in part, why certain groups are more frequently labelled as having 'psychiatric' problems. The incidence of mental health problems among women, certain groups of Black men, unemployed people and disabled people is greater than for the whole population.

Such examples suggest that the importance of ideology and discourse is not restricted to the way they 'map' the world but that these maps lead to practical consequences. How problems are defined, and who defines them, affect what response will be made to the problem. In the example of domestic violence, the dominant definition of it as a 'private matter' ensured that no intervention took place. As the definition has shifted, so have the responses. Its definition as a criminal act brings such violence into the realm of possible intervention by the police and courts, who prosecute some offenders. Where it is defined as a failure in the interpersonal relations between the particular couple, it may become the focus for intervention by a counsellor aimed at helping the couple to 'cope' with 'their' problem. For some women's groups it became the focus of mutual self-help, establishing refuges and support networks to create the chance for women to escape direct violence. All of these tend to operate at the level of the individual, in spite of the attempts to define such violence as a structural problem involving power differentials between men and women and the exercise of violence within such unequal relations. On the ground established by the distinction between normal and deviant and the linkage between deviance and individual defect, intervention tends to be directed towards particular 'cases' – individuals, families, groups who are identified as having a defect, rather than at structural conditions. In the same way, the disadvantages of ethnic groups as a consequence of racism throughout the social structure can be constructed as the result of cultural, educational or even biological defects.

We can see that ideologies or discourses are both systems of ideas and have real consequences for people's lives. For example, discourses about physical and mental impairment have created significant changes in the lives of people with disabilities. In the early twentieth century, some people were labelled 'mentally defective' and seen as a threat to society. Intervention was designed to segregate these people from the rest of society and from each other according to gender. Subsequently, the growing authority of the medical profession led to this same group being defined as 'sick' (suffering from mental illness rather than being mentally defective). Under the medical model, segregation was allied to forms of medical treatment, regimes of drug therapy in particular. Subsequently, a further discourse was added which focused on the idea of 'subnormality' – their 'defect' lay in a lack of certain characteristics which qualify the rest of society as normal. Different regimes of treatment developed to try to compensate for these 'lacks'. More recently, a more functional discourse has been added which identifies the same people as having 'learning difficulties' within a wider framework of individuals and groups with 'special needs'. Intervention framed by this discourse is concerned with skills training, aimed at helping individuals to be functionally independent. Although each of these variants has a somewhat different view of disability and different patterns of intervention, they all share some underlying features. Each is framed by the assumption that it is possible and necessary to distinguish the normal from the impaired, that some degree of segregation of the two populations is necessary and that intervention needs to be directed at the impaired population. None of them embodies the arguments from within groups of physically and mentally impaired people that they are disabled by social expectations of what being normal means.

Both ideology and discourse are concerned with producing and reproducing the distinction between normality and deviance. In industrial societies the core definitions of normality have tended to be drawn around the intersection of work and the family. Those not engaged in a 'good and useful life' in either production or reproduction are on their way to being deviant by virtue of being marginal to what are seen as the major life activities. Around these two poles of normality, one can see the sketch map of potential deviants: the 'wilfully' unemployed; the old (after the age of production and reproduction); the young (before the age of production and reproduction); women who do not marry and have children; single parents; lesbians and gay men; and those who do not fit the requirements of 'able-bodiedness' imposed during the period of industrialization. These all constitute 'problem populations', defined by deviance from the norm and defined as requiring special attention ranging from punishment, surveillance, segregation and control through to care, assistance and being made dependent. To fill out the picture properly, one would have to add more specific sets of cultural norms about how to live this pattern of work and family, which would add more problem populations defined by the ways in which they are not 'English', since deviance is also distributed ethnically.

This ideological distribution of normality and deviance around the institutions of work and family gives a clue to the power and persistence of ideologies, discourses and theories of deviance as individual defect. They sustain a view of the main institutional arrangements of society as normal/natural/satisfactory and position deviant groups as problems to be 'managed', while 'normality' can be left alone to get on with its business. In reverse, we can see why structural explanations tend to be marginalized and excluded, since they insist that social problems and deviance cannot be understood or solved apart from the way 'normality' works. They challenge the assumption that the world can be separated into an unproblematic normality and a few problems around the edges. On the contrary, they suggest that it is the way in which 'business as usual' works that accounts for the problems.

As Figure 5 indicates, what distinguishes structural theories is not just a matter of the way they identify a different array of causes for social problems arising from patterns of inequality in the society but that they also link one aspect of power inequalities to the process of defining social problems themselves. That is, among the capacities which are unequally distributed is the power to define situations and the power to make those definitions 'stick' so that they have effective consequences. Around any problem condition there is likely to be a wide range of alternative definitions, but only a limited range will become dominant and will guide what action is taken by the society as a whole in relation to the condition.

Figure 5 *A structural model of social causation and construction*

Finally, we need to admit that the field of social problems is more complex than our starting point of a distinction between individualist and structural explanations allows for. Attempts to explain the causes of social problems range from pure individualist to structural theories, with a variety of 'middle range' explanations between these two poles: the range might be expressed as something like the following: individuals; interactions between individuals; family and socialization processes; groups ('gangs'); geographical areas (the 'slum'); schooling or other social institutions such as the media ('copycat crimes'); through to the structural patterns of opportunity, wealth and power. These different explanations reflect resistance to elements of the dominant ideology and resistance within specific discourses. Dominant explanations (and the types of social intervention which follow from them) tend to cluster in the first part of this list. Similarly, dominant political ideologies tend to focus on the first part of the list, too – identifying defective individuals, families or areas as the causes of social problems.

For most of the period after the Second World War in Britain, the dominant ideologies of social problems have clustered around the nexus of individual–family–area and have been associated with professional discourses of individual and social improvement or reform. Intervention has mostly been directed through the state to improve the functioning of particular individuals, families or communities – to 'normalize' them. There have been occasional attempts to intervene at the structural level, as suggested by the community development projects (CDPs) of the late 1960s and early 1970s. Using community action instead of individual or group work, these projects addressed political and economic structural causes of disadvantage in certain areas. Such initiatives are often short-lived and the Home Office quickly terminated the CDPs. Since the middle 1970s, however, there has been a stronger development of 'pure' individualism, associated with the Conservative Party under Margaret Thatcher's leadership. This view has seen individuals and families as responsible for their own circumstances and is sceptical of the benefits of state intervention. The alliance between dominant political ideologies ('reformism') and the professional discourses of social improvement has been threatened by this revival of individualism. This variety of Conservatism has linked its individualism to a highly normative view of family life, British culture and traditional values. Not surprisingly, perhaps, such normative views provide a strong framework for the definition of social problems: 'defective' individuals (who *choose* to be deviant); incompetent families (parental failures); 'alien' cultural traditions and belief (subverting the British way of life), and 'liberals' and 'radicals' of all kinds who challenge traditional values and traditional sources of authority.

In summary, then, the study of social problems is complex because it requires attention to two processes: on the one hand, how social problems are caused and, on the other, how social problems are socially constructed. The social construction of problems contains ideas of causation which tend to be hidden or taken for granted. Social construction operates as if biological or individual explanations of cause were unquestioned. Social causation examines a range of causes beyond the natural–biological–individual group. One social explanation of the cause of problems includes the concept of social construction. The concept of social construction describes the dominant approach to the social definition of problems and is part of a critique of that process of definition. As a final example, 'child abuse' is a social construction which largely assumes individual defect as the cause of the problem. Child mistreatment is an actual social condition which can be identified and measured. Explanations of child mistreatment range from biological and individual through to structural ones like the patterns of male dominance in patriarchal relations. Social causation refers to explanations, beyond individualist ones, able to take account of various social factors.

Notes

This chapter has been developed from a talk given at a D211 day school in Cambridge in June 1990. We have resisted the temptation to turn the talk into a fully referenced academic article.

1 For further discussion, see the chapter by Jennifer Platt in this volume.

References

Becker, H.S. (1963) *Outsiders*. New York: Free Press.

Lombroso, C. (1911) 'Introduction' to Gina Lombroso Ferrara, *Criminal Man According to the Classification of Cesare Lombroso*. New York: Putnam.

Parkin, S. (1990) 'She's Leaving Home', *New Statesman and Society*, 6 April: 12–14.

Smith, P. (1989) 'Perfect Murders', *New Statesman and Society*, 7 July: 14–16.

2
The undeserving poor:
unemployed people, then and now

John Ditch

A dominant theme running through the history of social policy and still current in much of social welfare thinking and practice is the distinction drawn between the deserving and the undeserving poor. This distinction, implicit in the provisions of the New Poor Law of 1834, was first clearly articulated by the Charity Organisation Society in the 1870s and legitimated by an edifice of prejudice and rhetoric woven together into a social theory of Herbert Spencer towards the end of the nineteenth century.[1] But more than just a means whereby the poor can be classified against some moral criteria as part of the social construction of welfare, the dichotomy symbolizes a potent theme in the development of both social work and social security in Britain, even in the late twentieth century. Janus, the two-faced gatekeeper without equal, is alive and well, but not so much a patron saint for the poor as a malign spectre for social policy: constantly separating the deserving from the undeserving, caring for the former and disciplining the latter. This apparently simple and convenient dichotomy is being constantly reformulated and redeployed in social policy, from the early practice of the Poor Law and the Charity Organisation Society, through the means tests of the Public Assistance Boards of the inter-war years, to the changes in social security in the 1980s. In this chapter the implications of drawing such a distinction for the status of being unemployed and the operations of social security will be described, but above all the validity of such a dichotomy, redolent of moral rather than diagnostic differentiation, will be questioned.

The New Poor Law of 1834, reflecting strands of both classical political economy and utilitarianism, was predicated upon seeing the necessity of poverty as a spur to human labour. The early part of the nineteenth century, which saw Great Britain involved in a costly European war at the same time as it attempted to cope with the social, economic and political consequences of the industrial revolution, was dominated by a fear of social unrest and growing hostility to state intervention. The problems of rural destitution and periodic bouts of economic dislocation posed contradictory difficulties for the government. Contrary to much contemporary thinking which was firmly in favour of the abolition of the Poor Law, the political realities of the time, fearful of widescale social unrest, were such that its reform and retention were required. Classical political economy, dismal science that it was, asserted that a labourer's wages could not rise above subsistence level, except for short periods: this was seen as virtual justification for abandoning any attempt to raise wage rates artificially. In such circumstances the pressures for reform were concerned with limiting the cost of the Poor Law and disciplining the workforce. As Brian Inglis has suggested, 'The capitalism which developed in Britain was not laissez-faire, in the original sense; but what the employers preferred to call "laissez-nous-faire"'. In other words, they were asking not that the economic system should be left alone, but that they should be' (Inglis, 1972: 32). Rising costs, a quest for administrative rationality and fear of social unrest sparked by the Swing Riots of 1830 led to the appointment of the Royal Commission on the Poor Laws in 1832. Its report of 1834 is a major landmark in the history of social policy and despite the thinking and evidence being confused and deficient,

> in this crucially important period we must understand the motivation and philosophy of the report itself, however wrong-headed that report might appear. What the Commissioners may have believed may not have been the truth, but the subsequent legislation was based on that belief: what people thought was happening was, for the purpose of social policy, more important than what was actually happening. [Fraser, 1973: 33]

The central tenets of the report and the subsequent legislation declared the principles of 'less eligibility' and 'workhouse test', and also provided for large-scale administrative reorganization under the overall charge of the newly created Poor Law Commission. Of these provisions, the most important and persistent has been that of less eligibility, a principle intended to encourage people to work rather than receive support from the state. Under this principle no unemployed person could receive assistance (and thereby a standard of living) which was greater than that which could be achieved by the lowest-paid labourer in the immediate locality.

> The first and most essential of all conditions, a principle which we find universally admitted, even by those whose practice is at variance with it, is, that his [the able-bodied person's] situation, on the whole, shall not be made really or apparently so eligible as the situation of the independent labourer of the lowest class...Every penny bestowed, that tends to render the condition of the pauper more eligible than that of the independent labourer, is a bounty on indolence and vice. [Webb and Webb, 1929: 61–2]

So is the status of the undeserving described; they were both feared and despised. However the principles of 'less eligibility' and the 'workhouse test' had rather less to do with poverty than to do with pauperism: the former being regarded as an absence of material resources whereas the latter betokened a moral defect in the individual (Procacci, 1978: 55–72). Indeed, and of some significance in the development of nineteenth-century social policy, the latter was construed as posing a threat to the political order requiring a strong and controlling intervention from the state. This frequently described combination of fatalism ('The poor ye always have with you') and moralism ('So far from rags and filth being indications of poverty, they are in the large majority of cases, signs of gin drinking, carelessness and recklessness' [Rose, 1972: 7]) represented the backbone of Poor Law practice for the next sixty years. Under outdoor relief the unemployed or destitute (and their families) could receive assistance from Poor Law Guardians (either food or small sums of money) without having to go into the workhouse. The introduction of indoor relief meant that the unemployed or destitute (and their families) lived in the workhouse, where they received food and accommodation but were subject to its rules and regulations.

In reality, the move away from outdoor and indoor relief heralded by the legislation of 1834 was not always observed in practice, and least of all in the industrializing areas of Lancashire and the West Riding of Yorkshire (Rose, 1972: 11). As early as the 1830s the structure of the labour market was changing such that ever more workers were employed in the new factories as waged employees and subject to the fluctuations and vicissitudes of the growing British economy. The New Poor Law may, or may not, have been an appropriate instrument for the problems of rural destitution but it was quite insensitive to the problems of the 'new poor' in the urban centres.

The Poor Law regime was strict and without generosity but was not inhumane to the point of barbarity as was sometimes claimed. It did, and this is not something to be dismissed lightly, depend upon stigma to make it work and represented, in the words of Peter Townsend, the quintessential system of 'conditional welfare for the few' (Townsend, 1979: 62). Both the principles and the practice of the Poor Law dominated social policy in Britain for in excess of a century and, as we shall see, still cast a dark shadow.

If the range of services available from the state was restricted, there was, by way of contrast, a massive expansion in the number of charities providing support: it was estimated that in 1860, in London alone, there were 640 charitable bodies with an annual income of two and a half million pounds (Perkin, 1972: 122). The disorganization which characterized charitable and philanthropic activity in the mid-nineteenth century was the justification for the formation of the Charity Organisation Society in 1869. The COS, committed to the application of rational and proto-scientific techniques to charity, was predicated on a belief that industrial society was fracturing traditional relationships of social reciprocity by uprooting stable communities. Most particularly, the face-to-face relationship which had historically been the symbol and practice of giving and receiving had been destroyed. The result was that the massive expansion in charitable activity in the nineteenth century, far from contributing to an alleviation of the problems of poverty, was, by default if not design, contributing to an increase in the problems generated by pauperism. The COS was emphatic that the problems of poverty would be neither alleviated nor eradicated by the simple giving of money. The deserving had to be separated from the undeserving and the former supported by a series of structured and supportive casework visits: the twin facets of care and control are to be found here. Even Sidney and Beatrice Webb, who contributed so much to the historical exploration of the Poor Law while simultaneously cultivating the role of the expert in social policy matters, were critical of the COS without totally dismissing its value:

> What was wrong about the COS, as may now be seen, was its deep-rooted censoriousness; its strange assumption that the rich were, as such, intellectually and morally the 'superiors' of the poor, entitled to couple pecuniary assistance with a virtual dictatorship over their lives. [Webb and Webb, 1929: 456]

These are the origins of social work practice and as such demanded training and an increasingly secular and professional approach based on careful record-keeping with a view to encouraging a return to independence for the client.

However, the COS did not stand in opposition to the Poor Law but was more a complement to it; indeed there was a considerable overlap in personnel. The COS filtered out the deserving cases and passed on those who were judged to be the undeserving residue to the Poor Law Guardians. By identifying those who had fallen on hard times through no fault of their own, and supporting them to return to independence, the COS was claiming to reduce the incidence of pauperism by nipping the causes in the bud.

Statistics on the incidence of poverty in the nineteenth century were impressionistic. It was not until the publication of the findings of Booth and later Rowntree that any attempt was made to systematically explore the extent of deprivation. Indeed, even the official Poor Law returns on the number of paupers receiving relief were far from being accurate: the distinction between able-bodied and non-able-bodied was often confused and the tendency to record 'constructive pauperism' a further complication. This was a procedure whereby if any member of a family were receiving relief then all members of the family were deemed to be in receipt of relief (Rose, 1972:14). This tended to work to the advantage of the Poor Law authorities, as the overall impression given was that the incidence of pauperism was declining. This rather complacent assumption that poverty was a declining problem was shattered by the publication of Charles Booth's study of working-class life in the East End of London in 1887 which demonstrated that over 30 percent of the population were in poverty. This general finding was confirmed by Seebohm Rowntree's study of York (published in 1901) which showed that 27.8 percent of the domestic population were living in poverty (Veit-Wilson, 1985: 77). Findings such as these, together with a pervasive recognition that growth in the economy was beginning to slow, contributed to a growing awareness of unemployment and the consequences of under-employment as a major social problem.

Indeed it was only at this time that the word 'unemployment' came into the English vocabulary (Harris, 1972: Introduction). The emergence of socialist politics and the formation of the Fabian Society, together with a reorientation of traditional liberalism such that the role of the state became more interventionist, all contributed to a growing debate about the adequacy of existing arrangements for dealing with those out of work, and a growing realization that the phenomena which had economic dimensions were not amenable to solutions based on social discipline and enforced deprivation. Very gradually the possibility of dealing with unemployment by 'methods of economic, fiscal or monetary control' was contemplated (Harris, 1972: 6). Hitherto unemployment, in so far as it had been recognized as a serious question at all, was regarded 'as a localized "crisis" phenomenon rather than a problem that was more or less endemic throughout the industrial labour market' (Harris, 1972: 3). However, it was common for many contemporary observers to simultaneously hold that unemployment was the product of labour market dislocation while also believing that the unemployed were responsible for their own circumstances. As Harris writes, '. . . the growth of a scientific analysis of unemployment was paralleled by the growth of a harsher and more pessimistic attitude towards its victims, which was directed primarily against those who failed to support themselves but extended also to all who became unemployed' (Harris, 1972: 43). Echoes of this kind of double-think still ring in our ears some ninety years later.

The trade depressions of 1892–5, 1903–5 and 1908–9 generated considerable public debate about unemployment and the unemployed. The absence or unreliability of appropriate statistics did not prevent solutions being canvassed. The growing socialist movement called for work-sharing schemes based on the principle of an eight-hour day; when tried there was little impact on aggregate employment as productivity tended to increase. Other proposals included the transportation of the habitually unemployed to labour colonies: Charles Booth advocated emigration as a means of relieving pressure on the congested labour market.

The Liberal government of 1906–14, and in particular the dual influence of the Lib-Lab pact and associated parliamentary pressure for reform, together with New Liberal thinking which both suggested and legitimated progressive legislation, significantly advanced policies and services for the unemployed. First, under the aegis of Winston Churchill (at the Board of Trade) and William Beveridge (who had previously gained experience dealing with the provisions of the less than successful Unemployed Workman Act of 1905), labour exchanges were established to smooth out discontinuities in the labour market. Secondly, unemployment insurance was introduced and although the scope and scale of benefits may have been limited the principle was of great symbolic significance because it conferred rights on individual workers by virtue of past contributions. Moreover, 'it had to be separate from the Poor Law, yet cater for the vast mass of workers not organized in trade unions, without involving civil servants in discriminating between the poor individually' (Hay, 1975: 50). That the scheme was based not on citizenship but on status as an employee with an appropriate contributions record was reflected in the crisis faced by the insurance fund in 1934.

The economist J. A. Hobson, who had an ambiguous relationship with the New Liberal 'movement', prefigured much later thinking about the role and responsibilities of the state in the alleviation of unemployment. The full significance of this period for the so-called undeserving is that for the first time government acknowledged its potential role in both the prevention and alleviation of unemployment. The principles of 1834 had crudely expected that the market would spontaneously generate job vacancies and fill them from amongst the ranks of the able-bodied: its failure was inevitable because the market is neither that efficient nor that sensitive. Recognition by government that it could, with both legitimacy and political goodwill, intervene in the macro-economy so as to merge both social and economic policy objectives was recognized at this time and was subsequently to be formalized as a cardinal policy responsibility in the Employment White Paper of 1944. But this is to anticipate.

In the inter-war period, the scourge was, once again, unemployment. The massive increase in the numbers unemployed posed great problems for the government. Commitments entered into via the National Insurance scheme of 1911, expectations raised by the First World War, a growing and practical conception of citizenship reflected in the extension of the franchise and an almost subterranean but nevertheless potent fear of the political consequences of unemployment led to a series of extension Acts to further the rights of unemployed males under the National Insurance legislation. However, the old bogies were still present. As Alan Deacon has argued, the popular historical impression given is that the government attempted to make the best of a difficult job in pressing economic circumstances by extending National Insurance provisions (Deacon, 1976). But Deacon shows that the levels of benefit were minimal and the quest for the scrounger was unrelenting. The administration of the National Insurance scheme was complicated by regulations designed to determine that the claimant was 'genuinely seeking work', a procedure which is remarkably similar to the 'available for work' test introduced by the Conservative government in the autumn of 1986. Some 3 million claims were refused during the 1920s on the grounds that this condition had not been satisfied, and it is expected that the effect of the 1986 regulations will be to reduce the unemployment register by about 4 percent. As Deacon notes when writing about the 1920s: 'At no time in these years did any prominent politician or government official seriously suggest that the work they were supposed to be seeking actually existed' (Deacon, 1976: 9).

Another major aspect of the inter-war period was the spectre of the means test. Under the provisions of the National Insurance scheme and the extension legislation of 1920 (providing extended cover to 12 million workers) a series of rights were established on the basis of previous contributions. It is important to note that these rights conferred a status on the recipients, a status fully compatible with full citizenship. Most importantly they were quite distinct from the Poor Law and were not conditional upon a means test. As such the recipients of these benefits regarded themselves, and were regarded by others, as being deserving. The shock of the 1930s was their effective reclassification as undeserving as a result of extension of the means test in 1931. The potency of the household means test as a focus for political agitation and collective folk memory has been remarkable. It was crucially instrumental in persuading politicians and administrators alike during the Second World War that if, in the words of Derek Fraser,

> the essential theme of the 1930s had been selectivity, that of the 1940s was universalism. That specious universalism which in 1931 had required the unemployed to share in the national sacrifice by a 10 percent cut in income did not hide the fact that society and social policy were riddled with arbitrary distinctions and selective treatment. [Fraser, 1973: 192]

Throughout Great Britain, though not in Northern Ireland, the Second World War saw a notable return to full employment. The Beveridge Report of December 1942 promised not only a restructuring of the complete social security system but assumed that full employment would be regarded as a legitimate policy objective for government, a commitment adopted in the Employment White Paper of 1944. With the unexpected return of a Labour government in July 1945, there was a burst of legislative activity across a wide front of social policy issues giving effect to many of the proposals contained in the Beveridge Report: National Insurance was reformed and extended and backed up by a new scheme to be known as National Assistance, to be available without reference to contributions records but on the basis of a means test. Whereas in 1911 the Labour leader Keir Hardie had strongly opposed the introduction of a contributions-based National Insurance scheme on the grounds that it reinforced Victorian ideas of thrift and self-help, by 1946 the extended scheme appeared to give effect to the Labour principle of either work or maintenance and was therefore accepted as a pragmatic rather than socialist solution to the problem of want. However, the National Assistance Act of 1948 did formally abolish all existing Poor Law legislation and separated the payment of benefits from the provision of welfare services. With the exception of only a few MPs the Second Reading debate was characterized by enthusiastic or embarrassed approval. But the notes of warning and caution are salutary. Silburn quotes the words of one far-sighted MP:

> If this Bill is successful in removing that stigma from the minds of the poor, then it will indeed go down in history as a great measure. But if that stigma is to go, it will need something more than this Bill, or an Act of Parliament, or regulations. It will need a different attitude of mind on the part of the administrators of outdoor and other relief for the poor. They have a difficult job if they are to remove the stigma of the Poor Law. They have to humanize the relationship between the poor and authority – a difficult and complex task, and one which cannot be done merely by passing legislation. [Silburn, 1983: 135]

It is remarkable in this context to note that over a million people had recourse to the National Assistance Board in 1949, and were therefore subject to a means test, without there being a massive outcry from the left of the Labour Party. The distinction between the dreaded household means test of the inter-war years and the individual test of means in the post-war period is crucial. Certainly the position of women as dependents within families was unsatisfactory but was entirely consistent with a traditional distinction drawn within the labour movement, paralleling deserving and undeserving categories, as between productive (male) labour and unproductive (female) activities. As Deacon and Bradshaw have noted: 'An enormous shift towards universalism has occurred, and the areas of means testing that remained were seen as unimportant by Labour but were sufficient to reassure the Conservatives' (Bradshaw and Deacon, 1983: 48). But at this time – in the immediate post-war years – and for some years to come, the problem was not one of unemployment but one of labour shortage; once again, new supplies of labour were tapped, in particular from Ireland and later from the New Commonwealth (Addison, 1985: 173–5; Morgan, 1985: 180–5).

The 1950s were not the period of unbridled prosperity and consensus that is often suggested, but they were (with the exception of Northern Ireland) times of full employment. Popular attitudes (both public and professional) assumed that the benefits of economic growth were being diffused throughout society. Greater access to a range of consumer goods, from television sets to motor cars, suggested growing prosperity. However, beneath the complacency the old problems continued to exist: Silburn records that during the 1950s there was little public concern with the activities (or responsibilities) of the National Assistance Board, 'a minor service operating on the periphery of public concern' (Silburn, 1983: 135). Nevertheless, a faint theme is detected, which concerns the apparent reluctance of many pensioners (the deserving poor) to claim their entitlement. Only spasmodically were there outbursts prefiguring a later and more widespread hysteria concerned with the payment of benefits to the undeserving – strikers, malingerers, immigrants. The position in Northern Ireland was somewhat different in that throughout the post-war period a more widespread concern about the undeserving poor was articulated. Against the background of unemployment consistently in excess of 6 percent, there were accounts of alleged social security abuse such that the National Assistance Board for Northern Ireland was obliged to deal formally with the allegations in its annual reports (Ditch, 1984a: 27–31). The existence of a land border with the Republic of Ireland meant that there were also frequent allegations of fraudulent claiming by 'Southerners'. There was no evidence to confirm that this was a widespread problem but a popular construct merged the unemployed and 'Free Staters' as a necessary but threatening out-group. Such judgements were based on moral and political criteria and in part are reflected in the official five-year United Kingdom residence qualification for Supplementary Benefit which (still) operates in Northern Ireland (but not elsewhere in the United Kingdom where entitlement is established after six months).

The rise in unemployment from the 1960s, a greater emphasis on welfare rights together with a change in popular attitudes to authority placed growing demands on the social security system. The National Assistance Board was restyled as the Supplementary Benefits Commission in the mid-sixties, with a greater emphasis on claimant rights and closer integration with the National Insurance scheme. Although the largest proportion of the new claimants were pensioners seeking a Supplementary Pension, it was apparent that the number of unemployed (and their dependents) was also increasing. It was during the 1960s that the aggregate level of unemployment began creeping up in the United Kingdom. Many unemployed people had irregular contributions records under the National Insurance scheme and therefore were often ineligible for support other than via Supplementary Benefits. Even for those with established entitlements there was often a need to 'top up' National Insurance benefits from Supplementary Benefit because the former did not take into account family size or housing costs. A further difficulty, a by-product of economic policies and wage restraint, was a growing awareness of the 'unemployment trap', a situation which describes the position of those families who would be better off 'on the dole' because their net income from employment is less (or only marginally better) than when in receipt of benefits.

The massive increase in the numbers registered as unemployed (despite the no less than nineteen changes to the way in which the statistics are collected between 1979 and 1987) show that registered unemployment in the United Kingdom is in excess of 3.28 million (Unemployment Unit, 1986). Furthermore, and government data confirm this, unemployment has displaced old age as the main reason for low income in the United Kingdom (DHSS, 1985: 13). However, the Government is anxious to further subdivide this group and in particular to identify those families with children; those unemployed without dependent children are to be accorded lower priority (and lower benefits) in the reformed social security system. The categories of deserving and undeserving are endlessly elaborated in the light of changing circumstances.

The growth in long-term unemployment is no longer restricted to the older worker. Over the United Kingdom as a whole by July 1986 there were 1,303,976 people calculated, on the claimant basis, to be unemployed for in excess of one year: this is equivalent to 40 percent of the claimant population. Of these, 50 percent were aged 25–54, the age during which family responsibilities tend to be greatest. Of special concern in this context has been the growing significance of Supplementary Benefit as the principal source of income support for the unemployed. A minority of unemployed claimants now receive National Insurance Unemployment Benefit. But of even greater importance is that unemployed claimants, unlike all other categories of claimant receiving Supplementary Benefit, do not establish entitlement to the long-term Supplementary Benefit rate, which is worth about 25 percent more than the short-term rate. This is explicitly related to the apparent need to maintain work incentives by applying the principle of less eligibility; but the consequences are punitive, especially for families with children (Sinfield, 1981: 49–57; Bradshaw and Deacon, 1983).

As the numbers of unemployed increased throughout the 1970s so the pressure on the social security system also increased. This contributed to a review of the Supplementary Benefits scheme under the Labour government and the implementation of radical reforms under the Conservative administration. But in addition to changes in the operation and regulations of social security it is important to reflect on the macro-economic policy of governments in the past fifteen years, because a number of important themes can be discerned. In the immediate aftermath of the increase in oil prices in late 1973, many European governments responded to the increase in unemployment sympathetically (Sinfield, 1984: 42–3). However, as the levels of unemployment were sustained and the duration of unemployment increased, so governments became ever tougher in their treatment of the unemployed. Within the context of monetarist economics, emphasis is placed on 'pricing the unemployed into jobs' both by reducing wage rates and by lowering the range and level of benefits to increase work incentives. A more vigorously articulated vocabulary distinguishing between deserving and undeserving groups re-entered the public domain. As Sinfield has observed:

> While support remains relatively generous for some groups, others may only be eligible for programmes which appear to be less concerned to do something for the unemployed than to them. The difference in prepositions reflects a different perception of the causes of being out of work and so a different view of government's responsibilities. [Sinfield, 1984: 43]

Evidence on work incentives and wage rates is incomplete but vitally important and may be investigated by comparing the level of net income from work with net income when out of work, a relationship known as the replacement ratio. A recent report from the DHSS Cohort Study of the Unemployed (Moylan, Millar and Davis, 1984) does engage in some quantitative analysis to determine replacement ratios and comes to the conclusion that the majority of unemployed men in their sample suffered a severe reduction in income when out of work. Of men who were out of work for more than three months, about 50 percent received benefit income of less than 50 percent of their net earnings when in work. Benefits were greater than previous net earnings for only 6 percent of the sample. The basic idea is straightforward even though the arithmetic gets a little complicated. The problem with interpreting the results is neatly summarized by Smee:

> If the concern is with benefit adequacy, the discovery of significant numbers of high replacements rates might be interpreted as implying that benefit levels are more than adequate. An alternative interpretation would be that incomes in work are inadequate either because of low wages or because of a failure to claim in-work benefits. It requires judgement and detailed information on actual cases to distinguish between these interpretations. [Smee, 1984: 125]

Dilnot, Kay and Morris, re-analysing the Family Expenditure Survey, came to the conclusion that replacement rates changed through time:

> . . . in 1983 very few people (2.9 percent) would have received over 90 percent of their income in work when they were unemployed for a short period, and even fewer in the long term. But this has not always been the case. As recently as 1978 some 21 percent of working family heads had replacement rates in excess of 90 percent. [Dilnot, Kay and Morris, 1984: 59]

As they note, this was largely attributable to changes in tax regulations and the abolition of the Earnings Related Supplement. Any problem there may have been regarding incentives in the 1970s had been eradicated by the mid-1980s. Furthermore, their general conclusion was that 'there had never been a serious problem over longer spells: throughout the period, long-term replacement rates have been, on average, as low as 50 percent, and the proportion with long-term marginal rates in excess of 90 percent has never been above 3 percent' (Dilnot, Kay and Morris, 1984: 59). Finally, any convergence between income tax and social security benefits has been due to the changing burden on low incomes: Supplementary Benefit represents the same proportion of average gross earnings in 1980 as it (in the form of National Assistance) did in 1955 – 55.8 percent as opposed to 55.1 percent (National Consumer Council, 1984: 128). As aggregate levels of unemployment increase so the importance of benefit levels for determining the duration of unemployment is reduced in significance. Evidence from Northern Ireland, where the ratio between notified job vacancies and number registered unemployed is in the order of 1:75, is consistent with this (Ditch, 1984a: 18). Re-analysis of a cohort survey of the unemployed in Northern Ireland provides further evidence concerning replacement rates. Among the long-term unemployed (over one year in 1976) only 8.3 percent received benefits equal to, or within £5 of, previous income from employment. As the authors of the study conclude, this presents 'further evidence of the unimportance of "scroungers" in this large-scale sample of the unemployed' (Miller and Osborne, 1983: 90).

The dominance of a crude and one-dimensional model drawn from classical political economy and which presents workers as economistic utility maximizers, relentlessly pursuing every extra penny, is not without its critics. For example, Tipping identifies three traditions of explanation accounting for motivation to work. First there is the economistic approach which regards labour as a commodity, the price (and net financial gain) for which is determined by the interplay of the forces of supply and demand within the market. Secondly, there is a needs-based approach, which argues that labour is necessary as a means for the satisfaction of certain human requirements, ranging from necessities such as food and shelter to more elaborate psychological needs which may be in part satisfied by the very act of work itself. However, increasing attention is being paid to a third approach which stresses certain ideological forces: this 'views the desire for work as rooted in the dominant ideologies in our society in portraying work as an intrinsically "good thing" or as inevitable if an individual is to have a socially satisfactory life' (Tipping, 1985: 84). In other words people work because they are expected to work, because they enjoy work, because they like meeting other workers and not simply because they get paid for it. There is more to employment than the cash nexus relationship. Indeed the evidence on the extent of low pay within the workforce is overwhelming: the DHSS estimated that in 1981 some 230,000 full-time breadwinners, supporting 670,000 people, were living at net incomes below the prevailing Supplementary Benefit level. Moreover, in excess of 3 million people were living in families between 0 and 40 percent above Supplementary Benefit level where the head of household was in full-time work or self-employed (National Consumer Council, 1984: 126–7).

However, the range of evidence questioning economistic approaches has not deterred the proponents from advancing their arguments. Professor Patrick Minford (1983) has advocated setting a ceiling on benefits on 70 percent of previous income (net of tax, work expenses and the like). In effect the Government have followed his advice because in 1982 the Earnings Related Supplements were abolished (at the time they were worth about £11 per week) and long-term benefits were 'de-indexed' from movements with wages (Loney, 1986: ch. 4). Since the early 1970s there has been a distinction drawn between the short-term and long-term rates of Supplementary Benefit. The justification for this difference was originally based on the principle of 'deferred expenditure' which argues that in the short term various household expenditures can be postponed pending a return to work. In practice, pensioners with eligibility for

Supplementary Benefit immediately go onto the long-term rate and all other categories of claimant (including the sick, disabled and single parents, but excluding the unemployed) move on to the long-term rate after one year. Over the past thirteen years the gap between short-term and long-term Supplementary Benefit rates has increased and now remains constant at 27 percent for a single person and 25 percent for a couple. Nowhere is the principle of 'less eligibility' more vividly displayed than in the treatment of the unemployed with long-term needs but short-term rates of support. But even if motivation to work was reducible to a simple calculus rooted in the lure of incentives, there is another way of responding to the apparent challenge. Far from reducing benefit levels (and considerable evidence now exists to question their adequacy) the alternative is to either increase wage rates or improve the range and take-up of benefits for those in work. To increase wage rates is anathema to the present government, who are anxious to reduce wage costs as a means whereby employment can be stimulated. Changes in the terms of reference of Wages Councils and the establishment of Enterprise Zones are indicative of a disposition which wishes to create an employment culture free of as much state regulation as possible. The other strategy is to increase net income by reducing the tax burden on the low paid and by increasing benefit levels for families. Campaigns to increase the take-up of means-tested benefits such as Family Income Supplement and Housing Benefit are consistent with this objective. But programmes to stimulate benefit take-up are fraught with difficulties and conflict with other aspects of the policy process such as keeping down costs. A cross-national study has reported:

> ...the assumption seems to prevail that 'the' client, armed with comprehensive information, well versed and pugnacious in dealings with official departments, has sallied forth to 'extort' the maximum social benefits from an absolutely defenceless administration, to exploit legislation to the full and if necessary to resort to illegal practices. In fact, however, the interaction between applicants and official departments is probably more like a 'bargaining process' – or in other words involves a 'negotiable element'...In a political environment that is 'economy-minded' and attuned to 'combating abuse', there is probably no need for written instructions to induce the staff of welfare offices to observe the principle that 'good management means turning down as many applications as possible'. The rigid observance of this 'guiding principle' can without question have the result that persons who are in fact entitled to benefits fail to take the hurdle of official defence mechanisms and do not receive their due benefits. [Henkel and Pavelka, 1982: 5]

The imperative to restrict access to benefits is nowhere more noticeable than with regard to the unemployed. The recent (1985) reviews of the social security system make much of the importance of work incentives and the role of social security in relation to the broader economic objectives of the government. The review document clearly stated that one of its objectives is to underline the importance of incentives.

While it is one of the functions of the social security system to help those who are unemployed, it is self-defeating if it creates barriers to the creation of jobs, to job mobility or to people rejoining the labour force. Clearly such obstacles exist if people believe themselves better off out of work than in work; or if employers regard the burden of national insurance as a substantial discouragement to providing new jobs...If we wish to encourage individuals to provide for themselves then the social security system – public and private – must not stand in the way. [DHSS, 1985: 3]

The specific changes involve a translation of Supplementary Benefit into Income Support and the introduction of standard rate personal allowances to be supplemented by a range of special client group premiums: families with children, the disabled and elderly will be entitled to the new 'booster benefits', but the young unemployed and those unemployed without dependent children will not be eligible. The government did not accept that the long-term unemployed should be treated on the same basis as other categories of claimant.

The prospects for the unemployed remain bleak despite the range of labour market programmes being sponsored by the Department of Employment. The ideology of the unemployed being an undeserving group continues to be powerful, and not only among the ranks of monetarists. The distinction between deserving and undeserving groups is deeply embedded in popular attitudes to social policy issues. Considerable evidence now exists to suggest that services and benefits for such 'deserving' groups as the elderly and the disabled are favoured among the general public but that equivalent services and benefits for such 'undeserving' groups as the unemployed, single parents and the low paid are not. More surprisingly, however, there is evidence to suggest that there is little difference between the attitudes of people living in deprived areas and people living in more prosperous areas (Ditch, 1984b). But this complex and apparently contradictory picture of public opinion does not add up to a decline in support for the welfare state in general. The most recent studies (Taylor-Gooby, 1985; Jowell and Witherspoon, 1986) clearly indicate continued support for the major spending programmes.

However, the argument can be taken a stage further, because the undeserving poor become, in effect, a subordinated group (MacGregor, 1981: 132) who are not only stigmatized and forced to live on inadequate benefits but are effectively excluded from the public domain of political discourse and influence. The historical difficulties of organizing the unemployed are well known, but even in the 1980s it is remarkable that the unemployed remain marginal to the dynamics of the political process. The long-term unemployed are among those least likely to vote in parliamentary and local elections. The trade union movement has been rather more concerned with preventing their members from becoming unemployed than supporting those who are; most of the poverty lobby groups are concerned with other categories of deserving claimant such as the disabled or children; and the impact of the specialist groups such as the Unemployment Unit in the present cold climate has been minimal.

The unemployed have always been regarded as an undeserving group. This view is a product of a dominant ideology, and one which is endlessly recreated, to the effect that individuals are responsible for their own circumstances and prospects, such that the unemployed (given half a chance) would prefer to scrounge rather than work. This malign and inaccurate conception of human nature (a popular but erroneous term which is often used in this context) can be empirically refuted – but to little effect – because ideas about the deserving and undeserving poor, in the final analysis, are not a reflection of unemployment levels or the adequacy of benefits: they are embodied in and transmitted by the artefacts of popular culture such as novels, plays, soap operas and newspapers. These spurious divisions are drip-fed into popular consciousness wrapped in the coating of fiction so that truth and untruth, fact and fantasy become blurred. For over 150 years the unemployed, and their families, have been criticized and deprived for being the victims of circumstances mostly beyond their control. The principle of 'less eligibility' continues to inform and underline both the principles and the practice of social security. But more than this, and again consistent with the legacy of the past, certain political judgements are made about the unemployed which cast them in the guise of pariahs, not merely beyond the boundaries of formal political activity but actually thought of as morally undermining its foundations. The treatment of the unemployed is based not on economics alone, but on political philosophy; the challenge must be to reincorporate the unemployed within the status of citizenship. In this context future prospects for levels of unemployment and in consequence the status of the unemployed remain gloomy. In such circumstances, and in the absence of a well-informed public debate about the need to redefine the status of employment, and thereby restructure public attitudes and understanding of the activity of work (as opposed to employment), the probability is that the unemployed (and in particular the expanding numbers of long-term unemployed) will continue to be regarded as undeserving with all the pejorative implications associated with such undeserved status.

Note

1 Herbert Spencer was strongly opposed to what he detected as a growing trend towards collective social welfare. He was a firm believer in the development of 'good character' and the withdrawal of social services as a 'disciplinary agent'. More specifically, he approved of there being a close relationship between charitable donors and recipients: '. . . when the miseries of the poor are dilated upon, they are thought of as the deserving poor, instead of. . . the undeserving poor, which in large measure they should be' (quoted in Pinker, 1971: 27). Furthermore, Spencer believed that support of the so-called undeserving would lead to an inevitable deterioration in the 'biological and moral quality of the nation' (ibid., p. 27).

References

Addison, P. (1985) *Now the War is Over*. London: BBC.

Booth, C. (1970) *Life and Labour of the People of London*, Series 1: *Poverty* (5 vols), imprint of 1902 edn. New York: Kelley.

Bradshaw, J. and Deacon, A. (1983) *Reserved for the Poor*. Oxford: Blackwell and Martin Robertson.

Deacon, A. (1976) *In Search of the Scrounger (Occasional Papers in Social Administration, No. 60)*. London: G. Bell & Sons.

Department of Health and Social Security (1985) *Reform of Social Security*, Volume 1, Cmnd 9517. London: HMSO.

Dilnot, A. W., Kay, J. A. and Morris, C. N. (1984) *The Reform of Social Security*. London: Oxford University Press.

Ditch, J. S. (1984a) *Hard Times: Unemployment and Supplementary Benefit in Northern Ireland (Working Paper No. 3)*. London: National Consumer Council.

Ditch, J. S. (1984b) 'The Perception of Poverty in Northern Ireland' *Policy and Politics* 12(2): 167–81.

Fraser, D. (1973) *The Evolution of the British Welfare State*. London: Macmillan.

Harris, J. F. (1972) *Unemployment and Politics*. London: Oxford University Press.

Hay, J. R. (1975) *The Origins of the Liberal Welfare Reforms, 1906–1914*. London: Macmillan.

Henkel, H. A. and Pavelka, F. (1982) 'Abuse and Social Welfare Policy', *Eurosocial Newsletter* 25: 3–8.

Inglis, B. (1972) *Poverty and the Industrial Revolution*. London: Granada.

Jowell, R. and Witherspoon, S. (1986) *British Social Attitudes: the 1986 Report*. Aldershot: Gower.

Loney, M. (1986) *The Politics of Greed*. London: Pluto Press.

MacGregor, S. (1981) *The Politics of Poverty*. London: Longman.

Miller, R. L. and Osborne, R. D. (1983) 'Religion and Unemployment: Evidence from a Cohort Survey', in Cormack, R. J. and Osborne, R. D. (eds) *Religion, Education and Unemployment: Aspects of Equal Opportunity in Northern Ireland*. Belfast: Appletree Press.

Minford, P. (1983) *Unemployment: Cause and Cure*. London: Martin Robertson.

Morgan, K. O. (1985) *Labour in Power, 1945–1951*. London: Oxford University Press.

Morrissey, M. (ed.) (c. 1985) *The Other Crisis: Unemployment in Northern Ireland*. Ulster Polytechnic.

Moylan, S., Millar, J. and Davis, C. (1984) *For Richer, For Poorer? Cohort Study of Unemployed Men*. London: HMSO.

National Consumer Council (1984) *Of Benefit to All*. London: NCC.

Organization for Economic Co-operation and Development (1984) *High Unemployment: A Challenge for Income Support Policies*. Paris: OECD.

Perkin, H. (1972) *The Origins of Modern English Society, 1780–1880*. London: Routledge & Kegan Paul.

Pinker, R. (1971) *Social Theory and Social Policy*. London: Heinemann.

Procacci, G. (1978) 'Social Economy and the Government of Poverty', *Ideology and Consciousness*, Autumn.

Rose, M. E. (1972) *The Relief of Poverty*. London: Macmillan.

Rowntree, B. S. (1980) *Poverty: a Study of Town Life*. New York: Garland (facsimile of 1910, 2nd rev. edn).

Silburn, R. (1983) 'Social Assistance and Social Welfare: the Legacy of the Poor Law', in Bean, P. and MacPherson, S. (eds) *Approaches to Welfare*. London: Routledge & Kegan Paul.

Sinfield, A. (1981) *What Unemployment Means*. Oxford: Martin Robertson.

Sinfield, A. (1984) 'The Wider Impact of Unemployment', in OECD (1984).

Smee, C. H. (1984) 'Unemployment Compensation Replacement Ratios: A United Kingdom View', in OECD (1984).

Taylor-Gooby, P. (1985) *Public Opinion, Ideology and State Welfare*. London: Routledge & Kegan Paul.

Tipping, B. (1985) 'Work Incentives Amongst the Unemployed and the Ideology of Work', in Morrissey (c. 1985).

Townsend, P. (1979) *Poverty in the United Kingdom*. Harmondsworth: Penguin.

Unemployment Unit (1986) Briefing, September.

Veit-Wilson, J. (1985) 'Paradigms of Poverty', *Journal of Social Policy* 15(1): 69–99.

Webb, S. and Webb, B. (1929) *English Poor Law History: Part II: The Last Hundred Years*, Volume I. London: Longman.

3
The social construction of dependency in old age

Alan Walker

Introduction

Elderly people in all industrial societies occupy a generally low social and economic status in relation to younger adults. This is characterized chiefly by financial dependency on the state and can be illustrated by reference to their low incomes and restricted access to a wide range of other resources (Walker, 1980). In Great Britain about two-thirds of elderly people, 5.7 million people, live in or on the margins of poverty, as defined by the state, compared with around one-fifth of the non-elderly. In the USA about one in every five elderly people have incomes below the federally established minimum (Hendricks and Hendricks, 1977: 236). In Japan 90 percent of elderly people have incomes in the lower half of the income distribution (Maeda, 1978: 61). A considerable body of similar information could be adduced to demonstrate the generally low level of income and other resources commanded by the elderly (see Walker, 1986).

This low social and economic status has been accepted by society, including many social scientists, as an inevitable consequence of advanced age, and as a result has received very little critical attention. One important reason for this acceptance is the domination in social policy, gerontology and popular discussion of the life-cycle approach to need. Following Rowntree's (1901) pioneering studies of poverty and the life-cycle of family need, typical patterns of family development are superimposed on a chronological age scale and it is then assumed that periods of need are the natural result of age itself (Wynn, 1972). This effectively obscures inequalities between the elderly and younger poeple and amongst the elderly, as well as other social factors which play a part in determining need.

Secondly, until very recently consideration of the activities of the state in relation to elderly people was largely confined to an assessment of the beneficial or potentially beneficial aspects of pension provision, residential accommodation and other social services. Although these social policies may be criticized for being inadequate in scope and coverage, they are usually accepted as wholly positive additions to the welfare of elderly people. The role of the state and state 'social policies' themselves in creating and enhancing dependency, therefore, have been largely overlooked.

The purpose of this chapter is to argue that the 'dependency' of many elderly people and its severity consist of a structurally enforced inferior social and economic status in relation to the working population and, secondly, that social policies sponsored, directly or indirectly, by the state occupy a central role in the creation and management of that dependency. On this basis we can explain not only the increased dependency among the elderly in the twentieth century, but also the attitude of the state towards this group in periods of economic crisis. I am concerned primarily with the experience of Great Britain, but similar conclusions may well be drawn concerning the relationship between social policy and elderly people in other capitalist societies (see, for example, Guillemard, 1986; Hendricks and Calasanti, 1986). My starting point is the relationship between social policy and social welfare.

Social policy and social welfare

All societies have social policies and all societies have policies on ageing. These may be implicit or explicit in the social institutions and groups developed and managed by different societies to achieve social ends. My concern here is primarily with social policies which stem directly or indirectly from the state, although social policies may also be based on purely private institutions. Indeed the assumption that public policies are synonymous with social policies is wholly false (Walker, 1981b) and has resulted, in Titmuss's words, in a 'stereotype of social welfare which represents only the more visible parts of the real world of welfare' (Titmuss, 1963: 53). Analysis of state social policies has, in turn, been restricted by a major misconception about the nature of the welfare state which has a direct bearing on our subsequent analysis of policies towards the elderly.

The epithet 'welfare state' is applied to all advanced capitalist societies to characterize, on the one hand, the different forms of intervention by the state in the private market to modify or change social conditions and, on the other, the state provision of social services in cash or kind, usually in the form of social security, housing, health and social welfare, and education. According to the traditions of social administration, but also more importantly political and popular discourse, the purpose of this form of state intervention, quite simply, is to enhance welfare. The social construction of the welfare state represented in this dominant liberal-pluralist theory of society depends, firstly, on a limited conception of the state as a value-neutral coalition of all interests in society and of similarly neutral welfare state institutions, which are distinct from the social relations and values of other dominant institutions. Secondly, it rests on the assumption that welfare state institutions and social policies have the single function of promoting welfare.

There is no doubt that the welfare state in all capitalist societies has improved the absolute welfare of some groups, particularly elderly people, over the post-war period. But it would be wholly misleading to assess the impact of the welfare state in this one-dimensional way. It fails, for example, to account for the repressive aspects of the operation of some parts of the welfare state and the antagonism of many of its clients and claimants who do not always *experience* benefits and services in a straightforwardly beneficial way. This ambivalence is revealed in studies of public attitudes to welfare (Taylor-Gooby, 1985). The reluctance of elderly people to claim social security benefits and to enter residential institutions is also well documented (Walker, 1980, 1986; Hendricks and Hendricks, 1977; Tobin and Lieberman, 1976). To explain these aspects of the welfare state it is necessary to recast the dominant social construction and examine welfare state services within the context of the society (or social structure) in which they have been developed – in our case, a modern capitalist society.

In fact the welfare state in capitalist societies reflects the conflicts of interest embedded in those societies, and particularly the primary conflict between the forces of production, the increasing productive power of labour, and the relations of production, the continued private appropriation of surplus value (Gough, 1979: 11). Thus the state will operate to ensure the continued accumulation of capital and therefore the continued existence of the dominant mode of production and its attendant social relations (O'Connor, 1977). This process may be advanced through welfare state, as much as other, institutions in the form of social policies which both promote welfare and exert control. In other words the welfare state '...simultaneously embodies tendencies to enhance social welfare, to develop the powers of individuals, to exert social control over the blind play of market forces; and tendencies to repress and control people, to adapt them to the requirements of the capitalist economy' (Gough, 1979: 12). So rather than representing an antithesis of capitalist values and social relations, the welfare state reflects them. The welfare state, therefore, embodies the same conflicts of interest or 'contradictions' as any other social institutions in capitalist societies (Ginsburg, 1979: 2). The result is a welfare state which may at the same time enhance welfare and perpetuate unequal social relations, which may establish non-market principles of distribution, such as need, while reinforcing the prevailing system of distribution.

It is clear then that a consideration of the relationship between ageing and social policy must take as its starting point the dominant values of the society in which those policies are framed. The social policies and institutions within which the 'problems' of ageing are defined and managed reflect rather than contradict dominant values in society. These 'social' policies cannot be disassociated from the organization of production and decisions about the management of the economy, because these are even more crucial in determining the social status and living standards of the elderly. Changes in the way in which production is organized, for example, have a direct bearing on the development of retirement and age-restrictive employment practices. The goal of profit maximization has provided the economic rationale for the superannuation of large numbers of older workers from the labour market at an earlier age due to ill-health (Walker, 1981a). If, in turn, the economy is deflated and managed at a reduced level of production in order to further neo-monetarist economic and social goals, as under the Thatcher and Reagan administrations in Britain and the USA between 1980 and 1986, there are important implications for elderly people. Recent economic policies in Britain have increased unemployment and reduced public expenditure on the social services; both have had a direct impact on elderly people by reducing their economic activity, cutting their pensions and reducing the support they receive from the personal social services (Walker, 1985a, 1986). When these implications of economic management are coupled with values in capitalist societies which, partly due to assumptions about relative productivity, favour youth over elderly people, and more importantly, with the necessity of maintaining the work ethic amongst young people in a period of high unemployment, the economic and social status of elderly people is clearly precarious.

Ageing and social policy
The approach to social policy and ageing discussed here differs from the more familiar tendency in the social administration and gerontological literature to discuss ageing and elderly people as if they were a distinct social minority, in isolation from social values and processes, particularly the process of production. We are concerned primarily with the relationship between the way production is organized and the social and political institutions and processes of society, such as pensions and retirement, and therefore the starting point is the organization of production and the social relations which it fosters (Walker, 1981a). In other words there is a *structural* relationship between elderly people and the rest of society and among different groups of the elderly based on the social relations of production. The social and economic status of elderly people is defined not by biological age but by the institutions organized wholly or partly on production. Social policies are, therefore, part of the process of defining old age in different societies. Policies on social security, education and retirement determine the period of working life and since work is the main source of economic status in all industrial societies, those outside of the labour market occupy a relatively deprived status.

The stereotype of elderly people as a homogeneous group with special needs has tended to dominate public attitudes and social policies towards this group. Approaches to age and ageing based on the implicit assumption that the elderly can be treated as a distinct social group, in isolation from the rest of the social structure, have not provided an adequate basis for an explanation of the reduced social status of elderly people and the subordinate status of some groups among them. Some policies have been related closely to age, particularly retirement age, rather than the specific needs associated, say, with disability. Needs are assumed to arise at different stages of the life-cycle, one crucial stage of which is retirement. Little attention has been paid, therefore to the *differential* impact of retirement and other social processes on elderly people, especially the class and sex divisions in retirement experience. Secondly, the life-cycle approach to need has tended to obscure inequalities between elderly people and younger adults. Thirdly, by creating or reinforcing negative stereotypes through the portrayal of elderly people as a group with unique needs, there is a danger that a 'dysfunctional tension' will be set up between the elderly and the rest of society (Etzioni, 1976: 21). Resentment towards the elderly has not been openly and consistently articulated in British society, but periodic expressions of alarm at the 'burden' of dependency – for example in the recent (1985) debate about the future of the State Earnings-Related Pension Scheme – may be seen as one result of socially divisive attitudes and policies. Although they reflect a crude 'ageism' these attitudes cannot be dismissed so easily, since to do so would ignore significant variations in status and experience between different groups of elderly people. Alternative explanations are called for of both widespread dependent status and deep-seated deprivation among some elderly people.

It is important for policy-makers and practitioners to recognize that the process of assigning dependent status on the basis of age is a social and not a biological construct. There is no necessary relationship beween chronological age and need or dependency (Walker, 1980). Even at the extremes of age, physical dependency is associated with functional ability rather than with age as such. But even this relationship between disability and physical dependency is by no means clear cut, because financial resources, aids and adaptations may mitigate this need to some extent. Yet the social security systems of most countries do not recognize the financial need created by disablement in old age.

The combined effect of different policies in the spheres of industrial organization and income maintenance is to disengage many of the elderly from the working population and from participation in productive activity. On the one hand society defines work as the main device for establishing a normal family life and on the other it denies access to work in some groups, including the elderly. Yet in the face of this *social* creation of dependency our categorization of, and response to, the 'problem' of old age are individually based. Stress is placed on individual response to ageing through different social service agencies, rather than on the structural relationship between the elderly and the rest of society and the link between dependency and the creation of need. Moreover, use of apparently neutral terms such as 'helping' and 'care' hide the fact that the social definitions are *imposed* on elderly people by social policies and the agencies which apply them (Edelman, 1977: 67). As I have argued, this approach stems from the fact that social policies reflect ideological assumptions concerning industrial and social values and these are the same values which also underlie the growth of dependency.

Thus as well as ensuring the welfare of elderly people in advanced industrial societies, state social policies are an important aspect of the social process which defines the boundaries of old age, its membership and social status. Social policies are one of the means by which such societies are made more rigidly stratified. The definition of old age in Britain also effectively sets the limits to full working life and, therefore, there is a critical relationship between policies on ageing and policies on employment; a relationship that is obscured by concentrating on a set age as a criterion for the allocation of resources to elderly people. This socially constructed relationship between age and the labour market is one crucial component of the creation of dependent status in old age.

Creation of dependent social and economic status
Having established the dual nature of social policies in increasing control of dependency as well as welfare, the remainder of this chapter is concerned with an analysis of the specific role of social policies in increasing age stratification in British society and in distinguishing the elderly as a dependent and deprived minority. Over the course of this century various social policies have combined to create, enhance or maintain this dependent status. Three main sets of policies may be distinguished (Walker, 1980, 1986; Townsend, 1981): those concerned with retirement, pensions and social security, and social services. In addition, recent employment and public expenditure policies in Britain have increased the tendency for elderly people to become economically and socially dependent.

Retirement policies
Fundamental to the increased significance of the age boundary between independent and dependent status this century have been retirement policies. The growth of retirement has ensured that an increasing proportion of elderly workers have been excluded from the labour force, at a fixed age, and therefore from access to earnings and the other economic, social and psychological aspects of the workplace. This major social change has progressed rapidly and is continuing to do so. Between 1931 and 1971 the proportion of men aged 65 and over who were retired increased from under one-half to 78 percent and by 1984 the figure was around 94 percent. Thus, in a relatively short space of time 'old age' has come to be socially defined as beginning at retirement age and, whether by institutional rule or customary practice, the age at which older workers have to leave the labour force (Parker, 1980: 13).

This major social development has not occurred independently of the policy, organization of production and industrial demand for labour. Accounts of the emergence and development of retirement suggest that elderly people have, in fact, been used as a reserve army of labour to be tapped when labour is in short supply, and to be shed when demand falls (Phillipson, 1978; Graebner, 1980; Walker, 1985b). Retirement is largely a twentieth-century phenomenon, which has been managed to remove from employment older workers in order to reconstitute and re-skill the labour force. This is not to suggest a narrow functionalist theory linking the growth of retirement with industrialization or the process of production. Retirement has *not* grown as a result of industrialization – large numbers of older people were economically active in all industrial societies during the first half of this century – but changes in industrial processes and in the organization of employment have been developed and managed in ways intended to exclude older workers. Work processes have been reorganized, the division of labour has increased and the labour process has been rationalized (Braverman, 1976).

Various factors have combined to ensure that older workers were the most likely to be affected by these changes: for example, the influential scientific management school of thought in the United States argued that efficiency in the labour process depended on the removal of those with relatively low levels of marginal productivity, which was crudely related to age (Myles, 1981: 16); the historical tendency of capital is to reduce its necessary labour to the minimum in order to maintain profitability; the process of technological innovation and the high birth rate of the early 1960s provided some impetus for the displacement of older workers and, where necessary, their replacement with younger workers. Finally, the advent of large-scale unemployment in the 1930s was crucial in the institutionalization of retirement, and its return in the early 1980s has resulted in the growth and institutionalization of early retirement (Walker, 1982a, 1985b).

These main factors in the twentieth-century development of British society have combined to reduce the demand for older workers. At the same time, on the supply side, as retirement and early retirement have been encouraged by employers and the state they have been accepted as customary and have become part of trade union bargaining in production processes (such as the spread of assembly line production), have reduced the attachment of workers to employment (Beynon, 1976) and, together with the failure of employers and state to improve the working conditions of many, have contributed to a desire to leave work. Thus the perceived needs of capitalist enterprise and older workers have increasingly coincided on the issue of retirement. This consensus rests partly on the awful, health-destroying working conditions that many people are forced to endure and partly on the belief by older workers that retirement is a status to be earned and looked forward to, a belief that is socially constructed and fostered in order to encourage retirement. One facet of this social construction involves the restricted perception of retirement as a short-term status (Walker, 1982a) to be enjoyed by the 'young-old' (Neugarten, 1974). The paradox that this social construction of a desired status represents in a society in which the market is pre-eminent in the distribution of rewards is glaring. Poverty and deprivation in retirement are not likely to be eradicated until the relationship between age and the labour market is altered. So, the structural dependency among the elderly that superannuation creates rests on the predominance of wage labour and distribution through the market. The existence of welfare state provision, for reasons outlined earlier, does not challenge the prevailing system of distribution but supports it and therefore institutionalizes economic dependency through pension rules and regulations.

Like the experience of work the experience of retirement and attitudes towards it are socially divided. There are those, mainly salaried workers in a career structure, who are able to choose whether or not to leave work at the retirement age or to leave prematurely or perhaps to work on (Walker, 1985b). Then there are those, predominantly manual workers, who are effectively coerced into retirement and sometimes early retirement by poor working conditions, ill-health, redundancy and unemployment (Palmore, 1978; Olsen and Hansen, 1981; Walker, 1985b). Thus in industries which have arduous working conditions or boring and repetitive work workers are likely to welcome retirement at the earliest opportunity (Barfield and Morgan, 1969). There is also a sexual division, with a higher proportion of both married and non-married women than men remaining in work after the normal retirement age (Jolly, Creigh and Mingay, 1980: 114).

Thus for large numbers of older workers dependency is created by ill-health, redundancy and unemployment *prior* to retirement age. In fact sickness and unemployment account for nearly two-thirds of men and one-quarter of women who retire prematurely (Parker, 1980: 10). A recent study of 'voluntary' early retirement found that two important factors were health and dissatisfaction with their job (McGoldrick and Cooper, 1980: 860). The nature and organization of production is responsible for the exclusion of a significant proportion of elderly people but social policies have failed both to ensure adequate safety standards and to secure the return to work of injured and disabled workers. So for a significant proportion of older workers the retirement age is effectively lowered by unemployment, sickness or injury. As with unemployment itself, semi-skilled and unskilled workers are over-represented among the early retired (Parker, 1980: 16).

The policy of disengaging older workers from the labour force was formalized in January 1977 by the introduction of the Job Release Scheme, for women aged 59 and men aged 64, which is intended to 'alleviate unemployment among younger workers' (DHSS, 1981: 16) by 'encouraging older workers to leave their jobs' (Department of Employment, 1980). The scheme was extended in 1981 and 1982, to cover disabled men aged 60–63 and other men aged 62–63, and in October 1983 to include part-time work. Those taking up job release allowances must not take a job or set up in business on their own, and their employer must undertake to recruit as soon as possible a registered unemployed worker. In view of the close relationship between retirement and low incomes, the Job Release Scheme may be seen as an attempt to shift the social costs of dependency from younger to older workers. Similar policies have been introduced in other countries, such as France and Sweden (Laczko and Walker, 1985).

Pension policies

The corollary to this process of exclusion from the labour force is that elderly people are heavily dependent on the state for financial support – about 90 percent of them receive some form of social security benefit. Elderly people are, in effect, trapped in poverty by their reliance on state benefits. The process of retirement results in the average fall in income of about one-half.

The implicit rationale, or social policy, underlying the differential between those in employment and those dependent on state benefits is the assumption that social benefits are intended to maintain monetary incentives and the work, or rather, employment ethic. Thus paradoxically, even those groups, such as the elderly, who have worked for a full term are not entitled to non-dependent status, nor, for a large proportion, freedom from reliance on minimum subsistence income support; unless, that is, it has been earned through contributions paid to a *private* pension while in employment. We have seen that retirement has a differential impact on elderly people – depending primarily on prior socioeconomic status and the access it grants to resources which can be carried into retirement – but, in addition, because of the social limitation on the level of state pensions and other benefits for this outside of the labour force, retirement imposes a lowered social status on the vast majority of the elderly in relation to younger adults in the labour market. For some 5.7 million elderly people out of a total of 8.9 million, this reduction means life in poverty or on its margin and, within that total, there are one million elderly people living on incomes *below* the supplementary benefit poverty level.

Recent policy changes and proposals in the pipeline are likely to increase still further the proportion of elderly people in poverty. The Conservative government de-indexed the basic pension from earnings in 1980 and, as a result, pensioners' living standards have been declining steadily relative to wage-earners and will continue to do so. The main hope for a significant increase in the incomes of the elderly towards the end of the century – the

State Earnings-Related Pension Scheme (SERPS) – was a major feature of the reviews of social security which culminated in the publication of a Green Paper in June 1985. The government believed that SERPS represented an unacceptable 'burden' on future generations and proposed to abolish it (DHSS, 1985a: 5), thereby removing the right of future pensioners to full earnings-related protection from the state. However, the weight of influential opinion against abolishing SERPS – including the CBI and the private pension funds and insurance companies – was so great that the government was forced to rethink its plans. Thus the White Paper on the reform of social security, published in December 1985, proposed to modify SERPS rather than to abandon it. Briefly the intention of the proposals is twofold: to cut the projected cost of the scheme by half and to provide incentives that will encourage the spread of private pensions (DHSS, 1985b: 15). These proposed changes have been deferred until 1988.

The dependency relationship between elderly people, the state and the labour market was institutionalized by the 'retirement condition', introduced in 1948, whereby state financial assistance is conditional on retirement rather than age. Older workers must retire before the receipt of the National Insurance Retirement Pension to which they have contributed throughout their working life. This has encouraged an end to labour force participation and has established an arbitrary retirement age as customary. Ironically, Beveridge (1942: 96) had hoped that the retirement condition would encourage workers to defer retirement, but it has resulted in the adoption of the pension ages as the retirement ages. Together with the high marginal rates of taxation levied on pensioners who take up employment, it militates against the continuation of work by the elderly. More recently the social security system has been used to further encourage the disengagement of older men from the labour force by awarding the higher long-term rate of supplementary benefit to those over the age of 60 who are unemployed. At first this was conditional on their not registering as unemployed.

The social security system is also used to enforce women's dependence on men prior to and after retirement (see Peace, 1986). Most women still receive pensions as dependents on their husband's contributions and, regardless of their age, have to wait until he reaches 65. Although the Social Security Act 1980 contained some improvements in the status of women these were only a tentative first step towards 'similar treatment' for women and men rather than equal treatment. A significant step in the direction of equal treatment between men and women as far as retirement ages go was forced on the government by the European Court of Justice. It ruled, in February 1986, that Britain was guilty of sexual discrimination in compelling women to retire five years earlier than men and the Department of Employment announced subsequently that the Sex Discrimination Act would be amended to take the ruling into account. However, there have been serious reverses too. One of the main reasons behind the government's proposals to modify SERPS is that it is considered to be 'over-generous' to women who were the main beneficiaries from the best twenty years calculation of earnings for pension purposes.

Elderly married women are less likely than men to receive a National Insurance Retirement Pension in their own right and are overwhelmingly less likely to receive an occupational pension from a former employer (Hunt, 1978: 28). Moreover, the dependent status of married women under the social security system in earlier adult life is one contributory factor behind the certainty that, on reaching retirement age, they are likely to be poorer than men: 39 percent of elderly women live in families with incomes on or below the poverty line, compared with 26 percent of men and 16 percent of couples. In other words, just as discrimination against women, and married women in particular, in working life disadvantages them relative to men, further discrimination against women in the social security system and in the control and allocation of financial resources within families (Pahl, 1980) superimposes on them dependency and reduced social status in retirement.

Finally, the failure of the state through the social security system to meet the needs created by disablement in old age means that the increasing numbers of elderly and especially very elderly people who become disabled experience even deeper deprivation than their non-disabled counterparts (Walker and Townsend, 1981).

Health and personal social services
Related to the crucial role of retirement and pension policies in the creation of dependency has been the development of care in the health and personal social services. In fact, the existence of a poor, dependent minority resulting from exclusion from the labour force and the resulting restriction of access to resources has an important part in shaping policies as well as attitudes in the personal social services. There is a wide range of groups in the health and personal social services – from the consultant geriatricians to domestic staff in old people's homes – who exert a considerable degree of control over the lives of elderly people, and who may enhance or reduce their dependence. Policies in the health and personal social services, like other social policies, have been treated as distinct from the dominant social structure and social values. But the pattern of residential and community care cannot be explained without reference to this structure, particularly the sexual division of labour within the family, the distribution of resources between different classes and age groups and assumptions about the role of elderly people in society.

There is a wide literature about the exercise of professional pow' particularly on the part of doctors, in pursuit of narrow group inte'

(Friedson, 1975). The dominant elements in the medical profession have favoured institutional care as opposed to community care for a very long time, and they are one of the important pressure groups resisting the switch to the latter form of care for elderly people. Through membership of planning and resource allocation agencies, from the Department of Health and Social Security to the Area and Regional Health Authorities, as well as through the proselytization of institutional models of curative medicine, some sections of the medical profession represent a powerful countervailing force to community-based forms of care.

Other interest groups – such as architects, caterers, builders, local politicians, administrators and planners – may also tend to favour institutional forms of care. Achievements can be registered permanently in the form of bricks and mortar. Also, as staff unions have increased their influence, they too have tended towards narrow interpretations of their members' interests. Consequently despite the fact that an explicit policy of community care has been in operation for over twenty years and that only 5 percent of elderly people live in institutions, this form of care dominates resource allocations within both health and social services (Walker, 1981b, 1982b, 1985a).

Residential institutions like other social organizations perform different functions, providing, as well as care, the control of 'difficult', 'confused' and 'forgetful' residents and a relatively cheap substitute for public housing and community services. Independent evidence collected over the last twenty years indicates that a significant proportion of residents are capable of living independently and are not, as the relevant legislation requires, 'in need of care and attention'. These studies have provided conclusive evidence that a substantial proportion of residents do not need constant care and attention (Townsend, 1981: 16). Moreover there are important social divisions between residents, suggesting that institutionalization has social determinants. For example, there are differences based on marital status, with 37 percent of single men and 44 percent of single women aged 90 or over living in institutions, four times as many as married men and married women respectively of the same age. Those with close relatives, especially daughters, are less likely than others to enter institutions. In addition, there is homelessness and lack of community support underlying the entry to residential institutions by relatively fit elderly people.

There is also a body of evidence showing that once in residential institutions elderly people are likely to become increasingly dependent. A long history of research suggests that the interests of the staff of residential homes are likely to tend towards the creation of dependency rather than independence amongst elderly residents (Townsend, 1962; Booth, 1985). Independent research indicates, among other things, that the desire of staff for increased 'nursing' status and rewards is an important contributory factor in the dependence of elderly people in residential accommodation.

In other words, in the definition and practice of their role residential staff may, unwittingly, enhance the dependence of *both* the less physically disabled and the more severly disabled. Of course, staff are not free to define the content of their roles – they are circumscribed by management, professional and training authorities – but they do have considerable flexibility in how they choose to carry out their role and in how they treat elderly people on a day-to-day basis.

Other aspects of the social organization of residential care also contribute to the loss of liberty and independence on the part of elderly people. Administrative regulations such as fire and safety rules impose constraints on elderly people living in 'homes' which go far beyond their experience of independent living in their own homes. Moreover they have no influence over the formulation and application of these regulations. Ironically, however, research by the Tavistock Institute of Human Relations suggests that old people are not necessarily safer when they are in care. Out of 133 fatal accidents among those aged 65 and over, 35 percent were in institutional care, although only 5 percent of that age group live in institutions (Norman, 1980: 17).

Clearly there are variations in good practice between residential institutions and therefore variations in the quality of life experienced by elderly people, but a long series of research studies have shown that they deny freedom, privacy and comfort and are very far from resembling the commonly understood concept of a home. Consultation with the residents is still rare and democratic organization virtually unknown. Management is often strict and rigid, with hospital-like daily routines for meals, bed times and visiting, lacking privacy and possibilities for self-care. The loss of independence suffered by elderly people on admission to a hospital or residential institution has been forcefully summarized by Norman:

> Old people are taken from their homes when domiciliary support and physical treatment might enable them to stay there; they are subjected in long-stay hospitals and homes to regimes which deprive them of many basic human dignities; and they are often not properly consulted about the care or treatment to which they are subjected. [Norman, 1980: 7]

It is not wholly surprising, therefore, that elderly people themselves associate moving into institutions with loss of independence (Tobin and Lieberman, 1976: 18). In turn, the likelihood of admission to a residential institution is increased by public expenditure cuts and the failure of successive governments to develop community care services (Walker, 1981c, 1985a). In the face of increasing need the failure of community care policies falls on those least able to bear them as only the better off are able to buy home care in the market. For many the only alternative is to enter the private sector of residential and nursing homes, which have mushroomed in the last five years under the encouragement of supplementary benefit subsidies. The inadequacy of community care thus increases institutionalization in both public and private sectors.

In combination, these policies in employment, pensions and social services have played an important part in creating and legitimating dependency among elderly people. It is on this foundation, moreover, that the impact on the elderly of recent policies in public expenditure and employment can be understood. The exclusion of older workers from the labour market has formed the basis for a more general devaluation of the contribution and social status of the elderly in British society, a judgement which, incidentally, is confounded by the contribution of elderly people to family relationships (Walker, 1981c). Since the mid-1970s governments of both Labour and Conservative parties have reduced the growth of expenditure on the social services; because they are the main client group of these services, this has affected elderly people more than others (Walker, 1985a, 1985c). Furthermore, the massive rise in unemployment under the Conservative government has hit older workers as well as younger ones, but their employment policies have positively favoured younger workers to the detriment of the employment prospects of older workers.

Conclusion

The increasing dependency of elderly people in Britain has been socially engineered in order to remove older workers from the labour force. At the heart of this social change has been the narrow financial goals of capitalism, and particularly its constant desire to increase profitability. In this interest mass superannuation has been managed through the retirement, early retirement and unemployment of older workers. Age-restrictive social policies have been used by the state both to exclude older workers from the labour force and to legitimate that exclusion through retirement. Retirement pensions are one of the means by which capitalism is able to enforce changes aimed at reconstituting the workforce. This changing social relationship between age and the labour market has formed the basis for a more general spread of dependency among the elderly. Age-restrictive policies in health and personal social services have been reviewed, but also in housing the failure to provide a sufficient stock of sheltered housing for older people has tended to increase the likelihood of institutionalization, and therefore increased dependency. Similarly in education and training, age-restrictive policies have relatively disadvantaged elderly people in relation to changing knowledge and technology.

Increasing economic and social dependence may also contribute to increasing physical and mental dependence outside as well as inside institutions. What is certain is that dependency imposes reduced social status on *carers* as well as elderly people. Community care policies in the allocation of home helps, meals-on-wheels and other assistance are based on assumptions about the division of care within the family, particularly the sexual division of labour, and the responsibility of the family in caring for their own members (Walker, 1981b, 1982b, 1985a). Thus social services substitute for rather than support families (Moroney, 1976). Carers are usually women, and social policies which allocate social services in preference to those without wives or daughters to care for them effectively lead to isolation, low incomes and restricted opportunities for these, predominantly female, carers. It is not surprising, therefore, that loss of status is frequently expressed by women who care for elderly relatives (Nissel and Bonnerjea, 1982).

Increasing dependency among the elderly in Britain has stemmed from conscious changes in the structure and organization of capitalist production. These changes have encouraged an unnecessarily narrow age-restrictive approach to employment and, therefore, to social policies in the field of pensions and social services. The key to the dependent relationship between the elderly and the state is the labour market, and policies such as the abolition of age-barrier retirement and the encouragement of flexible retirement would necessitate changes in pension and other policies. This change would provide an alternative interpretation of the role to be played by the elderly in modern British society, from an increasingly dependent one to an active and productive one. Such a change in the social status of elderly people would be accompanied by increased incomes, and by better and more appropriate housing and improved social services.

References

Barfield, R. and Morgan, J. (1969) *Early Retirement: the Decision and the Experience.* Michigan: Institute for Social Research.

Beveridge, Sir W. (1942) *Social Insurance and Allied Services* (Cmnd 6404). London: HMSO.

Beynon, H. (1976) *Working for Ford.* Harmondsworth: Penguin.

Booth, T. (1985) *Home Truths.* Aldershot: Gower.

Braverman, H. (1976) *Labour and Monopoly Capital.* London: Monthly Review Press.

Department of Employment (1980) *Job Release Schemes.* London: HMSO.

Department of Health and Social Security (1981) *Growing Older.* London: HMSO.

Department of Health and Social Security (1985a) *Reform of Social Security* (Cmnd 9517). London: HMSO.

Department of Health and Social Security (1985b) *Reform of Social Security: Programme for Action* (Cmnd 9691). London: HMSO.

Edelman, M. (1977) *Political Language.* New York: Academic Press.

Etzioni, A. (1976) 'Old People and Public Policy', *Social Policy* 7: 20–4.

Freidson, E. (1975) *Profession of Medicine.* New York: Dodd, Mead.

Ginsburg, N. (1979) *Class, Capital and Social Policy.* London: Macmillan.

Gough, I. (1979) *The Political Economy of the Welfare State.* London: Macmillan.

Graebner, W. (1980) *A History of Retirement.* New Haven, CT: Yale University Press.

Guillemard, A-M. (1986) 'Social Policy and Ageing in France', in Phillipson and Walker (1986: 263–79).

Hendricks, J. and Calasanti, T. (1986) 'Social Policy and Ageing in the United States', in Phillipson and Walker (1986: 237–62).

Hendricks, J. and Hendricks, C. D. (1977) *Ageing in Mass Society*. Cambridge, MA: Winthrop.

Hunt, A. (1978) *The Elderly at Home*. London: HMSO.

Jolly, J., Creigh, S. and Mingay, A. (1980) *Age as a Factor in Employment*. London: Department of Employment.

Laczko, F. and Walker, A. (1985) 'Excluding Older Workers from the Labour Market: Early Retirement Policies in Britain, France and Sweden', pp. 100–22 in Brenton, M. and Jones, C. (eds) *The Year Book of Social Policy in Britain 1984–5*. London: Routledge & Kegan Paul.

McGoldrick, A. and Cooper, C. L. (1980) 'Voluntary Early Retirement – Taking the Decision', *Employment Gazette* (August).

Maeda, D. (1978) 'Ageing in Eastern Society', in Hobman, D. (ed.) *The Social Challenge of Ageing*. London: Croom Helm.

Moroney, R. M. (1976) *The Family and the State*. London: Longman.

Myles, J. F. (1981) 'The Aged and the Welfare State: An Essay in Political Demography', paper presented to Roundtable on Ageing and Social Policy, Paris, July 8–9.

Neugarten, B. L. (1974) 'Age Groups in American Society and the Rise of the Young-Old', *Annals of the American Academy of Political Science* 415: 187–98.

Nissel, M. and Bonnerjea, L. (1982) *Looking After the Handicapped Elderly at Home: Who Pays?* London: Policy Studies Institute.

Norman, A. J. (1980) *Rights and Risk*. London: National Corporation for the Care of Old People.

O'Connor, J. (1977) *The Fiscal Crisis of the State*. New York: St Martin's Press.

Olsen, H. and Hansen, G. (1981) *Living Conditions of the Aged 1977*. Copenhagen: National Institute of Social Research.

Pahl, J. (1980) 'Patterns of Money Management Within Marriage', *Journal of Social Policy* 9(3): 313–35.

Palmore, E. C. (1978) 'Compulsory Versus Flexible Retirement: Issues and Facts', in Carver, V. and Liddiard, P. (eds) *An Ageing Population*. Sevenoaks: Hodder & Stoughton/The Open University Press.

Parker, S. (1980) *Older Workers and Retirement*. London: HMSO.

Peace, S. (1986) 'The Forgotten Female: Social Policy and Older Women', in Phillipson and Walker (1986: 61–86).

Phillipson, C. (1978) *The Emergence of Retirement*. Durham: University of Durham.

Phillipson, C. and Walker, A. (eds) (1986) *Ageing and Social Policy*. Aldershot: Gower.

Rowntree, B. S. (1901) *Poverty: A Study of Town Life*. London: Macmillan.

Taylor-Gooby, P. (1985) *Public Opinion, Ideology and State Welfare*. London: Routledge & Kegan Paul.

Titmuss, R. M. (1963) 'The Social Division of Welfare', in *Essays on 'The Welfare State'*. London: Allen & Unwin.

Tobin, S. S. and Lieberman, M. A. (1976) *Last Home for the Aged*. London: Jossey-Bass.

Townsend, P. (1962) *The Last Refuge*. London: Routledge & Kegan Paul.

Townsend, P. (1981) 'The Structured Dependency of the Elderly: A Creation of Social Policy in the Twentieth Century', *Ageing and Society* 1(1): 5–28.

Walker, A. (1980) 'The Social Creation of Poverty and Dependency in Old Age', *Journal of Social Policy* 9(1): 49–75.

Walker, A. (1981a) 'Towards a Political Economy of Old Age', *Ageing and Society* 1(1): 73–94.

Walker, A. (1981b) 'Social Policy, Social Administration and the Social Construction of Welfare', *Sociology* 15(2): 225–50.

Walker, A. (1981c) 'Community Care and the Elderly in Britain: Theory and Practice', *International Journal of Health Services* 11(4): 541–57.

Walker, A. (1982a) 'The Social Consequences of Early Retirement', *Political Quarterly* 53(1): 61–72.

Walker, A. (ed.) (1982b) *Community Care*. Oxford: Blackwell.

Walker, A. (1985a) *The Care Gap*. London: Local Government.

Walker, A. (1985b) 'Early Retirement: Release or Refuge from the Labour Market?', *The Quarterly Journal of Social Affairs* 1(3): 211–29.

Walker, A. (1985c) 'Getting the Elderly to Pay', *New Society* (18 April): 76–8.

Walker, A. (1986) 'Pensions and the Production of Poverty in Old Age', in Phillipson and Walker (1986: 184–216).

Walker, A. and Townsend, P. (eds) (1981) *Disability in Britain*. London: Martin Robertson.

Wynn, M. (1972) *Family Policy*. Harmondsworth: Penguin.

4
The future of social work: a pragmatic view

Joan Cooper

Introduction

The popular image of social workers as middle- or upper-class women doing good for the poor while successful businessmen managed charitable funds and property was a nineteenth-century legacy which persisted until the Second World War (Walton, 1975: 258). It was largely dispelled by a fanfare for social workers as mediators between individuals and the welfare state systems which developed during and after that war. As Titmuss, the influential philosopher of the welfare state, observed in 1965, 'It is an interesting and often overlooked fact that, during the last twenty years, whenever the British people have identified and investigated a social problem there has followed a national call for more social work and more trained social workers' (Titmuss, 1979: 86). Various committees pronouncing on medical, penal and social issues had come to recognize social work's contribution as able to humanize bureaucratic systems, to protect the rights of individuals through casework and counselling, through advocacy and mediation leading to the effective use of services. Their employment was both compassionate and prudent.

Although scattered and peripheral within the health, welfare and penal systems, social workers had evidently demonstrated their skills particularly in psychiatric and medical settings. With the establishment of children's departments in local government in 1948, social workers – who have always needed to be attached to resources – learned to manage services and to be accountable to democratic process and the local electorate. The final administrative gesture of the welfare state was the creation of local authority Social Services Departments (SSDs) in 1971, combining the scattered personal social services for children including juvenile delinquents and families with children, for sick and disabled people, and for elderly, mentally ill and mentally handicapped people. This organizational reform was more limited than the Seebohm Committee's vision (Seebohm, 1968: 11). That committee, when reviewing the organization and responsibilities of the personal social services in England and Wales, had recommended a universal service to 'reach far beyond the discovery and rescue of social casualties' and to 'enable the greatest possible number of individuals to act reciprocally, giving and receiving service for the well-being of the whole community'. Social work departments in Scotland were more comprehensive and included adult offenders, but in the rest of Britain these remained the responsibility of the probation service. Northern Ireland formed Health and Social Service Boards outside local government. The aim was to make day, domiciliary and residential services available to all groups, and to make the services acceptable, accessible and comprehensive (Cooper, 1983: 85). The collective response of the welfare state to meeting social need finally ran parallel with the education, health, housing and social security systems.

Since 1971 the vast majority of professional social workers have been employed by SSDs but numerically they are a minority of the total staff. Importantly, they provide and guard the dominant ethic in these bureaucratic systems. This social work ethic pursues social equity and, within the imposed legal limits, the provision of appropriate services to all citizens, irrespective of their condition, creed, race or contribution to society. Social work is a moral activity. This is significant, for social workers intervene to preserve 'life, liberty and the pursuit of happiness', and act as gate-keepers to the resources assessed as necessary to pursue these ends. Without an ethical code it would be dangerous for social workers to be exercising the powers, vested in their agencies, which permit them to intervene in the delicate relationship between state and citizen. Their role in the redress of structural inequalities is minimal, particularly in an increasingly conscious capitalist society, but their impact remains symbolically significant within systems, and their intervention may be crucial to individuals and groups. Social workers retain elements of a rescue service, open to the criticism that they fail to achieve radical solutions, and have barely achieved a promotional service.

Areas of intervention
Local authorities are agents of law. More than thirty Acts of Parliament confer powers and duties on them to provide personal social services administered by SSDs. This is an untidy legal legacy which takes complexity to the point of strangulation. For social workers to act outside their powers is illegal, while to fail in their duties is liable to put them in peril of a public inquiry, an Ombudsman investigation for maladministration or a prosecution. Yet within the context of SSDs and the probation service, discretionary social work is also practised, notably the probation officers' role in counselling and conciliation in divorce proceedings, and SSDs' involvement in preventive and rehabilitation work. The exercise of legal duties and discretionary powers leaves social work in an equivocal position.

The main categories or client groups who are deemed in law to require service or protection are an historical legacy derived from the Poor Law (abolished in 1948) and from medical and penal services. They are vulnerable or dependent people because of age or condition, or deviants from the accepted norms of society, but assessed as likely to benefit from support, counselling and care or benign social control.

One view is that those whose welfare needs were long term and peripheral to a medical and largely hospital model were of low priority, and the obligation to care and protect ranked below that of caring and curing (Pinker, 1978: 21). A social model was gradually evolving which recognized that humans have a social entity, and throughout their lives live in social relationships. Social work and the personal social services required their own identity if they were to be effective in promoting social functioning at times when people were beset with difficulties and impediments. For effective intervention, as social work increasingly moves from an institutional to a community base, the inherited categorical and distinctive client group approach becomes stigmatizing, restrictive and outmoded. Social work is needed by newly emerging groups in response to social change. Yet it is on the horns of a dilemma. Its intervention through offering care, support and practical assistance commands public approval and sympathy for handicapped people of all ages. These are the deserving. This is an unsophisticated view, for given adequate support and technical aids, increasing numbers of handicapped people demonstrate their independent social functioning and rightfully resent being labelled. With elderly people intervention is designed to protect, to promote capacity and maintain independence for as long as practicable and this intervention wins social approval. Intervention is more ambiguous and is viewed more controversially when protection requires a measure of control under the legal powers and duties vested in local authorities but exercised by social workers. The law may be invoked to protect children from mental, physical or sexual abuse by adults. Social workers, including probation officers who are themselves qualified social workers, intervene in and out of court to protect adolescents from unnecessary custody. Recent legislation requires specially approved social workers who have had additional training to intervene in mental illness crises to prevent self-damage or avoid danger to others, and to ensure that community resources are explored before compulsory hospital admission is imposed. Very occasionally, social workers intervene to seek the removal of an elderly person living in unsafe or neglectful circumstances. This continuum of care and control, necessary because any society needs a social defence system, makes social work a very public activity and vulnerable to public scrutiny.

Social work settings

Conceptually, this care/control function is positive and defensible, if uncomfortable. In protecting people from deterioration and damage, individual freedom is guarded. Social work is non-punitive and aims at the least detrimental intervention. This remains true whether social work is practised from an SSD base which commands immediate access to day, domiciliary and residential services or when social workers respond to referrals from the public or from other professionals or when they are guests rather than the primary workers in the education, health or justice systems. Their formal absence from the employment, housing and social security systems is historical rather than logical.

Unlike law and medicine, social work in Britain has no tradition of private practice. Historic tradition lies in the voluntary movement and philanthropy which also encompassed unpopular groups such as delinquents or alcoholics. The voluntary service-providing organizations which sagged during the heyday of the welfare state have now re-flowered, with political support, to supplement or substitute for public provision. Increasingly, voluntary organizations are being professionalized and employing social workers for day and residential services where care and control covertly merge. With the exception of the National Society for the Prevention of Cruelty to Children (for historical reasons), powers of statutory intervention are not vested in voluntary organizations on the grounds that infringement of liberty is better limited to accountable public bodies.

Potential developments lie, and have already occurred, in the expansion of voluntary and commercial provision to offer variety and increase choice. These developments raise the question of users' rights outside public accountability, the management of adequate standards in all sectors and issues of class distinction in service provision. There is the possibility that the image of the public service could be one of a controlling service, and a 'poor service for poor people'. This is alien to a welfare state philosophy, as distinct from the existence of welfare state mechanisms which ensure bedrock services administered but not personalized.

Means of intervention

Philosophically, the purpose of social work has developed beyond a rescue service, a nineteenth-century concept largely based on administrative procedures, to intervention based upon a skilled assessment of need and a matching of available or created resources to provide opportunities for adequate personal care, social development and creativity for individuals and groups. Intervention covers a range of activities which span personal or group counselling, arranging access to day and residential services or supporting people in their own homes with domiciliary services. Social workers are involved in staff roles in residential and day care to offer social skills and a therapeutic experience.

Social workers are frequently called upon when people are in crisis, whether environmental or personal. The task is to reduce difficulties to more tolerable proportions. The protection of vulnerable people and the support of dependent people and of those tending them, sometimes unremittingly, are social work tasks. But so are experimental responses to meeting old and new forms of social need and associated behavioural responses. It is now incumbent that such responses must be so designed as to be amenable to evaluation and research.

The legacy of the casework or counselling tradition in social work remains an important one in professional practice. Its emphasis on individual reaction is a constant challenge to collectivism and bureaucratic prescription. It preserves the perspective that each individual is unique, and respects the particular meaning and construction that a person or family puts upon their situation (England, 1986: 7). Without an understanding of that meaning, sometimes an irrational one, and the social workers' insight into their own perceptions and reactions, quite obvious forms of help can be rejected or misused, or behaviour may be unmodified. The consequences may be serious in cases of violent, aggressive or antisocial behaviour. The trend is towards integrated methods or using a fuller range of measures of intervention based on common principles cutting across client groups, harnessing resources and practical skills 'in dealing with social problems as they are manifest in a single individual, group or a community' (Specht and Vickery, 1977: 15).

Both approaches, and there are others, such as task-centred social work, are open to criticism from left and right, from theorists and researchers. There is no intention here of examining social work methodology. The illustrations serve only to emphasize that professional social work practice is the application of knowledge and skills which have to be learned. And it is important to recognize that, like all dynamic activities, social work is subject to styles and fashions which reflect public attitudes, expectations and development in knowledge. Put dramatically, social work is a combination of 'applied love', relevant knowledge, skilled practice and organizing ability.

Cultural aspects of intervention

Social work is practised worldwide and reflects social and cultural patterns and values which may stress overt family, tribal or group systems. In developing countries, subject to rapid social change and urbanization, social work concentrates largely on community projects and group intervention but still aims to protect and promote the needs of the vulnerable, powerless and disadvantaged, especially in relation to children and young people since Third World population structures are youthful.

In Britain, highly specialized and skilled social work practised in relation to a particular client group with an emphasis on specialist teams, is in rivalry with a neighbourhood or 'patch'-based approach which links back to specialist practice but seeks to maximize accessibility and community resources. In theory, the method and action derive from local study, dialogue and consent (Beresford and Croft, 1986: 288). This is a pragmatic approach as yet largely described rather than tested and evaluated. The neighbourhood approach confined to 'patches' of 5000–10,000 population is to be distinguished from the community development projects popular during the 1960s and at first designed to change the system by co-ordinating all the social services horizontally rather than vertically, and so increase their responsiveness to consumer demand while at the same time articulating that demand. This radical approach collided with fears of politicization of social workers and voluntary organizations (Loney, 1983: 30). The patch approach is more traditional in re-emphasizing a geographic base for social work, inviting local participation and mobilizing local statutory, voluntary and informal carers, to capitalize on community resources (Hadley and Hatch, 1981: 154).

Although social work has always articulated its perceptions of social need and been associated with social reform, it claims neither the knowledge nor the role to reform society politically or economically. To claim such a role would be impractical, diversionary and a desertion of the essential function of responding to people undergoing social stress. In practice, this limitation of role does not exclude those who enter social work for political reasons in order to influence the working of systems in the interests of the disadvantaged.

Debate in social work

Debate about whether local government provides the most appropriate base for social work and the personal social services, especially in view of its increasing politicization, is evident. There are other debates about specialized teams practising with particular client groups or neighbourhood-based work and community participation, about the length and content of social work education and training, about the emphasis to be placed on planning and sharing resources across education, health and housing and about the role of social workers in securing welfare rights for clients. These debates are frequently ascribed to malaise, poor management and bad practice. The occasional tragedy fans the criticisms and vividly illustrates the complex role of social work in society.

There is some consensus that social work is about change in people and their environment. A relevant question is, who needs to change? It may be the parent rather than the child, or the carer rather than the elderly person, who is likely to deteriorate. It may be that society needs to change its attitudes, its policies and its administrative systems so that inequality and hardship are reduced.

One critique is that social work papers over the cracks of problems which arise from social disorganization and disadvantage, thus ignoring the economic and social deficits of poverty, unemployment, bad housing, urban decay, racism, class discrimination or inadequate and insufficient public services. Faced with such apparently intractable but tolerated problems, it is argued that individual or family social work is at best over-persuasive, or at worst downright manipulative, and that therapy does not stand up to scientific proof. Social workers might well respond that loss, stress, depression, violence, resistance to maintaining and repairing relationships inhibit social functioning, and that without positive motivation, resources which can be mobilized are not constructively used and conflict is increased. This is an incremental rather than radical position, though radical change may be the objective.

Social care planning is also regarded as an essential element of social work intervention (Barclay, 1982: 51). The social worker is equipped with knowledge of the other relevant social services which typify a welfare state model, and increasingly adds knowledge of facilities available in the voluntary and private sectors and of informal networks of helpers. Knowledge of relevant services implies negotiation and advocacy with other agencies, and an ability to work in a multi-disciplinary context or team. Social care planning and organization is followed by the review and monitoring of social care to assess effectiveness and risk. Risks may be high in packages of care for housebound, even bedbound, elderly people and for handicapped people, and the risks of overstraining carers are high too.

Programme provision is part of social work, and may range from residential care, across day centres for families or for a mixture of client groups, projects for adolescents, family placement schemes for children, now being extended to elderly and handicapped people for respite care, groups for mentally disturbed people and drop-in centres for advice and information. While there is a lack of programme evaluation, constant decision-making, re-appraisal and modification characterize social work programmes, and trial and error must be accepted features as in any other inexact science. The increasing involvement of family, friends, neighbours and volunteers adds both resources and complexities to programmes and to evaluation.

Is social work in crisis?
Since the amalgamation of the personal social services in 1971, social work has survived constant pressures from over-demand for services, an over-zealous response to all social problems, high public expectation, government policy statements urging service development for each client group apparently in competition, major mental health legislation and a stream of incremental legislation in child care. Establishing priorities has defeated central and local government for two main reasons. The first reason is the extent of economic and social change. Economic recession and unemployment have imposed constraints on service expenditure and increased social stress markedly in areas where heavy industries once flourished as major employers. Social change, which is always ahead of social policy and the law, has involved new family styles which reflect the prevalence of divorce, remarriage, single parenthood and the existence of the four-generation family for the first time in history. The now well-established pattern of women's employment outside the home has influenced family roles and functioning.

One effect of all these changes has been a decrease in adoption and an increase in the support needed by parent(s) and children. Another is the growing volume of disputed child-care cases, when parental and children's interests appear to be in conflict, and the interested parties invoke the law for resolution. Another social change to which social work has had to respond is the traffic in drugs and the spread of addictions. Social work has to react to crises in society and has to learn fast, but that does not mean that it is itself in crisis. It has never been more innovative and experimental, and this is true of both the public and voluntary sectors.

The second reason lies in the difficulty of long-term planning to prepare an effective response to change. Neither the mechanisms nor the knowledge exist in central or local government for planning ahead, even if the resources existed. There has been knowledge of the demographic change affecting the elderly population for forty years: planning then would have been unlikely to match current life-styles and aspirations. It is immediacy rather than crisis which is characteristic of social work.

The recognition of child abuse, which came to prominence in the early 1970s, illustrates this state of immediacy. Public concern, which sets its own priorities, provided little option to SSDs but to concentrate on statutory duties towards children and families. Abuse of elderly people, or any category of dependent people, is predictable unless those caring for them receive adequate services and respite, a need which fortunately is achieving public recognition and political response. All client groups demand due service on grounds of need, humanity and equity, and many are effectively supported by powerful lobbies, which may challenge official priorities.

Social work has to contend with the dilemmas over setting priorities when every group has a justifiable claim, and some are well served by voluntary organizations but other are not. The dilemma was well illustrated in the DHSS publication, *Priorities for Health and Personal Services in England*, issued in 1976 and immediately castigated by its critics as a document of non-priorities. The lifeboat principle of women and children first has found no current substitute. Social work is exposed to immediacy and conflict rather than being in crisis.

The current and future financial restraint over public expenditure presents a threat to social work. It has to accommodate to the rationing of resources to meet need, sometimes at near survival level. There is an extra burden: as other social services suffer reduced budgets, casualties are off-loaded onto the personal social services from housing, social security and health services. This means that social workers are increasingly called upon to work with clients in severe difficulty. Similarly, unemployment has produced its special demands, but social work is no substitute for work and financial stability. One result is that social work is constantly fighting for a promotional role and resisting an enforced residual function. In this context, social work is a political activity in that it has to confront crisis and conflict, and yet seize opportunities. If a crisis mentality prevails, the publicly provided personal social services will be reduced to offering minimal service to applicants and a return to the Poor Law deterrents of disgrace and stigma as a means of controlling demand.

Meantime there are new expectations. Social work has been slow to learn about the feelings and aspirations of black groups in society. The white assumption of assimilation has been confronted with a demand for different cultural patterns and habits in the delivery of personal social services. Acknowledgement is too little and too late. Social work needs more black social workers in a multiracial society.

There is evidence that social work is surviving despite the exposure of poor practice in mental health and child care. The demand for social work training is buoyant. The resurgence of the voluntary sector and developments in the private sector particularly for elderly people, provided the social work ethic prevails, may well produce a co-operative partnership, rather than a power struggle, and may also expand resources. There are problems. Social workers have led the way in identifying with clients in their situation, and in avoiding an elitist professional stance which makes decisions for people rather than with them. This attitude has attracted some criticism from other professionals, and has sometimes increased risks in what is a high-risk activity.

The image of social work

A recent government-established committee studying the roles and tasks of social workers pronounced:

> In spite of all the complexities and uncertainties surrounding the functions of social workers, we are united in our belief that the work they do is of vital importance in our society, as it is in other modern industrial societies. It is here to stay, and social workers are needed as never before. But it is important that we use a scarce and costly resource – the trained social worker – in a creative and effective manner. [Barclay, 1980: xi]

This is a statement of faith born of study and investigation inevitably biased by representations from social work interests, but counterbalanced by the committee's examination of relevant published literature and by visits made to sixteen areas for discussions with statutory, voluntary and informal agencies. Pragmatism is, however, no substitute for empirical or theoretical research, nor for the controlled trials conducted in the pure and applied sciences, and such research is needed to develop good practice. But interventions which aim to harmonize or develop family or group relationships are neither easily measured nor accurately repeated because of the human variables involved.

The current demand for extended social work education and training, for professionally supervised practice, for post-qualifying specialized training (Short, 1984: paras 279–90) and for evaluation and research reflect social work's proper aspiration for knowledge and skills which confer both the image and reality of professional competency in the interests of clients.

Research prospects

Social work has been under-researched, but prospects on this front are improving. Further research and evaluation to assess the efficacy of modes of intervention varying for individual, group and neighbourhood are needed. Studies of the quality of life, the risks and the costs associated with domiciliary, day and residential care for all client groups are required. These are needed for the analysis of policy, for example the current community care policy, to promote the competence and confidence of social workers, and to specify more closely their social utility. Research has already influenced attitudes towards institutional care as being both expensive and dysfunctional in personal development terms. Paradoxically residential care with its hotel-like services is a marketable commodity among elderly people who can realize capital on house sales or have other financial means. Some claim that the purchase or rental of residential care or sheltered housing is a direct result of a social policy which has encouraged home ownership. When official policies for community care and consumer choice run counter, as they sometimes do, social workers are placed in conflict.

One commentator, approvingly noting twenty-eight controlled experiments testifying to the tangible impact of social work services, concludes not uncontroversially, that

> when social workers clearly identify target problems; work extensively with them; apply task-centred or behavioural approaches; help co-ordinate the other services concerned with an agreed and definite policy; adopt a contractual style with people they are trying to help; rehearse possible solutions to problems rather than just talking about them;...then social workers are very likely to be effective. [Sheldon, 1985: 15]

This statement remains a hypothesis, which may or may not validate a problem-solving form of intervention, and may not impress supporters of a community-oriented model, but it clarifies aspects of social work.

The universities and the personal social services have been laggards, when compared with North America, in harnessing research capacity to the analysis and illumination of social work practice and service delivery effectiveness. 'The key challenge for the future is how to make good use of our growing knowledge and to ensure that it feeds through into practice' (Goldberg, 1984: 1).

The complementarity of research, policy and practice requires social workers to be educated to analyse and evaluate practice, for they are uniquely able to reflect a consumer perspective into policy-making.

The prognosis is hopeful. Universities and polytechnics are establishing research units extending over planning, policy and practice. The marketing of academic and practice research is the key to its influence. This is particularly important lest cost-effectiveness studies, very marketable commodities, predominate and recreate administrative rather than human services. The Audit Commission's Study on managing services for elderly people provides a logical framework for planning resources and provides a useful analysis of the home help service (Audit Commission, 1985: 47). A corrective to the careless use of expensive resources is important, but human input and consumer satisfaction still need to be tested.

Future developments

Unless another profession is invented, whatever the structural framework for service provision and service delivery through public, voluntary and commercial enterprise, social workers will still be needed to protect and promote the individual and group interests of people experiencing social difficulties. The overlap between professional intervention, informal service and community involvement seems likely to gain ground, but it still leaves social workers with the demanding task of making an empathetic and alleviating response to needs and problems exposed by social, cultural and economic change.

To be effective in intervention, social workers need a knowledge of the political economy of the society in which they work. They will be conscious that social and economic policies do not necessarily share the same values. To be effective, social workers must also be knowledgeable about the mores of the community in which they work, and about the resources it produces or lacks so that they can help people and influence policy. As Davies puts it, 'The social worker and the probation officer are at the hub of a network of services, and until knowledge of the network is mastered they can only provide a second-rate service' (Davies, 1985: 230). The crux of the matter is that social workers are in business to challenge in social terms the doctrine of the survival of the fittest, to do more than ensure that those at the end of the queue get support, care and some priority. They have moved beyond a rescue and maintenance function towards a positive mobilization of people and resources to provide time and space for people in serious difficulties, and to enable marginal groups to participate in the community as well as to receive service from it. They aim to ensure that service giving and receiving are invested with dignity, and confer freedom by reducing restriction.

References

Audit Commission (1985) *Managing Social Services for the Elderly More Effectively*. London: HMSO.

Barclay, P. (1982) *Social Workers: Their Role and Tasks*. London: Bedford Square Press.

Beresford, P. and Croft, S. (1986) *Whose Welfare: Private Care or Public Services?* Brighton: Brighton Polytechnic.

Cooper, J. (1983) *The Creation of the British Personal Social Services*. London: Heinemann.

Davies, M. (1985) *The Essential Social Worker*. Aldershot: Gower.

Department of Health and Social Security (1976) *Priorities for Health and Personal Services in England: a Consultative Document*. London: HMSO.

England, H. (1986) *Social Work as an Art*. London: Allen & Unwin.

Goldberg, E. M. (1984) *Research, Policy and Planning*. Social Science Research Group, University of Sheffield.

Hadley, R. and Hatch, S. (1981) *Social Welfare and the Failure of the State*. London: Allen & Unwin.

Loney, M. (1983) *Community against Government*. Aldershot: Gower.

Pinker, R. A. (1978) *Research Priorities in the Personal Social Services*. London: Social Science Research Council.

Seebohm, F. (1968) *Local Authority and Allied Personal Social Services* (Cmnd 3703). London: HMSO.

Sheldon, B. (1985) 'Yes, and the Prospects are Good', *Social Work Today* (7 October).

Short, R. (1984) *Second Report from the Social Services Committee, House of Commons*. London: HMSO.

Specht, H. and Vickery, A. (eds) (1977) *Integrating Social Work Methods*. London: Allen & Unwin.

Titmuss, R. M. (ed.) (1979) *Commitment to Welfare*. London: Allen & Unwin.

Walton, R. F. (1975) *Women in Social Work*. London: Routledge & Kegan Paul.

5
The role of the social services: a view from the New Right

Patrick Minford

The personal social services are an integral part of the 'welfare state' which has been the main reason for the explosion of public expenditure over the last forty years. They cannot be discussed in isolation, for their growth and the philosophy behind their provision have been inspired by the more general philosophy of the welfare state. I shall therefore spend much of this chapter on general issues concerning the welfare state; I shall then try to draw out the implications for the personal social services.

Two concepts of 'welfare'
Two concepts have struggled with each other in British welfare history. The first, which seems to be close to Beveridge's, is that of the *safety net*. The object of welfare in this version is to ensure that people in our society do not drop below a certain minimum living standard due to personal misfortune. The principle is that of social insurance, therefore: people contribute in normal times to this insurance and in hard times they can claim assistance. But as with any insurance policy, assistance is not forthcoming if the 'hard times' could have been avoided by the efforts of the insured: in this case, the insured person is asked to pay some proportion of his or her costs in order to provide an incentive to avoid false, avoidable claims for assistance.

This is one concept. But there is another, and it has significantly influenced our welfare state as it has actually evolved from Beveridge's intentions. This is *paternalistic egalitarianism*. Here the objective is to ensure equality at least in the 'basic' things of life: the list varies but would include at the minimum education, health care and pensions. In this view people's incomes and behaviour are determined essentially by forces outside their control, whether birth or environment, and thus the redistribution required by social justice is assumed not to affect their behaviour significantly: the poor will not 'exploit' the system (therefore there is no 'moral hazard'); the better off will not reduce their efforts (in this case there is no 'incentives problem'). It is further assumed that the poor require guidance and supervision in the use of the assistance given to them, because the same forces that made them poor also tend to make them incompetent, negligent or immoral.

Many people are ranged passionately on either side of this conceptual divide. Personally I favour the safety-net concept. But from the start we must be aware that what really matters in the view of the typical British voter, i.e. the floating voter. Ultimately they will decide what is done. What professionals, such as economists or social workers, have a duty to do is to advise their fellow nationals about the most efficient ways to achieve what *they* want. Such professional advisers should not let their preferences intrude; though they are of course free as citizens to try to persuade others to share their preferences, they should try to separate that activity from their activity as professional advisers. In the next part of this chapter, therefore, I shall try to set my preferences on one side and, after characterizing my fellow citizens' preferences in what I hope is an uncontroversial way, discuss how best these wishes might be achieved. In a later part I shall urge the reasons why those preferences should evolve towards the safety-net approach.

Welfare aims and public expenditure

I assume that the typical Briton's preferences are more or less reflected in the present, apparent aims of the welfare state. These aims appear to be to provide minimum support of living standards (through such programmes as housing benefit, Family Income Supplement and Supplementary Benefit) and to ensure supervised access to basic services, including health, education, pensions and, of course, the personal social services. Widespread means-testing suggests a safety-net view but much supervision (health care and education are transferred *in kind* by state officials) suggests elements of paternalism. The degree of egalitarianism seems very limited: wide disparities of personal expenditure even on health, education and pensions are tolerated, as is obvious from flourishing private sectors in all three cases. So, as you might expect in Britain, the preferences are a mixture: there is no dogmatic adherence to either side.

Are these preferences being well served by the mechanisms of production and consumption through which we now attempt to satisfy them? Broadly, we satisfy them via public expenditure. There are three aspects of public expenditure which require to be distinguished: public production, state purchase and taxation.

Much state expenditure involves public production. In these cases the state itself provides the capital and the management and hires the labour for such services as primary and secondary education and the National Health Service and products from the nationalized industries.

Much state expenditure involves state purchase on behalf of the public to whom goods and services are provided at prices different from those they would have paid if they had bought them privately. Examples of government purchase from the private sector are defence products for the armed forces, drugs and equipment for the NHS, road construction and maintenance and council house building. Where the state (local or national) owns the production, it is usually the main or only customer in its role as government purchaser; the prime examples here are primary and secondary education and the NHS. But in nationalized industries this is not so; the private sector – companies and individuals – are the major customers.

Finally, much state expenditure does not involve public purchase of goods but cash transfers (such as pensions and supplementary benefits), which go straight into people's pockets for them to spend in the open market, and payment of debt interest. These are best thought of as part of the tax/transfer system by which the state distributes income both *within* one generation and (by borrowing and deferring tax) *between* generations.

State expenditure invariably requires taxation, whether present or future (if funds are borrowed). It is usual in discussing state expenditure theoretically to assume that this taxation takes the form of 'lump sum transfers' (i.e. a poll tax – the only sort of tax which causes *no* economic inefficiency or 'disincentive effect'). But in practice no modern government has so far made significant use of poll taxes for the obvious reason that they are very 'regressive', hitting the poor as hard as the rich (or harder relative to income). Rather, governments have used expenditure taxes such as VAT and income taxes, including National Insurance Fund contributions.

I shall now evaluate the efficiency dimension of each of these aspects.

State production

In principle we can visualize the state being a producer of 'widgets', operating alongside competing private producers (who thus deprive it of monopoly power) and enjoying no subsidy (or equivalent privileges such as preferential tending for government contracts). But this is very rare. For once the state *is* a producer of widgets, its direct interest, as a corporate entity consisting of managers, tax-gatherers, employees, public sector unions and politicians, becomes the maximization of its returns (broadly defined to include non-monetary returns such as prestige, power and security of tenure) by hedging the company around with protective devices. The most effective device is monopoly power, which in practice is enjoyed by the vast majority of state producers. Examples are nearly all the nationalized industries, schools and the NHS (a monopoly of 'free' medicine, best treated as a different product from private medicine under present institutions).

But monopoly is not always so readily to hand. When the government took over British Leyland (BL) (now the Rover Group), it was unable to confer on it a monopoly of car production; the British consumer would not have tolerated it. Instead the state can subsidize the producer or erect a tariff (or equivalent) barrier which is the same as simultaneously subsidizing the producer and taxing the consumer by equal percentages. For BL, the government *both* gave a direct, overt subsidy (which continues) *and* installed a covert tariff barrier by sanctioning a UK cartel arrangement (i.e. price fixing) for cars. This double subvention enabled *all* the producers in the UK – both British and foreign – to raise their UK prices. The Japanese, who might not have co-operated with the European multi-nationals operating this cartel, were coerced by the British government into accepting 'voluntary' quotas and, since they could not compete for extra business, were content to let their car prices rise in line. This cartel also continues, though it has come under attack, particularly under EEC trading laws, and the present government has agreed in principle that it should end.

The cost to society, the residents of the UK, its 'consumers' and 'tax-payers', of such protective devices can be measured by a well-known technique originally developed by the pre-Keynesian Cambridge economist Alfred Marshall, that of 'consumer surplus' lost, which can measure the pure waste of resources due to the *inefficiency* fostered in their use. The monopolist has a tendency to raise prices above the competitive equilibrium, that is above the price at which the amount of a product which sellers wish to sell is exactly matched by the quantity that buyers want to buy; and in doing so wastes resources. In the UK, the openness of the economy has meant that, if tariff and equivalent barriers were eliminated, foreign competition might often be sufficient to eliminate monopoly power in the markets for goods. Such indeed has been UK policy in general – to ensure that trade barriers come down on the products of the private sector, but to apply this policy only loosely, if at all, in the state sector since much government production is of non-traded goods and services (education, medicine, rail and road transport, electricity). Where imports could have meant competition, as with coal and the Rover Group, they have been restricted. In the state sector, therefore, monopoly is likely to be serious.

Long experience of political pressures shows that, if something is produced by central or local government, it is very hard to avoid the addition to it of substantial monopoly power or protection. It is utopian to think that production could remain 'public' and yet be disciplined by competition. The only remedy is for production to be private and, simultaneously, for any residual monopoly power to be broken up, and protection to be removed; in short, simultaneous privatization and competition.

This process has no necessary implications for the existence of the welfare state. Defence production is mainly private but its products are bought by governments. In countries where the defence industry is government owned, the government has to spend more resources on defence (or get worse quality) to allow for the waste involved in state production. Thus, if the total resource budget were to be maintained, privatization and competition would certainly *increase* the value for money, probably rather substantially, of that unchanged spending by cutting out the waste in *production*.

Once this crucial conclusion is fully grasped, and it has not been in much recent debate, it should become common ground between defenders of total welfare spending *per se* and those who wish to see less of such spending by the state (for reasons to be examined below) that, if nothing else, privatization *and* competition (from now on 'privatization' for short) should be pushed ahead. Coal, gas, electricity, railways, hospitals, schools, car producers and all the other now state-owned production units should compete for private and government customers' business as private *production* units.

State consumption

We now turn to the second aspect of state expenditure, consumption. We now have to ask the key question: is there justification for the state to buy goods and services (such as medicine, doctors' services, education, armaments, bridges and roads) on behalf of the public, using their taxes, rather than let individual consumers/taxpayers buy these goods and services with their own untaxed money directly from the producers?

There is one type of product or service for which government purchase can be justified under certain circumstances, i.e. something which, once bought and installed, can give an extra person pleasure or benefit at 'low' or zero cost ('low' means smaller than the average cost of buying it) whatever the direct cost of utilization or indirect cost of inconvenience to other users. The classic example is a park: once bought and set up, extra people can enjoy it (at least up to the point where congestion sets in) without imposing costs on the park budget or on other people using it. Arguably, therefore, it pays society for the park to be used to the point where an extra person doesn't use it simply because he has better things to do and not because he can't pay the price; it should, in other words, be free because it costs society nothing for an extra person to use it. The park is said on this argument to be a 'public good' because, if it were privately bought by individuals at the average cost of park provision from a private operator, it would be under-used; thus it is 'natural' or 'right' that society should buy it and provide it to taxpayers at no further cost.

In practice, the argument has applicability but must be used with care. Many goods have the feature that, once bought and installed, their marginal cost of use is at times lower than their average cost of installation. Once all overheads have been met, an aeroplane could carry any extra passengers for nothing. It is clearly not a public good, however. Even when governments buy aeroplanes, as unfortunately they do, mainly for prestige reasons, they hesitate (except in some lunatic cases) to give seats away in this manner. The reason is that to vary prices according to capacity is too complicated and hence expensive (in information costs, for example) to operate. Hence airlines are classed as private goods.

The question to ask about state provision of goods with 'public good' qualities is: is the state the natural provider of this product? And this boils down to whether its benefits are sufficiently widely spread (either directly in the sense that everyone will or may use it or indirectly in the sense that everyone enjoys the availability; for example, air/sea rescue facilities may give the public in general pleasure because they want people not to perish in sea crossings, mountaineering, etc.). This is the question and it must be posed very carefully and answered by those in the debate. A few examples of fairly obvious 'public goods' (*full* status) are: defence, police and economic infrastructure such as trunk roads and sewers.

Having attempted to define public goods in principle, I now discuss the cost to the public if a *non*-public good (henceforth a 'private' good) is provided free (or at a subsidized rate) to the public and financed by taxation.

We can use the same Marshall technique as above for measuring this waste in public consumption. If the state provides *all* that people want of the good, it is obvious enough that the cost of over-provision could be massive because people will take a lot of it as if it were free, whereas the state has to pay the full cost. It is for this reason that the state would typically *ration* goods that it provides free. This conclusion introduces a new modification of the problem: now some goods may be rationed to amounts *less* than consumers would want at cost price, while others may be rationed to *more*.

We can simplify this problem if the state allows private purchase as well as public. In this case under-rationing will not arise because the private sector will fill the gap between government provision and private demand at the full cost price. This in the UK is the typical case; think, for example, of plastic surgery, where the state rations *below* what people are prepared to pay for at cost price, and the private sector steps in at the margin.

It follows that the problems of state purchase arise with the cases where the state 'over-provides'. These costs are potentially substantial, because the rationing process is politically vulnerable; if the public *want* more expensive medicine in the NHS, politicians find it hard to deny it, because they are too easily cast in the role of the niggardly villain. The political problem of holding subsidies to zero or a lower number is in practice insuperable; free services are 'open-ended' subsidies, in the sense that demand at a zero price is 'infinite' (compared with Exchequer resources) and politicians are under constant pressure to increase the quantity supplied. The 'pure waste' element will tend towards its maximum under this political pressure.

Taxation

We now turn to the third aspect of public expenditure, taxation.

In practice, all taxes raised are wasteful, because of political factors. A 'lump-sum transfer' or poll tax was from time to time practised in some European colonies but in a modern democracy it would be unacceptable because it would be the most regressive form of taxation in a society where it is expected by the populace that the 'rich' should pay 'more', even 'most'. Hence the emergence of 'graduated' income tax. Even expenditure taxation is not liked in many democracies because it bears less heavily on high incomes than an income tax can be made to bear. A further feature is that a high degree of protection (or safety net) is stipulated for the poor, presumably because most people feel there is a significant chance of slipping into that category. The result of this general tendency is that marginal tax rates on labour input (i.e. personal effort) are typically high in two main areas of the income scale, high and low incomes: high because high earners have to carry a bigger burden of tax, and low because the desire to protect low incomes often results in extra work for the poor bringing little extra income.

The effects of these high marginal tax rates are well documented, less indeed at the top end of the income scale (where evidence is more elusive, perhaps because it involves individuals rather than large groups) than at the bottom end in the 'poverty trap' and 'unemployment trap'. The most recent evidence for the UK comes from my own research of post-war behaviour for the economy and for seventeen individual industries (Minford et al., 1986); it suggests that on average across the whole economy a 10 percentage point fall in marginal tax rates on working among the poor unemployed, whether it comes from lowering rates on the low paid or benefits *to* the unemployed, would reduce unemployment by half a million (a rise in *employment* of 2 percent).

If one accepts that a reduction in government expenditure would lower taxes on the low paid, and even facilitate a reduction in unemployment benefit, because *post-tax* wages that the unemployed could then obtain in the labour market are higher, the gain to society from lower spending is swelled very substantially. Suppose we allow that every 1 percent reduction in state spending would permit a fall in *marginal* tax rates on the low paid (because of skilful distribution of the gains across the tax structure) of 3 percentage points: employment and national output would on my calculations rise by about 0.6 percent. This means that, at present tax rates, 60 percent of the *total* cost of any government expenditure is a pure burden of waste on society, a staggering indictment of our management of public finance.

For what we are saying is that, because of political difficulties in raising taxation, the inefficiency cost of extra taxes is now up to 60 percent of their yield. It follows that there is a strong absolute case for government expenditure cuts simply to avoid Exchequer outlays and regardless of the other, more subtle, arguments above. Of course, as these bad taxes are reduced (high marginal tax rates on low- and high-income groups eliminated), this factor will disappear from the calculation. But at present it must be rated as of very high importance in the debate.

An ideal system

We have argued that there is a strong case for reducing state expenditure, on three main grounds:

1 the waste in state production;
2 the waste in state purchase, except that of truly 'public goods';
3 the waste in taxation.

Unfortunately there is insufficient space to discuss relevant policy remedies in detail here, but the following are my main recommendations (see Minford et al., 1986, esp. Ch. 3):

(a) Public sector production should be privatized, unless there are over-riding reasons (such as strategic) for keeping it public.
(b) People and firms should pay for goods and services currently provided by the state, unless they are 'public goods'.
(c) Poverty should be assisted via a Negative Income Tax (that is, an income subsidy to those in employment), and the unemployed should be assisted to a lesser extent than those in work, in order to maintain incentives to take a job.
(d) Using the proceeds from savings under (a) to (c), taxes should be cut to increase incentives.

These principles apply in general across the public sector; below we will apply them in a little more detail to the personal social services. Before we do so, however, we turn from issues of efficiency to normative ones.

So far this chapter has been analytical in thrust. I have argued that there are more efficient ways of achieving our welfare aims than those pursued at present. All these ideas stem from the potency of incentives in affecting human behaviour. In this respect there is a conflict with the ideas of paternalistic egalitarianism; but it is a conflict about fact not preferences, and it can in principle be resolved by evidence. There is a lot of evidence of this potency, produced by thousands of economic researchers over the last two decades; and it is pretty compelling on this point.

If this evidence is accepted, then paternalistic egalitarianism starts to require qualification even for those with strong ideas of 'social justice'. For the paternalism is less necessary if the poor respond to incentives in a rational way, while the costs in lower incentives and performance by the better off reduce the attractiveness of egalitarian redistribution.

There is also a deeper concern, both ethical and practical. The ethical concern of writers such as Nozick, Hayek and Flew has focused on the legitimacy of taking away from people their accumulated assets. 'Finders keepers' is a principle with strong legitimacy in human history. The right of a finder to transfer his assets to those whom he chooses is similarly deep-seated. And the right to the fruits of one's assets and efforts has similar status. *Ethically*, the right of those who have *less* than these finders et al. to *help themselves* to their assets is doubtful. There is little doubt that those who are fortunate should have pity on and help those who are less fortunate. But should they be *compelled* to, and if there is some public level of charity to which they should be compelled, does this level include large-scale expropriation? Reflection brings doubts, at least to my mind.

It has been pointed out now frequently by such writers that 'social justice' is a contradiction in terms. *Justice* concerns the adjudication of legal *rights*; it awards equal treatment to all before certain principles of law which have evolved as legitimate and accepted within a society. Social redistribution, however, involves violating the rights under common law of certain citizens, namely the better off; this is achieved by a parliamentary majority overruling the common law by *force majeure*. Ethically, redistribution may be defensible, at least to some extent; but it is obfuscatory to identify it with justice.

The practicalities are more worrying, however. The force of recent economic research on incentives suggests that the inefficiencies produced by quite modest redistribution may be very serious. The accumulation of long-lived capital, the mainspring of economic growth with its pay-offs over several generations, is hit by inheritance taxes; it becomes more attractive to 'eat, drink and be merry'. If governments compete to attract high-level personnel (as they do; witness recent US tax reforms), then emigration may impoverish a highly taxed nation. Work-effort and risk-taking are also affected by the expectation and risk of partial or total confiscation. Attempts to stop these side-effects through instituting a police state merely worsen the problem, as we have seen from the sclerosis of the Russian and Chinese systems which are now being belatedly opened up to market forces. The comparative 'macro' performance of economies like Hong Kong, Taiwan, the US and Japan relative to highly taxed economies like Sweden, the UK and Belgium supports the evidence on micro behaviour. It suggests that attempts to pursue 'social justice' will be self-limiting: the societies who take them too far will decay, while others flourish and attract the more productive citizens. The natural order will tend away from redistribution back towards common-law systems of protective rights.

A safety-net approach to welfare is essentially the organization of private charitable instincts and informal social insurance across a society recognizing mutual bonds. The provision of charity is a public good, in the sense that if I provide it, you benefit from seeing less distressing deprivation as you go about your business. There is therefore a case for everyone being compelled to contribute to its provision. People will also insure themselves directly. The combination is the 'safety-net'. More than this seems (to me at least) to violate deep ethical and practical objections.

Personal social services: an agenda for change

Under the present arrangements, state resources are devoted to assisting people, either indirectly through social workers or directly through allowances, to cope with the personal vicissitudes of life. The elderly are cared for in state homes, unmarried mothers draw special rates of benefit, home helps are provided for some categories of mothers who have just given birth, children can be taken into care under certain conditions, and so on; the supplementary benefit recognizes a huge number of cases of disadvantage where benefits are payable. How much of this would be consistent with the safety-net philosophy I have described? That is one question of interest. Another, which can be answered more easily, is how far this general system can be made more efficient by the sort of proposals described earlier.

How should help be provided?

I shall begin with the second question. Many of these personal social services are capable of being privatized. Nothing decrees that, for example, homes for the elderly be run by the state or that home helps and district nurses be paid by the state. The principles set out above suggest that these services could be supplied by private companies.

As for how benefits are provided, a system of vouchers for these services would enable consumers to exercise choice, something which is lacking under the present state monopoly. A mother who qualifies for a home help should be able to 'shop around' if she is unhappy with the one she has. The elderly person who is in a home he or she dislikes should be able to choose to go to another. Vouchers here would give that choice. They would ensure that the services were provided in the combination suitable to the user and, because of the spur to competition between private producers (who can otherwise bargain with the state), at the lowest possible cost.

The scale and distribution of benefits is another aspect. There are some efficiency aspects to this. If the state provides a subsidy to old people's homes, that weakens the incentives of families to look after their old people. If the state subsidizes unmarried mothers, there will be more illegitimate children. There is a trade-off here between alleviating distress and encouraging the conditions for more distress. This is a value judgement to which we turn next. But there are also cases such as that of the elderly where a voucher – or an element in the pension – avoids the problem, since the voucher could be transferred in payment by the elderly to their family, so leaving the choice to the old and their family whether they go to a home or stay with their family (society does not 'load' the choice if it gives a voucher).

So, given the decision to intervene with help for people suffering certain categories of misfortune, then the following principles apply:

1   All services should be privately provided.
2   The help should be given in the form of vouchers.
3   The vouchers should discriminate as little as possible against 'natural' sources of help (i.e. the family in most cases).

How extensive should help be?

Having shown how such help could be applied more efficiently, we can now turn to the first question: the *extent* of help under the safety-net system. To focus our minds, let us ask how the world would look if there were only the sort of help being outlined under this new system. Some of what this means is:

(a)   no special help to the elderly. They receive the pensions for which they contributed. Under our 'plan' for pensions, they were assisted as necessary by Negative Income Tax when in work and they had to subscribe to some approved 'minimum pension' plan (more if they chose). Out of this pension they would be expected to provide for their old age;

(b)   unmarried mothers helped only through Negative Income Tax;

(c)   similarly, handicapped people would obtain NIT only;

(d)   visits by home helps, midwives, district nurses to be paid for. No state help (other than NIT).

Negative Income Tax is central to this plan. Society is concerned to help the poor to achieve an above-subsistence living standard but without damaging incentives. This help is best given through NIT which makes net income slip back very slowly as gross income falls towards the subsistence level. This maintains the incentive to work harder and earn more; it also protects the poor in a general sort of way, i.e. via income. It is assumed to replace *all* means-tested benefits (rent and rebates, Family Income Supplement).

Coupled with this, it would be made compulsory by law to contribute to medical insurance and a pension scheme, as well as to pay for the education of any children. Payment of NIT could be made conditional on the production of the appropriate receipts, etc. (This is equivalent to a voucher scheme but administratively simpler.)

This may seem harsh. But presumably misfortune shows up in low income relative to the needs on which Negative Income Tax is based. NIT is not an ideal system but it does maintain some incentive to avoid misfortune because the marginal rate in NIT is less that 100 percent; technically, the individual 'co-insures' his or her state, to reduce 'moral hazard'.

Some people are unfortunate through no action of their own (or anyone else's), as, for example, a handicapped person. Should such a person not be 100 percent 'compensated' for his or her handicap? But to enunciate such a principle is to reveal its difficulty. How are we to establish what he or she would have achieved without handicap? Or even if we limit the compensation to some 'minimum living standard', how could we compensate someone for the loss of an enjoyment he or she is unable to obtain (for example, running for someone with an amputated leg)? Or where do we draw the line for a 'handicap'? Is lack of a good brain a 'handicap'? Or lack of sporting ability?

Nor is it true that all handicaps are unaffected by personal action. Handicapped people can improve their abilities to deal with their predicament. Their family can also contribute in various ways. If a family has a handicapped child, for example, they should *expect* to look after and equip him or her for life as best they could.

Nevertheless, this brings us up against the dilemma posed by personal social assistance. Many would be uncomfortable with giving *no* special needs allowances to someone handicapped with little way to help him or herself or to parents with a severely handicapped child. Surely the state should provide a special needs allowance, calculated on the same principles as NIT? In fact, the logic of the NIT, which is based on 'need', is that 'need' should also include such unavoidable problems as handicap, for quite clearly a family with a handicapped person has higher expenses to achieve the same basic living standard as a family without. The distinction being sought is between *avoidable* and *unavoidable* need. (Avoidable need includes insurance risks.) NIT is designed to alleviate unavoidable need. Avoidable need should not be alleviated. The safety net applies to misfortunes that are outside personal control.

Suppose we take this definition, which is designed to deal with at least some of the harshness of our original proposition. Clearly, it will not satisfy those affronted by the suffering caused by misfortune which is self-inflicted, either directly or indirectly by failure to insure against it. But there is no system which can costlessly avoid suffering. Under the system we have described, those elderly who saved conscientiously for their old age will be rewarded: they will be better off than those who merely put aside the minimum. That is both just and good for the economy. Under this system, those who have illegitimate children will suffer; illegitimacy is therefore discouraged. Families which choose to have many children will have less income per head than those which have fewer; the number of children chosen then reflects their costs and benefits to those who have them and society does not create an incentive to propagate large families among those unable to support them. And so on. The system discourages avoidable need, which is of course a good thing. The inevitable penalty is the suffering incurred when people fail to avoid such need. Conversely, a system which abolishes or alleviates this suffering (as at present) will generate more avoidable need, ultimately possibly a lot more as people learn to exploit it efficiently. The alternative system described may ultimately produce very little avoidable need, as insurance spreads and people adjust their behaviour.

Issues of responsibility and the scope of the law

In all this, I have written as if the rights of individuals *within* the family were respected; I have taken the family as the unit with which personal social services deal. For example, I assumed the unmarried mother would look after her illegitimate child. Yet these services deal also with individuals whose rights within the family have been violated: that illegitimate child may need to be looked after, the mother having abandoned or neglected it. Should not the state intervene here? Of course it should. But in this case the child's rights must be upheld; the mother must be compelled to look after the child or, if she refuses, she must pay for the child's upkeep and be punished for her violation.

Rights of this sort are not always clearly defined, but the courts of law exist for their better definition. The point of principle here is clear, however: those who violate the rights of dependents must be punished and forced to respect them. At present this law is more honoured in the breach (with the accompanying subsidy of the 'unfortunate' breachers) than in the observance.

Conclusions

I have attempted to cover two main issues in this chapter. One is to do with efficiency: how best can the 'welfare' services currently on offer be provided? The second is normative: how much 'welfare assistance' should be given to people? I have given answers both in general and in the particular case of the personal social services. Naturally, my answers to the normative question reflect my own values, which incline to the safety-net concept of welfare as opposed to that of paternalistic egalitarianism.

However, I would like to end with a caveat. My answers become more tentative the more detailed the level of the discussion, for I am no expert in the details of the many services dealt with here. Others who know will be able to improve greatly on my fumbling attempts to illustrate the principles involved. These principles are the point, and it is because they have been lost sight of that, first, we define our aims less rigorously than we should, thus allowing our programmes to spread beyond the proper target area, and, secondly, we implement those programmes with such a degree of waste. It is my hope that we will return to a properly thought out set of principles.

Note

I am grateful to the Editor of *Economic Affairs* for permission to use some material from my article in Vol. 4, No. 3.

Reference

Minford, A. P. L., Ashton, P., Peel, M. J. Davies, D. H. and Sprague, A. (1986) *Unemployment: Cause and Cure*. Oxford: Blackwell (2nd edn).

6

Hazardous lives – social work in the 1980s: a view from the Left

Ann Davis

People who live in poverty live hazardous lives. They battle constantly against poor health and disability. They survive in overcrowded, deteriorating accommodation and run a higher than average risk of becoming homeless. If they are in paid work they are in the dirtiest, most unstable occupations. If they are unemployed they have little chance of finding work. Inadequately clothed and nourished, they exercise little choice in the way they live their lives. They often feel helpless against the forces which are shaping their world.

The 1980s in Britain have produced increasing numbers of individuals struggling with such hazards. Despite active attempts by government to suppress or 'interpret' it, the evidence mounts of the increased toll that poverty is taking. More people of all ages are living at or below the state's own poverty line (CSO, 1986: 91). Gaps are widening between the classes when the incidence of disease and mortality are measured (Townsend and Davidson, 1982; OPCS, 1986). The frustrations faced by dispossessed young people and black communities have surfaced in inner-city riot and rebellion (WMCC, 1986; Scarman, 1982).

One of the many hazards that poverty brings is an increased chance of contact with social work. This is not because social workers can relieve poverty. Unlike most European countries and the United States, Britain in the post-war era did not make social workers guardians of its means-tested social security system. Instead the provision of state benefits was centralized and separated from the provision of local authority social work services. The implementation of the 1986 Social Security Act is modifying this. But it is still the case that most poor people do not have to contact a social worker when they need to claim social security benefits. Local authority social workers in Britain, working with clients who use drugs or drink excessively, cannot, like their Swedish counterparts, withhold benefit payments if a client refuses to join a treatment programme. In local authority social services departments, the probation service and voluntary agencies, social workers do not have statutory responsibilities for income maintenance. Despite the administrative separation of social work from the state's financial support of poor people, around 90 percent of local authority social work clients are dependent on state benefits for all or part of their income (Becker and McPherson, 1986: 18). Poverty does not guarantee you a social worker but it certainly helps you get one. Social work remains, as it was in the nineteenth century, primarily a service for the poor and destitute. Despite its professional aspirations in the post-war period, it is a service of last resort.

Social work has developed and been financed by the state as a means of distributing a particular range of welfare goods and services. This range encompasses services which individuals are routinely expected to provide for themselves and with assistance from family and friends. It includes the care and control of children and adults; support of both an emotional and material kind when illness or disability strikes; and basic domestic servicing. In providing these services social work agencies are often supplementing or substituting for the family when it fails to deliver what is expected of it – in terms of both caring for and controlling its members. As a consequence social workers find themselves constantly negotiating between the expectations of the state and people who have failed to meet those expectations. This is difficult, sometimes dangerous, territory to work in. Social workers survive using a variety of tactics, which range from verbal encouragement to the removal of individuals from their homes. The resources which they have at their disposal are experienced as both rewards and punishments by those who receive them. The grounds on which they are dispensed are rarely made clear to recipients.

Of course, social work agencies are only one way of replenishing family and friendship networks. There are other alternatives which are regarded more favourably by most sections of society. As Jordan has pointed out, contact with social work agencies has always carried contagion. Even in the late 1960s and early 1970s when the climate towards state welfare provision in Britain was more positive, 'everyone with the means to do so avoided state social work services like the plague, and bought the expensive private services of counsellors, nannies, clinics, special schools, housekeepers, convalescent homes and companions, in the private sector' (Jordan, 1984: 142). The recipients of social work services are people whose lack of resources, vulnerability and behaviour cannot be adequately met and dealt with by their own social networks or privately purchased alternatives. They are therefore amongst the most marginal people in British society.

Explanations as to why it is overwhelmingly poor people who find their lives investigated, serviced and monitored by social workers are central to a great deal of debate in social policy. From the political Right commentators continue to argue, as they did in the days of the Victorian Poor Law, that the poor have only themselves to blame. They view the association between social work help and poverty as a reflection of the kind of individual pathology and lack of moral fibre which jettisons people into poverty in the first place. From this perspective it is not just social work but all forms of state welfare consumption that serve both to confirm the presence of, and spawn, fecklessness and deviant behaviour.

In the welfare climate of the 1980s the speeches of Conservative ministers have been replete with examples of the demoralizing effects of state provision of health, education and income. Geoffrey Pathe, speaking as information and technology minister, added council housing to the list. He claims it 'breeds slums, delinquency, vandalism, waste, arrears and social polarization' (*Guardian*, 17 June 1986). His solution to this problem echoes those of other ministers concerned with the welfare plague. All have pointed to the need to resist demands for expanding the state sector and to turn instead to private provision. From the Right, then, the relationship between poor people and social work is just one example of the way in which the failure of individuals to 'stand on their own two feet' is amplified by state intervention.

From the perspective of the political Left the relationship between poverty and social work is seen as reflecting deep-seated structural rather than individual characteristics. It is the product of a capitalist society which is organized in such a way as to create and perpetuate want amongst a substantial section of its population. Denied the means to fulfil themselves, people in poverty are denied membership of society and are trapped on its margins. For some (a minority) this results in contact with social workers. They become 'clients' not because they and their situations are unique but because they have precious little choice. They approach social workers either because they lack basic resources or because other people in positions of power prescribe social work for them. Given this analysis the Left view the welfare solutions proposed by the Right with alarm. Cutting back on the state's provision of basic welfare services and leaving individuals to privately purchase or provide alternatives can only increase the burdens carried by poor and vulnerable people. Any extension of the social division of welfare reinforces the social and economic divisions within society.

From a Left perspective the provision of adequate levels of state welfare is essential if the needs of the disadvantaged in society are to be recognized and met. Welfare provision in itself cannot eradicate disadvantage and deprivation because they are the products of our political and economic system. Nothing less than a fundamental change in the social order is required to tackle disadvantage and deprivation at their root. Adequate state provision of welfare, which guarantees a basic minimum for all, is an essential prerequisite of full citizenship. The Left would argue that to meet this basic minimum state welfare provision must take into account the situation of the most vulnerable sections of the population, for example by directing increased resources to support parents bringing up children, in order to reduce the incidence of neglect and abuse currently associated with stressed family situations.

Clearly this is not an argument for more of the same. The Left have developed a substantial critique of the form which British state provision has taken in the post-war period. As Jordan says: 'Social services set up during the social democratic era tended to be bureaucratic and paternalistic; they were relatively large-scale organizations which made unilateral decisions about people's needs, and dispensed their services according to their own criteria. They tended to be relatively inflexible and unresponsive to local opinion and pressures, and were unfitted to deal with the growing crises associated with economic recession' (Jordan, 1984: 134). The Left are all too aware that contact with such provision has exacerbated feelings of alienation and hopelessness amongst the poorest sectors of society.

It is because of this that the Left argue that change is needed in the organization and delivery of state welfare provision, the kind of change which promotes participation and control by users. This promotion of collective participation in state welfare services contrasts sharply with the Right's attempt to individualize responsibility for welfare provision. It reflects a vision of a social order in which co-operative endeavour and collective responsibility are central.

Debate about the relationship between poor people and the social work services has been noticeably revived in the welfare politics of the 1980s. Increasing poverty and the limits placed on personal social services expenditure have fuelled discussions about what social work is and who needs it most. But the mainstream social work literature has not been drawn into this debate. The economic and political dimensions of the social work task continue to be omitted from the professional social work agenda. The increasing presence of poverty on the caseloads of social workers is a phenomenon which receives little attention. It is implicitly accepted as a fact of social work life, unpalatable perhaps, not only for clients but also for its tendency to muddy therapeutic waters, but not one to be debated. This stance is not reserved for poverty alone. Recently feminist social workers exploring the position of women in social work agencies have commented:

> This is not a topic that has attracted a great deal of attention in social work literature over the last thirty years. Its neglect is interesting, given that the changes that have taken place in the scope and organization of social work during this period have resulted in an increasing number of women being drawn into its sphere. The significance and consequences of the predominance of women in the day-to-day negotiations between social workers, clients and their families have not been explicitly discussed. Most social work literature has taken for granted that this is a normal, and therefore unimportant, fact of professional life. [Brook and Davis, 1985: 5]

In practice, of course, poverty – like gender, race and class – is not so easy to ignore. They all raise complex and painful issues which clients and social workers have to grapple with. Whatever professional texts might say, private troubles cannot be divorced from political and economic forces. As feminists argue, the personal *is* political, and an occupation which is as concerned with the personal as is social work cannot ignore this.

Ignoring the structurally common components of clients' situations, the mainstream social work literature has focused primarily on methods and techniques of working with individuals and groups. Social work methods are presented as the tools which the professional worker needs to 'fix' situations. Or, as Martin Davies has put it in a recent, influential text: 'Social workers are the maintenance mechanics oiling the interpersonal wheels of the community' (Davies, 1985: 28). Such a view of social work is firmly rooted in a belief that the world we live in, however imperfect, is one in which common interests and beliefs outweigh conflicts. It is a view of society as a machine, which fails to function smoothly at times, but within which each part is designed to work in harmony. Such a view is at odds with socialist, feminist and anti-racist perspectives. The Left argue that it is conflict of interest and oppression which characterize the way society functions. Social workers cannot therefore be viewed as mechanics or fixers; they too represent interests which can fuel conflict and contradiction.

The critiques of social work literature and education which develop this perspective have grown over the last decade. Originating outside the professional field – in sociology, feminism and social policy – they now have a representation amongst social work texts, as, for example, the series edited by Peter Leonard on Marxist practice in social work, and some of Bill Jordan's work (e.g. Jordan, 1984; Jordan and Parton, 1983). There are also the beginnings of a feminist contribution to social work (for example, Hale, 1983; Wilson 1977; Brook and Davis, 1985) and a multicultural analysis (for example, Cheetham, 1982; Ohri et al., 1982; Ahmed, Cheetham and Small, 1986). But like the clients of social work, these contributions continue to be marginalized. On social work courses they are likely to be referred to as offering interesting 'insights' but having little to offer 'real' social workers in the 'real' world (Davies, 1985: 13).

Meanwhle – in the real world – vulnerable people living insecure lives find themselves faced with additional hazards if they have contact with social work.

Stigma is the first major hazard. People who become social work clients find themselves judged as not being able to manage their own lives. Such judgements are not just made by social workers. Courts, other professionals and a range of state agencies can confirm such judgements. The impact they have on an individual's sense of their own worth, strength and status can be profound. As the designation *personal* social services suggests, the territory of the welfare system that social workers occupy is characterized by individualized investigation of, and intervention in, people's lives.

Such professional activity can arouse angry and depressed feelings in people who are being judged and found wanting. There seem to be two related processes at work here.

Firstly, social workers tend to focus on the negatives. They highlight the difficulties clients present and their failures to resolve troublesome situations. This approach results in a view of clients' experiences which is frequently at odds with clients' own perspectives. Mary, a young woman who had been in nine foster homes in sixteen years, was shown the file in which a succession of social workers had recorded their contact with her. She was devastated: 'I hoped the files would explain my life to me, help me make sense of it all. But over all those years, all they've been doing is put in what went wrong. I don't know whose life that is. It's not mine' (Williams, 1986: 23).

Contact with social workers can, therefore, undermine self-esteem and confidence. It can reinforce the oppression experienced by the poor in our society. It can give rise to clients' responding and behaving in ways which confirm the social worker's view that they are 'helpless', 'hopeless' or 'dangerous'.

Secondly, exchanges of this kind take place in a society in which success, status and reward are represented as the fruits of individual effort and responsibility. Standing on one's own two feet and looking after oneself and one's dependents is portrayed as the way in which the responsible citizen behaves. Contact with a social work agency is a public declaration of failure to make the grade as a citizen. To look to a state service to supplement or substitute for one's own efforts is to be branded as an inadequate. This sense of failure can, then, be reinforced by the way in which social work help is delivered.

Social work research has examined the way in which stigma can attach itself to those using social work services (for example, Mayer and Timms, 1970; Robinson, 1978; Sainsbury, Nixon and Phillips, 1982). Stigma has been revealed to have a number of hazardous properties. It strengthens the resolve of some people never to seek help again, however desperate they are. It confirms in others their worthlessness: ' ''How do kids like me get to be in children's homes? Well I suppose it's when no one else will have them, as a last resort. The lot living here – they're a real ragbag. You can understand families not wanting to be bothered with most of them. We're all the left-overs.'' (Boy, aged 13)' (Berridge, 1985: 88).

From a Left perspective such stigma is endemic to the kind of state provision which has characterized the personal social services in post-war Britain. Its roots lie in a society whose social divisions are reflected in welfare provision. It is maintained not only by the media's and politicians' portrayal of welfare spongers, scroungers and deviants, but also by the manner in which services are delivered to individuals who have no other options but to turn to the state for assistance. The reception areas of social work agencies where responses from harassed receptionists and the often public scrutiny of private pain and confusion all confirm to potential social work clients that they become a different class of person once they are designated as 'a case'.

For many people such experiences may just confirm a lesson they have learned in other welfare queues, for benefits, health care, education or housing. But the individualized nature of social work contact, which locates clients' problems firmly in their own hearts, minds and lives, uniquely underlines their personal responsibility for their predicaments.

The casework approach adopted in most social work agencies is one which lies at the centre of this process. Traditionally it has masked the social and political forces which shape individual lives. It has served to deny the collective problems faced by those who are oppressed and in poverty. This does not mean that from a Left perspective, working with individuals has no place in the repertoire of social workers. As the women's movement has shown, individual contact, discussion and support can be productive. It can strengthen understanding and the motivation to tackle private sorrows which are shaped by the political and economic interests operating in society (Hale, 1983). But to fully realize this potential in individual work, the Left argue that social work and social work agencies must change radically. The direction of such change needs to be towards dialogue, and involvement with the communities which workers and agencies serve. These processes must permeate both worker–client relationships and the management of services.

This vision of change does not just challenge the Right's notion of the relationship between the individual and state welfare. It also challenges the quest for a more 'professional' relationship between social workers and their clients which is part of the mainstream social work position. Professional distance and mystique have no place in efforts to work together with clients. The Left suggests that social workers must recognize the disabling consequences of adopting a quasi-medical professional stance towards working with people who are poor.

If they work in a more open, participative way with dispossessed people, social workers cannot afford to deny the power which they have to intervene in such people's lives. This power is derived from the fact that social workers are representatives of the state. Poor people experience state oppression and contact with social workers will inevitably involve conflict of interests and denial of rights. Working together rarely means working in harmony. Dispute is bound to enter negotiation and dialogue between clients and social workers. Changes which move towards a more participative style of working will test the nature of the relationship between the state and its most deprived citizens. It will not eradicate the stigma attached to the use of social work services. But it could provide people who become clients with a firmer sense of their strength and their collective potential to change their situation.

A second major hazard of contact with social work is that it involves pressure to change. This may be explicitly declared. Some social workers draw up 'contracts' with clients which are written agreements about change in life-style or behaviour over a given period of time. Some social workers attach conditions to the provision of particular resources. For example, a place at a day centre for people suffering mental disorder might be offered if a client agrees to leave psychiatric hospital and live in the community. All too often the expectations which social workers have of individual or family change take little account of either clients' views or the material circumstances of their lives.

As Holman has shown in relation to child care, the expectations which most professionals place on poor parents ignore the structural inequalities which exist in our society (Holman, 1976). The fact, for example, that current rates of supplementary benefit are insufficient to adequately clothe and feed a child is not often acknowledged as having an impact on the quality of parenting. Parents have to perform adequately whatever their financial situation. Failure to change in order to meet social workers' expectations about 'good parenting' tends to be viewed as an indicator of personal inadequacy, not structural inequalities.

During the 1980s the number of children who are homeless has increased. Many are being brought up in bed and breakfast accommodation because this is all that local authorities are prepared to offer their parents. Families in this situation who have to walk the streets during the day find that public toilets or parks are the only places in which it is possible for parents to toilet train their children. When parents in this situation fail to produce continent children they are more likely to be described by social workers as inconsistent parents than people struggling against impossible odds.

Women are more likely to find themselves facing pressures to change than men. This is because, 'viewed as the linchpin of family life, women are held responsible by welfare agencies, not just for their own behaviour and attitudes, but also for the behaviour and attitudes of their children, husbands and relatives' (Brook and Davis, 1985: 4). Contact with social workers can therefore reinforce the oppression women experience within both the family and the community. When they seek help from social workers they are likely to find themselves pressured to change their lives in order to keep the family 'together' or to 'save' a dependent from going into 'care'. The personal costs of such change can be enormous, as research into the lives of carers by the Equal Opportunities Commission and others has shown (EOC, 1982; Finch and Groves, 1983).

The Left argue that questions need to be asked about the class and cultural values which underpin the expectations and exhortations of social workers. The history of social work with working-class families and communities has been characterized by concerns to 'rehabilitate' or 'train' clients in order to help them reshape their lives in accordance with middle-class norms. This approach has also been adopted in work with people from different cultures. Social work education has not yet taken sufficient account of the multicultural nature of British society. It has not concerned itself with the plight of clients who are faced with insensitive, patronizing and racist expectations about themselves and their situations.

To be confronted with pressure to conform to expectations you do not share or understand is confusing and oppressive. Failure to conform to those expectations is hazardous. Clients can lose resources they need. Their resistance to change can be taken as evidence of pathology which requires more intensive 'treatment'.

Finally, contact with social work is not just a public acknowledgement of the marginal position of clients in our society. Contact can increase marginality. Social workers have powers to act to remove individuals from their homes. The exercise of these powers under the Children Act, the National Assistance Act and the Mental Health Act can have profound effects on the lives of individuals and families. As the research on institutional and foster care reveals, decisions of this kind can result in loss of rights and further deprivation.

Physical removal from home is just one example of the way in which social work contact can increase the marginalization of poor people. Some clients run risks when they comply with the criteria devised for rationing social work resources. The scarcity of day nursery provision means that most social services departments only make it available to children who are at risk of being received into care because of physical abuse. Some parents, desperate for help with child care and with no viable alternatives, learn to declare themselves as abusing or potentially abusing, in order to secure their children a nursery place. Such behaviour usually results in an entry on the local authorities' register of families where children are at risk. Registration of this kind increases a family's chances of welfare surveillance and loss of parental rights.

In focusing on the hazards which poor people face in their contact with social work agencies, the Left are critical of existing social work practice and the delivery of state welfare services. However, the Left's agenda for change, drawn up on the basis of their critique, contrasts sharply with the Right's concern to roll back state provision and promote private and individual enterprise in meeting welfare needs.

From a Left perspective the state has an important role to play in providing basic welfare goods and services. The distribution of adequate housing, income, health and education provision cannot be left to the operation of 'market forces'. In a society which generates inequality and deprivation 'market solutions' serve to reinforce and exacerbate existing social divisions. State services reflect a collective recognition of, and provision for, welfare needs. This is not to argue that state provision of welfare can alter the economic and social structure of Britain. It can, however, promote alternative means of distributing goods and services which are fundamental to personal well-being. To fully realize the possibilities of such alternatives, the economic and political organization of society needs to change radically. It is only in the context of such radical social change that the potential of social work to assist individuals and groups to tackle their problems of daily living can be fully explored. Meanwhile within existing structures social workers can move towards and raise people's consciousness of an alternative vision of society.

Social work is a small part of the public welfare services in Britain. The Left would argue that located where it is – negotiating between the state and its poorest citizens – it can both affect and develop that relationship. Within existing political and organizational constraints social workers can take steps to work with individuals, groups and communities in more open and participative ways. Such steps will necessarily challenge assumptions about professionalism in social work which are held by the Right and the mainstream. But the Left emphasize the role of social workers as state employees rather than professionals concerned to guard their privileges, exercise discretion without discussion and build a mystique around their skills and knowledge.

Taking on the Left's agenda about participative working is not an easy option. Over the last decade social workers have found themselves being pilloried in the media and by politicians for their failure to prevent the deaths of and injuries to vulnerable clients of all ages. Given this climate and increasing rates of poverty and stress amongst clients, social workers may feel understandably reluctant to discard their claims to be recognized as 'real' professionals. Doctors and the legal profession have demonstrated the advantages of a strong profession in protecting individual members from investigation and loss of livelihood. However, social workers need to ask themselves whether, placed as they are in a territory in which they deal with the least considered and valued members of society, it will prove possible to gain equivalent occupational status.

The future for social work must be in working to encourage the involvement of poor and marginalized groups in society. This can be promoted through social work contact if such contact takes forms which reduce the risks of stigma, pressure to change and marginalization. The alternatives are to seek to identify and build on people's strengths and talents, increase opportunities for people to meet and work with others who share their oppression and openly share, in negotiations, information about the way in which the state seeks to impose itself on its citizens.

The room which social workers have to share and develop their work in this way will be determined by a number of facts including wider political and economic forces. The encouragement social workers give to political participation by those with whom they come into contact may challenge the current welfare agenda. But only by making a start, exploring the possibilities and contradictions which result from such an approach, can social workers hope to make a positive contribution to dismantling the hazards faced by peole who become clients.

References

Ahmed, S., Cheetham, J. and Small, J. (1986) *Social Work with Black Children and their Families*. London: Batsford.

Becker, S. and MacPherson, S. (1986) *Poor Clients: the Extent and Nature of Financial Poverty amongst Consumers of Social Work Services*. Benefit Research Unit, Department of Social Administration and Social Work, University of Nottingham.

Berridge, D. (1985) *Children's Homes*. Oxford: Blackwell.

Brook, E. and Davis, A. (1985) *Women, the Family and Social Work*. London: Tavistock.

Central Statistical Office (1986) *Social Trends*, No. 16. London: HMSO.

Cheetham, J. (ed.) (1982) *Social Work and Ethnicity*. London: Allen & Unwin.

Davies, M. (1985) *The Essential Social Worker*. London: Heinemann.

Department of Health and Social Security (1985) *Reform of Social Security: Programme for Action* (Cmnd 9691). London: HMSO.

Equal Opportunities Commission (1982) *Caring for the Elderly and Handicapped: Community Care Policies and Women's Lives*. Manchester: EOC.

Finch, J. and Groves, D. (eds) (1983) *A Labour of Love: Women, Work and Caring*. London: Routledge & Kegan Paul.

Golding, P. (ed.) (1986) *Excluding the Poor*. London: Child Poverty Action Group.

Hale, J. (1983) 'Feminism and Social Work Practice', in Jordan and Parton (1983: Ch. 11).

Holman, R. (1976) *Child Care and Inequality*. London: Child Poverty Action Group.

Jordan, B. (1984) *Invitation to Social Work*. London: Martin Robertson.

Jordan, B. and Parton, N. (eds) (1983) *The Political Dimension of Social Work*. Oxford: Blackwell.

Mayer, H. and Timms, N. (1970) *The Client Speaks*. Oxford: Blackwell.

Mayo, M. (1977) *Women in the Community*. London: Routledge & Kegan Paul.

Office of Population Censuses and Surveys (1986) *Occupational Mortality: The Registrar General's Decennial Supplement for Great Britain, 1979–80, 1982–3*. London: HMSO.

Ohri, A., Manning, B. and Curno, P. (eds) (1982) *Community Work and Racism*. London: Routledge & Kegan Paul.

Robinson, T. (1978) *In Worlds Apart*. London: Bedford Square Press.

Scarman, Lord (1982) *The Scarman Report*. Harmondsworth: Penguin.

Sainsbury, E., Nixon, S. and Phillips, D. (1982) *Social Work in Focus: Clients' and Social Workers' Perceptions in Long-term Social Work*. London: Routledge & Kegan Paul.

Townsend, P. and Davidson, N. (eds) (1982) *The Black Report* (Report of the Department of Health and Social Security Working Group on Inequalities in Health, Sir D. Black (Chair)). Harmondsworth: Penguin.

West Midlands County Council (1986) *A Different Reality*. WMCC.

Williams, S. (1986) 'Exclusion: The Hidden Face of Poverty', in Golding (1986: Ch. 2).

Wilson, E. (1977) 'Women in the Community', in Mayo (1977: Ch. 1).

7

Child sexual abuse: challenging the orthodoxy

Mary MacLeod and Esther Saraga

> We need to have confidence in our ability to read and interpret. Rather than believe in 'experts' who imply they know it all, we must look for the gaps and the hidden agendas. If knowledge and power go hand in hand, it is the responsibility of feminists both to acquire knowledge and to transform it. [Cameron and Frazer, 1987: xv]

In all the storm of words about child sexual abuse, there has been a deafening silence on why it happens. This is strange. For finding a meaning is a central concern of everyone touched by child sexual abuse. Why did it happen? Why did he do it? are questions which obsessively preoccupy sufferers of abuse and their relatives. The abusers who can accept some responsibility for their actions also struggle to find answers.

Child sexual abuse is also at the centre of many ideological debates, bringing together as it does sexuality and the family; yet the debates seldom address why child sexual abuse occurs. Rather, anyone with an issue to explore or a point to make attaches child sexual abuse to it as the clinching argument. Seabrook, in the *New Statesman* (1987), adopts it to argue the debauchery of the market economy; Labour MP Stuart Bell, the integrity of the north-east working-class family; critics and apologists of psychoanalysis use it to attack or defend; James Anderton, Chief Constable of Greater Manchester, to argue for more repressive policing and draconian sentencing.

confused

Why then is there evident in political, professional and journalistic writings such a curious absence of discussion on why abuse occurs? The answer should come as no surprise to feminists; it enables an avoidance of the most glaring feature of child sexual abuse: it is something that, overwhelmingly, men do to children. The men come from every social class, and from all kinds of families and cultures; they are brothers, uncles, babysitters, friends, strangers, grandfathers, stepfathers and fathers. They have in common that they are men, but little else that we know. Very little attention has been paid to studying them, and none to the study of non-abusive men.

Interestingly, the focus of frantic study and hypothesis are the children who are abused, the families they come from and, more than almost anything else, the women who are their mothers. One particular theoretical approach, family dysfunction theory, has, in locating child sexual abuse in 'problem families', dominated lay and professional discourse and achieved the status of common sense. Its main attribute, certainly not logic, is the comfort it affords to the establishment and the great general public. It calms the collective anxiety about the 'family' which erupts, as in the furore over Cleveland, when the reality of sexual abuse of children within families emerges.

Though family dysfunction theory currently holds the position of orthodoxy among professionals, it is actually one of many explanations of child sexual abuse. In this chapter we want to look at, and offer a feminist critique of, three influential approaches: the *libertarian* view, *psychoanalysis* and *family dysfunction*, before elaborating a feminist approach. The approaches are worth exploring in some detail because they have powerfully constrained the ways that child sexual abuse is talked and thought about, and influenced the kinds of intervention and help that occur. These broad approaches are not theoretically pure; they often share assumptions, starting points and arguments. This also is not surprising, since these ideas have all developed within a very old set of discourses, within European culture, about sex, men, women, children and incest.

The furore set off by Cleveland shows us how child sexual abuse arouses a deep collective anxiety about the family: an anxiety that troubles equally the Left and the Right. The new wave of right-wing interest in idealizing the family merges with the anti-interventionist line of the Left; the usual signposts to people trying to find a way to understand and take charge of a difficult issue are missing. There is no clear left or right line on child sexual abuse; indeed it is often hard to distinguish the politics of any piece on child sexual abuse.

However, the confusion, the contradiction, the absence of politics and the sheer difficulty of untangling the debates on an issue which has painful emotional resonances for all of us, must not deter us from attempting to articulate and impose a feminist analysis. It is time to cast a cold eye on the whole business. This is especially true for professionals, for those who choose to and those who are asked to help. Sarah Nelson, in an admirably cool book, *Incest: Fact and Myth*, says:

> The first step in designing a programme among social work, medical, legal and other agencies involves reaching a consensus on what incestuous abuse is about. That means agreeing a theory . . . decisions on how you deal with each family member depend crucially on how you theorize about them. [Nelson, 1987: 96]

There is without doubt just such a clear link between theory and practice. Practice (statutory, voluntary and therapeutic) has to be born of theory. The outstanding success of the initiatives of the women's movement (Rape Crisis, Women's Aid) on sexual violence against women and children is a testimony to this, and it is of course to the women's movement and the courage of survivors that the credit must go for publicly establishing child sexual abuse as the scandal it always was. However, feminist theory is still 'out in the cold' when it comes to the professional establishment.

The first step in agreeing a theory would seem to be establishing what child sexual abuse is and how common it is. This, however, is fraught with difficulties, and cannot precede theory. The way that experiences are understood by children themselves, and by lay and professional people, depends on the ways these events are commonly theorized and categorized. This affects the statistics and definitions, because research too is conducted in a culturally specific way. For example, the *Guardian* letter (11 August 1987) on the Mori poll results which have given such a welcome boost to the forces of denial can say that sexual experiences such as 'showing/touching sex organs', 'fondling/kissing in a sensual way' and 'erotic talk/indecent suggestion/showing pornographic material' cannot and should not be included in figures for 'serious abuse'. Yet anyone who has a nodding acquaintance with casualties of child sexual abuse knows that children have been horribly traumatized by being the object of, for example, 'mere' verbal sexual abuse by their fathers. So it is not such a simple exercise to count the incidence of 'serious sexual abuse', or to define it.

Definitions

A number of definitions of child sexual abuse are used in the literature. They vary according to the activities, and the relationship of abused child to abuser, which are included or excluded. The most widely used definition in the professional literature, usually attributed to Kempe and Kempe, but actually from Schecter and Roberge (1976) is:

> The involvement of developmentally immature children and adolescents in sexual actions which they cannot fully comprehend, to which they cannot give informed consent, and which violate the taboos of social roles. [Quoted in Kempe and Kempe, 1984: 9]

This definition has been criticized for not including the idea that force may be used, or the threat of force, and that the adult's power over the child may constitute sufficient coercive power (Ash, 1984). The inclusion of the idea that abusive acts must 'violate the taboos of social roles' also suggests that some acts are abusive only because they are not socially acceptable.

Recent research by the London Rape Crisis Centre (LRCC) has shown that the 'legal definitions of sexual offences are inadequate in representing the real pattern of violence' (LRCC, 1987: 39). This is particularly true of the crime of incest, which must involve penetration and is restricted to a particular set of family relationships. The term 'incest' has been further criticized by some feminists because it can imply mutuality or complicity, and because it underplays the sense of violation or trauma. Others, such as Herman (1981), Russell (1986) and Nelson (1987) choose to use 'incest' in a wider sense to include all abuse occurring in a familial context, or by any relative, however 'distant'. They believe that it is important to distinguish between abuse that occurs within and outside the family. Even this is problematic, though, because their terminology does not include abuse by someone like a teacher or friend of the family, who is not a relative but who is nevertheless close to the child and in a position of love, trust or responsibility.

Kelly (1988) and Herman have suggested that it is important to include the child's subjective experience as part of the definition: abuse is not defined by what happens, but by how it is experienced. Russell takes a contrary view – that abuse is not dependent upon being experienced as such; many children may not have the knowledge or understanding to know that it is abuse. Many survivors find it difficult to apply 'such value-laden words' as 'rape' or 'sexual abuse' to their experiences (Russell, 1986: 24). Nelson (1987) and the Incest Survivors' Campaign both emphasize the dependent relationship of the child on her/his abuser, the inequality of power and the betrayal of trust.

Another problem with definition is the upper age limit of childhood, and the appropriate age of consent. British surveys usually take 16, the legal age of consent for heterosexuality for girls, as the upper age limit; but this is contested by those who argue the appropriateness of young adolescents having sexual experience with their peers. Some researchers therefore count experiences as abuse only if the abuser is at least five years older than the child. However, for intrafamilial abuse, or any sexual experience involving an adult in a position of power in relation to the child, 16 years is in our view too young; in fact age becomes more or less irrelevant, Nash and West (1985) found that some of the women in their survey felt that 'the cutoff point for childhood at age 16 was arbitrary and that their own sexual experiences with older men, when they were still too young to cope emotionally, should have been included' (Nash and West, 1985: 82). One example cited is of a 16-year-old raped by her employer while working as an au pair.

It is clear that the definition derives from theory; like all aspects of this subject, it is a matter for debate and discussion. The constant concern about finding the correct definition is another diversion from the real issue. Most adults, men and women, know perfectly well that certain actions and activities, from verbal abuse and harassment to rape, are abusive to children. We are not convinced by the 'worried' fathers who write to the press that they no longer dare be affectionate with their daughters for fear of being accused of abuse. Most abusers know exactly what they are doing, and hence find ways of silencing the child.

We are concerned in this chapter with abuse that is defined in terms of three key elements: the betrayal of trust and responsibility, the abuse of power and the inability of children to consent. An assessment of trauma may be important to decisions on intervention, but it should not be part of the definition. We agree with the use of the broad definition, given by the Incest Survivors' Campaign (1981):

> The sexual molestation of a child by any person whom that child sees as a figure of trust or authority . . . we see the questions of age, blood relationship and taboo as red herrings which obscure the central issue: the irresponsible exploitation of children's ignorance, trust and obedience. Incest is the abuse of power. [Quoted in Nelson, 1987: 14]

The 'statistics'

The obsession with numbers following Cleveland is another false trail into the undergrowth. Nevertheless, we need to be prepared with information about the 'incidence studies' in order to counter the arguments that it really isn't as common as everyone is claiming, and shouldn't be taken so seriously.

We cannot say exactly how common child sexual abuse is. Different interpretations of the available statistics, plus the fact that most people have no direct access to any of the research, mean that it is very difficult to draw clear conclusions and easy to believe what we want to believe. However, as more and better research has been done over the last few years, and as more people have been prepared to listen to the findings, ideas have changed dramatically and, whatever the prevalence actually is, it *is* much more common than was ever imagined. The hairsplitting discussion of what is abuse, and what not, obscures the fact that children are constantly exposed to unacceptable sexual attentions from adult men.

Until recently research in this area was very limited, because of lack of interest and the very real problems about doing good research on such a painful, sensitive subject which is shrouded in secrecy. Early research (pre-1978) was based on small clinical samples, 'cases' that were on the files of some authority: police, social workers' or doctors'. These samples were obviously skewed, because very few incidents were ever reported to anyone.

One early exception to this focus on 'cases' was the Kinsey reports (1948, 1953), which surveyed more than 5000 men and more than 4000 women. No numerical data were reported for sexual contacts between boys and adults, but the survey on women did address this issue, looking at 'adult–child sexual contact'; terms like incest or sexual abuse were not used. Careful analyses of Kinsey's data suggest that 24 percent of the women had been sexually abused before puberty; between 3 and 5.5 percent by a family member (Russell, 1986; Herman, 1981). In *all* cases, the abuser was a man.

Work in the USA on child sexual abuse has been several years ahead of the UK. Following the feminist initiative on rape and domestic violence during the 1970s, 'new feminist research and thinking on incest victimization finally started to surface in 1978' (Russell, 1986: 9), and several large-scale retrospective surveys have been conducted. In Britain there are two: the well-known Mori poll (Baker and Duncan, 1985) and a study by Nash and West (1985).

In order to interpret the results of these studies, which conclude that between one in ten and one in three girls have been incestuously abused, in the wider sense of that term, it is necessary to consider the issues of definition discussed earlier: is all abuse being included or only that within the family? What age limits are put upon childhood? However, these do not pose the only difficulties; some problems in research may be more or less inherent to the nature of child sexual abuse itself:

> Memory failure over time, subconscious or even deliberate blocking, and the rationalisation or the reinterpretation of emotive childhood

events, render problematic the interpretation of information gathered retrospectively from adults. [Nash and West, 1985: 5]

How the research is carried out will have a major effect on the information obtained. Russell's study is impressive because it started from an understanding of, and sensitivity to, the nature of the phenomenon being investigated. Interviewers and respondents were matched where possible according to age, race and class. No other major study replicates this methodology.

> In summary: Some of the main methodological features that may explain why our survey obtained a 19-percent prevalence rate for incestuous abuse of women of all ages include use of face to face interviews; use of a range of questions that helped to tap women's memories of experiences, some of them long repressed; avoidance of words like 'incest', 'molest', 'rape' (used only once); careful selection of interviewers who did not subscribe to the usual myths about sexual assault; and rigorous training of interviewers in both the administration of the interview schedule and education about rape and incest. [Russell, 1986: 25]

The Mori poll, which is extensively quoted in Britain, has been criticized for overestimating 'serious abuse' by not having a 'tight' enough definition. The reserve is true. The methodology failed to take account of the emotional impact on respondents of questions on sexual abuse, so that the results were bound to be an under-estimate of the 'true' prevalence rate. The questions asked seem hardly likely to have encouraged disclosures. The interviewers presented respondents with a card on which was printed the following definition of sexual abuse:

> A child (anyone under 16 years) is sexually abused when another person, who is sexually mature, involves the child in any activity which the person expects to lead to their sexual arousal. This might involve intercourse, touching, exposure of the sexual organs, showing porno-graphic material or talking about things in an erotic way. [Baker and Duncan, 1985: 458]

They were asked whether they had had such an experience before the age of 16, so that only experiences which fitted into this definition, which they themselves defined as abuse, were included in the survey.

The definition itself uses a lot of very specific words which might cause anxiety. The details of respondents' experiences could not be described in their own words, but had to fit into pre-chosen categories. Answers were given by choosing options from a 'multi-ple response format'. 'To minimize any embarrassment' respon-dents could answer by referring to the options by 'identifying letters' (Baker and Duncan, 1985: 458), a procedure which reduces personal experience to a category. Moreover, the formulation of the definition is grammatically loose: whose sexual arousal are we talking about?

The figures on the sexual abuse of boys are also a subject of disagreement. Those studies which looked at boys as well as girls (Finkelhor, 1979; Baker and Duncan, 1985) found that the proportion of girl to boy 'victims' is about 3:2 when all sexual abuse is included, but that this proportion changes significantly (about 5:1) when the figures look only at 'within family abuse', and some research suggests that boys tend to be abused within the family only if a girl is being abused (Weir, 1987: 5). Most abuse of boys, whether within or outside the family, is by heterosexual men. Here, and for similar reasons, we are likely to be dealing with an underestimate, though whether, as some people claim, there is an even greater silence on abuse of boys is impossible to say. There has certainly been a denial that boys will find adult–child sexual contact abusive; Kinsey did not even report on this. On the other hand, it is commonly argued that sexual abuse is even more damaging to boys because being passive or submissive is a greater distortion of male sexuality (Kempe and Kempe, 1984). Stereotyped thinking about boys' sexuality has done them a considerable disservice.

Some very important conclusions can be drawn from these retrospective studies. In the majority of cases, the abuse had *never* been reported to any authority, and in many cases the abuse was being disclosed for the first time to the interviewer. Race and class were not significant, with the exception of Asian women, among whom Russell (1986) found that there was significantly less incestuous abuse. While for the reasons discussed here it is difficult to give accurate incidence figures, abuse by stepfathers was proportionately much more common than abuse by biological fathers. The evidence suggests an increase in child sexual abuse during this century.

While some of these conclusions may be important in our arguments, it is, we believe, a matter of insignificance to the position taken on theory and practice how *many* children are sexually fondled, masturbated, raped or 'merely' flashed at. Much more important than establishing a prevalence rate is agreeing a set of rules about what is permissible and what is not.

Don't women sexually abuse too?

The first step in establishing a theory is, then, a recognition of gender as a centrally important feature of child sexual abuse: the gender of the perpetrator rather than the victim. Whenever one argues the feminist position on child sexual abuse, the question is put: but don't women sexually abuse too?, as if the rare incidence of women abusing undermines the argument. Numbers are useful here.

All the research studies agree that the overwhelming majority of abusers are men. For example, in Russell's sample of 930 women, only ten cases of incestuous abuse by women were reported, despite a wide definition of abuse (Russell, 1986: 297). Few of the 'orthodox' experts choose to make this explicit. Although their statistics look at gender of 'victim', they rarely consider the gender of the 'perpetrator'. Instead, as happened in Cleveland, they talk about 'parents' or whether the abuse is within or outside the family. The report of the Mori poll is a good example of this; the tables distinguish between 'intrafamilial', 'extrafamilial' and 'stranger' abuse; the gender of the perpetrator is never mentioned (Baker and Duncan, 1985: 461).

Currently in the UK, many people are suggesting that the extent of sexual abuse by women is probably much greater than we think. The number of *cases* involving a female abuser has increased, but this is in the context of a rapid increase in the total number of cases. Feminists are often accused of being resistant to the idea that women may ever sexually abuse their children, but how much more resistant have the 'experts' been to the acceptance of sexual abuse as a predominantly male problem.

Women are quite capable of abusing power and trust, and of using children to fulfil their own emotional needs. They extremely rarely *sexually* abuse. To accept this is not to say that women never do, nor that women are morally superior. Simply, if we do not accept it, then we lose important clues to understanding *why* child sexual abuse occurs.

The increasing concern in the USA about the hidden incidence of sexual abuse by women led Russell and Finkelhor to carry out a detailed review of the research. Extraordinarily, they discovered that many of the early studies included women in the figures for perpetrators, not only when they had abused a child, but also when they had 'simply "allowed" sexual abuse to occur' (Russell, 1984: 219). Many of the cases of 'sexual abuse' by women were better described as inappropriate behaviour, such as overinvolvement with the child or continuing to sleep in the same bed, and were more likely to constitute emotional abuse. They found evidence that male abusers may be responsible for more serious and traumatic levels of sexual abuse than female abusers (Russell, 1984: 230).

They concluded from their review that 'the theory that perpetrators of sexual abuse are primarily men seems clearly supported' (Russell, 1984: 224). The most important question to come out of this research is one they themselves pose: 'So why are so many experts in the field currently arguing that the number of female perpetrators has been seriously underestimated?' (1984: 230).

The answer has to be because feminist theory is too threatening an opposition. Feminist theory, in taking account of gender in the examination of the phenomenon, does not exclude other inequalities. It must also take account of class and race and, crucially, the inequality and power relations associated with age. In most approaches to child sexual abuse, a great deal of attention is focused on 'the nature of childhood'. A number of 'childhoods' people the discussions. Some are very persistent: child as 'innocent'; child as 'seductress'; child as 'unliberated'; child as 'fantasizer'; child as 'home wrecker'; child as 'self-protector': all of these are roles set by adults for children to fill. But understanding the nature of childhood is not the key to understanding child sexual abuse.

Libertarianism: the legacy of Kinsey

This, we think, is the failure of the libertarian position: its apologists concentrate on proving a childhood sexuality, which is repressed and denied; thus, they say, a perfectly straightforward area of human sexuality is problematized. The libertarian arguments on 'adult–child sexual relations' were particularly important in the 1970s. They influenced the recommendations of the Criminal Law Revision Committee in 1976. They have enshrined in the discourse on child sexual abuse two ideas that have proved remarkably difficult to shift and that continue to have a profound impact on intervention: it is intervention rather than abuse which causes trauma; and children can participate willingly in sexual activity with adults – indeed they desire it.

The recent history of these ideas, as they apply to child sexual abuse, can be said to begin with Kinsey:

> In many instances the law, in the course of punishing the offender, does more damage to more persons than was ever done by the individual in his illicit sexual activity. The child has been raised in fear of all strangers and all physical manifestations of affection may ruin the lives of the married couple who had lived as useful and honorable citizens through half or more of a century, by giving her parents and the police a distorted version of the old man's attempt to bestow grandfatherly affection upon her. [Kinsey, 1953: 20]

Further:

> Some of the more experienced students of juvenile problems have come to believe that the emotional reactions of the parents, police officers, and other adults who discover that the child has had such a contact, may disturb the child more seriously than the sexual contacts themselves. [Kinsey 1953: 121]

Throughout the 1970s, while the libertarian view was the predominant approach to child sexual abuse, women were beginning to voice their own experience and open the door to children's voices. At the same time important research studies (Finkelhor and Russell) were undertaken, influenced in their approach to interpreting their data by the women's movement campaigns on rape and domestic violence. Gradually the evidence was established which could challenge the liberal view, but it has persisted as an influence, and should be questioned.

The libertarian view is that there is nothing inherently harmful or problematic about adult–child sexual relations; it is the way childhood is constructed within a society that sets up a problem/panic where none need exist. If knowledge was available and guilt about sex abolished, children would not be traumatized by 'consensual sexual activity', would be empowered to say no to 'unwanted sexual contacts' and, presumably, since this is not explicit, sexual liberation would have stopped adults from wanting to have sex with unwilling children. The extreme form of the libertarian view is that of PIE (Paedophile Information Exchange) as argued in O'Carroll (1980), but libertarian arguments are adopted by some feminists. It is of course a utopian argument, because it fails to take account of power relations between adults and children.

Libertarian politics has an honourable history as a force arguing for sexual freedoms: lesbian, homosexual and heterosexual, and it is not possible to argue that freedoms have not ensued. Equally convincing is the general argument about the repression of childhood sexuality and the repressive nature of the image of child as 'innocent'. What does not follow is that adult–child sexual relations are 'unproblematic'.

One of the results of the sexual fix is the intense reluctance we have to envisage that there are real political-ethical problems in the area of sexual politics, that we really do need to develop a critical sexual politics. [Heath, 1982: 164]

As the forces of reaction gather, in a number of unholy alliances, it is crucial that just such a critical sexual politics is produced by feminists on this issue. We must not allow debate to be polarized as it is now: pleasure versus repression, family versus the state, decriminalization versus castration. The new initiatives produced by this confusion are very troubling. The whole movement to introduce so-called prevention programmes in schools is an excellent example of the inconsistencies, and the danger, of current government-supported practice. The support for 'educating children to say no' is happening at exactly the same time as the government is making ordinary sex education less and less possible; thus sex as danger becomes the constant message received by children; but children have been badly served by libertarian views.

The libertarian position on adult–child sexual relations was most emphatically put in a collection of essays called *Adult Sexual Interest in Children*, published in 1981, possibly as an intervention in the hounding of O'Carroll and PIE (Cook and Howells, 1981). In the summing-up chapters by Plummer and West, the common erroneous assumptions are put. On children's experience of adult sexual attention: 'It is comparatively rare that the sex act is forced upon the child' (Plummer, 1981: 225). 'It is probable that most child "victims" could have removed themselves from the situation rather easily had they chosen to do so' (West 1981: 264).

Survivors' accounts differ startlingly: 'I would have had to kill him to stop him'; 'he said he did it because he loved me, all fathers did it' (Channel 4, 1984); 'I was so entirely frightened of him . . . he was the sort of person that you would have to do what he told' (quoted in Nelson, 1987: 42).

We know from women's accounts that a threat to kill their mother is often used. Research in the UK and USA bears out absolutely the range of threat, coercion, material and emotional bribery and blackmail used to enforce children's submission and ensure their silence. We also know that the power the adult has by virtue of his relationship to the child may be sufficient.

On the impact of adult sexual attention on children, Plummer and West have this to say: 'Although there is some evidence of the child experiencing short-term shock the evidence for any long-term impact seems thin' (Plummer, 1981: 227). 'The effects of anxious probing by parents, followed by police interrogations, court proceedings and the imprisonment of someone to whom the child has been much attached, are certainly worse than the effects, if any, of the sexual activity itself' (West, 1981: 256). 'If sex by genuine consent were to be decriminalized, it would seem inconsistent to maintain incest as a crime, in the absence of force, coercion or abuse of parental authority' (West, 1981: 268). The evidence which most overwhelmingly dismisses these contentions is that of women and men survivors who have not had the experience of any state intervention, as well as the growing body of evidence on the connection between child sexual abuse and severe mental health problems.

The most serious and considered recent expression of the libertarian position is in Jeffrey Weeks' book *Sexuality and its Discontents* (1985). Weeks reports the strength of feminist arguments on the powerlessness of young people, particularly girls, in relation to adult men, and argues that young people are not fully aware of the sexual connotations of their actions. He also makes a distinction between children and adolescents. Yet he continues his argument by quoting heavily from the literature on paedophilia, which is biased towards stranger homosexual and heterosexual attacks on children, and especially quotes from O'Carroll's *Paedophilia: The Radical Case* (O'Carroll, 1980). Thus he argues for adult sexual relations with young people on the basis of an argument that children are sexual beings, that the trauma involved in intervention is greater than the trauma of the act itself, and that the paedophile has been given a bad name, being chiefly, in reality, distinguished by 'an intense, but often highly affectionate and even excessively sentimental regard for young people' (Weeks, 1985: 227).

This line of argument has a number of disturbing features. First it uses a particular language of euphemism to persuade: adult–child sexual relations are described as inter- or cross-generational, by which is not meant sex between 30-year-olds and 60-year-olds. Secondly this *particular* view of childhood sexuality derives from a particular Eurocentric history of childhood which takes no account of the gender differences which existed, and seems to assume a lost golden age of childhood sexuality drawn from Aries' examples of the childhood of Louis XIII (O'Carroll, 1980; Langfeldt, 1981). A cursory reading of Aries' description of the childhood of Louis XIII reveals a childhood sexuality no less socially constructed and no less a product of adult definition than now.

Incongruously in Weeks' work, which has contributed so much to the notion of a socially constructed sexuality, it appears to incorporate an essentialist view of sexuality as a biological force requiring particular expression; thus paedophilia is entirely taken for granted. We are offered no deconstruction of paedophilia.

Though women have benefited from sexual liberation arguments, they are 'male' arguments. They have no politics of relationships, and women just do not feature. Of course women and children are sexual beings, but this is no argument for the acceptability of any male desires.

Finally we come to consent, the subject of much debate within the libertarian approach, and for centuries an issue within sexual politics. In our view there is no debate about whether children can consent to sexual relations with adults. To be meaningful, consent must be freely given on the basis of knowledge, understanding and equality of relationship. We cannot conceive of a situation where children and adolescents could be deemed to have such knowledge and understanding. Apart from the risks associated with sexual activity – pregnancy, VD, AIDS, cervical cancer, risks which adults have to attend to with forethought and planning – sex in this society is, as Weeks says, heavily burdened with meanings and consequences hard enough for experienced, 'liberated' adults to understand.

This position does not rule out a childhood sexuality, nor an adolescent one. No one should argue against changing the ways in which people speak to children about sexuality, nor against openness about children's own sexuality; and we should strongly oppose the government's policies on sex education. There is, however, no evidence of a simple relationship between children's knowledge and understanding of sex, and protection from abuse (Nash and West, 1985: 76). An age of consent must be maintained, below which consent has to be deemed ungiveable. Whichever age the boundary is, it will be an imposition on some young people and an inadequate protection for others. How much of an imposition it is to adult men is a complete irrelevance.

Psychoanalysis: the legacy of Freud

Psychoanalysis also has things to say about child sexual abuse, but especially incestuous abuse. It is extremely difficult to do justice to the many aspects of incest which psychoanalysis addresses. We therefore propose to do no more than briefly survey psychoanalytic ideas, their currency and their influence on practice.

Though psychoanalysis is not the dominant theory on child sexual abuse, it is powerful in the influence it has had, and continues to have on the way that incest is thought and talked of, and the impact it has had on all casework and therapeutic practice.

Freud's influence on the meaning of 'incest' is profound. He clearly found 'incest' a deeply apt metaphor for the transformation of animal into civilized 'man'. His description of the sexual as the instinctive force which requires restraint, control and channelling to allow the existence of a stable social order continues to appeal to the collective imagination. He saw the incest taboo as the primary restraint, and he found in Greek myth a fruitful source. In Sophocles' *Oedipus the King*, Jocasta says: 'Nor need this mother-marrying frighten you; many a man has dreamt as much' (Sophocles, 1947: 52).

In Sophocles' play and Freud's incestuous world, incest is mother–son (the least common); the 'Father' is absent as a character, being present as the punishing superego, the holder of the Law. It is a truly patriarchal imaginary world, the 'goddess' nowhere to be seen; but Freud was a man of his time, and we should not berate him for being so. The furious debates about whether Freud or psychoanalysis recognized the existence of widespread sexual abuse of children are to some extent irrelevant. Exculpatory myths and denial are produced in avoidance of painful realities: that the law-givers have feet of clay. What was important in constructing the mythology of incest (seductive children asking for it, and children making it up) were the conjunction of particular psychoanalytic ideas with a particular time and place, and a long extant discourse about children, men, women, sexuality and incest.

The collective anxiety, panic and confusion set off by discussion of child sexual abuse can be seen as the unsurprising response to the challenging of a founding idea of our civilization: that incest is the boundary between stability and chaos. If, as the supposed facts show, incest is rife everywhere, then chaos is foreclosing on us.

Psychoanalysis, in supporting this meaning for incest, has assisted in the denial of actual abuse; but it should not be accused of minimizing the trauma of incest. Indeed, quite the reverse. Anna Freud has argued that:

> Far from existing as a phantasy, incest is thus also a fact, more widespread among the population in certain periods than in others. Where the chances of harming a child's normal development growth are concerned, it ranks higher than abandonment, neglect, physical mal- treatment or any other form of abuse. It would be a fatal mistake to underestimate either the importance or the frequency of its actual occurrence. [Freud, 1981: 34]

Winnicott says that seduction brought children 'to a real, instead of an imaginary, sexual life, and spoiled the child's perquisite: unli- mited play' (Winnicott, 1961: 109).

Psychoanalysis, then, has a great deal to say about the meaning of the event to the individual child or adult, and much of this is acute, sensitive and complex. Only the literature of women survivors can better communicate the terrible confusion that a sexually abused child feels: 'Could I tell her [mother] now? The terrible pain assured me that I couldn't. What he did to me, and what I allowed, must have been very bad if already God let me hurt so much' (Angelou, 1984: 79)

The major contribution psychoanalysis makes to theory and practice on child sexual abuse is the understanding of this ambiva- lence, the support that it gives sufferers in the confusion of their feelings, and the discipline that enables its practitioners to hear the unspeakable and thus allow it to be said. In having a place for childhood sexuality, for fantasy, and a 'morality' for parents and adults (which is often crushing in its demands), it has a way of theorizing the internalization of guilt which abused children and adults feel. It is a common experience that children feel love as well as hatred or fear for their abuser. Sometimes, sadly, they say that the abuser was the only person in their lives who gave them any attention or affection. This is then sometimes interpreted to mean that the girl's *real* feeling was to welcome the abuse, or that it wasn't really harmful. Or there is an attempt to weigh up which of the two feelings is the stronger. What psychoanalysis enables us to under- stand is that both feelings can exist simultaneously.

There are, however, difficulties in the traditional therapeutic method in helping recovery:

> The greatest difficulties come when there has been a seduction in the patient's childhood, in which case there must be experienced in the course of treatment a delusion that the therapist is repeating the seduction. [Winnicott, 1961: 86]

The vehicle of transference within the therapeutic process, and the emphasis on the patient being responsible for the journey to insight and meaning, may provide overwhelming stumbling blocks to a sufferer's capacity to use psychotherapy. In order to achieve a meaning other than self-blame or self-hatred, the 'rewriting' of a survivor's history may require, if it is to start, the relocation of the patient in a different landscape. This is something that women know well; consciousness-raising is perhaps the most effective way of beginning the challenge to an internalized ideology.

In theorizing about child sexual abuse, psychoanalysis is within a patriarchal ideology. Where this is most evident is in what psycho-analysis has to say about abusers. The abuser's progress to abuse is generally understood as the man's response to a childhood history, featuring acute anxiety about sexual adequacy, fear of castration and rage at the 'mother'. This of course individualizes the problem and takes for granted a particular construction of male–female relationships and masculine sexuality. It asks no questions about this association of powerlessness, violence and sexuality in male sexuality and none about the 'mother', and thus abandons men and abusers to a theory and practice that offer little hope of rescue from the idea of uncontrollable male sexuality and misogyny.

The orthodoxy: family dysfunction

Though libertarian and psychoanalytic ideas have a place in con-structing the current discourse on child sexual abuse, the discourse is dominated by another approach. It focuses on the 'family' in which abuse occurs, not in order to expose problematic sexual politics, but in order to enshrine 'normal' family relationships. The approach is not presented as a 'theory' supported by evidence, or as an interpretation of a set of 'facts', but instead is put forward as an orthodoxy, as the *truth*, by a particularly influential, mainly male, group of professionals in Britain.

No debates are ever posed, nor any public discussion of these ideas offered. They are associated with various 'institutions', such as Great Ormond Street Hospital for Sick Children, the Tavistock Clinic, the National Society for the Prevention of Cruelty to Children (NSPCC) and the National Children's Bureau, and are embodied within the DHSS guidelines on how to intervene in cases of child sexual abuse. These professionals are the accepted authorities in the field, and they advise the DHSS and the Home Office. Their power and status in this area means that they are difficult to challenge, and their ideas are couched in technical language which serves to mystify people and to hide what is actually being said. The approach is chilling in its incorporation of the most reactionary sexual politics into an apparently reasoned, reasonable and caring theory and practice.

Until recently, there has been a complete split between the work and ideas of Rape Crisis, Women's Aid and Incest Survivors on the one hand, and the orthodox approach on the other. Individual feminists working in the statutory agencies have been isolated. The presentation of feminist ideas on theory and practice at conferences and in articles has been a revelation and almost a liberation to many professional workers, who have been troubled by the orthodoxy and relieved to discover that there is an alternative way of working. The orthodox approach is seductive in its certainty. People faced with child sexual abuse desperately desire certainty about what to do and what to say.

The approach derives from 'systems theory', which has been increasingly influential in social work and family psychiatry. It has been adapted from electronics and applied to the study of families and groups, and is the theory underlying 'family therapy'. What is crucial for our purposes is that the focus of concern is the *family*, rather than particular individuals who may have abused or been abused. Indeed, they frequently refer to 'sexually abused families' (NSPCC, 1984: 14). Simply, it describes families as 'systems' which organize themselves so as to maintain a 'homeostatic' or 'steady state'. This is achieved by each part of the system influencing and being influenced by other parts. Interaction is governed by rules which are usually observed from outside by a trained therapist/ observer, but which are not agreed explicitly by the family members. 'Family dysfunction' is a particular brand of systems theory, unsophisticated in its conception of family members' roles, and of power relations, which are completely unquestioned.

The presentation of this approach usually starts with an acknowledgement that child sexual abuse is far more common than professionals had accepted until recently. The idea that children either lie or fantasize about sexual abuse is explicitly rejected, and it is categorically stated that the child is not to blame, that the abuser is wholly responsible. However, the explanation which follows takes account neither of how common child sexual abuse is, nor of the majority of child sexual abuse which is not father–child incest, nor of how a 'family dysfunction' explanation draws responsibility away from the abuser. The approach does not even follow through the logic of its position.

The family, then, is seen as a system with two levels of functioning: a 'surface action' of the roles and relationships which can be observed in the family, and a 'depth structure' of underlying needs and emotions. In a normal, healthy or 'functional' family, the 'depth' needs for care, warmth and sex are satisfied through the surface action of the family, and traditional gender and age roles are an important way of achieving this. In a 'dysfunctional' family, however, the surface action of the family does not satisfy the underlying needs of the family members. There are various 're-medies' or 'solutions' to this dysfunction, one of which may be a 'sexualization of what should be nurturant physical contact' (Mrazek and Bentovim, 1981: 168). Thus sexual abuse is a *symptom* of what is wrong in the family, or even a 'solution' to the dysfunction. It is argued that there are 'many different routes' (Mrazek and Bentovim, 1981: 168) to this incestuous family surface action, and other workers have distinguished between different sorts of sexually abusive families. In all cases the problem is not the sexual abuse, but the underlying dysfunction. Once the family system is analysed in detail to see why it has broken down, then in almost every case it is the mother who is seen as ultimately responsible. There is an unwritten assumption that families are functional when men's needs are met.

The textbook of this approach is *Child Sexual Abuse Within the Family*, published in 1984. In it, Furniss distinguishes between 'conflict avoiding' and 'conflict regulating' families (Porter, 1984: 11), in which the sexual abuse serves the function either of avoiding conflict between the parents, or of helping to regulate it. He argues that: 'Two different patterns of maternal behaviour occur in the two different types of family' (Porter, 1984: 12). In the 'conflict avoiding families' it seems that the mother 'sets the rules for emotional relationships and for the way sexual and emotional matters are talked about' (Porter, 1984: 12). She is emotionally distant from the daughter(s) who are being abused, although she may compensate for this by compulsive caretaking. If the child tells her mother about the abuse it will be denied or dismissed.

By contrast, in the 'conflict regulating family', 'the mother is deficient in practical as well as emotional support for the children. She becomes their "pseudo-equal" ' (Porter, 1984: 12). In this kind of family it is said that the girl who is being abused may have adopted the role of mother. Conflict, and even violence, between the parents is overt, and 'the child is "sacrificed" to regulate this conflict and avoid family breakdown' (Porter, 1984: 12). In all this there is no discussion of the father or his role, except to suggest that in the 'conflict avoiding' family, the 'non-spoken collusion increases the father's emotional dependence on the mother and keeps him firmly bound to the family' (Porter, 1984: 13): mother is ultimately responsible again.

Elsewhere in the same book there is a discussion about whether some children are more vulnerable to abuse than others. There is a suggestion that children denied affection are at risk. In addition:

> A child is at risk when a mother is over-punitive over sexual matters; not close or affectionate with the child; often ill or absent – rejecting or rejected by her family; poorly educated; socially isolated or with few friends . . .; depressed, psychotic, or dependent on drugs; and most importantly, sexually abused in her own childhood. [Porter, 1984: 8]

The father's behaviour is discussed only as a response to the mother's rejection or withdrawal, which may lead to the father and children turning to each other 'for support, practical assistance, or comfort and the foundations of an incestuous relationship are laid. In other cases a man deprived of his conjugal rights may turn to the nearest available source of gratification – a dependent child' (Porter, 1984: 9).

Furthermore, there is no attempt to explain why it is *men* rather than women who sexually abuse their children. So male sexuality is seen as driven and uncontrollable: 'These men may misunderstand the adolescent's behaviour and be sexually aroused by it; or physical chastisement may lead the perpetrator to the excitement that blends into sexual activity' (Porter, 1984: 9). Poor men! It is up to women not only to nurture and care for their men adequately, and to control their own desires, but also to control men's sexuality, since men are not able to control their own desires. Since men are not able to control themselves, and are seen as being 'addicted', there is always the danger that it will happen again. Bentovim and others argue that children are safe within the family only if their mothers can protect them.

In all these accounts women are described as actively withdrawing, being punitive or depriving men of their conjugal rights, while men are described as if they were children, more frequently passive, aroused by what others do to them, or spontaneously acting and in need of control. Thus Bentovim speaks of a man 'finding himself' touching the genitals of a 5-year-old, just as we might 'find ourselves' assaulting a policeman or robbing a bank.

While the approach concentrates on abuse within the family and in particular by fathers, it is suggested that families in which children are neglected or not valued as individuals may also fail to protect their children from abuse from the wider family, friends and even strangers, At the same time, and without picking up the contradictions, it is argued that responsibility and blame should be removed entirely from individuals and placed on the family system: everyone's a victim of the family breakdown. This removal of blame is followed by a plea for rejection of a punitive model and its replacement with a therapeutic one, since 'the emphasis on punishing the perpetrators which was prevalent in the English approach and in the media meant that victims would conceal the problem and make it harder to identify' (Bentovim, quoted in the *Guardian*, 8 September 1987).

There are feminists who are family therapists (Bograd, 1984; Pilais and Anderton, 1986). They suggest that feminism and family therapy need not be incompatible, but they distinguish between the *explanation* given for the abuse happening and the therapeutic methods adopted. Family therapy may provide a useful way of helping a secret in the family to be disclosed. The incestuous assault could be described as the cause, rather than the symptom, of family dysfunction. These refinements have not yet reached Great Ormond Street.

Subcultures and cycles
The family dysfunction approach often incorporates other popular views, which need to be questioned: the 'cultural theory' and the 'cycle of abuse'. Thus it is often suggested, despite no evidence, that 'there are isolated communities or subcultures in which incest is accepted readily' (Kempe and Kempe, 1984: 51), or that incest is more likely in cultures which do not conform to traditional sex roles. These ideas feed racist myths about 'pathological' Black families and class stereotypes about so-called 'chaotic' or 'disorganized' working-class families. Many abusers tell children that abuse is quite normal in their family/culture: they are 'good cultural theorists' (Nelson, 1987; 48).

The other notion, the 'cycle of abuse' is taken as a 'fact': men abuse because they were abused in childhood; women who were abused in childhood do not themselves abuse, but they marry abusers and become 'colluding' mothers. These ideas are not based on sound research, but are derived from the experience of clinicians. No one has investigated either the number of men who were abused in childhood who do not go on to abuse their children, or the women survivors who do not marry abusers. Given the frequency of child sexual abuse, any relationship that does exist between mothers who were abused in childhood and abused daughters may well arise by chance. Indeed, if all men who abuse their daughters had been abused themselves, it would mean a disproportionately huge amount of undisclosed abuse of boys. Finally, there has been no attempt to describe a causal link between childhood abuse and adult abusing or collusion.

It is important not to underestimate the power of these ideas. Not only do they have a spurious liberal appeal, by saying that individual men are not to blame, but they are also internalized by many women. Their effect is to absolve the abuser of responsibility (he's a victim of his own childhood) and to add to the abuse done to women by claiming that their abuse in childhood is largely to blame for their own children being abused.

Mother blaming

The extent of mother blaming in the family dysfunction approach is quite breathtaking:

> Incest . . . is not initiated by the child but by the adult male, with the mother's complicity. Stories from mothers that they 'could not be more surprised' can generally be discounted – we have simply not seen an innocent mother in long-standing incest, although the mother escapes the punishment that her husband is likely to suffer.
>
> Why do mothers play such an important role in facilitating incest between father and daughter? Often a very dependent mother is frantic to hold on to her man for her own needs and the financial support he provides, and sees the daughter as a way of providing a younger, more

attractive sexual bond within the family than she can offer. This is
specially true if she is frigid, rejected sexually, or herself promiscuous.
[Kempe and Kempe, 1978: 66]

We want to expose in some detail the mother blaming in the
professional literature, before suggesting an alternative way of
understanding the ways that women respond to the sexual abuse of
their children. For it is the view of 'mothers', and the implication of
this view for practice, that most clearly divides the 'family dysfunction' and feminist positions. Earlier we unpicked the theory and
demonstrated that, in this approach, families are dysfunctional
when 'mothers' are not adequately performing their role. This
criticism has been made before and often. Yet as Sarah Nelson says:

> Where incest is concerned, many assumptions are being swept away by
> the tide. Yet professionals cling to the collusive wife theory like
> drowning men grasping at flotsam. Could it be because it is such a
> powerful defence against admitting the male abuse of power? And
> because without it family therapists might be like emperors without
> clothes? These are harsh questions which they owe it to their own
> integrity to ask. [Nelson, 1987: 108]

On the surface it appears that some feminist ideas have had an
influence on professionals, but scratch it, and we are back to the
mothers again. For example, in a recent paper, Baker and Duncan,
working within a model of family dysfunction, both acknowledge
that it is *men* who sexually abuse and *appear* to have taken on board
some feminist arguments. Thus they argue that in order to understand why it is men who sexually abuse children we have to look at
the way men are socialized to separate sex from affection, and to be
aroused by people smaller and less powerful than themselves. They
go on to argue that 'men are not helpless victims of their own
uncontrollable sexual urges (Baker and Duncan, 1986: 262) and that
most men, even if they have fantasies about children, will not act on
them. However, they suggest that some men will overcome their
internal inhibitions, because they themselves were abused in childhood (cycle of abuse), or because of their social or material
situation (poverty, unemployment). In these cases the men require
'external constraints', and again one person in the family is
ultimately responsible for these!

> In families where the mother is absent, sick or powerless or spends large
> amounts of time away while others, including the father, care for the
> children there is an increased opportunity for abuse to take place. The
> father whose self-esteem has been damaged by redundancy or unem-
> ployment may have ample opportunity to reassert himself by abusing a

child as he is cast into the role of primary caretaker. [Baker and Duncan, 1986: 263]

It is interesting to note in passing that if 'opportunity' were an important factor then one might expect a very high level of abuse from women.

So, starting from some ideas that we might have sympathy with, we have been taken on a tour of several theories and ended right back in the same place, with the ideas of uncontrollable male urges, female responsibility to control men, the collusive wife, and the absent, withdrawn or rejecting mother. It is these ideas that are the most dangerous and damaging parts of the current orthodoxy.

It is encouraging to find that some workers within the 'family dysfunction' framework are finding that the practice does not always bear out the theory. Thus, an account of 'Group Work with Mothers Whose Children Have Been Sexually Abused', carried out at Great Ormond Street, states:

> In our experience it is unwise to assume that all mothers contribute to or condone the abuse. Indeed it may be that less weight should be given to psychological explanations of mothers' roles in child sexual abuse and more to factors which lead to them perceiving themselves as powerless to alter their own or their children's situation. [Hildebrand and Forbes, 1987: 288]

What is not recognized in the theory of the 'collusive' mother is that we have all absorbed the ideology of motherhood: mothers are supposed to care for and protect us; we blame them when things go wrong; often they are the only safe recipient of children's anger. If children are being sexually abused, then it is assumed that their mothers *should* somehow know it and stop it. Child and adult survivors' anger at their mother, and their belief that she must have known, is taken as evidence that she did in fact know, but practitioners must not assume this. They would easily perceive the distinction between feelings and reality in another context, for instance bereavement.

Some mothers do refuse to believe that sexual abuse has occurred, or know and do nothing, or are angry with and blame their daughter, or feel that they are themselves to blame. This is taken as evidence of collusion. Yet we know that denial, anger and guilt are common responses to loss. This kind of event, especially if it occurs within the family, is a tragic loss for everyone. The woman has lost her view of herself as 'wife' and mother. She has lost the fantasy family; her family and her relationships with other family members will never be the same again. The desperate desire of many mothers is: 'let it not have happened, let it not be true'. Jan

Macleod and Patricia Bell of Glasgow Women's Support Project sum it up beautifully:

> A woman does not commit her life and security to a man she believes capable of molesting his own children. Psychiatrists and experts in this field cannot find any 'identifying' features among abusers – so how are women supposed to identify an abuser before they marry him? People will very readily talk about 'colluding mothers' but we should ask ourselves: if you were told, or began to suspect, that your brother or husband or friend was abusing his children, would you go straight to the police? In [their] powerless position women are expected to be more aware, more resourceful and more courageous than the doctors, teachers, social workers etc, who make up a society which through denial colludes with child abuse. Professional workers often condemn 'colluding mothers' in one breath, and in the next say 'I'm sure that there is incest in such and such a family, but I don't know what to do about it.'
> [Quoted in Nelson, 1987: 70]

In criticizing the idea of 'mother collusion', we also have to be careful not to put in its place our own idealization of mothers. We should not insist that mothers are always perfect; we know they aren't, and why should they be? Many women *do* believe their daughters, *do* protect them, *do* act in their best interests, and have always done so (Clark, 1987: 101), but a feminist analysis also explains why some women may be unable to protect their children, and why the failure to do so 'is regarded as particularly loathsome' (Wattenberg, 1985: 203).

It is not possible to overestimate either the power of 'mother collusion' ideas on lay people, on mothers and on abused children themselves or their enormous influence on practice. Practitioners will engage in lengthy discussions at case conferences on the mother's role. Some will see all mothers as collusive; others will look at the mother's response to the information that her child has been abused, interpreting anger and denial as evidence of 'collusion'. From this will come decisions about appropriate measures for child protection and therapeutic plans. In protection work, children are seen as equally unsafe with their mother as with the abuser, and are received into care, as appears to have happened in Cleveland. Therapy starts from an assumption of mother's collusion and pursues this through family meetings and individual work. This leads to a belief that the 'best' outcome for a woman who has been abused is that she understand and forgive her father and recognize her mother's responsibility, in the context of a 'rehabilitated' family system (Baillie, 1983; Owen, 1987).

A collusion *is* at work here: a collusion with a set of assumptions which allows families to remain exactly as they are, and which can have a ruinous effect on children and families. Clearly the attitude of the therapist toward the mother is pivotal. 'The therapist's unstated pursuit of evidence for the therapist's *assumption* of the mother's collusion will threaten the entire therapeutic process' (Wattenberg 1985: 209). It can also drive a wedge between mother and daughter, widening difference and exacerbating distress. For many survivors, part of their anger with their father is that he denied them the possibility of a good relationship with their mother; therapy ought not to collude with this.

While it is true that women's and children's interests are not identical, it is also true that if workers attempt to build an alliance between mother and daughter at the time of disclosure, both do benefit emotionally: the child in feeling less rejected, less alone; the mother in feeling less guilty, less detached.

If we adopt a feminist perspective we will not automatically condemn a mother as 'collusive' if she does not want to believe what has happened, or even if we discover that she did know and did nothing. We will concentrate on giving care and attention to women, recognizing the difficulties of their position, the complexities of their feelings, the meaning for them of what has happened.

The feminist challenge

And so to feminism, and its challenge to the orthodoxy. Feminist theory starts with gender. In looking at why children get sexually abused we are not looking at some 'Neanderthal' drive, nor at problem families, but at problematic sexual and adult–child politics.

If we look at the history of child sexual abuse as an issue, we find that it was not discovered by sociologists, psychiatrists, social workers or journalists. Like rape and domestic violence, child sexual abuse was brought to public attention by women, particularly women survivors. The voices of women survivors and workers in Women's Aid, Rape Crisis and Incest Survivors' groups have told child sexual abuse as a different story. It is an overwhelmingly convincing story. It says: don't tell us we like it, we want it, we need it or we agree to it. Don't tell us you're freeing us from sexual repression, educating us for a more fulfilling adult life. Don't tell us you do this because you love us, don't tell us you do this because nobody loves you. Don't tell us we are dirty. Don't tell us we are worthless. And don't tell us we can't recover. You may have fucked our bodies, but you're not going to fuck our minds.

The process of recovery, of moving from victim to survivor, has a central phase of anger. The process of developing a feminist theory mirrors this. There is plenty of scope for rage in reading the annals of academic inquiry into child sexual abuse; but if we are to move from conspiracy theory to a revolutionary one, we have to move from anger to analysis.

The elaboration of a feminist analysis of child sexual abuse began with Florence Rush's book, *The Best Kept Secret*, published in 1980. Herman (1981) in the USA and Nelson (1987) in the UK have developed the arguments, which are borne out by the research on child sexual abuse undertaken by feminists and others, and by the autobiographical and fictional accounts of incestuous abuse.

Adults, women and men; adolescents, boys and girls, have the means to abuse (age, power, status, love) and they have or can easily arrange the opportunity within the family; but only men (and a very few women) have the motive, the desire. Though both men and women abuse power over children by engaging in physical or emotional abuse, it is men who abuse children sexually. Child sexual abuse is, then, one part of a spectrum of male violence against women and children. Instead of asking why it is that we problematize children's sexuality, feminists ask why it is that men wish to objectify children's sexuality. Why is it that male rage is turned on women and children? Helped by analyses of the ideology of racism, feminists look for answers to the history and the cultural representation of masculinity, femininity and sexuality. For the objectifying of others' sexuality is not a biologically determined masculine characteristic; women can and do arrive there too. Finding the representations is only too easy. From the rape of the Sabine women, a potent artistic image for generations of painters, rape, personal power and state power have been linked. Rome, says the history, was established on rape: the founding of a dynastic, imperial state depending on the male as sexual aggressor.

The long history of misogyny in western Europe has its current expression everywhere from violent and degrading pornography to respectable films and novels, from working-class pubs to Oxbridge colleges. The long-established discourse on male sexuality as subject and everything else as object dominates cultural expression. The association of masculinity with domination, of sexual dominance with personal 'success', is all-pervasive.

In western culture, there has for 500 years also been an association of sexual domination and racism:

> I want to suggest to you that rape bears a direct relationship to all of the existing power structures in a given society. This relationship is not a simple mechanical one, but rather involves complex structures reflecting the complex interconnectedness of race, gender, and class oppression which characterizes that society. If we do not attempt to understand the nature of sexual violence as it relates to racial, class and governmental violence and power, we cannot even begin to develop strategies which will allow us to eventually purge our society of the oppressiveness of rape. [Davis, 1985: 9]

This is the ideology that not only makes possible sexual violence of every kind, but also renders it invisible. It is only the latter part of the ideology, the invisibility, that is currently threatened. It is a mistake to separate off any particular manifestation of the spectrum of violence and to see it as a special case. Simply, these politics, that history, this culture ensure that some men will be able to abuse their own daughters.

The impact of the ideology on the collective and individual male internal world is also easy to narrate. Generally boys and men learn to experience their sexuality as an overwhelming and uncontrollable force; they learn to focus their sexual feelings on submissive objects, and they learn the assertion of their sexual desires, the expectation of having them serviced. Obviously this is a crude account of a complex phenomenon; male sexuality is not one-dimensional, and within a culture oppositional ideologies exist (for example, men as caretakers of their families, gentle lovers and protectors of their daughters), and have their impact on self-definition and cultural practices. Thus all men do not abuse, and sexual violence against women and children will have a different meaning, and different prevalences, within different societies at different times.

Even if the demand of the ideology on male self-esteem is high (as many will argue), and the resulting anxieties and inadequacy crushing, then all men do not escape from inadequacy and anxiety into sexual violence. For some men, an escape may be managed and reinforced through fantasy and pornography. But those who do abuse seem to find this conjunction of sexual pleasure and domination so heady a mixture that they feel constantly driven to repeat it. Some say they are tormented by remorse or self-disgust and want to be stopped. Beyond this we know very little about the men who abuse, or why they do. What is clear is that there is no help to be got in answering this from studying their children, their 'victims', their mothers, wives or girlfriends.

Some men are turning their attention to the 'problem of masculinity'.

> Some theorists . . . draw attention to differential patterns of conscious and unconscious socialization for boys and girls which, together with wider social images of masculine sexuality, have the effect of constructing men as alienated from intimate relations and from our sexuality . . . . The characteristic patterns of masculinity, focusing on independence and 'hardness' and turning away from intimacy and nurture, follow from this. In particular it produces a severely narrowed rendering of sexuality, operating primarily in two convergent ways. First, sex is one of the few means by which men aspire to closeness with others, and as such it becomes the carrier of all the unexpressed desires that men's emotional illiteracy produces. However this same process makes sex dangerous to men whose identity is built on the denial of emotion; sex then becomes split off, limited to the activity of the penis, an act rather than an encounter. At the same time, sex becomes tied up with competition, separation and power – something used to bolster a man's sense of masculinity rather than to create a bond with another. The link between such a form of masculinity and sexual abuse is apparent; it is not just present, but *inherent* in a mode of personality organization that rejects intimacy. Sex as defence and as triumph slides naturally into sex as rejection and degradation of the other . . .
>
> This is not, of course, to say that all men actually abuse children, nor that there are no differences between those that do and those that do not. . . . There are also important and difficult questions concerning the processes whereby most men learn *not* to abuse children – processes presumably connected with the quality of their relationships in early life, internalization of moral constraints, and the development of capacities to form positive sexual and emotional relationships with adults. But if there are systematic factors that make men more likely to sexually abuse children, then these factors will be present more or less strongly in all men. [Frosh, 1987: 335]

Frosh explains sex as defence, triumph, rejection and degradation, but not sex as rage. He sees the embargo on emotional expression as on affection, softness, tenderness, sadness; he does not mention anger and rage. It seems to us that men get every encouragement to express anger. If emotion is sexualized this explains why men sexually abuse and perceive it as non-abusive; it does not explain the sexualization of rage and anger, unless what is suggested is an inability to separate tenderness and brutality. If this is so, then instead of seeing the source of sexual violence in rage at the mother, perhaps it should be seen as rage at men, at the father, at the self, that is displaced on to and acted out against women and children, and instead of perceiving other men as threatening, which is terrifying and unacceptable, the threat is perceived in women, where it can be controlled.

The wilderness of the playground, where boys learn so much about domination, submission and the basics of misogyny – the worthlessness of girls – may have a lot to say about 'those who do and these who don't'. Certainly the figure, pathetic in the face of authority and brutish at home, which peoples the clinical accounts, bears a striking resemblance to the school bully, ingratiating and terrifying by turn.

Whatever difficulties exist in childhood, family, relationship, work and lifestyle, whatever freedom or repression exists about child and adult sexuality, it is a particular construction of masculinity that enables men to sexually abuse children. A feminist analysis places at the centre of an explanation of child sexual abuse the 'problem of masculinity'. It attempts to stop the collusion of theory with sexual politics, to make sexual violence visible, and to construct a different meaning for it. This is not simply academic. From a different meaning arises a different practice.

From theory to practice

Feminist critiques of the orthodox approach draw out the woman, mother, and child blaming, and the essentialist view of male sexuality that it incorporates, be it ever so apparently scientifically and academically respectable. The first aim of feminist practice is to attack this and to argue an alternative theory. This is already under way: witness the burgeoning feminist literature on child sexual abuse.

The next step is influencing policy at all levels, and this too is well under way: for example, the moves to enable the exclusion of abusive men so that children can stay in the non-abusive parts of their family, as outlined in the Islington policy and guidelines and recent discussion at the Labour Party conference. There have been changes in police practice, and the government proposes changes in the rules of evidence. Some feminists fear the gifts of a Tory establishment, wondering whether other less acceptable outcomes are the real motive behind the change.

What should a feminist policy and practice look like? Is such a thing possible within a statutory agency? If our analysis of child sexual abuse leads to the conclusion that it is a product of the construction of male sexuality within a particular form of society, then how can single state agencies, let alone individual workers, do anything more than alleviate the consequences of such abuse?

There have tended to be two feminist responses to this dilemma; either feminists should remain outside the statutory sector, and continue to offer women and children an alternative service through Rape Crisis, Women's Aid, and Incest Survivors' groups, or feminist social workers should see their work as part of the process of overthrowing the capitalist patriarchal state (Dominelli, 1986). Recently, however, a more complex analysis of state intervention has brought the work and ideas of feminists and some statutory agencies closer together.

It is not surprising that the issue of child sexual abuse should expose the inadequacies of the Left's position on state intervention. The Left has generally seen social work as the instrument of state control of working-class families. The use women and children have made of voluntary and statutory social work agencies to redress some of the imbalance of power within the family has long been invisible, and only recently written about (Gordon, 1985). It has been possible in looking at the physical abuse of children to argue a relationship between poverty and stress and abuse (Parton, 1985). No such relationship exists for child sexual abuse: sexual politics has to be taken into account. We cannot continue to see the family as a monolithic structure serving everyone's needs. We have to admit the inequalities of power and the conflicts of interest that exist within families. The 'traditional' Left is no less threatened by a feminist critique of the family in its male hegemony than the Right, as crudely argued pieces in the *News on Sunday* (2 May 1987) and the *Socialist Worker* (22 August 1987) show. This is not to argue for no debates about intervention: only for a more complex appreciation of the issues.

Intervention and racism

There never has been a 'golden age' of no intervention in people's lives. Constraints and controls on how people 'parent' have always been exercised by communities, though of course the form of these has been historically specific, and has incorporated the dominant ideology on 'good parenting'. This leads to a heavy class and racist bias in the practice of intervention, the imposition of white middle-class heterosexual norms of good parenting on people and the assumption that poor single parents, Black parents or lesbian

Sad

parents need 'improving'. Inequalities in child care are just that –
the result of unequal resources – but there is nothing wrong, racist
or anti-working class in saying that certain behaviours toward
children are unacceptable. It is possible for workers to make
judgements in groups other than their own, though an understanding of racism and different cultural patterns is essential if accurate
conclusions about the meaning of interactions are to be made. The
problem comes in acting on a judgement.

In a racist society, it is extremely important to be aware of the
injustice into which a Black family may be delivered in invoking
criminal proceedings, in taking children into care and in separating
children and families. If the family has a central place in people's
identity, how much more so for Black people, for whom it may be
one of the few places of retreat from racism. It is also necessary to
recognize the impact that racism can have on the meaning of the
event. A Black child who has internalized racism may equate being
Black with being bad, and the guilt that all abused children
experience may confirm those feelings. She may also find it harder
to 'tell', since it may feel like an even greater betrayal of her family
than it is to a white child.

We cannot, however, simply be anti-interventionist, thinking we
are being progressive, because this does mean closing our eyes to
the abuse of children in families; but we do have to take cognizance
of the implications of state intervention. Feminists have a lot to say
on this.

Feminist practice
Feminist practice has been born from the initiatives of the women's
movement on rape and domestic violence. The growth of awareness
of child sexual abuse started from hearing women talk about

childhood abuse, from women asking for help to protect their children, and from girls and young women ringing the crisis lines because of abuse. These groups have built up a formidable body of knowledge and experience, from working with women and children who have been assaulted, on what their feelings may be, on the process of recovery, and on what is helpful. This expertise should be acknowledged, and the knowledge used to improve practice elsewhere. (See the articles in *Feminist Review*, no. 28, January 1988, and London Rape Crisis Centre, 1984.)

However, these women's resources are not adequate to protect children, because they do not have statutory power; and the principles underlying their practice – that women have the right to complete control over what action is taken following an assault – cannot be straightforwardly extended to children, though ChildLine appears to be doing so. Statutory services are essential, but they must be organized to empower not oppress women and children.

Feminist social workers, often isolated in their work, have begun to organize specifically around child sexual abuse. The power and potential of this is demonstrated by the development of the Islington policy and guidelines. A conference held in April 1987, 'Child Sexual Abuse: Towards a Feminist Professional Practice', attracted a large number of women working within a wide range of voluntary and statutory agencies. The interchange of ideas and experience was exciting, and it has enabled many workers in statutory and 'non-feminist' voluntary agencies to initiate discussions within their own workplace on a different, feminist policy and practice. From these initiatives have come suggestions for a feminist social work practice.

Protection work
Most concern and attention is devoted to the 'crisis of disclosure' – what to do when sexual abuse has been identified. This is not surprising; it is a crisis for all involved. Social workers who have a statutory duty to investigate *all* allegations of child abuse have to act to protect the child(ren) involved. This poses a painful dilemma: they *have* to act, often in the absence of clear ideas of what is the best thing to do, of training, and of the resources required to do the job. Teachers, nursery workers, health visitors and doctors usually work to guidelines which instruct them to inform social services but it is not compulsory for anyone to report abuse to 'the authorities' or the police.

Though this work is emotionally painful and demanding, it is not fundamentally different in the issues and dilemmas it raises from all other social work with children. Undertaking it well requires time, resources and good legal advice. Following disclosure, the aim is to ensure the safety of the child while decisions are made on how best to stop the abuse and help the child recover. If the abuser is a family member, this should be done by removing the abuser and not the child.

The focus of work must now be with mother, child, siblings and extended family. Two workers with a lot of time may be needed. (Some authorities now allow one worker to focus on work with the child and one to work with the mother.) The aim should be to empower the non-abusing adults, enable the expression of feelings and encourage emotional support for the child. Work of this quality cannot be done in agencies with no facilities for interviewing individuals and families in private, and with no resources for working with children. Adequate provision in not a priority for the present government.

Many mothers on learning of the abuse immediately assume responsibility for protecting the child. Some women are unable to do this. If their response is understood, and they are supported, then many more are able to make that choice. We are not suggesting that this is easy for either the mother or the worker, but the evidence is that it often does lead to a good outcome. If this cannot be achieved, then it may be possible to find an immediate safe solution within the framework of the wider family network, in order to avoid the need to remove the child. More resources are required to enable women to safeguard children: in particular, the provision of refuges, including, where necessary, separate provision for Black women, or women from particular communities; legal advice for women and children; material support, and financial support for voluntary agencies which can offer help outside the umbrella of the state.

However, invoking statutory powers to protect children should not be seen as a sign of failure. Many survivors describe how they longed for someone to intervene to stop the abuse, and many children taken into care have been grateful. Public care can be a desperately inadequate solution for children, and too often it is; but it can be and has been a refuge. Feminists need to begin thinking about what safe and good public care should be, and to work for change.

The second aspect of intervention which is widely discussed is the longer-term outcome. This is often posed as a question about the future of the 'whole family': will the 'family' break up, or is family rehabilitation possible? Most writers/commentators assume that to break up the family in any way is the worst thing that can happen to a child and is to be avoided at all costs. This was certainly voiced constantly in response to Cleveland. We are in no doubt that this is not true. To be abused by someone you love and trust, especially when he is your father, is worse, much worse, than family break-up. Separation of the child from the abuser does not have to mean that the child is immediately taken into care; if the family is not viewed in a monolithic way, then it is possible to distinguish between the abusing and non-abusing parts of the family.

Many women have to make an agonizing choice between their 'man' and their child, and this is a choice that they may need help to make. For some commentators, this is an unacceptable choice to pose to any woman. Here children's rights, which have been ignored in most of the post-Cleveland discussion, are central, and come into conflict with the rights of adults, about which we have heard so much. In this context we have no hesitation in putting the rights of children above the rights of adults, or the rights of women to choose who they live with or marry.

Survival

Protection and long-term arrangements are only one part of the process; there is also emotional work to be done with children, and we have argued that *how* you intervene to protect the child also has enormous implications for the process of emotional survival. There is of course direct therapeutic work to be done at the time of disclosure. This is recognized by most professional workers, and there is agreement on many aspects. Specifically, it is agreed that the child must be believed, assured that it is not her/his fault, that s/he has been both brave and right to tell, and that s/he is not alone – that this has happened to other children too.

This formula is terribly important in conveying to children the way they are being perceived by 'authority', but it is not necessarily very effective in changing their perception of themselves. To avoid exacerbating the child's plight, workers must use their knowledge, their imagination and their own experiences of abuse and betrayal to enter into the child's world and to begin to judge what this abuse means for this child. This involves working directly with children and listening to them. The process of recovery is a long journey to which every bit of the child's current and future experience will contribute. Every intervention has to be thoroughly thought out and carefully executed. Some feminists argue that part of the abuse in all forms of sexual violence is the loss of control; emotional survival therefore depends on the abused woman or child being in control of what happens following disclosure. But child sexual abuse is an abuse of adult power, and many children have carried a dreadful burden of responsibility in protecting their abuser, themselves and their mother by keeping the secret. The experience of a positive use of adult power, of someone else making the decisions and taking the responsibility, may be very therapeutic. Children who have been abused have been deprived of their childhood; they need to be allowed to be dependent, so long as they are safe in that dependency. We cannot have absolute rules about how much control children and young people can take at different ages. It is a matter of delicate judgement.

Many people argue that to prosecute a man and to send him to prison only makes the child feel guilty or doubly punished. This may be the case if the child has to make that decision (as they do if they contact ChildLine). Part of the work that needs to be done with children at disclosure is to help them accept and understand their possibly ambivalent feelings towards their abuser, and that they are not in any way responsible for any consequences that follow for him. This is where a systems approach is particularly unhelpful in trying to see the family system as responsible. Blame is not a problematic emotion. We cannot sanitize what has happened. Someone has been wronged and somebody is blameworthy. Perhaps the most 'therapeutic' thing an abuser could do is to say, 'I was to blame; I shouldn't have done it.' They seldom do. Instead blame is taken by the child who, in the very confusion of her sexual desires and fantasies, is emotionally vulnerable to this. For a child who is sexually abused has a 'real' world within her fantasy world; undoing this requires the most careful and sensitive therapy.

The most important single contribution to recovery is changing the child's circumstances for the better, so that abuse is ended and the child is living with loving and caring adults, preferably those she already knows and loves, and if possible adults with whom she can talk about the abuse and her feelings. That children do survive without this does not affect its importance; we know that many don't.

Among feminists there are debates about what constitutes emotional survival and how best to achieve it. Incest survivors/self-help groups have been an invaluable resource for many women, but for some they are only a first step. If survival is conceived as a long journey towards meaning, then it is clear that the theory underpinning any therapeutic work communicates meaning, and this has to be taken into account in assessing its effectiveness. Yet this is not done within non-feminist approaches. Therapy is never an equal relationship; there is always the possibility of the therapist abusing power. Such an abuse of power is never satisfactory, but in work with child and adult survivors it is disastrous. Those who offer therapy have a clear responsibility to examine the implications their theory has on meaning, and to examine rigorously their conduct and countertransference.

Thus within the orthodox approach it is assumed that family therapy is useful in helping everyone to see what has gone wrong, assuming that abuse has happened because of family dynamics. However, it is probably most helpful in exposing the secret and facilitating discussion and negotiation about what is to happen. Similarly, it is assumed that group therapy for groups of abused children, for their mothers or for abusers is helpful in changing their perceptions of themselves, but depending upon how it is conducted (what theory informs the group leaders), it may merely confirm a whole range of disabling ideas about sexuality and parental roles. Finally, it is assumed that individual psychotherapy can help a survivor towards an understanding of the past, but it may merely exacerbate confusions about real and fantasy, desire and action, guilt and self-blame. Many workers claim that their approach is neutral; that it is not up to them to judge who is responsible or to blame. One cannot be theoretically neutral. We know, for example, that many survivors will feel that they are at least partly responsible, that perhaps they could have stopped it, that maybe their behaviour was interpreted by their abuser as consent. A therapist at this point has a choice: to ask in what way they feel responsible, or to ask whether they believe that a small child can consent.

Disclosing, talking, telling is important in challenging the power of the secret, of shame, in facing and confronting the pain, and in reaching catharsis, but it is not everything and it may not be enough.

There has to be a range of resources for self-help, therapy, and for women who need to 'break down' within a safe environment.

What is to be done about abusers?
In this account we, too, have concentrated on issues for children. The literature on child sexual abuse has astonishingly little to say about abusers. Whether he is described as a 'paedophile'; a pitiful rejected husband, as the product of his own abused childhood, or as a sadistic brute, he is always described as being 'driven'. The fact that many abusers repeat their behaviour on other children leads orthodox therapists to use the term 'addiction' to describe the quality of obsession in this repetition. In the face of all this, there is a collective sense of helplessness. Many therapists, like those at the Portman Clinic in London, which specializes in work with sex offenders, continue in this difficult work as the only alternative to 'locking them up and throwing away the key'. While many feminists may feel that this is a good idea, or that it is 'not our problem', we cannot just leave it at that. While we argue for the removal of the abuser rather than the child from the home, many of these men will join or form new families and subsequently abuse other children.

Statutory workers will sometimes have to work with abusers, directly or as part of their work with children (for example, an abuser may be granted supervised access to his child(ren)). Within the orthodox framework, children will be expected to be part of family meetings with their abuser, and they propose that abusers, prior to family rehabilitation, must not only accept their responsibility for what they have done but must say so to their child. We do not believe that children should *have* to experience this; but some children will want to see/have contact with their abuser, and workers will have to handle this.

The first questions usually posed about abusers are whether criminal proceedings are the appropriate way of dealing with sexual offences against children and young people, and whether abusers should be sent to prison. Arguments for decriminalization come from a very wide range of people – from those who argue that it is a 'family matter'; from those who believe that it punishes a child still further; from those who argue that the 'punitive' climate is preventing abusers from admitting their guilt; and from those who believe that prosecution and prison will achieve nothing whereas therapy might.

There are three separate aspects to this issue: the impact on the meaning of the event; the impact on the children involved, and the best way of changing abusers. Of the first we are in no doubt: to decriminalize child sexual abuse is to say that it is not very serious; it is to support the idea that abusers are pathetic or disturbed, and certainly not responsible for their actions. Child sexual abuse, like rape and domestic violence, must be seen as a straightforward crime against the person. Anything else is an injustice to those assaulted. While it is clear that prison is not successful at reforming anyone, to abandon it for sexual offences (before, for example, crimes against property) is to regard sexual offences as a special category of behaviour and to collude with the notion of men's 'uncontrollable drive'. While many abusers, having internalized the ideology, may perceive themselves thus, it is quite wrong for the state to concur. Finally, a custodial sentence does guarantee the safety of women and children for a period of time.

The second argument looks at the impact on children, arguing that children's feelings of self-blame are worsened by the responsibility they feel for sending their father to prison. Without wishing to play down the pain of this, we believe that children can be helped to deal with it. Moreover, this view takes account of only *one* aspect of a child's painfully ambivalent feelings at this time. One way of helping a child not to feel responsible may be for society to say clearly: 'He is responsible.' Survivors' accounts demonstrate both their ambivalence, and their desire to see their abuser punished in some way: 'I hated him and I wanted him punished, but he was my father and I loved him' (Channel 4, 1984), said one adult woman of her distress as a child giving evidence against her father. Clearly the debates on these questions will continue; we have to be sure that our arguments about what should be done do not come from *denial*, from an inability to face up to and accept the reality and seriousness of child sexual abuse.

Finally, what about changing men? It is true that prison, as currently organized, is not very effective at changing men's behaviour; but then neither is therapy. 'There can be little question that the strongest predictor of future sexual offences is past sexual offences' (Dreiblatt, 1982: 3). This is not surprising. If therapy is also a search for meaning, then much of it confirms, rather than challenges, their own story to themselves: they have an overwhelming obsession; they are lonely, rejected, unhappy. Traditional approaches to 'treatment' may not be useful:

> Mental health practitioners are trained to adopt a helping, accepting and caring posture. They are discouraged from taking an authoritative and controlling stance. The mental health approach emphasizes client support: one attempts to trust and believe one's client and have confidence in him. Although not completely so, this posture is the antithesis of the authority-based treatment approach one takes with a sex offender. Effective assessment and treatment of the offender requires a degree of skepticism and cynicism on the part of the professional. I tell my clients that I do not operate on a trust basis. Trust is what is abusable. I communicate to them that I have no intention of feeling confident in them. Feeling confident in them can be dangerous. [Dreiblatt, 1982: 3]

What is required is something altogether more bracing, less collusive and more challenging, aimed at exploring power, anger and fear, more than sex, love and desire:

> A direct, focused approach to the offence . . . confrontative and challenging . . . . Although we are often taught to focus on *why* behaviour has occurred, your assessment will be more effective if you focus on *what* has happened. The tough-minded approach. [Dreiblatt, 1982: 5]

Until and unless it is recognized that child sexual abuse is a gender issue, and a product of the social construction of masculinity, there can be no change, either in individual men or in masculinity, no counter to the dominant messages, no way of providing boys with an alternative view of masculinity. Posing an alternative explanation of child sexual abuse, and giving it a different meaning, is an essential part of the wider political struggle towards real prevention.

Training, prevention and the way forward
The little money available for child sexual abuse work from this close-fisted government is for training and prevention. These are the way forward, says the establishment; but its conception of training and prevention are a monument to the wrong-headedness of the theory. There are to be more specialist workers, more specialist units in the orthodox mould; and children are to be taught

how to say 'no' to sexual assault by special programmes developed for use in schools: 'My body's nobody's body but mine', say the eager children in a Rolf Harris video. 'Please leave it alone when you hear me say "No!" '[1]

There is nothing wrong or malevolent about the desire to do something; nothing wrong with wanting to help children be more assertive; nothing wrong in trying to improve, through wide training, the service to children and families. However, if the problem of masculinity is edited out of the discourse on child sexual abuse, we are left with children waging a war armed only with words, the adults having left the front. As all the feminist writings on child sexual abuse show, we do have ideas, resources, possibilities, weapons for a different fight, aimed at transforming knowledge and instituting a different practice.

Note
We would like to thank all the women with whom we have discussed these ideas. Drawings by Kerry.

1 Chorus and one of the verses from 'My Body' by Peter Alsop, sung in the video *Kids Can Say No!* produced by Rolf Harris Video, 43 Drury Lane, London. WC2B 5RT.

References

Angelou, Maya (1984) *I Know Why the Caged Bird Sings*. London: Virago Press.
Ash, Angie (1984) *Father–Daughter Sexual Abuse: The Abuse of Paternal Authority*. Bangor: University College of North Wales.
Baillie, Beverley (1983) 'All For the Love of Ann', *Community Care*, 489.
Baker, Anthony W. and Duncan, Sylvia P. (1985) 'Child Sexual Abuse: A Study of Prevalence in Great Britain', *Child Abuse and Neglect*, 9: 457–67.
Baker, Tony and Duncan, Sylvia P. (1986) 'Child Sexual Abuse', in Meadow (1986).
Bograd, Michelle (1984) 'Family Systems Approaches to Wife Battering: A Feminist Critique', *American Journal of Orthopsychiatry*, 54(4).
Cameron, Deborah and Frazer, Elizabeth (1987) *The Lust to Kill*. Cambridge: Polity Press.
Channel 4 (1984) 'Child Sex Abuse' Programme 1: 'The Evidence'. 20/20 Vision.
Clark, Anna (1987) *Women's Silence: Men's Violence*. London: Pandora Press.
Cook, Mark and Howells, Kevin (1981) *Adult Sexual Interest in Children*. London: Academic Press.
Davis, Angela Y. (1985) *Violence Against Women and the Ongoing Challenge to Racism*. Latham, NY: Kitchen Table/Women of Color Press.
Dominelli, Lena (1986) 'Father–Daughter Incest: Patriarchy's Shameful Secret', *Critical Social Policy*, 16.
Dreiblatt, Irwin S. (1982) 'Issues in the Evaluation of the Sex Offender', A Presentation at the Washington State Psychological Association Meetings.
Finkelhor, David (1979) *Sexually Victimized Children*. London: Free Press.
Freud, Anna (1981) 'A Psychoanalyst's View of Sexual Abuse by Parents', in Mrazek and Kempe (1981).
Frosh, Stephen (1987) 'Issues for Men Working with Sexually Abused Children', *British Journal of Psychotherapy*, 3(4).
Gordon, Linda (1985) 'Child Abuse, Gender and the Myth of Family Independence: A Historical Critique', *Child Welfare*, 64(3).
Heath, Stephen (1982) *The Sexual Fix*. London: Macmillan.
Herman, Judith Lewis (1981) *Father–Daughter Incest*. London: Harvard.
Hildebrand, Judy and Forbes, Constanze (1987) 'Group Work with Mothers Whose Children Have Been Sexually Abused', *British Journal of Social Work*, 17: 285–304.
Kelly, Liz (1988) 'What's in a name? Defining child sexual abuse', *Feminist Review*, 28(Spring): 65–73.
Kempe, Ruth S. and Kempe, C. Henry (1978) *Child Abuse*. London: Fontana/Open Books.
Kempe, Ruth S. and Kempe, C. Henry (1984) *The Common Secret*. New York: Freeman.
Kinsey, Alfred C. *et al.* (1948) *Sexual Behaviour in the Human Male*. Philadelphia: Saunders.
Kinsey, Alfred C. *et al.* (1953) *Sexual Behaviour in the Human Female*. Philadelphia: Saunders.
Langfeldt, Thore (1981) 'Sexual Development in Children', in Cook and Howells (1981).

London Rape Crisis Centre (1984) *Sexual Violence*. London: The Women's Press.

London Rape Crisis Centre (1987) *Strength in Numbers*. London: London Rape Crisis Centre.

Meadow, Roy (1986) *Recent Advances in Paediatrics*. Edinburgh: Churchill Livingstone.

Mrazek, Patricia Beezley and Bentovim, Arnon (1981) 'Incest and the Dysfunctional Family System', in Mrazek and Kempe (1981).

Mrazek, Patricia Beezley and Kempe, C. Henry (1981) *Sexually Abused Children and their Families*. Oxford: Pergamon Press.

Nash, C.L. and West, D.J. (1985) 'Sexual Molestation of Young Girls: A Retrospective Survey', in West (1985).

Nelson, Sarah (1987) *Incest: Fact and Myth*. Edinburgh: Stramullion. First published 1982.

NSPCC South West Region Working Party (1984) *Developing a Child Centred Response to Sexual Abuse*. London: NSPCC.

O'Carroll, Tom (1980) *Paedophilia: The Radical Case*. London: Peter Owen.

Owen, Marika (1987) 'Laying Ghosts to Rest', *Community Care*, 643.

Parton, Nigel (1985) *The Politics of Child Abuse*. London: Macmillan.

Pilais, Jennie and Anderton, Joy (1986) 'Feminism and Family Therapy – A Possible Meeting Point', *Journal of Family Therapy*, 8(2).

Plummer, Ken (1981) 'Paedophilia: Constructing a Sociological Baseline', in Cook and Howells (1981).

Porter, Ruth (ed.) (1984) *Child Sexual Abuse Within the Family*. London: Tavistock/ CIBA Foundation.

Rush, Florence (1980) *The Best Kept Secret*. New York: McGraw-Hill.

Russell, Diana E.H. (1984) *Sexual Exploitation*. London: Sage.

Russell, Diana E.H. (1986) *The Secret Trauma*. New York: Basic.

Seabrook, Jeremy (1987) 'The Corruption of Childhood', *New Statesman*, 114(2937).

Sophocles (1947) *The Theban Plays*. Harmondsworth: Penguin.

Wattenberg, Esther (1985) 'In a Different Light: A Feminist Perspective on the Role of Mothers in Father–Daughter Incest', *Child Welfare*, 64(3).

Weeks, Jeffrey (1985) *Sexuality and its Discontents*. London: Routledge & Kegan Paul.

Weir, Kirk (1987) 'Report of AFT Research Meeting: June 1987', *Association of Family Therapists Newsletter*, 7(3).

West, D.J. (1981) 'Adult Sexual Interest in Children: Implications for Social Control', in Cook and Howells (1981).

West, D.J. (ed.) (1985) *Sexual Victimization*. Aldershot: Gower.

Winnicott, Donald (1961) *Home is Where We Start From*. Harmondsworth: Penguin.

II
PUBLIC POLICY AND THE FAMILY

The family provides the major reference point for distinguishing between the 'public' and 'private' worlds of our society. Outside are the worlds of work and politics, inside is the space for personal relationships. The distinction is an apparently clear one: the outside world stops at the front door. But this seemingly simple distinction conceals a more complicated set of interrelationships between politics, work and the family. In particular, the family is intimately linked to the field of public policy and the provision of social welfare. The history of welfare policy is unintelligible without reference to the family as a central organizing principle. Much welfare policy assumes the existence of the family as providing the primary source of care and support for its members, and state intervention is sought when the family fails or is absent. Similarly, welfare policies assume that most people live, most of the time, in social arrangements which resemble the 'normal family': two adults, of whom one is a wage-earning male and the other a female home organizer, accompanied by a number of dependent children. Welfare policies aim to work with and through this 'normal' pattern of arrangements and to find ways of dealing with 'deviant' cases, such as single-parent families.

For the most part, this interconnection of welfare policy and the family has appeared to be so natural and obvious that it has not required comment. Its invisibility has been challenged by two, very different, processes over the last twenty years. The development of feminist politics and scholarship since the late 1960s has opened up the family, and its intersection with the world of public policy, to critical scrutiny. Attention has been directed to the easy assumptions about the natural fit between the family and welfare. On the one hand, the idea that it is the family that provides care has been displaced by a more careful analysis of who it is within families that does the caring. Not surprisingly, such studies have revealed that the disproportionate burden of care falls on women. On the other hand, such studies have also shown the extent to which state policies both rest on this assumption of a gendered division of labour and reinforce it through their consequences. Feminism, then, has highlighted the social construction of gender divisions and roles which have been passed off as the 'natural' assumptions on which social policy rests.

The second challenge to the taken-for-granted links between the family and state welfare came from the Conservative governments of the 1980s, which identified a major aim of policies intended to 'roll back the state' as being to make the family more independent. They argued that the expansion of the state in the post-war period had been at the expense of the family: taking over its caring functions, undermining its authority and weakening its strength. Freeing the family from the state was a precondition to restoring its proper position as the premier social institution. In doing so, they juxtaposed the 'natural' institution of the family with the corrupting and demoralizing 'unnatural' interference of the state. Parental choice, parental rights and parental responsibilities became the key themes of Conservative welfare policies – the basis for encouraging families to take back what they had lost to the state and become revitalized in the process. Although Conservative 'privatization' was most explicitly associated with selling off public assets to the private investors, privatization also had a second sense of returning care from state institutions to the private world of the family. In turn, transferring the burden of care to the family meant reproducing the gender structure of the traditional family, so that women – the 'natural' carers – faced increased demands of caring.

The chapters in this section explore some of these issues about the intersection of public policy and the family. The first, by Felicity Edholm, examines the anthropological evidence which challenges the assumptions about the 'naturalness' of the family, and about the nuclear family form in particular. She draws attention to the implications of viewing the nuclear family form as natural, in the way that other forms of household arrangement are positioned as 'unnatural' or 'deviant'. When such assumptions occupy a major place in the organization of welfare policies, other household arrangements are, as a result, made vulnerable to being devalued, pathologized and put under surveillance.

Carol Smart's chapter examines the impact of family assumptions on social policy. Looking at policy developments in the 1980s in the related fields of social security, pensions and taxation, she considers their impact upon gender patterns and different types of household, particularly single-parent families. She argues that Conservative policies towards the family cut across their policies on employment. Where women have been encouraged into employment in increasing numbers during the 1980s, family policies have aimed at the restoration of the traditional family in which women should be at home providing care and nurturance.

Her chapter draws attention to the continuities in this view of social policy and the family, stretching back to before the Second

World War. Social policies have continued to be dominated by the assumption that if men are economically active (breadwinning), then the institution of the family ensures that women and children are safeguarded. This chapter underlines the impossibility of viewing social policy and the family as if they were two entirely separate spheres of social life, and the necessity of understanding the interaction of the two, shaped by the assumptions which the state makes about the family and gender roles within it.

Malcolm Wicks' chapter examines the relationship between family policy and political rhetoric. Where Carol Smart focuses on Conservative policy-making, Wicks examines the range of political claims about the family in Britain in the middle 1980s and their implications for family policy. Although there have been political changes since Wicks wrote this chapter, it provides an overview of the main political arguments around the family in the 1980s. More importantly, it offers an introduction to ways of assessing the connection between political claims and the policy outcomes for families.

Finally, Yvette Rocheron's chapter explores the relationship between assumptions and policy through an analysis of one specific form of intervention – the Asian Mother and Baby Campaign of the middle 1980s. Her discussion of this campaign situates it in terms of how state institutions and policies respond to the welfare needs of ethnic minorities. The recognition of different needs itself marks a move away from the dominant assumptions of 'universalism'. Universalist policies have been founded on the assumption that everyone has the same needs. Perhaps not surprisingly, this assumption embodies the belief that the ways of life and needs of white British middle-class families are the norm, and that groups who differ from that norm are 'deviant' or 'unnatural'. Attempts to move away from this normative universalism towards a recognition of difference open up a new set of problems. We might distinguish two types of response to the place of ethnic minorities in British society. One recognizes the presence of differences, and attributes them to different cultural traditions: language, religion, patterns of family organization and so on. This 'multicultural' view has three effects. First, it recognizes the existence of difference. Secondly, it suggests that racism or racial prejudice can be removed by a better understanding of cultural difference. Thirdly, it assumes that the result of better understanding will be the accommodation of differences by small adjustments of the existing patterns of provision. The alternative view sees culture as only one aspect of the place of ethnic minorities within Britain. Ethnicity involves not only cultural difference but social division. Racism is, therefore, not a matter of understanding but involves structures of power and inequality. Such divisions require more than better understanding before their consequences can be overcome. Rocheron argues that interventions which adopt a multicultural view of ethnicity stop short of confronting the impact of 'race' in British society and in its welfare policies and practices. The result is to reduce divisions to difference, and to fail to challenge the 'pathologizing' of Black and Asian families and cultures as deviant.

In one way, Rocheron brings this section back to its starting point. Social policy is profoundly shaped by dominant ideas about the family, about its naturalness as a social institution and about the unnaturalness of family forms and practices which do not fit the norm. Racial divisions highlight the significance of such assumptions and are a focal point for their consequences in social intervention. Ideas about the family determine who is served by social policy and on what basis. They also shape who is excluded and pathologized as the cause of their own problems. While specific political claims about the family may have changed since the middle 1980s, ideas about the family continue to occupy centre stage in the field of public policy. This central position of normative views of the family means that they also become a focal point for conflicts about the intersection between social policy and wider patterns of gender and racial divisions.

8
'The unnatural family'

Felicity Edholm

A recent anthropological textbook defines the family as 'a cluster of positions to and through which an individual traces crucial kinship links, particularly links with others which give him/her rights and positions, etc.' (Keesing, 1976: 292). It is further emphasized that the family is not a necessary social group in either social or economic terms, and that households and families are not identical, similarly bound units. This definition seems to have little to do with any of the elements that we commonly assume to be central to the kinds of family with which we are familiar. There is no mention of gender, none of co-residential units, of domesticity, of marriage or sexual relations. We are only given the idea of rights and positions, and the mystification of 'crucial kinship links' related to these. What, then, has happened to what we commonly conceive of as the family? Why are we given such a removed definition? What are these kinship links?

Anthropologists, in their attempt to understand the ways in which societies other than their own function, have inevitably constructed unfamiliar social relations in terms of those with which they are familiar; they have developed conceptual tools which have been formulated from within the constraints of their own culture, which inevitably relate to their own world.

It was, and still is, widely argued that some form of the family, and, in some cases, of the nuclear family, was universal, and was found in all societies. Only recently has this accepted wisdom been challenged and it has still not been dislodged. One major reason for its resilience in anthropology, apart from the crucial political, economic and ideological significance of the family in the nineteenth- and twentieth-century western world, is that groups very similar to those which we identify as the family do exist in the majority of societies known to anthropologists. Furthermore, anthropologists have tended to assume that an adequate explanatory definition of any given social or cultural trait can be extended to similar traits in other cultures. But as one anthropologist has commented: 'because the family seems to be the predominant unit we must not be bemused into thinking that it is the "natural" or "basic" one' (Fox, 1967: 38).

We have to look similarly at the crucial exceptions, to re-examine the seemingly familiar, family-like groups, to question the given assumptions about human relations and social forms that we almost inevitably have. In the light of the new self-consciousness about the dangers of generalization, when all-embracing definitions are given they now tend, as the already quoted definition of the family demonstrates, to become minimalized and abstracted to the point of identifying no immediately recognizable social form. Definitions are now guidelines and tools rather than explanations.

But what are the kinship links referred to as so crucial in the same definition? When anthropologists talk about the family, it is primarily in terms of kinship. At its simplest, kinship refers to the ties which exist between individuals who are seen as related, through birth (descent) and through mating (marriage). It is thus primarily concerned with the ways in which mating is socially organized and regulated, the ways in which parentage is assigned, attributed and recognized, descent is traced, relatives are classified, rights are transferred across generations and groups are formed. Such relationships are seen as constructed within the basic constraints and imperatives of the organization of human life; production and reproduction, mating, dependence, the need for enculturation and the life cycle. Kinship is above all concerned with relationships which are socially constructed; relatives are not born but made.

When we look at the societies studied by anthropologists and at the variation in kinship systems, it is clear that the range of social options is enormous, that the constraints on human behaviour do not produce uniformity, and that those assumptions we make about what is 'natural' in respect of fundamental human kinship relations are profoundly challenged by the evidence from widely different societies. If we take some of these assumptions, we can then look at some anthropological data on kinship and become aware of the extent to which we are profoundly ethnocentric in our outlook.

It is usually assumed that the family, a co-residential unit containing parents and their own children, is the natural primary unit within which domestic and sexual relations and socialization will take place; that relationships between members of a family are unique and specific, and are recognizably different to relationships with individuals outside the family; that there is, at least for the early years of life, an inevitably deep and necessary dependence between a mother and her children, and that there is some sense of obligation and interdependence between those who are members of the family, particularly between parents and children, that incest taboos operate within the family unit, and that property, status and positions pass within the family. It is also usually assumed that there is considerable interdependence, both social and sexual, between men and women and that this is revealed within the family/the household.

The most critical areas of kinship to examine in order to have some understanding of the family are those which offer the greatest challenge to preconceptions and which have significant effect on the construction of kinship relations in so far as they affect the assumptions we have outlined above. Five areas will be explored: conception, incest, parent/child relations and adoption, marriage, households and residence.

Conception

The question of who our kin, our relations are is answered in numerous ways, even for the primary parent–child relation. Notions of blood ties, of biological connection, which to us seem relatively unequivocal, are highly variable. Some societies of which we have anthropological record recognize only the role of the father or of the mother in conception and procreation. The other sex is given some significance, but is not seen, for example, as providing blood – as any biological connection. Only one parent is a 'relation', the other parent is not. In the Trobriand Islands, for example, it is believed that intercourse is not the cause of conception, semen is not seen as essential for conception (Malinowski, 1922). Conception results from the entry of a spirit child into the womb; the male role is to 'open the passage' to the womb, through intercourse, and it is the repeated intercourse of the same partner which 'moulds' the child. A child's blood comes from its mother's side and from her siblings, her mother and mother's brother, not from the father. A child will not be related by blood to its father, but will look like its father since he has through intercourse created its form. Fathers continue after birth to have a very close and intimate relationship with their children and it is this contact which is also seen as creating the likeness, as moulding the child in his/her father's image.

Other societies recognize the crucial importance of semen in the formation of a child, but believe that it is essential for conception that either the semen of more than one man is involved or that fertility is only possible given a mixture of different semen; thus a newly married woman in Marind Anim society (in New Guinea) is gang-raped at marriage, and on subsequent ritual occasions (Van Baal, 1966). Semen is understood as being necessary for growth throughout childhood and adolescence and elaborate male homosexual activities ensure that adolescent boys are in receipt of semen.

The Lakker of Burma on the other hand consider that the mother is only a container in which the child grows; she has no blood connection with her children, and children of the same mother and different fathers are not considered to be related to each other (Keesing, 1976). These cases are extreme but have important implications in that they indicate not only that relations which seem to us to be self-evidently biological are not universally seen as such. 'Natural', 'biological' relations are not inevitably those which organize human relations at a very fundamental level, since what is understood as 'biological' is socially defined and therefore is expressed in different ways.

Incest

Incest is another area of human relations which is widely discussed in terms of some kind of innate, instinctive abhorrence for sexual relations with 'close kin' and is often attributed to a subconscious realization of the genetic danger of inbreeding. (It is not uniformly accepted that inbreeding is inevitably disadvantageous.)

Incest taboos, defined as prohibitions on sexual relations between individuals socially classified as kin, as relations, are nearly universal. But the prohibition does not inevitably apply to the individuals whom we would identify as primary kin. The most dramatic exceptions to incest are found in certain royal dynasties (Egypt, Hawaii) where inbreeding (brother–sister) was enforced in order to keep the purity of the royal line, as well as in Ptolemaic and Roman Egypt, where apparently father–daughter and brother–sister sexual relations were relatively common. In most other known societies, sexual relations between those socially recognized as 'biologically' related are taboo. The Trobrianders, for example, do not consider the children of one father and different mothers to be related and sexual relations between those children are thus entirely legitimate, whereas sexual relations with women who have the same mother, or whose mothers are siblings, are taboo. The Lakker of Burma do not consider that the children of the same mother have any kinship links. 'Incest' does not apply to these non-kin and sexual relations are permitted. In other societies in which, for example, the category of brother or sister is extended to include all males or females of the same generation who are descended through one parent from a common grandfather, or great-grandfather, it is frequently this whole group which is sexually unavailable. It is the social definitions of significant kinship relations that are important in defining incest rather than any concept of natural biological imperatives militating against sexual intercourse within a 'natural family unit'.

Parent/child relations: adoption

It is nearly universally accepted in all anthropological texts on the family, however prepared they are to accept the fact that the nuclear family is not ubiquitous, that 'the mother–child tie is inevitable and given', that 'the irreducible and elementary social grouping is surely the mother and her children'. This is seen as determined by the imperatives of infantile dependence and the need for breast-milk, and is also related to other psychological needs on the part both of the mother and of the child. In this context it is instructive to consider the implications of the widespread practice of adoption. In many societies children do not live with their 'real' parents, but often stay with their mothers until some time after they have been weaned, when as they say in North Ghana, they have 'gained sense' (at about six). However, throughout Melanesia and Polynesia, children are adopted just after weaning or, in some instances, well before – a phenomenon which is considered absolutely acceptable. In some instances, babies are adopted and breast-fed by their adopted mother. Margaret Mead describes such a situation among the Mundugumor in New Guinea:

> even women who have never borne children are able in a few weeks, by placing the child constantly at the breast and by drinking plenty of coconut milk, to produce enough, or nearly enough milk to rear the child, which is suckled by other women for the first few weeks after adoption. (Mead, 1935: 193]

In Tahiti, young women often have one or two children before they are considered, or consider themselves to be, ready for an approved and stable relationship. It is considered perfectly acceptable for the children of a young woman to be given to her parents or other close kin for adoption, while she is freed to continue what is seen as the 'business of adolescence'. The girl can decide what her relationship to the children will be, but there is no sense in which she is forced into 'motherhood' because of having had a baby; 'motherhood' in such a situation can be seen as a status reached by women at a particular stage of development, as involving a psychological and social readiness, not something inevitably attached to the physical bearing of children.

In nearly all the societies in which adoption of this kind is common (and where anthropologists have discussed it at length), it is clear that the adopted child will still maintain contact with its 'natural' parents, and will know what their relationship to each other is. A Tahitian man (himself adopted) was asked about children's relations to their parents:

> if you are not adopted you are grateful to your biological mother, because she gave birth to you. On the other hand, when you are taken in

your infancy by somebody it isn't worthwhile to think anymore about your mother. The woman who took you is just the same as your biological mother. Your gratitude is because you were an infant and you were taken in. [Levy, 1970: 81]

One of the interesting aspects of this definition of the relationship between parents and children is the sense in which it is seen as so critically dependent on gratitude – from child to parent – since it is recognized that adults choose to bring up the child, and do not have a necessary sense of responsibility, or instinctive love for it. The implications of such attitudes for all social relations are clearly considerable.

Again, in most of these societies it is agreed that the adopted child is more the foster father's than the true father's. Margaret Mead (1935), writing on the Manus of New Guinea, describes the very considerable personality similarities she saw between fathers and their adopted children. The relationship between fathers and children is extremely close, fathers feed and spend a lot of time with their children. The 'likeness', of which the Trobriand Islanders speak, between father and children, is also, in many other Melanesian and Polynesian societies, seen as due to the close personal contact between them. The father–child relationship is seen as a crucial, and above all as a social, relationship; one which is created by social contact, not one which exists because of a 'blood relationship'. In Tahiti it is considered an ultimate shame for adopted children to leave the house of their adopted parents since the relationship between those who have lived together and who have grown 'familiar' (matau) with each other (the essential ingredient for all good relations) is seen as inevitably far closer than that between biological 'natural' parents.

It is instructive in this context to consider the United Nations' study, *Adoption of Children in Western Nations*, in which it is argued that in the West, society attributes 'a sacred character . . . to family bonds' (Levy, 1970). The extent to which this attribution is ideological is even more evident once we have understood the extraordinary narrowness of our definitions of familiar 'natural' relations.

Marriage
It has been claimed that some form of marriage is found in all human societies. The definitions of marriage, however, again give some indication of the kind of complexity that is involved in the attempt to provide universals. One famous definition by Goodenough defines marriage in these terms:

> Marriage is a transaction and resulting contract in which a person (male or female, corporate or individual, in person or by proxy) establishes a continuing claim to the right of sexual access to a woman – this right having priority over rights of sexual access others currently have, or may subsequently acquire, in relation to her (except in a similar transaction) until the contract resulting from the transaction is terminated, and in which the woman involved is eligible to bear children. [1970: 12–13]

Other definitions stress above all the significance of marriage in determining parentage – in allocating children to different groups. The definitions have to be understood in relation to the kinds of social arrangement which are entirely inconsistent with our notions of marriage.

The Nayar of Northern India provide one of the most problematic cases of 'marriage' (Schneider and Gough, 1972). The basic social group among the Nayar is the Taravad, a unit composed of men and women descended through the female line from a common ancestress. Thus it is brothers and sisters, mothers and children who cohabit. A child becomes a member of the mother's Taravad, not the father's. A Nayar girl was involved, before she reached puberty, in a formal ritual with a man from an equivalent caste to her own, and then was able to take as many lovers as she wished; the 'husband' – the man who had been involved in the ritual – only had a very minimal ritual attachment to his 'wife', although he too could be one of her lovers. (Not all lovers came from the same caste.) Husbands and fathers, in such a context, are entirely peripheral to the domestic life of their wives and children – and never cohabit.

Among the Nuer of the Nile Basin, one of the most common forms of marriage is what has been called 'ghost' marriage. (The anthropologist Evans-Pritchard who worked among the Nuer estimates that nearly 50 percent of all marriages correspond to this form.) Ghost marriage refers to the situation in which a man dies, unmarried, or with no children of his own. If this happens, a close kinsman (related to him through his father's line) will marry a wife 'to his name' and children born of this union will be seen as the dead man's children. A man who has been involved in marrying in this way and bearing children for another man will, when he dies and if he has not contracted a second marriage in his own name – only possible if his wife dies – have to become in his turn a proxy father and a subsequent ghost marriage will be contracted. If a married man dies, his widow then should ideally be married by a brother or close male kin of the dead man and again, children born of this union will be considered to be those of the dead man, not of the living husband.

The Nuer also have another contractual form of 'marriage' in which an old and important, usually barren, woman may marry a younger woman. Nuer marriages are contracted through the 'husband' giving the bride price (cattle) to the wife's group. The children born to this younger woman will then, for particular purposes, such as inheritance, be considered as the children of the old woman, their 'father'. Marriages of this kind indicate the importance among the Nuer both of becoming a parent, or rather a male parent, in order to become an ancestor – for only 'fathers' with offspring are remembered and have status as ancestors – and also of the inheritance of property. Nuer marriages also demonstrate that the marriage indicates a contract between the group of related 'men' who are seen in some sense as equivalents and a woman married to one of them.

These two widely differing examples illustrate one of the other critical elements in the relations defined by marriage: the difference between the 'legally' recognized father or mother and the person who was involved in conception, or birth. In both the cases cited above, the person we would see as the father, he who had impregnated the woman, is not given any social recognition at all, it is the person, not necessarily male, who is given the social position of father who is recognized through the ritual of 'marriage'. The two males are distinguished in anthropological literature thus: the biological father is the *genitor*, the biological mother the *genetrix*, the 'socially' recognized father the *pater*, socially recognized mother the *mater*. In cases of polyandry – where a woman is 'married' to more than one man, as is the case among the Toda, one of the men will perform a ritual which makes him the pater, and the child, and subsequent children, will belong to his group. In some of the societies (very few) in which polyandry exists, it is a group of brothers who share a wife. In some cases a group of sisters will be 'married' to a group of brothers, and in such situations the children belong to the family group. Individual paternity is thus socially less important than membership of a family unit.

Paternity is of crucial importance in societies in which status, position and property are transmitted through the male line. The notion of the group, related through the male line, can in some societies have such force that sexual relations between a woman and any male from the same group as that into which she was born (and such a group can include a considerable number of individuals, all the descendants of a common great-grandfather, for example) are regarded as incestuous. We can see with the example of the Nayar (although the Nayar do constitute an exceptional case) that paternity has far less social significance if all important social attributes are gained through inheritance down the female line. (It is important to recognize that such a system of inheritance does not imply that men are marginalized in such an inheritance system, but that it is brothers rather than husbands who are the significant social males.)

Even in situations in which the attribution of paternity is so important we cannot simply assume that the concepts of legitimacy and illegitimacy are clearcut. In many societies of this kind there are all kinds of arrangements for the allocation of children – which are not wholly dependent on the concepts of the determining factor of parenthood.

Household and residence

Our conception of what constitutes the family is dependent not only on what we have called kinship ties but equally residence, domestic units or households. Given the range of kinship relations that we have briefly explored, it is inevitable that a wide range of different residential patterns exist. Moreover, households will not only be composed of individuals whose relations to each other are based on different criteria, but the size and composition over time of such households will vary, as will their relation to production, to other units and to social position.

There are three basic forms of residence as isolated by anthropologists: vivilocal, where a married couple and their children live with the kin of the husband; matrilocal, where the couple live with the kin of the wife; and neolocal where the couple live independently of either group of kin. This scheme is however further complicated by the fact that in many societies in which descent is traced through the female line (matrilineal societies), the children might initially live with the mother and father with the father's kin, and then later move to live with their mother's kin; in other words, with their mother's brothers, those from whom they will inherit property, status or position. Often in such societies (such as the Trobriand Islanders) daughters never live with their mother's kin – they stay with their father's until they marry and then move to their husband's kin. The complication of residence patterns is considerable – one of the factors which these different patterns demonstrate is that households as units of parents and their children are not a necessary or permanent social arrangement. The extent to which individuals are identified with any one household, both as children and as adults, varies considerably. In most matrilineal societies men will circulate and often a man will split his available time and space between kin and conjugal roles. In some societies of this kind, men will live alternately in two places, or will frequently visit two different units, or move at different stages from one to another. In the case of the polyandrous Toda, a woman married to different men will circulate between their different households (Rivers, 1906). Children similarly will shift residence in many societies – in many instances, because of the 'institution' of fostering whereby, from the age of about 5, children are sent to be brought up by non-parental kin. Claims to have a foster child are formally expressed as the rights held by a man in his sister's children – and by a woman in her brother's daughter – but it is much more extensive than this, and there are many instances of children living with their grandparents (Goody 1969: 192). Households then can often be extremely fluid units, with shifting membership.

In most of the known societies of the world, monogamy is the exception rather than the rule. Some anthropologists claim that over 90 percent of the world's cultures involve plural polygamous marriages. We have already referred to polyandry, one woman with several husbands, but by far the most common form of polygamy is polygyny – one man with several wives.

In some polygynous societies, almost invariably those in which descent is traced through the male line, households consist of a series of relatively self-contained living quarters, in which a man and his wives, each with her own children, live, one wife in a relatively autonomous domestic unit. In others, domestic arrangements are dominated by a group of brothers, with their wives and their offspring.

The domestic existence of each smaller unit within such a group is determined by the existence of the larger group and is ultimately dependent on the authority of those males who are in control of the unit as a whole.

In such situations it is again difficult to arrive at a useful definition of such a unit if we are concerned to consider households purely as kinship entities. Is such a mother and children unit an entity, or is it a sub-household within a much larger household?

The Tiv of Nigeria provide an example of this latter form of 'household'. Tiv kinship groups live in compounds, a circular arrangement of huts and granaries, in the centre of which is an open space – 'the centre of Tiv family life'. The compound head is the senior, eldest man. He settles disputes, supervises the productive activities of the group and controls magic. His several wives live in separate units in the compound, which is also inhabited by his junior children, unmarried daughters and married sons and their families.

In addition, there may be a younger brother and his family, and/or outsiders.

As is argued by the anthropologists involved, while in a sense each wife who has a separate hut and her children constitute a separate domestic unit, the larger compound group – a patrilineal extended family augmented by outsiders – is the central domestic unit of everyday Tiv life and of collective economic enterprise (Bohannon and Bohannon, 1968).

It is only when we consider the household in terms of this latter – its productive capacities – that we can make sense of this kind of domestic unit usually found in agricultural communities. Households and domestic units are not only an arrangement of people related to each other through parent–child ties, but in societies such as the Tiv, they form units of production and have to be analysed and understood as such.

Kinship ties have thus been seen by some anthropologists as constituting the relation of production. The Tiv compound, for example, is essentially a means of reuniting and controlling necessary labour, both productive and reproductive. Clearly households in many societies have to be analysed as units of production and consumption, and as providers of labour. The form of the household must therefore be analysed in terms of the economic structure of the society as a whole and cannot simply be seen as a unit containing the 'family', essentially defining sets of affective relations. Precisely because the western ideal of the nuclear family is so ideologically and spatially separated from wage labour, the recognition of the profound economic significance of household formation in other societies has posed considerable problems for anthropologists. It has been even more difficult for western sociologists to re-examine the economic role of the family within their own society in the light of the understanding gained through anthropological analysis.

Polygynous households of the kind described above are common in Africa, south of the Sahara, and however different their form, they are usually crucial productive units. In New Guinea, very different domestic arrangements exist and these cannot be analysed in terms of the same economic determinants. In Marind Anim and many other New Guinea societies, domestic organization constructs very considerable separation between men and women. Special men's houses provide the focal point for all male life (often including sleeping and eating) and there are often stringent taboos on women having access to such houses and, in general, on contact between males and females.

Conclusion

The family, particularly the nuclear family, can be seen, through comparative analysis, as just one very specific means of organizing the relations between parents and children, males and females. It is not, as has so often been claimed, some kind of 'natural' instinctive and 'sacred' unit. Even the bond between mothers and their own children, which is seen in almost mystic terms as the fundamental biologically determined relationship, can be seen as far less important than we are generally led to believe. Universal definitions of human relations must be constantly questioned and the whole notion of the 'natural' must, in terms of human relations, be challenged, and the 'unnatural' – in these terms the social construction of relationships – must be fully recognized.

References

Bohannon, P. and Bohannon, L. (1968) *Tiv Economy*. Evanston: North Western University Press.

Carroll, V. (1970) *Adoption in Eastern Oceania*. Honolulu: University of Hawaii Press.

Evans-Pritchard, E.E. (1951) *Kinship and Marriage among the Nuer*. Oxford: Clarendon Press.

Fox, R. (1967) *Kinship and Marriage*. Harmondsworth: Penguin.

Goodenough, W.H. (1970) *Description and Comparison in Cultural Anthropology*. Chicago: Aldine.

Goody, J.R. (1969) *Comparative Studies in Kinship*. London: Routledge & Kegan Paul.

Keesing, R.M. (1976) *Cultural Anthropology, a Contemporary Perspective*. New York: Hunt, Rinehart & Winston.

Levy, R.I. (1970) 'Tahitian Adoption as a Psychological Message', in Caroll (1970).

Malinowski, B. (1922) *Argonauts of the Western Society*. London: Routledge & Kegan Paul.

Mead, M. (1935) *Sex and Temperament in Three Primitive Societies*. New York: William Morrow.

Rivers, W.H.R. (1906) *The Todas*. New York: Macmillan.

Schneider, D. and Gough, E.K. (1972) *Matrilineal Kinship*. Berkeley: University of California Press.

Van Baal, J. (1966) *The Dema, Description and Analysis of Culture (South New Guinea)*. The Hague: Martinus Nijhoff.

9
Securing the family? Rhetoric and policy in the field of social security

Carol Smart

In the mid-1980s the family became the focus of much political and policy attention. Of course, in many ways there is nothing new in this. It is hard to find a time since the early development of a centralized state, with its ability to deploy policies to affect whole populations, that the family has not in some way exercised the minds of law- and policy-makers. It is possible to argue that 'family policy' (albeit in a very different form to that adopted today) is coterminous with the growth of centralized political power. Moreover, not only does 'family policy' predate the nineteenth and twentieth centuries, it is possible to identify common themes within this 'policy' which have emerged in different historical periods. One example is the way in which the Elizabethan Poor Law placed punitive sanctions in the way of unmarried mothers and their children, subjecting them to varying degrees of economic hardship. These measures were designed as a way of giving priority to 'legitimate' family life based on monogamous marriage. In this respect they have been in common with the proposals for divorce reform in the 1960s. Although these measures might seem worlds apart – one attempting to force women into marriage, the other attempting to provide greater access to divorce – in fact they were both put forward on the basis that they would give priority to married family life. In the case of the 1960s' legislation it enabled unmarried, illicit unions to be regularized by freeing partners from the 'empty shell' marriages that they had left in person, but not in law. In this way divorce was constructed not as an end to marriage, but as the beginning of a new, better marriage. In all events primacy was given to the married state.

This is not an attempt to argue that nothing has changed in relation to family policies, but to establish that the family has been central to policy development, and that the family has been on the political agenda for a very long time. Hence the family has never been *outside* politics, a haven where the state dares not intrude. On the contrary it is social and legal policies, whether on marriage, taxation, property ownership, child custody or inheritance, which have created the conditions for the reproduction of particular family structures.

This, of course, raises the question of why, if the family has been a political issue for a very long time, there is any particular significance to its re-emergence on political agendas in the 1980s. I hope to show that even where rhetoric is relatively unchanging, there is always a different political significance to such discourses which derives from the economic, political and social climate in which they gain ascendancy. In consequence there will be two main themes to this paper. The first will look at a specific variant of political concern for the family, that engendered by the New Right (see David, 1983; Levitas, 1986). The second will examine the links between the rhetoric and recent attempts to embody these values in concrete policy provisions. It will become apparent that, even for a government in power, it is no simple matter to turn 'ideals' into policies. I shall take as my example the Review of Social Security set up by the Secretary of State for Social Services in 1984 and subsequent legislation.

This review (DHSS, 1985a and b) is a particularly interesting example of the development of policies central to New Right ideals of family life. Indeed the Conservative government came to power in 1979 and again in 1983 with the promise to 'roll back' the influence of the state and to alter welfare policies which undermined the stability and self-sufficiency of the family. The advent of the public review system (whereby all manner of interested bodies from the Confederation of British Industries to the Child Poverty Action Group were called to give oral and written evidence to the Government on how social security legislation should be changed) gave considerable opportunity for the rehearsal of New Right rhetoric on the family. It provided a scenario in which radically different policies closely aligned with views about traditional family values could be espoused.

It is important at this point to understand the context of these discussions on welfare. In the increasingly vocal political rhetoric of the New Right, the family is seen to be failing both its members and the wider society. Two points of view are espoused. First the 'normal', nuclear family has become submerged under a welter of concern over 'abnormal' families (such as one-parent families, divorced families, immigrant families) and hence cannot assert its real value and importance for society (Anderson and Dawson, 1986). The second is that there is too much family disintegration, resulting in delinquency and social disorder (Morgan, 1986; Johnson, 1987). One universal theme is that the family, or its members, have become far too dependent upon the state. Hence even 'normal' families are at risk of being undermined in their efforts to retain traditional values, whilst 'less desirable' families are able to waste scarce resources and become trapped into a spiral of unemployment and declining moral values. The concern over too much dependence upon the state has been made to apply to issues as diverse as the provision of welfare benefits and the provision of sex education in schools.

As a consequence of the ascendency of such views – many deriving from inside the government itself – the Conservative administration of the early 1980s began the process of turning these sentiments into policy. Under pressure from its own right wing (for instance the Bow Group, 1986),

New Right ideologues (Johnson, 1987) and the pro-family lobby generally, there was a growing urgency to turn the rhetoric into action. Before turning to the specific case of the Social Security Reviews, however, it is important to consider the development of social security policy affecting the family since the inception of the modern welfare state.

The family in social security policy

The family is generally treated as a homogeneous unit in social policy. With regard to social security this has meant that there is an underlying premiss that the standard of living of all members of a family can be judged by the income of the wage earner or earners. The Beveridge Report (1942), which provided the basis of our system of social security in the post-war years, elevated this principle to a dominant policy objective. Hence Beveridge ensured that benefits would be designed around the unit of the family, with married women having very different claims to benefit from men or single women. Married women were required to be insured through their husbands, and all their benefits depended upon his work record. All benefits were also to be paid to the husband on behalf of his wife and children. (The exception to this was the Family Allowance introduced in 1946 but this was paid to mothers largely through the political lobbying of Eleanor Rathbone and other feminists.)

The Beveridge Report, and hence subsequent policy on Social Insurance and National Assistance, as it was then called, did not take into consideration the 'discovery' of Rowntree (1902) in York at the beginning of the century, namely that a clear distinction could be made between primary and secondary poverty. Primary poverty was caused by inadequate income to cover the basic needs of a family. Secondary poverty was caused when there was an adequate income but this was not distributed in such a way as to meet the basic needs of all members of a family. Hence the discovery that women and children in a household might be malnourished whilst the 'breadwinner' was not. This 'discovery' has never featured very highly in social security policy in spite of the fact that secondary poverty and the uneven distribution of resources within households has been 'rediscovered' at regular intervals.

In the 1950s Michael Young (1952) drew together a wide range of material to show that maldistribution of scarce resources created a situation in which family members could be co-residing at different standards of living. In the 1980s Pahl (1980, 1983) has produced further evidence to this effect, while Graham (1984) has shown that women and children can find themselves better off on Supplementary Benefit (i.e. the official poverty line) than when living in households with husbands earning an average wage.

Social security policy has continued to disregard the distinction between primary and secondary poverty. It is argued that secondary poverty is too hard to assess for policy purposes, but more recently the reason put forward has rekindled ideas of the sanctity of the private sphere and the value of personal – as opposed to collective or state – responsibility. For instance, as I shall outline below, the government Green and White Papers on social security (DHSS, 1985a, 1985b respectively) stated clearly that men, as breadwinners, must be trusted to distribute their wages responsibly and that it is not the business of the state to interfere in private arrangements of this kind. So whilst the family has been the major focus of social security policy in the post-war years, this policy has refused to address itself systematically to inequalities within families. Such strategies are supportive of the idea of the sanctity of the private sphere and it is significant that, with the exception of Family Allowances (later to become Child Benefit), post-war governments have retained policies that ensure the financial dependence of women in families.

The link between rhetoric and policy

It is not easy to assess the link between rhetoric and policy in the form of legislation and in practice. Certainly it is not the case that policy merely implements the rhetoric. The Beveridge Report, if it were taken as a routine example of the transposition of a specific familial ideology into very practical policy measures, could be very misleading. This is because the Beveridge Report was essentially the work of a very influential individual with compelling, if unrealistic, ideas about how families operated (Macnicol, 1980). Moreover his rhetorical statements and most of his practical policy recommendations on the family were taken over directly into legislation. There were dissenting voices about both Beveridge's views on family life and the final policy proposals (see Clarke, Cochrane and Smart, 1987) but these did not manage to change the course of policy development in 1945 when the National Insurance Act brought the proposals into operation.

   This was an unusual situation and one that does not usually apply. Even where a government has a large majority in the House of Commons and can, in theory, introduce what legislation it wishes, it is rare for there to be so few compromises in the formulation of legislation. One major difference between the Beveridge era and the present is that policy documents, like the Green Paper on social security, are not the work of individuals but of committees and civil servants. This inevitably introduces compromises and modifications. In any case, the government does not speak with a unitary voice on all matters concerning the family. It may be that certain positions assume ascendancy at certain moments, but there are always contradictory voices. For example, the Conservative government of 1972 planned to abolish the Family Allowance based on the influential idea that it was wasteful of resources and that it was administratively more convenient to turn it into a tax credit (payable mainly to husbands). However, this policy was defeated by a coalition of political and voluntary organizations which included the Conservative National Women's Committee and various other Conservative women's organizations.

In addition, the field of social security is now far more complex than it was at the time of Beveridge. This means that it is much harder to be certain of the long-term effects of certain policy measures. For example, Family Income Supplement (FIS) was introduced to help those in low-paid jobs and to encourage those on benefits to take up work (even if it were poorly paid). However, in practice FIS contributed to the massive complexity of the benefit system and added a new problem, namely the employment trap. This meant that people were discouraged from working more hours or earning a few extra pounds because their benefits would be drastically reduced by the withdrawal of FIS, leaving them worse off than before. Quite simply this means that even where the government has clear views on what it intends (i.e. to encourage two-parent families, to create an incentive for men to work), it may fail to achieve these ends in practice.

Finally, it is increasingly apparent that even where there are clear objectives these may be in contradiction to one another. The best example of this in the area of the family is the conflict between the wish of the Conservative government to encourage two-parent families (and therefore to discourage one-parent families) and the wish to prevent child poverty (in other areas of government policy this is referred to as protecting the best interests of the child). Children in one-parent families are extremely vulnerable to poverty, yet when the state provides for these children it necessarily gives financial support to lone mothers as well. This was seen by some members of government, as well as by the New Right generally, as lending support to marriage breakdown and as counterproductive to the aim of encouraging two-parent families.

It is, of course, arguable that different family structures are neither encouraged nor discouraged quite so easily, and that a few extra pence on one-parent benefit can hardly be said to be a deciding factor in the increase in the divorce rate or illegitimacy rate. Yet when all the effects of different policies were taken together, there was a clear concern in government circles that social security policy might 'distort' the proper (natural) structure of the family.

Recent developments in social security:
the Fowler Reviews and the 1986 Social Security Act

Shortly after the Conservative Party was returned to office to serve a second term in 1983 the Secretary of State for Health and Social Service, Norman Fowler, announced his intention to begin a major review of the social security system. The welfare state, and particularly the social security system, had come increasingly under attack from the Left, the Right and from feminists and other pressure groups. Discontentments with the system, although widespread, arose from very different sentiments and experiences. The government too had its own concerns, in particular the cost to the Exchequer of the system of benefits paid to the unemployed, disabled, lone parents and so on. The second paragraph of the Green Paper, Volume 1, made it clear that expenditure was identified as the main problem. It stated: 'The cost of social security will this year be over £40 billion. Since the Second World War, it has grown five times faster than prices, twice as fast as the economy as a whole; and it is set to rise steeply for the next forty years' (DHSS, 1985a: 1, para. 1.2).

As well as the concern for the costs of the system, the government expressed concern at the complexity of the system, the fact that '(to) be blunt the British social security system has lost its way', and the blurring of responsibilities as between the individual and the state. The Green Paper sought to replace the rhetoric of Beveridge's call for the abolition of poverty and the idea of benefits as a right, with the idea of a new partnership between the individual and the state – 'a system built on twin pillars'. The Green Paper, however, went on to state that

> The proposals in this Green Paper will bring the social security system firmly back under control. Social security will be based on twin pillars of provision – individual and state – with stronger emphasis on individual provision than hitherto. The proposals will make it more worthwhile for individuals to work and to save. [DHSS, 1985a: 45, para. 13.1]

The overall aims of the Review were therefore to reduce costs, to identify the individual as having greater responsibility for his or her own impoverishment, and also to produce a system whose aim was not 'benefits as a right' nor the 'abolition of poverty', but the provision of assistance on a means-tested basis to individuals and families once they had *become impoverished* (and not before).

While the focus of the rhetoric of the Green Paper was the individual and the state, many of the policies were in fact directed towards families and the idea of reconstructing the 'responsible family' whose breadwinner would be motivated to work and whose stability would not be jeopardized by the malign influence of social security benefits.

Unfortunately, in focusing solely on social security, the Green Paper overlooked the influence of other areas of state policy, namely tax policy, legal policy (especially on divorce, custody and maintenance), and employment and economic policies. It overemphasized the impact of social security and gave weight to the oversimplified view that cash benefits 'distort' the family, whilst tax allowances, matrimonial legislation or employment protection rights and other areas of employment policy have no real bearing on the family. Before turning to look at the policies introduced by the White Paper on social security and the subsequent legislation, it is important to consider how other areas of family policy might bear upon the family. It is, however, necessary to be very selective in this review and I shall discuss only the issues of income tax and marriage, divorce and pensions policy and employment policy. These are all areas identified by the New Right as being in need of policy changes.

Taxation
The actual effects of existing taxation policies on the family are far from clear but there has been a general wish on the part of successive post-war governments to construct policies that give priority to marriage and which treat the husband and wife as one person as far as the Inland Revenue is concerned. The New Right has developed a critique of the tax system, however, based on two main arguments. The first argument is that the tax system rewards couples for cohabiting rather than marrying and the second is that it also encourages breakdown. Hermione Parker (1986), for example, has made this point, compiling statistics to show that two single people living together can benefit from two single person's income tax allowances (amounting to more than one married man's tax allowance), and from a mortgage interest tax relief on £60,000 (twice the allowance for the married couple). On the basis of this somewhat untypical model, she argues that government have really been following an anti-marriage policy. There are, however, problems with her argument because her comparisons operate only when both the individuals in the statistical model are in (well-paid) employment. As soon as one of the cohabiting parties gives up work to look after a child the situation is reversed and the married couple receive more benefit from tax allowances. For example, if the woman in the cohabiting couple gives up work she loses her mortgage interest tax relief (£30,000) and she also loses her single person's allowance, but her partner's tax relief does not increase as he is not entitled to receive the married man's tax allowance.

So although actuarial figures based on hypothetical household arrangements can establish that in some situations there is a premium on cohabitation, it is equally possible to find examples where it does the opposite. It is also questionable as to whether people contemplate their tax position prior to marriage (or divorce), and then decide not to marry on the basis of this. Yet this seems to be the basis of the New Right's concern. Clearly there are other social and legal benefits associated with marriage which may prove to be more significant than some potential tax gain (such as the fact that children born outside marriage may still be subject to some form of stigma). The concern shown by the New Right over the damaging effects of tax policies on the family is therefore misplaced, but it does reflect a desire to treat those who do not marry in a punitive way in tax terms in order to ensure they conform to the ideal of married, family life. Paul Johnson (1987) has after all argued that 'The legally-defined (i.e.

married) monogamous family unit has always been a civilizing element in society.' Presumably the cohabiting couple must be an uncivilizing element.

It is, of course, possible to analyse the tax system in quite a different way. An argument which is put forward by the poverty lobby and feminist critics of the tax system is that it is actually structured to favour marriage as against parenthood. In this perception of the system, it is argued that priority should go to people with children, whether married or not. The married man's tax allowance, for example, is paid to all married men whether or not their wives are in paid employment and whether or not they have children. This is, in effect, a premium on marriage and a waste of resources (amounting to £3 billion per annum in 1985) which could be better directed towards children or families with children.

Divorce and the problem of pensions

It is a major element of the critique of social policy by the New Right that state benefits 'destabilize' the family. It is held that benefits undermine responsibility so that men will not support their families by working. But it is also argued that the availability of benefits means that women can easily choose to divorce or separate from their husbands because they have a financial cushion. It has been suggested that policies and legislation which have this effect should be reversed (Johnson, 1987). At the same time the ideal of the mother who stays at home to look after the children, or who looks after elderly or infirm relatives, is celebrated (Bow Group, 1986). To a large extent, of course, existing policy on divorce, public child-care provision, community care and so on already reflects this view. The Conservative administrations of 1979 and 1983 did nothing to help women with domestic responsibilities to go out to work, they provided little in the way of care for the infirm elderly who are able to stay in the community and they ensured that divorced or separated women continued to find themselves impoverished by the failure of the social security system or the wage labour system to support them adequately (see DHSS, 1974; Smart, 1984). Notwithstanding this, the New Right wishes the government to take more stringent measures to ensure that the family ideal is maintained.

There is, however, a very profound flaw in the arguments being put forward, and also in existing policy affecting married women and carers. Basically the policy requires that in order for women to take on their 'traditional' duties they should be entirely dependent on their husbands whilst caring for children or elderly relatives. Such women are not to be allowed access to an independent income lest this should undermine the stability of the marriage. Yet there is nothing that can be proposed in policy terms that will ensure the husband supports his family and that he will not leave his wife. In such a situation the wife has no security; having given up work and having lost all access to an independent income she is completely destitute. This should then be considered in the light of the legislative measure taken in 1984 by the Conservative government which reduced the wife's right to claim maintenance from her former husband (the argument being that wives should be self-sufficient and self-supporting). It was precisely the revolt against a similar situation in the 1960s that created the demand for safeguards for married women (Smart, 1984).

Retirement pensions policy is a very good example of this problem. Prior to 1975 divorce for a woman also meant a 'divorce' from any pension scheme (state or private) unless she had her own policy or was paying the full contribution to the state scheme. (Most married women did not because it was financially punitive for them to do so, and in any case most women did not have sufficient contributions to establish a worthwhile pension owing to time out of the labour market to care for children.) Changes were made to pension policy in the mid-1970s to safeguard the position of older women whose only right to a pension was through their husband's contributions. However, the value of the state pension scheme was severely undermined with the changes made to the State Earnings Related Pension Scheme (SERPS) in 1986. At the same time the possibility that women who cannot establish private pension contributions in their own right because of child-care responsibilities could claim on their former husband's occupational pension schemes was being given a very low priority by the Conservative government. There is therefore a very real problem for women in the development of such contradictory policies which idealize the dependent family without providing safeguards.

Employment policy

The last example I wish to consider before turning to the case of the Social Security Review is that of employment policy. Again it was part of the Conservative government's rhetoric to state that welfare benefits undermine the motivation to work. However, it is clear that, with the exception of lone mothers, it was policy to motivate only men to enter the labour market. Of course, the fact that the general policy on motivation was 'gendered' (i.e. applied more specifically to men than women) was never made explicit. However, the lack of support for measures which would enable women with children to enter the labour market at a time when 're-motivation' was a central tenet of policy, gives a good insight into the preference given to men in jobs rather than married women. A very good example of this was the Government's approach to *Parental Leave and Leave for Family Reasons*, an EEC Draft Directive of 1983. It was widely acknowledged (for example, by the Equal Opportunities Commission, the Maternity Alliance and the National Council for One-Parent Families) that measures which would make child care more compatible with paid employment, as outlined in the Draft Directive, would enable many mothers (married and single) to go out to work. This would also reduce their dependence on state benefits which would accord with government policy. However, the UK government was unsympathetic to the Directive and voted against it in the European Commission in 1986.

This example is interesting in as much as it reveals that the government's policy on the family cuts across its policy on employment – only men are to be motivated to work, women should remain at home in their 'traditional' roles – and it is an insight into the difficulties of pursuing any one policy in ignorance or in isolation from policy developments in other spheres. This is perhaps one of the major problems of the reform of social security in 1985/6. The government *did* isolate the benefit system from policies on the family, on employment and so on and were simply content to blame the welfare state for problems they identified elsewhere. Hence juvenile delinquency, unemployment and divorce were all causally linked to the undermining influence of the welfare state. Yet having established this causal chain in its rhetoric, it proved more difficult to radically alter the welfare state in the way this 'analysis' seemed to dictate. I shall now turn to a closer examination of the so-called Fowler Review of Social Security and shall argue that it was a failure in terms of the Conservative rhetoric on family policy, but that it created the conditions for further radical reforms more in keeping with the demands of the New Right.

The proposals for reforming social security

As I have argued above, the basic aim of the Conservative government's proposals on social security was the 'relief' of poverty rather than its prevention. This meant that the measures under consideration were those which would act to reduce the worse rigours of poverty, rather than those that would redistribute wealth and income in such a way as to prevent poverty occurring. Given the structure of British society in the 1970s and 1980s, there emerged certain clear routes into poverty. For example, old age, sickness or disability, large families, low pay, unemployment and lone motherhood all carry the risk of grossly inadequate living standards. Notwithstanding the complexity of these routes into poverty, the proposals in the Green and White Papers focused mainly on one route. Their central concern was the two-parent family with children whose earning potential was lower than their entitlement to state benefits. This was not so much a concern that wages were too low as a fear that benefit levels were 'too generous', thus creating a disincentive to join the labour market. Hence the focus of early discussions at the consultation stage of the review procedure was the problem of keeping men in work in spite of low pay, and of making sure it was worth their while to work by ensuring that the benefits they might receive on the dole would not be higher than their wages (plus FIS) whilst in work. This meant that the poverty trap (where one cannot afford to work because of the steep loss of benefits) and the employment trap (where one cannot afford a raise or a slightly better paid job because of the effects of benefit withdrawal) became virtually the organizing principles of the policy review.

This in turn tended to result in a review whose focus was largely upon men as the persons most appropriate to a policy to revive the motivation to work. In practice, therefore, the Green and White Papers adopted the prevalent perspective of Beveridge which had become so dominant in the post-war years, namely the idea that as long as men were economically active then families as a whole would be adequately protected from poverty. It was absolutely taken for granted in the two government documents that if public policy measures address men, then women and children will be taken care of privately in the family.

This reaffirmation of the role of the head of household was signalled in the Green Paper. In this the government made it clear that they wanted the new version of FIS, called Family Credit, to be paid through the wage packet and hence usually to the husband. FIS, by contrast, had been paid through the Post Office and was usually collected by the wife along with Child Benefit. Serious doubts were also thrown on whether Child Benefit should still be paid to the mother and the idea that it too should operate as a form of tax credit was debated. It is clear that the Green Paper accepted a continuation of payments to the mother only very grudgingly. It is worth comparing the following two statements, from which it can be seen that, were it possible, all benefits would have been paid through the male head of household.

> Child benefit is simple, well understood and popular. The system of payment usually to the mother is also well established and appreciated and, *although the result is that the value of the benefit as part of general household income is often overlooked*, the Government do not wish to change it. [DHSS, 1985a: Vol. 2, p. 48; emphasis added]

> The [family] credit will be paid through the wage packet as an offset to tax and national insurance so that *people [sic] are more aware of the extra help they are getting alongside their earnings*. [DHSS, 1985a: Vol. 1, pp. 45–6; emphasis added]

It would seem from these statements that the Government considered that money paid to women is 'invisible' in the family, whilst money paid to men is 'visible'. But this raised the question, visible to whom? The Child Poverty Action Group survey of 2000 mothers' views on Child Benefit showed that 94 percent of all mothers receiving the benefit found it important in meeting their children's needs, while 75 percent said it was essential (Walsh and Lister, 1985). This, and further evidence collected by CPAG in the Save Child Benefit Campaign in 1985, revealed that Child

Benefit is hardly invisible to mothers, so the Government's concern was over its lack of visibility to husbands. On the other hand, evidence that many wives still do not know what their husbands earn (Pahl, 1980, 1983) might indicate that benefits paid through the wage packet will remain quite invisible to women.

What is at issue here is the power relations between men and women in the family. The government took the view that policies directing money to women were less desirable than those directing it to men. Moreover, the government adopted the view that to give money to a wife is an unwarranted interference into the private sphere and a form of redistribution which is not the business of the state. On the other hand, directing financial resources towards husbands was not treated as a form of intervention or redistribution, presumably because it is regarded as 'natural' that men should have the economic power in the family. The White Paper stated:

> But we do not accept the proposition that, uniquely among the people of this country, those in full-time work on low earnings cannot be trusted to allocate their other resources responsibly within the family and must have the state to do it for them. [DHSS, 1985b: 33]

In continuing to ignore the problem of the distribution of resources inside households, whilst in practice directing resources to men, the government proposals were set to ensure that secondary poverty of the sort discovered by Rowntree and Eleanor Rathbone would not simply continue but would be considerably worsened. However, these proposals fell as a consequence of strenuous opposition from a coalition of the poverty lobby, trades unions and women's organizations, yet it would seem that such proposals are likely to re-emerge in the event of further reforms to social security.

There is not space here to outline in detail all the proposals of the Green and White Papers and subsequent Social Security Act 1986 (see Land and Ward, 1986; CPAG, 1985; National Council for One-Parent Families, 1985). However, it is worth mentioning the main changes which will have the greatest impact on family members.

Income support
Income support will replace supplementary benefit in April 1988. It will be a means-tested benefit mainly for people outside the labour market. The personal allowance will vary according to age with dividing lines at 18 and 25 years. There will be a family premium for all married couples over 18 as well as separate children's additions. For so-called client groups (i.e. one-parent families, the elderly and the disabled) there will be additional special premiums which are meant to take account of their extra needs.

In terms of its impact upon families the most important aspect of this reform is the introduction of the new age bands. This is because young people under 25 will not be eligible to receive higher benefits if they live away from their parents. (Under the old supplementary benefit scheme they could claim more as 'householders'.) When this is combined with the severe cuts to be imposed on Housing Benefit, the outcome will be to prolong the dependency of the young unemployed on their parents. This is because it will be financially impossible to set up an independent household without suffering considerable hardship. Although it is possible that young unemployed people will still leave home, it is an important part of the new policy direction espoused by the Government that parents should be responsible for their children even when they are clearly of adult status.

Interestingly, under the first proposals in the Green Paper, only lone mothers would have qualified for the higher premium, in addition to which they were entitled to the lone parent premium. At least this was the case until it was recognized that this would make lone motherhood financially more attractive to young, unemployed women than marriage, a goal clearly antithetical to the Government's stated aims (CPAG, 1985). As the policy will stand in 1988, however, unemployed young people under 25 will have an option of remaining in their parents' home and extending the 'twilight' existence between youth and adulthood, or getting married and having children (or simply having children if they are young women), in order to achieve some independence.

Family Credit

The new Family Credit which will be introduced in 1988 is, in many ways, the cornerstone of the reforms. It is here that the focus on the low paid and the need to increase motivation is most clearly expressed. Yet critics on the Right have pointed out that it will do nothing for the lowest paid. Hermione Parker has used figures produced by the DHSS Tax/Benefit computer program based on those provided in the Social Security Bill to show that,

> Contrary to expectation living standards for those at the bottom of the earning distribution *go down*, as a result of which the gap between incomes in and out of work is further diminished. For two-child families earnings of £110 a week are necessary before the gains from family credit can offset the cuts in child benefit and housing benefit. [Parker, 1986: 83]

It would seem therefore that the overt purpose of the introduction of Family Credit will be undermined by government cuts in other benefits – a clear example of the gap between rhetoric and the practical effects of policy measures.

However, for the purposes of this discussion on family policy, the most important feature of the introduction of Family Credit is that it was introduced despite arguments from both Left and Right of the political spectrum (CPAG, 1985; Parker, 1986) that to increase Child Benefit would have been a much more effective way of directing resources to the low paid with families without creating more problems with the poverty and employment traps. However, Child Benefit ran counter to the ideological leanings of the Conservative Government. In many ways it epitomized the antithesis of the new policy direction. Child Benefit emphasizes the responsibility of the state for the care of children; it is a measure designed to prevent poverty rather than one that 'helps' people who have become poor; it is not means-tested and therefore has no stigma attached to it. Finally, it is paid to mothers, as I have argued above. All of these factors tend to make it unacceptable to the new thinking on social security.

Maternity benefits
The Social Security Act abolished the universal maternity grant as from April 1987. It will be replaced by a maternity needs payment from the newly created social fund. In other words it will become a means-tested benefit with a ceiling of £75. The loss of the grant is significant mainly because it means the loss of a universal benefit which acknowledged the state's shared responsibility for the health of children rather than for its monetary value. This is a concrete example of what is meant by rolling back the state and of putting more emphasis on the individual in the individual–state relationship. It is also firm evidence of the trend away from state responsibility which I discussed above in relation to Child Benefit. However, it is important not to overlook that there will also be a significant reduction in financial aid to the poorest pregnant women because they will no longer be able to claim much-needed single payments from the old supplementary benefit scheme, nor from the new income support scheme.

Various pressure groups responding to the proposals in the White Paper showed that the ceiling of £75 which was imposed on the new payment would be inadequate for the poorest mothers who would be forced to take a loan from the social fund to cover the rest of their costs. It was also argued that as a means-tested benefit the take-up rate amongst those eligible would inevitably decline with serious consequences for poor mothers, most especially young single mothers (National Council For One-Parent Families, 1985). In this respect the new proposals do not give priority to the health and welfare needs of mothers and babies. They reflect instead the ideological premiss that children are a private concern and not a matter for state policy.

Conclusion
It has been possible to raise only a few of the possible consequences for the family of the measures arising from the review of social security.[1] There is in any case, as I have outlined above, some problem in assuming

that there will be a simple cause and effect relationship between the stated aims of policy, its implementation and structural changes to the organization of households and child care. For example the government's desire to legislate in such a way that family stability will be increased is such a vague objective, and the meaning of stability and the means of securing it are so obscure, that it is unlikely that any clear outcome along these lines will be perceived. The resolve to make individuals more 'independent' of the state, in order to make them more dependent upon their relatives, is an example of this. The government appears to have assumed that this 'dependency' is synonymous with stability; the passage of time may show that it has little to do with recreating an idealized extended family of the Victorian era, and more to do with increasing hardship as people continue to opt for independence or as their relatives cannot or will not support them. But narrower objectives such as the shift away from universal benefits, or the reduction of benefits like Housing Benefit, will have clearly identified effects. Quite simply, they will increase poverty and hardship.

In many ways the family is becoming the main welfare agency of the 1980s. Whilst it has never abandoned this role as the conventional wisdom of the New Right would argue (Land, 1983), certain structural changes have occurred with the growth of the number of married women in the labour market, the extension of the period of children's economic dependence, the greater longevity of grandparents and, most recently, chronic unemployment. All these factors mean that families (or more correctly mothers and daughters) need support if they are to continue to provide care and welfare for other members whilst also joining the labour market. But it is this support that recent measures are undermining. The Fowler reforms may not transform the family overnight; indeed not all the rhetoric about reducing the role of the state may work when put in practice. But some measures will have damaging effects, and the rhetoric itself contributes to an ideological climate which in turn prepares the ground for other policy measures which may well go further. The Bow Group (1986) has recently produced a discussion document arguing that not enough support is being given to the traditional family and that measures should be introduced which should discourage married women from taking paid employment and which should penalize single mothers. The rhetoric of the Fowler review makes such policies all the more imminent.

Note

1 For more detailed comments on the Fowler proposals it is worth consulting the documents produced by groups like the Equal Opportunities Commission, the Child Poverty Action Group, Shelter, the National Council for One-Parent Families, the National Council for Voluntary Organisations, the Disability Alliance and Maternity Alliance. Papers are available from all of these organizations.

References

Anderson, D. and Dawson, G. (eds) (1986) *Family Portraits*. London: Social Affairs Unit.

Beveridge, W. (1942) *Social Insurance and Allied Services* (Cmnd 6404). London: HMSO.

Bow Group (1986) Article in the *Guardian* (7 July).

Child Poverty Action Group (1985) *Burying Beveridge*. London: CPAG.

Clarke, J., Cochrane, A. and Smart, C. (1987) *From Dreams to Disillusion: Ideologies of Welfare*. London: Hutchinson.

David, M. (1983) 'The New Right, Sex, Education and Social Policy', in Lewis, J. (ed.) *Women's Welfare, Women's Rights*. London: Croom Helm.

Department of Health and Social Security (1974) *Report of the Committee on One-Parent Families* (Hon. Sir Morris Finer (Chair), Cmnd 5629). London: HMSO.

Department of Health and Social Security (1985a) *Reform of Social Security* (Vols 1–3, Cmnd 9517/8/9 (Green Paper), Norman Fowler (Chair)). London: HMSO.

Department of Health and Social Security (1985b) *Reform of Social Security: Programme for Action* (Cmnd 9691 (White Paper)). London: HMSO.

Graham, H. (1984) *Women, Health and the Family*. Brighton: Wheatsheaf.

Johnson, P. (1987) 'Families under Fire', *Daily Telegraph* (5 January), p. 12.

Land, H. (1983) 'Family Fables', *New Socialist* 11 (May).

Land, H. (1986) *Women and Economic Dependency*. Manchester: Equal Opportunities Commission.

Land, H. and Ward, S. (1986) *Women Won't Benefit*. London: National Council for Civil Liberties.

Levitas, R. (ed.) (1986) *The Ideology of the New Right*. Oxford: Polity Press.

Macnicol, J. (1980) *The Movement for Family Allowances, 1918–45: A Study in Social Policy Development*. London: Heinemann.

Morgan, P. (1986) 'Feminist Attempts to Sack Father: A Case of Unfair Dismissal?', in Anderson and Dawson (1986).

National Council for One-Parent Families (1985) *The Insecurity System*. London: NCOPF.

Pahl, J. (1980) 'Patterns of Money Management within Marriage', *Journal of Social Policy* 9(3).

Pahl, J. (1983) 'The Allocation of Money and the Structuring of Inequality within Marriage', *Sociological Review* 31(2).

Parker, H. (1986) 'Family Income Support: Government Subversion of the Traditional Family', in Anderson and Dawson (1986).

Rowntree, B. S. (1902) *Poverty: A Study of Town Life*. London: Macmillan.

Smart, C. (1984) *The Ties That Bind*. London: Routledge & Kegan Paul.

Walsh, A. and Lister, R. (1985) *Mother's Life-Line*. London: Child Poverty Action Group.

Young, M. (1952) 'Distribution of Income within the Family', *British Journal of Sociology* 3(4).

10
Family matters and public policy
Malcolm Wicks

'We are the party of the family', said Margaret Thatcher in 1977, and her words have been echoed by politicians across the political spectrum in recent years. Yet this has not always been the case. The enthusiastic bear-hug of the family by the British political parties is in fact fairly recent. Indeed, back in 1970 Margaret Wynn observed that 'No political party in the UK has identified itself with the social and economic interest of the family' (Wynn, 1972: 279).

How things have changed since the early 1970s is illustrated by the fact that, shortly before the last election, a Cabinet committee – the Family Policy Group – achieved some notoriety when its papers were leaked (Dean, 1983). Some of the group's more whimsical ideas became controversial overnight – the suggestion that children should be trained to manage their pocket money, for example – but more fundamental ideas included encouraging mothers to stay at home and a greater emphasis on family responsibility in the provision of care. This episode revealed just how far family interests had moved towards the centre of the political debate.

Before current 'family policy' questions are discussed, however, let us go back somewhat. How can we explain today's interest in the family? After considering that question, some difficulties about the concept of 'family policy' can be examined.

The development of interest in family policy
While a number of different factors lie behind contemporary interest in family policy (see, for example, Craven, Rimmer and Wicks, 1982), two are of particular importance: the nature of family change (and responses to it) and the growing importance of debates about the future of the British welfare state.

The nature of family change
While any careful analysis of family life today needs to balance continuities against change, it is undoubtedly change which is of most interest. It raises a range of policy questions, and sparks off controversy – often fierce controversy.

Neglecting family *continuities* nevertheless produces an unbalanced debate. For this reason one recent account of family questions started its analysis this way:

> . . . the fact is that *most* young people in Britain will get married; *most* marriages will survive; *most* married couples will have children; *most* children will be born legitimate and be brought up by two parents. Indeed nine in every ten children are still born within marriage and seven out of eight are living in two-parent families. [Study Commission on the Family, 1982: 9]

While the picture has changed somewhat since that description was written – almost one-fifth of children are now born illegitimate, for instance – the point is still well made.

Nevertheless, family changes *are* dramatic. This is most apparent in relation to marriage. Indeed probably one in three *new* marriages will end in divorce, and this is true of a far higher proportion of those marrying in their teens. Large numbers of children are affected by divorce – currently some 155,000 children each year – for some six out of ten divorces involve dependent children. Parallel developments towards remarriage (but also more redivorces) mean that family life is changing – and will change – dramatically. Growing numbers of children are brought up in step-families, and there are many more one-parent families: about one and a half million children – one in eight – live with just one parent (Family Policy Studies Centre, 1986).

Other things are changing too. In particular, the developing role of women in society has affected family life. More women now work outside the home, as well as within it. In 1921 less than 10 percent of married women were in the formal labour force, but since the Second World War the proportion of married women in paid employment has risen rapidly and continuously. Today about half of all married women are economically active. This means that many mothers with dependent children work outside the home, most mothers working part-time, rather than full-time. But many mothers with quite young children now work – some 27 percent of those with their youngest child under five in 1980, for example (Martin and Roberts, 1984).

Such family change has generated controversy. For while these developments are now taken for granted by many, some see in them a grave threat to the family itself. Indeed in recent years there has been a strong backlash against moves towards family diversity. Of course 'traditionalists' have always had high regard for the family within the existing social order (see Craven, Rimmer and Wicks, 1982) but today such organizations as the new Conservative Campaign for the Family show the strength of feeling. Recently, a report from the Social Affairs Unit, *Family Portraits*, provided an important text for the traditionalists (Anderson and Dawson, 1986).

According to this report the case for the normal family needs to be powerfully argued because it is threatened from three directions:

> First there are brands of feminism which are deeply hostile to the family, most especially to the role of fathers. Secondly, the expansion of the modern state has led to the responsibility of the family for children and young people being

subverted by the state itself and by professional bodies of doctors and teachers whose autonomy from, that is irresponsibility to, the family, the state endorses. Further the web of incentives and penalties set by the tax and benefit system is now firmly loaded against the normal family. Thirdly, modern technological developments such as new techniques of embryo fertilization threaten, unless controlled, to dislocate traditional relations in the family. [Anderson and Dawson, 1986: 1!]

Opposing the traditionalists, feminists and others argue that the extent of family change has been exaggerated and, in fact, traditional family arrangements all too often still hold today. As noted later, they argue that within social policy traditional assumptions about the roles of men and women are still dominant. Moreover, they note, within the home there are still vastly unequal relationships between men and women, and unfair allocations of domestic responsibilities, including child care and the care of elderly relatives (Family Policy Studies Centre, 1987).

The welfare state debate
It is no coincidence that family concerns have come to the fore at the very time of renewed controversy about social policy and, consequently, the future of the British welfare state.

After a period of, what seems in retrospect, a great deal of agreement and consensus about the role of the state in human welfare in the period from the end of the Second World War through to the mid-1960s, there is now fierce disagreement about the state's role in such areas as health, education, housing and social security (see Wicks, 1987). The context for this disagreement is to be found in the increasing recognition, from the mid-1960s through to the late 1970s, that there were a growing number of problems about the welfare state. Both Left and Right were agreed about this, although the causes and remedies were open to argument.

By the late 1970s the New Right had become a major force in political debate and were arguing strongly that the welfare state was too large, too expensive, too bureaucratic and, moreover, not very effective in meeting genuine need. The prognosis was clear: the state should restrict itself to helping only those who could not get support from elsewhere, while most people should look to other institutions for their welfare. The New Right therefore sought the development of a 'residual welfare state', to use Titmuss's term, that is one 'based on the premise that there are two 'natural' (or socially given) channels through which an individual's needs are properly met: the private market and the family. Only when these break down should social welfare institutions come into play and then only temporarily' (Titmuss, 1974: 30–1). Thus the family became an important feature of social policy discussion. For those wishing to reduce the role of the state in welfare, it was important to emphasize that families should take greater responsibility for their own dependents, both children, particularly when very young, and elderly or disabled relatives. It was wrong, argued the New Right, to assume that somehow the state should take on such responsibilities. Families themselves should save and invest to meet such contingencies. In this way, argued the New Right, people themselves would get a better deal: they would be able to make proper choices; there would be more options; the private market was flexible; and there would be less danger of bureaucracy. Public expenditure would decline; taxation would be less burdensome.

The family and social policy

This chapter opened by saying that the 'discovery' of the family by British politicians was a relatively recent process. But this is not to say that there have not always been some very clear assumptions about the family underlying social policy. Though often not explicit, very clear views about the nature of family life and, in particular, the roles of men and women feature in social policy.

Sometimes these have been freely stated. When national health insurance was first being planned, for example, in 1910, government actuaries explained the exclusion of married women in the following way:

> Married women living with their husbands need not be included since where the unit is the family, it is the husband's not the wife's health which it is important to insure. So long as the husband is in good health and able to work adequate provision will be made for the needs of the family, irrespective of the wife's health, whereas when the husband's health fails there is no one to earn wages. [Quoted by Fraser, 1973: 155]

Later, Beveridge in his 1942 report made certain assumptions about family life and argued that:

> ...all women by marriage acquire a new economic and social status, with risks and rights different from those of the unmarried. On marriage a women gains a legal right to maintenance by her husband as a first line of defence against risks which fall directly on the solitary woman; she undertakes at the same time to perform vital unpaid service...[Beveridge, 1942: para. 108]

In framing his proposals for social security, which still substantially influence current policy provisions, Beveridge therefore had clear views about the pattern of family life in the post-war world and the role of married women. Despite the fact that, while he was writing his plan, women were taking on roles hitherto denied to them – as members of the armed forces, munitions workers, land workers and so on – he assumed that, come the peace, married women would revert to traditional roles, roles which Beveridge emphasized were of the utmost importance: 'In the next thirty years housewives as mothers have vital work to do in ensuring the adequate continuance of the British race...' (para. 117). Beveridge was anxious to ensure that the detailed arrangements for social security reflected the status of married women: 'Every women on marriage will become a new person, acquiring new rights and not carrying on into marriage claims to unemployment or disability benefits in respect of contributions made before marriage' (para. 339). The plan assumed therefore that women would be financially dependent on their husbands.

More generally, Abel-Smith has noted the assumptions underlining the Beveridge Plan:

(a) that marriages are for life: even if the parties do not stay together, the legal obligation to maintain persists until death or remarriage;
(b) that sexual activity and child birth takes place, or at least should take place, only within marriage;
(c) that married women normally do no paid work or negligible paid work;
(d) that women and not men should do housework and rear children;
(e) that couples who live together with regular sexual relationships and shared expenses are always of the opposite sex. [Abel-Smith, 1982]

Current social policy and the family

While the assumptions about family life which underlay the Beveridge Report were certainly explicit, current social policy also makes certain assumptions about the nature of families and the appropriate roles of men and women. This may be more implicit than in earlier policy, but the assumptions are no less important or pervasive in their practical implications. Recent developments concerning community care provide an important illustration.

Community care policy

Community care policy in the 1980s has firmly located 'the family' at its hub (Henwood and Wicks, 1985; Parker, 1985). As a broad policy aspiration for the health and personal social services, community care is long-standing. It is also a policy around which there appears to stand a remarkable political consensus: governments and parties of all shades and persuasions have advocated it in recent decades, and the role of the immediate 'community' of family, friends and neighbours has been stressed increasingly.

The growing emphasis on community care owes much to perceived demographic pressures. The ageing of the population is a long-established trend. In Britain between 1901 and 1981 the numbers of people aged 65+ rose from 1.7 millions to almost 8 millions, and increased as a proportion to the total population from less than 5 percent to 15 percent.

The ageing of the elderly population itself is now of growing importance. Between 1981 and 2001, for example, those aged over 75 are expected to increase by 31 percent (almost 1 million persons). At the same time, changes in the very elderly population are likely to be even more dramatic. Those aged 85+ are expected to virtually double to number more than

1 million. In the light of such changes, questions about the need for care and support, and who will provide it, are of obvious importance (Henwood and Wicks, 1985).

One of the clearest statements of the current policy approach was provided in the DHSS 1981 White Paper, *Growing Older*. The objective of community care was located in the context of public expenditure compression, a reduced reliance on statutory services, and an increased emphasis on 'the community':

> Whatever level of public expenditure proves practicable, and however it is distributed, the primary sources of support and care are informal and voluntary. These spring from the personal ties of kinship, friendship and neighbourhood. They are irreplaceable. It is the role of public authorities to sustain and, where necessary, develop – but never to displace – such support and care. Care *in* the community must increasingly mean care *by* the community. [DHSS, 1981a: 3]

'Community' care in practice

Whatever romantic images the phrase 'community' conveys, the research evidence has consistently found that the reality of community care is largely care by families, which in turn mainly means care by women:

> A growing body of evidence suggests that 'community care' has in reality meant care by individuals on an unpaid and often unaided basis in the home. . . They will often find themselves badly supported by statutory services and without any real choice as to whether they will care or not. Far from the community carrying the costs, the allocation of caring responsibilities has major implications in financial, social and emotional terms for the individuals involved. [Equal Opportunities Commission, 1982: iii]

The assumptions underlying such development reflect a belief in the primary responsibilities of the family in general, and of women as carers in particular.

Indeed there is now a keen awareness of, and interest in, 'carers' to complement the long-standing, and more obvious, concern about those in need of care. This term was virtually unknown, even in social policy literature, until the 1980s, but interest in the carers – those who care for dependent family members, such as frail elderly people, children, and adults with disabilities or chronic illnesses – is rising.

The performance of such caring functions is crucial to the operation of community-based care and to the government's estimation of its cost-effectiveness. A DHSS report on community care in 1981 noted that 'the strength of informal support available to people is often critical to the feasibility and cost-effectiveness of community-based packages of care . . . all depend for their success on a high level of commitment from informal carers' (DHSS, 1981b: 54). However, it was also noted that the cost-effectiveness of such service packages 'often depends on not putting a financial value on the contribution of informal carers who may in fact shoulder considerable financial, social and emotional burdens' (DHSS, 1981b: 3). As in other fields, underlying assumptions about the family within community care policy do not match the reality of family trends. As has been noted:

> The notion of 'family care' often assumes a particular model of family life. It is rarely specific, but is implicit in policy statements from government. It includes all or many of the following characteristics: an elderly relative either living with or near her family; a stable 'nuclear' family; and an able-bodied woman at home supported financially by her husband at work. [Rossiter and Wicks, 1982: 63]

Several trends now challenge this family model.

One of the most significant trends of recent times has been the increase in women's employment, particularly among married women. Today over half of all married women are in paid employment: they are not all 'at home ready and waiting to undertake the role of carer' (House of Lords, 1983). Changes in roles and expectations may, in the future, increasingly question women's 'cultural designation as carers' (Finch and Groves, 1980). There is therefore a potential discord between the interests of women and the pursuit of community care policies. While women today may have achieved considerable emancipation relative to previous decades, some fear that the thrust of current policies could undermine such advances by emphasizing the domestic unit and the supply of personal care as women's lot.

Other trends need also to be considered. The move towards smaller and more mobile families may mean potentially fewer people, especially women, 'available' to provide support and care for elderly relatives in the future.

Developments in divorce and remarriage may also be significant:

> The reconstruction of families has, as yet, unpredictable consequences for the supply of informal tending. On the one hand, it may widen the network of kinship by the addition of step-relatives. On the other hand, the sense of obligation to dependent step-kin may be weak, thereby reducing the tending available. [Parker, 1981: 21]

Does Britain need a family policy?
Growing concern about family life in Britain, as indicated by the rise of political interest in the family, has led, in turn, to the development of interest in 'family policy'. A number of different individuals and groups, across the political spectrum, have advocated specific family policies, or a more general 'family policy', or the appointment of a Minister for the family, or other proposals or mechanisms which would seek to reassert the importance of families within Britain and therefore in the policy-making process (Craven, Rimmer and Wicks, 1982).

Before considering some of the different ideas on offer, it is important to sound some words of caution, for certainly there are no grounds for feeling that family policies are *necessarily* a good thing, nor that they are somehow an easy answer to the many problems current in Britain. There are two specific cautions which need to be borne in mind when considering the idea of family policy.

First, history shows us that 'family' policies have often been disguised attempts by governments to manipulate families for 'national' interest – by, for example, promoting birth rates or by encouraging (or discouraging) female participation in the labour market. The Third Reich had a sophisticated family policy with a system of marriage loans, child subsidies and family allowances. Medals for motherhood were awarded, the gold one being reserved for mothers who produced eight or more children.

There have been more recent examples of governments projecting the image of the woman as 'mother' or 'worker' depending on demographic, social or economic factors and being prepared to implement national objectives through adjustments to social security and other policies. Recently the Soviet Union attempted to stimulate the low birth rate among ethnic Russians and accordingly increased family allowances and extended maternity leave. But while this was to be implemented immediately for women living in the northern parts of the country, it was planned to introduce it only later in Muslim central Asia, where a population explosion is causing concern.

The one-child-only policy in China is a further indication of 'family policies' in operation. The point is also illustrated graphically by the fact that two very different societies, Hungary and Kenya, both have governments advocating the desirability of the three-child family, but whereas Hungary extols this in order to increase the birth rate (out of concern that many urban couples are now having just one child), in Kenya the motives are very different. There the concern is to *discourage* large families, in a society where many families are typically *eight*-child ones (Clare, 1986).

A focus on families or individuals?
The second caution concerning family policy is raised by the question, should policies be supporting the family or individuals? Much recent interest in the family derives from the changing role and status of women with respect to work, child-rearing, their relationship with men and their overall position in society. As indicated earlier, there is a direct clash between traditionalists and feminists on this issue. And economic recession has made the question more controversial. Some argue that married women should return to their 'rightful place' – in the home. Moreover, advocates of this position would say that, given the importance of child care (which an over-burdened welfare state should not be providing), and in the light

of rising needs among the elderly population, it is crucial that women maintain or resume their traditional role.

This is, of course, anathema to others, particularly feminists. They analyse social policy in terms of still dominant assumptions about women as dependents and natural carers. Their concern is to enable women to become less dependent on men, and accordingly advocate social policy developments to equalize rights and responsibilities in respect of child care, the care of elderly relatives and other matters (Family Policy Studies Centre, 1987).

Issues 'inside the family' do not just revolve around the respective positions of men and women, however, for there are also important contemporary questions concerning the rights of children. Much social reform in Britain, both historically and more recently, has been concerned with protecting and promoting the interests of children – sometimes against parents' wishes. The current controversy about contraceptive advice for girls below the age of sixteen – whether or not doctors should inform parents – shows that the issue is a very live one. And some of the most difficult questions concerning child care revolve around whether (and when) to remove children from their natural parents in cases of child abuse or neglect.

What all this illustrates is that any simple call for 'a strengthening of the family' or policies 'to enhance family life' are more suitable to the rhetoric of the political platform than useful guides to effective social policy. They also show that there can be no *one* family policy. Rather, political parties, and other groups and institutions, need to argue their own family policies. Hence the public, as electors, will need to decide between rival packages – some supporting traditionalist demands, others quite different approaches.

Family policy agenda

What will the (different) family policy agenda include?

There are certain key policy questions, arising from contemporary problems and current trends, which cannot fail to be discussed under the heading family policy. They are all difficult questions not least because there is a sense in which the rights and responsibilities of families are less certain today than in the recent past. Changing family patterns have very often led to uncertain attitudes, or great controversy, about the proper response from society to change. A number of issues illustrate this point. The first two concern the family and employment.

Unemployment

Just as the question of employment features strongly today in debate, so it did in the 1940s when the modern welfare state was being fashioned. This was hardly surprising given the mass unemployment of the 1920s and

1930s. There was a wide measure of consensus that post-war reconstruction could only be based on a firm foundation of full employment (Wicks, 1987: Ch. 2). William Beveridge, the great social policy architect, recognized this more than most. Indeed when he presented to the public the 'Five Giant Evils' of Want, Disease, Squalor, Ignorance and Idleness, he emphasized that:

> Idleness is the largest and fiercest of the five giants and the most important to attack. If the giant idleness can be destroyed, all the other aims of reconstruction come within reach. If not, they are out of reach in any serious sense and their formal achievement is futile. [Beveridge, 1942: 43]

In retrospect perhaps it can be seen that the ideal of full employment, matched by the virtual reality of this in the late 1940s, the 1950s and the 1960s, represented an historic consensus between the demand from the Left that citizens should have a *right* to work, and the traditional emphasis from the political Right that the citizen (largely meaning men) had a *responsibility* to work for themselves and their family.

With the disappearance of full employment, there is no consensus in this area, and many, on both the Left and the Right, are uncertain as to whether full employment is any more a realizable goal. Hence, with three or four million people out of work, a major foundation for social policy has crumbled and the implications for families are severe. What are the rights and responsibilities in this fundamental sphere?

The two-worker family

Another employment trend with major implications for the family (and hence policy) is the rise of the dual-worker family. The evidence was noted earlier and it shows that typically today families with children are headed by both a mother and a father in work. And this raises particular challenges for social policy. Many of our social arrangements still assume that the traditional pattern holds and that the wife, as mother, is at home to care and tend for her children. Despite some movement towards child care for the under-fives, such facilities are still scarce in many areas (and far fewer than in many other European countries).

For some, a rapid development of such services – both care for the pre-school child and after-school care for the children of working parents – would seem a logical policy development in the light of trends. Nevertheless, the value questions raised are immense and are controversial. Many resist the idea that the state should take over this traditional family responsibility for children and this view is strengthened at a time when government wishes to reduce rather than extend public spending. The rights and responsibilities of dual-worker families are thus uncertain: there is a lack of fit between the way in which many families live and work today and the number and range of facilities that are available.

Marital breakdown

At the heart of much debate about the family in Britain today lies the state of marriage. As noted earlier, since the reform of divorce law in the late 1960s the number of divorces increased dramatically. While essentially a *private* matter, divorce has *public* consequences and raises a number of practical questions about housing and social security, as well as the law on maintenance.

Some of the most important questions are financial. Any look, for example, at the statistics on supplementary benefits shows just how many recipients are one-parent families (Family Policy Studies Centre, 1986). All too often the breakdown of marriage leads to poverty for many of the family members concerned.

This raises an important question. Where do responsibilities lie following divorce? At present there is an uncertain answer from society to this question. At one level, responsibility dwells within the realm of the private law on maintenance. At another level, it is a social security matter. And, given a large measure of default on maintenance orders, not to mention the complications created by remarriage – whereby many men have responsibilities for two families – there is much overlap, and muddle, between the two areas.

Given that, to take just one estimate, one and a half million children in Britain are likely to have parents who divorce within the coming ten years, the need for policy development in this area is obvious. But not only are the policy questions difficult, there is also a fundamental question about values that makes policy resolution uncertain. For while some see the major problem as the family poverty created by marital breakdown and hence argue the need for improved social security provision for one-parent families, others argue the issue very differently. Some argue that already non-traditional families receive too much support to the detriment of traditional families. Moreover, they advocate that problems in this area need to be tackled through a maintenance of traditional values, rather than painful state intervention.

Care of elderly people

A final illustration of the issues on the family policy agenda is the challenge posed by an ageing population.

The ageing of the population is a unique demographic development (Family Policy Studies Centre, 1984). Some of the key trends were noted earlier and they call for positive and imaginative policies if many of our elderly people are not to live out their last days in discomfort, misery and – sometimes – squalor. Circumstances and needs vary greatly but in general many very elderly people face problems. Compared with younger pensioners, they are more likely to suffer from ill-health and mental and physical handicaps, they are less able to carry out normal household tasks, they are more likely to live alone and to live in the least suitable housing and are more likely to be below or close to the poverty line.

As shown earlier, it is the family that provides the great bulk of personal care. Moreover, community care in practice normally means family care and that, in turn, means females within the family. Many of the frailest elderly live with their families, while many still living alone are only enabled to do so because of the devoted work of carers (Henwood and Wicks, 1984).

But what of the future? Can existing levels of family support for the elderly population be sustained in coming decades and even be increased to cope with the pressures and needs associated with demographic trends? As noted earlier, these are difficult questions and are, inevitably, controversial ones at a time of uncertainty about the future of the welfare state.

As our earlier discussion showed, some see the questions mainly as family matters, rather than ones for the state. It is for families to care for their elderly relatives, rather than social services, argue many traditionalists and conservatives; it is not, primarily, a state matter. Against this, others argue that to emphasize the family's role is, in essence, to argue that women should regard themselves as the natural carers of elderly relatives and should be prepared to take on this role, whatever sacrifices are called for in terms of individual aspirations and career consequences. This, they argue, is not acceptable in the late twentieth century.

What these different issues demonstrate is that no rhetorical gloss about the need for 'sensitive family policies' can get over the controversies that lie deep within the debate. While those seeking to strive for consensus are often tempted to overlook the controversies and the value questions that are implicit, this is a mistake.

Developing a family perspective

Much of this paper has been concerned to argue that the term 'family policy' needs to be disaggregated and looked at critically. It is important to look at questions on the family policy agenda, but naive to suggest that a focus on the family always leads to consensus rather than conflict. Despite this, however, it is possible to suggest ways in which family issues can be distinguished and properly evaluated within the social policy process.

The new interest in family and policy questions is partly due to a belief that policies are not always formed on the basis of a realistic and sound evaluation of how they will affect families of different kinds in practice. Policies often fail to relate specific issues and objectives to other policies; they do not then respond to critical questions of implementation, and are not firmly based on actual family circumstances and needs. These kinds of anxieties are not merely voiced by outside critics of government, but have also been put forward by leading politicians from different political parties. For example, James Callaghan, when Prime Minister, stated that:

'I don't believe that the Government has done enough, hardly started to consider as a whole the impact of its policies on the family when we take our decisions in Cabinet and in government' (Callaghan, 1978).

For the future, there is a need for a family *perspective* within the policy-making process. This would have three major components: a sensitivity to changing family patterns and relationships; a full recognition of family roles and functions; the monitoring and evaluation of the effects of public policy on families.

Evaluation

Evaluating the effects of policies on families is necessary at different stages of the policy process. It is important, firstly, at the early stages of policy development, when different policy options are being considered. Secondly, it is important at the stage when policies are being finalized and are put to Parliament. And finally, once implemented, it is important to develop monitoring and evaluation to look at the implementation of policy in practice. Such a process may well lead to policy adaptation and will feed back into more fundamental reappraisals of policy when these take place.

Family impact statements

When new legislation is being proposed – or when other policy proposals are being made – the idea of a 'family impact statement' is important. There has been interest among British politicians in this area.

A family impact statement is, simply, one that would spell out the intended effects of a new policy on families. The hope for such statements is that they would lead to policies which are more in tune with contemporary family life, which take more account of family functions and which meet family needs and aspirations. This, perhaps, is idealistic and it would be foolish to overstate the potential importance of impact statements, but such statements would encourage a family focus in policy-making. Thus, in the preliminary stages of the policy process, officials – aware of the need to produce impact statements – would be more likely than now to take into account family considerations. During the parliamentary consideration of new legislation, MPs would consider specific policy changes in the context of the statement, as would interest groups, local authorities and the media. Impact statements should also stimulate public debate. It follows that they should be published and they might well appear at the beginning of a Parliamentary Bill alongside the statements, which are already required, on financial implications and civil service manpower. In a Study Commission on the Family paper, it was argued that the kind of factors to be included in a family impact statement might be:

1 The impact of the proposed policy on *different* family units, including one-parent and dual-worker families, for example.

2 The assumptions made about family life, including male and female roles.
3 The association between the new policy and existing related policies and the likely cumulative impact of these measures.
4 The rights and responsibilities of families.
5 The intelligibility of the new policy – questions of access, complexity and so on.
6 The policy goals in relation to families and how these will be achieved, and procedures for monitoring and evaluation. [Study Commission on the Family, 1983]

The development of a 'family perspective' within the policy-making process is, perhaps, one step that all parties and groups concerned about the family might support. It offers a means of making public policies more sensitive to family trends as we approach a new century. It does not, however, resolve important family policy issues which are themselves subject to controversial value questions – about the relationship between the citizen and the state and the respective roles of men and women – which are at the heart of much contemporary debate.

References

Abel-Smith, B. (1982) 'Marriage, Parenthood and Social Policy', lecture at Liverpool University.

Anderson, D. and Dawson, G. (eds) (1986) *Family Portraits*. London: Social Affairs Unit.

Beveridge, W. (1942) *Social Insurance and Allied Services* (Cmnd 6404). London: HMSO.

Callaghan, J. (1978) Speech at Labour Women's Conference, 14 May.

Clare, A. (1986) *Lovelaw: Love, Sex and Marriage Around the World*. London: BBC Publications.

Craven, E., Rimmer, L. and Wicks, M. (1982) *Family Issues and Public Policy*. London: Study Commission on the Family.

Dean, M. (1983) 'Ministers Rethink Welfare State', *Guardian* (17 February).

Department of Health and Social Security (1981a) *Growing Older* (Cmnd 8173). London: HMSO.

Department of Health and Social Security (1981b) *Report of a Study on Community Care*. London: HMSO.

Equal Opportunities Commission (1982) *Caring for the Elderly and Handicapped: Community Care Policies and Women's Lives*. Manchester: Equal Opportunities Commission.

Family Policy Studies Centre (1984) *An Ageing Population* (Factsheet). London: Family Policy Studies Centre.

Family Policy Studies Centre (1986) *One-Parent Families* (Factsheet). London: Family Policy Studies Centre.

Family Policy Studies Centre (1987, forthcoming) *Inside the Family*. London: Family Policy Studies Centre.

Finch, J. and Groves, D. (1980) 'Community Care and the Family: a case for Equal Opportunities', *Journal of Social Policy* 9 (4): 487-511.

Fraser, D. (1973) *The Evolution of the British Welfare State*. London: Macmillan.

Henwood, M. and Wicks, M. (1984) *The Forgotten Army: Family Care and Elderly People*. London: Family Policy Studies Centre.

Henwood, M. and Wicks, M. (1985) 'Community Care, Family Trends and Social Change', *The Quarterly Journal of Social Affairs* 1 (4): 357-71.

House of Lords (1983) 'Invalidity Benefits for Married Women', *Hansard*, columns 754-71 (12 July). London: HMSO.

Martin, J. and Roberts, C. (1984) *Women and Employment: A Lifetime Perspective*. London: Department of Employment/Office of Population Censuses and Surveys.

Parker, G. (1985) *With Due Care and Attention: A Review of Research on Informal Care*. London: Family Policy Studies Centre.

Parker, R. (1981) 'Tending and Social Policy', in Goldberg, E.M. and Hatch, S. (eds) *A New Look at the Personal Social Services*. London: Policy Studies Institute.

Rossiter, C. and Wicks, M. (1982) *Crisis or Challenge? Family Care, Elderly People and Social Policy*. London: Study Commission on the Family.

Study Commission on the Family (1982) *Values and the Changing Family*. London: Study Commission on the Family.

Study Commission on the Family (1983) *Families in the Future: A Policy Agenda for the '80s*. London: Study Commission on the Family.

Titmuss, R.M. (1974) *Social Policy: An Introduction*. London: Allen & Unwin.

Wicks, M. (1987) *A Future for All*. Harmondsworth: Penguin.

Wynn, M. (1972) *Family Policy*. Harmondsworth: Penguin.

11
The Asian Mother and Baby Campaign: the construction of ethnic minorities' health needs

Yvette Rocheron

The DHSS and the Save the Children Fund sponsored the Asian Mother and Baby Campaign (AMBC), which was launched by Princess Anne in September 1984. The Campaign has been discussed both in the English and in the Asian press, and in professional health journals. The scheme is seen, by all parties, as a significant new development.[1]

Very few health authorities had, until then, been dealing with projects specifically concerned with the maternity care of ethnic minorities.[2] This would explain the interest raised by the campaign, the merits of which were yet to be demonstrated. Evidence for this view comes from the Select Parliamentary Committee who have been concerned with perinatal and neonatal mortality. In 1980, the Short Report recommended that health authorities should make 'positive efforts to seek out pregnant women in the minority groups, using every means in their power' (HMSO, 1980). In 1984, in its follow-up report, it repeated its concern for high perinatal and neonatal mortality rates among these groups of women and deplored DHSS slowness in implementing the campaign (HMSO, 1986). From its infancy, there had been great expectations of the campaign.

The AMBC aimed to improve the antenatal and postnatal care given to Asian women in the sixteen District Health Authorities (DHAs) which accepted its programme, and hoped to assist the development of a more sensitive service. To achieve these aims, a health education campaign was launched to 'inform Asian families about the importance of early antenatal care, and about the diet and care of the mother in pregnancy'.[3] A 'linkwork scheme' was established for a period of two years. It involved the full-time employment of up to eight Asian women in each district, fluent in several Asian languages and English, who 'will be trained and act as a bridge between health professionals and Asian mothers'.[4]

This chapter examines the medical, social and political context in which the campaign started. It is based on an ongoing evaluation of the campaign and deals solely with its origins. It does not survey the concrete improvements in the delivery of service to Asian women which the campaign has initiated in many areas.[5]

What is under consideration here is the extent to which the campaign can be seen as an instrument of social policy in the health care offered to Asians. I will examine how the campaign relates to distinct debates on such issues as the interpretation of perinatal mortality rates,[6] women's rights in obstetric care and racism in the NHS.

The overall argument is that the campaign, in its initial conception and objectives, represents an intervention by health authorities which seeks to enable Asian mothers to use the health service efficiently and to create a consensus among health professionals on how to meet their health needs. By doing so, the campaign defines these needs in such a way as to accommodate, rather than undermine, dominant professional practices. The problems which the campaign associates with Asian women's care (for instance, patients booking a hospital bed too late in pregnancy or the delivery of inappropriate and meaningless advice) are restricted either to the private-domestic field or the biological/medical. In either case, problems under scrutiny lose their reference to patients' race and class positions while they highlight their cultural elements. Thus, the reformist intentions of the campaign tends to collude, at the ideological level, with an image of a 'Black pathology', although they represent a genuine attempt to challenge personal racism.[7] It is this core tension in the campaign which needs unwrapping.

The Stop Rickets Campaign legacy

When managers and campaign staff explained how the idea for a national campaign on maternity health care for Asian women started, they unanimously saw it as an outcome of the Stop Rickets Campaign. This was a health education campaign initiated in 1979 by the then Minister for Health and the DHSS Working Group on Rickets, which aimed to involve health authorities and Asian organizations in creating a greater awareness, among Asians, of the nature of rickets and the role of vitamin D in the prevention of osteomalacia. The Save the Children Fund agreed to manage the campaign, which was funded by the DHSS and launched in 1982.

One year later, campaign staff and Save the Children Fund drew the conclusion that the Stop Rickets Campaign had been successful. They also recommended that health authorities could improve their services to Asian populations by 'the use of liaison workers whose functions are agreed with all health professionals involved and who are suitably trained' (Save the Children Fund, 1983).

From this emerged the idea of the 'linkworker'. She would be an Asian woman employed by health districts with the brief to ensure that consultations between the NHS staff and Asian patients were not handicapped by language problems and a lack of awareness of clients' culture. Also, the Rickets Campaign identified maternal health as a prime target for a future programme of action in which linkworkers would be a key component. (The roles of the link-workers will be discussed in greater detail later.)

There was much managerial continuity between the two campaigns. They shared the same director and management structures. They were both centrally managed by Save the Children Fund with a team of staff going out to the periphery – the districts – with the brief to promote the campaigns with local authorities and Asian families. Although the staff from the AMBC are all employed by the Save the Children Fund, the think-tank for the operation came from the DHSS and the Working Group on Rickets, now reconvened as the DHSS Working Party on Asian Health. Both initiatives were the brainchild of this committee and received public and internal endorsements by successive Ministers of Health.

The Stop Rickets Campaign also gave the AMBC an ideological legacy. It has been argued that the Rickets Campaign was ineffective and that there was no evidence that incidences of osteomalacia among Asians would be reduced significantly as a result of this campaign (see, for example, Donovan, 1983: 20–9). Its advice to Asians to westernize their diets, sunbathe and expose their skins, was said to be victim-blaming. It implied that Asian cultures were inferior to western culture while an alternative policy – to have chappati flour fortified with Vitamin D – was rejected.

It is inappropriate here to assess the Stop Rickets Campaign. Suffice it to say that it created a still unresolved controversy among Asian pressure groups around two issues (see Shelham and Quick, 1982). First, should public health policies in health promotion be advocated rather than private solutions, that is, changes in individuals' behaviour? Secondly, whose norms of behaviour and values should be fostered by health education programmes? These and other related questions which often lurk behind such initiatives are all the more pertinent when it is an ethnic minority that is singled out for state intervention. Why is this group selected now? Which solutions are put forward? Would they replace other policies?

Inevitably, the Stop Rickets Campaign was seen in political terms and the same is to be expected for the AMBC, especially as its scope, with the creation of linkworkers' posts, is more ambitious. The analysis of the causes of the main concerns that have influenced the second campaign will seek to answer some of the questions which have just been raised and thus map out the political orientation of the DHSS initiatives.

The concern with perinatal mortality rates

A member of the DHSS Working Party on Asian Health remarked on the causes for concern which led to the Campaign: 'We identified the area of mothers and babies because the perinatal mortality rates were almost double those of the indigenous populations.' Press releases and newspaper reports on the official launches of the campaign in the DHAs almost invariably pointed to the higher risks of having a stillbirth or a neonatal death among babies of women born on the Indian subcontinent.[8] Articles quoted the fact that babies born to women from Pakistan had exceptionally high mortality rates. Thus, to gain credibility, the campaign mobilized press support around the necessity to improve perinatal mortality rates (PMRs) for Asian-born women.

It is of interest to note that this concern emerged some time after the alarm on perinatal deaths had been raised in relation to all women (irrespective of race). Since the early 1970s, health professionals and lay pressure groups have campaigned to improve the provision of neonatal intensive care units.[9] This outcry culminated in the Short Report (1980) and its claim that 8–10,000 babies a year 'unnecessarily die or suffer permanent handicap in the perinatal and neonatal period' (HMSO, 1980: 158). It was to the campaign's and the health authorities' credit that public attention was at last drawn to alarming differences: for instance, in 1980, there were 26.3 perinatal infant deaths per 1000 mothers born in the UK (OPCS, 1982: 198). But what do these figures measure?

The concept of Perinatal Mortality Rate (PMR) was invented in the 1950s as a means of quantifying success and failure in births. But, since then, according to Oakley (1984), it has been used much more widely. It now links women's health status to the care delivered by health professionals. Therein lies the difficulty of interpreting crude PMRs as social indicators of health inequalities, since they refer to both the professional system of care and the lay world in which women experience their pregnancies. But, with the help of detailed analyses, positive associations can be made between, for instance, high rates and high parity, maternal age, low birthweight or the obstetric experience of family practitioners (see, for example, Lumb *et al.*, 1981; Terry *et al.*, 1980; Clarke and Clayton, 1983).

It is understandable that the campaign reflects the difficulty of interpreting high rates which are the result of complex biological and social events. However, in its reference to PMRs, the campaign tends to isolate the birthplace of first-generation immigrants as the main risk factor and overlooks the other variables which have clear associations with excessive rates. This has produced one unintended consequence. It has exposed the campaign to accusations of stigmatizing Asians because of their race, a theme which will be returned to in the final section of this chapter.

However complex the issues, it is reasonable to say that any public discussion of perinatal mortality would be more informative were it at least to refer to a correlation which has been frequently noted between the less favoured classes and PMRs. Thus, while PMRs have been steadily declining in England and Wales since the 1970s, social differences have tended to persist in relation to PMRs and low birthweight, which remains a significant element in stillbirth and morbidity rates. Thus, in 1980, in England and Wales, perinatal deaths among infants weighing 2500 g or less were 25 times higher than for those over 2500 g.[10] Also, babies born to unskilled manual workers were twice as likely to die within one year as infants born to professionals (Townsend and Davidson, 1982). In a review of the relevant literature up to 1980, MacFarlane and Mugford concluded:

> There is a tendency for the areas with a relatively high proportion of low weight births to have a high proportion of babies with fathers in the less favoured social classes, and high crude rates of stillbirth and death at different stages of the first years of life. [1984]

Thus, in 1985, the infant mortality rate for children born to mothers from professional and managerial groups (social class 1) was 8.9 per 1000 and 18.2 for children of unskilled workers (social class 5). But, as Doyal noticed for Greater London, infant mortality rates vary:

> significantly between boroughs, reaching 14.9 in Kensington, 15.1 in Lewisham, 16.1 in the City and Hackney, and 16.3 in Greenwich. These figures undoubtedly reflect the social class distribution and the number of people from ethnic minorities in the different boroughs . . . it is clear then, that while they are not the only factors involved, race and social and economic status have a strong influence on levels of infant mortality rates in London. [Doyal, n.d.]

Although national statistics do not routinely correlate information on PMRs and social class by parents' ethnic origins,[11] a few local studies have been conducted since the early 1980s which indicate that Asian-born women from the lower social classes are at a higher risk of having stillbirths and infant deaths (see, for example, Gillie *et al.*, 1984).

In 1982, Clarkson observed that the current tendency for the 'Asian low birthweight syndrome' to disappear as maternal health improves would suggest that 'environmental factors contribute to this high risk group'. This may be the case as more recent studies (which do not focus on Asian groups) suggest that types of occupation and working conditions may also influence the outcomes of pregnancy.[12]

Anybody examining statistics on PMRs has to consider these in the light of the deprived conditions in which many people of Asian origins live in inner cities.[13] In 1981, according to the Department of the Environment (1981), about 70 percent of Afro-Caribbean and Asian populations lived in declining industrial districts and over-crowded accommodation. At the same time, another report on London health services (LHPC, 1981) argued that the take-up of services in such deprived areas was likely to be less than in middle-class areas. Such evidence has been gathered since the late 1960s, and demonstrates that morbidity and mortality rates tend to be higher in inner-city areas than elsewhere in the country.[14] According-ing to a survey of health inequalities in the 1980s, there is a growing body of evidence (in Britain) that material and structural factors like housing and income can affect health (Whitehead, 1987). Social deprivation remains a serious health risk factor which the campaign does not discuss in relation to the health care of mothers and babies.

Campaigning messages on improving antenatal care which had been identified in an *ad hoc* way through the Rickets Campaign, gain a scientific authority from references to PMRs but the main remedy proposed, better communication, runs the risk, in the long term, of remaining tangential to the complex causes which deter-mine higher PMRs among some groups of Asian women. Conse-quently, the campaign becomes vulnerable to the criticism that it is engaged in the ideological construction of a 'Black pathology' by taking ' "ethnic groups" as the explanatory independent variable to which ill health is attributed' (Pearson, 1986: 41). This is regrettable as the campaign was inspired by a genuine concern with excessive PMRs.

Although the campaign's approach on communication has been constructed within a medical discourse, this development has merged with a lay view on maternity care which will now be considered.

The concern with the consumers' revolt
There is a striking parallel between the claims made by the campaign and those voiced by such organizations as the Association for Improvements in the Maternity Services or the National Child-birth Trust. The campaign is echoing, in the name of Asian women, the demands of white health consumerism while tending to leave aside the more radical demands made by workers in community health development projects.

The middle-class consumer groups[15] have rejected the techno-logical management of pregnancy and birth which have now become the experience of nearly all women:

> The brave new world of hospital-dominated obstetrical technology . . .
> has generated a new historical response: the consumer revolt . . . .
> Consumer dissatisfaction with antenatal care has always existed . . . but
> the health care and wider political climate of the 1960s and 1970s has
> allowed the dissatisfaction an organisational voice of its own. [Oakley,
> 1984: 236]

This mobilization together with women's self-help groups, inspired by the women's movement, has been arguing that antenatal care cannot be left solely in the hands of the medical professions and state policy-makers. Women with low obstetric risks should be offered midwifery-controlled and community-based care in the whole period of pregnancy and birth. All women should be able to discuss with doctors the benefits and disadvantages of particular interventions, such as Caesarians or inductions, before a clinical decision is taken. Other demands concern the need to give women, in a supportive and sensitive way, more help on diet and parenting generally.

The AMBC staff have repeated these demands: 'The AMBC is about providing an in-depth quality of care to all Asians on a personal level . . . . We should offer more choices, more home confinements, more midwifery care.'

Like the health activists, the AMBC staff who trained the linkworkers are concerned with the quality of antenatal care experienced by Asian women. They emphasize in particular the need for Asian women to 'communicate' with health professionals: 'We want women to express their feelings and not talk to health professionals through their husbands and children.' The AMBC staff did not just ask for non-English-speaking women to be provided with interpreter facilities. They saw the linkworkers' role as being more challenging:

> Linkworkers will speak for their patients. Health professionals shouldn't
> be rude and shout at a mother. If there is a problem like that, the
> linkworker can take it to her manager, who will put an end to the
> situation.

Behind this view is the notion that Asian women, like any other group, are entitled to personalized health care. There appears to be a shift of focus which, in effect, undermines the scientific framework of the campaign. Whereas the campaign's concern with PMRs singles out Asian mothers to bring them under a medicalized system of surveillance, its preoccupation with these mothers' experiences tends to shift the focus away from women as Asians and to identify them with white women who have organized themselves against medical control of their fertility.

What achievements of the consumer movement are relevant to an understanding of the AMBC? It has defined issues in antenatal care which medical and nursing staff cannot settle on their own any more without risking, in extreme cases, some form of protest by individual women or organizations. Since the late 1970s medical researchers have been encouraged to investigate routine hospital procedures and their effectiveness. They have shown that the benefits to be derived from routine antenatal care and education should not be assumed to be limitless.[16] The consumer movement has also suggested a few solutions. The hope for a more sensitive service is pinned on the recruitment of more female registrars and consultants. The extension of community services and preventative provisions like consultants' satellite clinics and pre-conception clinics has been called for. The consumers' revolt has also been a catalyst in the growth of community health projects, like interpreter schemes or health advocates' projects.[17]

Let us consider for a moment the health advocates' schemes, as there is much in common between these programmes and the AMBC. Projects like those from the City and Hackney Health Council were set up in the early 1980s with the aim of overcoming linguistic barriers between non-English-speaking women and the maternity services. They share the view that antenatal care, for too many women from ethnic minorities, had become a largely unsatisfactory experience.[18] But, unlike the campaign, they define the role of their health workers as 'health advocates' and not as 'link-workers'. There is a significant conceptual difference. Thus, as part of her role, the health advocate has 'to ensure that the right questions are asked and the right information sought or given'.[19] One of the main initiators of the City and Hackney scheme, Fedelma Winkler, develops further this conception of the health advocate as a 'watchguard':

> Patient advocates emphasise that they are there to speak for the 'whole patient' . . . they are the person whose job description enables them to cross departmental boundaries in seeking information or solving a problem. They can follow through until a satisfactory solution is found. They have to handle special situations for which no mechanism has been established for dealing with them . . . they can identify problems in interdepartmental communication. They reduce the number of people to whom a patient must explain a problem and/or request a service. [Winkler, 1984]

Health advocates are expected to press for the patients' perspective against the most entrenched practices of health professionals.[20] They are expected to advise the hospitals in which they work about reforms, like the policy of offering women the choice of having female doctors. In other words, their brief is not just to help to improve interpersonal communication but to develop procedures which meet local women's needs. In comparison, the AMBC has developed a more restrictive conception of the linkworkers' roles: 'Linkworkers cannot give any medical advice and they cannot give advice on personal matters but they can give commonsense advice, not professional advice' (AMBC staff). These comments suggest that the linkworkers, unlike the health advocates, are conceived as assistants to health professionals first and representatives of patients second.

These differences are conceptual. Short of evaluative and comparative studies, we do not know what they mean in practice. They are nonetheless significant here. They highlight the points where the rationale of the campaign departs from the more radical demands of consumers' revolt and, by the same token, they help to show how the relations between Asian women and the health services are being defined within the structures of the NHS.

The linkworkers are accountable to health professionals only through the steering committees which manage the linkwork scheme in each district, whereas health advocacy schemes are run mostly through community health councils in co-operation with the NHS and the community. According to Rosenthal (1983) and Dowling (1983), the strength of community projects lies in this managerial structure: they first articulate the needs of local people by working outside the NHS and exercise pressure on the services when they gain access to these.

This form of management does not apply to the AMBC, although the press has tended to present the campaign as a scheme based within Asian communities since a number of health authorities have held a few public meetings. The programme is managed by health authorities, and Asian communities have had only nominal representatives on the steering committees. The director of the campaign explained the managerial structure in these terms:

> My many years of experience in the NHS confirms my impression now that anyone outside the NHS remains an outsider, however good you are. People in the NHS identify with people within it because they are accountable to someone in the NHS. 'Who is any voluntary organisation answerable to?' is what health professionals tell me. . . . Changes have to come from within the services and it is the people working inside who

have to make them. I see the linkworkers working at the grassroot level and changing people's attitudes within the services.[21]

She identifies the question of control by the NHS over 'grassroot' activities as the main reason for opting for a model of change which departs from community-based initiatives. Policies to improve the delivery of service for Asians are expected to come from within the NHS and not from outside.

So the appraisal of the maternity services by the health consumers' movement is closely reflected in the campaign's concerns but with a significant difference. In the campaign's view, Asian women's needs are limited to issues of communication and do not include a demand for increased accountability by the services to Asian groups.

In sum, by publicizing the plight of non-English-speaking patients, the campaign's rationale has incorporated a consumerist perspective which claims that, in the patient–practitioner relationship, the views of the former must not be silenced any more. However, as low-status workers, it is neither within the role and power of the linkworkers to forcefully encourage in their clients qualities of self-reliance and self-assertion *vis-à-vis* health professionals nor to question, alongside the Active Birth Movement, routine medical procedures. Under the linkwork scheme, decision-making remains firmly in the hands of the maternity services, and thus the conception of the scheme deviates from the partnership model between client groups and the services which are advocated by many community-based health groups. The strategy to promote 'reforms from within' is seen by the campaign staff and their sponsors as the best practical solution to the problems as defined. Behind such differences lies the core issue of control over policy-making and the allocation of resources for ethnic minorities which has to be understood within the context of race relations and the NHS.

The concern with racism

The recognition that racial position may affect health has grown significantly in the last thirty years. This development has been uneven. In the 1960s, ministries and the medical professions were engaged in screening immigrants in ports of entry.[22] Their concern later shifted to the mentally ill among ethnic minorities and lately, back to their physical health.

These developments have taken place at a time when Black militancy and inner-city riots have put race relations on the political agenda while debates on how ethnic minorities form their social identities have been raging among militants and intellectuals (Sivan-andan, 1982). Radical organizations together with Black and Asian researchers have documented, and campaigned against, personal and institutional racist practices. They have, for instance, noted the absence of interpreters in areas with a high proportion of non-English-speakers, the absence of educational materials in minority languages, of hospital food acceptable to Asians and Afro-Caribbeans and above all, the failure by many health authorities to implement equal opportunities policies.[23]

Medical treatments have been questioned, such as the use of Depo-Provera (an injectable contraceptive) for women who are not fluent in English and are not informed of the side-effects of the drug.[24] What has been the NHS response to this rising militancy about health among ethnic minorities?

Since its earlier concern with 'a relatively heavy burden on the health services' (HMSO, 1965) which immigrants were (wrongly) feared to inflict on resources, the DHSS was remarkably inactive until the mid 1970s. In 1977, it supported the development of educational materials for (mostly) the nursing professions which aimed to inform them about Asian cultures.[25] The Department also urged local health authorities to follow the spirit of multiculturalism which the Race Relations Act 1976 invited all parties to embrace. Health authorities should consult ethnic minorities on local community care and give them 'suitable' representation on manage-ment boards. However, when circulars have been issued on such concerns, 'they have had little impact on the NHS' (McNaught, 1985). In his review of health care and race in the UK, McNaught observes;

> In the contemporary period the NHS response has been random and lacking in depth. There has not been the recognition that issues of race raise fundamental questions about the goals of health authorities and that race relations initiatives require skilled management at all levels. Race relations initiatives are generally introduced in the absence of clear management strategies and inadequate support. The other problem has been the tendency to pick off individual issues: the DHSS approach is classical in this respect . . . these initiatives can marginalise the issue and be perceived by black and ethnic minority people as stigmatising. [McNaught 1985: 35]

While agreeing with McNaught's conclusions, it is regrettable that he fails to comment on one important aspect of the DHSS interventions: it is the health of Asians and of no other ethnic minority group which is the subject of the three single projects which DHSS has directly funded so far.[26] This singular concern deserves some attention.

Several factors could be at play. First, people of Asian origin form the largest ethnic minority group. Secondly, there is a sizeable number of doctors from the Indian subcontinent who have been working in the NHS since the late 1950s. They have had to deal with racial discrimination within the services like the under-representation of Asian general practitioners on consultative bodies such as the General Medical Council or the over-representations of Black hospital doctors in lower grades and in the least attractive specialties (CRE, 1983; LACRC, 1985). But their representative organizations, like the Overseas Doctors Association, have grown in influence in the health and policy divisions of DHSS. The setting up of the Stop Rickets Campaign and the AMBC are a measure of their success in combating the marginalization of race in health policies. Thirdly, Asian health professionals may share with the ethnic majority a view on race relations which became dominant in the 1960s. Sivanandan's seminal comments on this are relevant here:

> They [Asians] may not be assimilable, but they were certainly made for integration – a parallel society to be accommodated in a pluralist set-up. All that was required was an acceptance of the principles of cultural pluralism on the part of the 'host' population. [Sivanandan, 1982: 115]

The strategy of the state in relation to Asians has been to turn cultural antagonism into cultural pluralism:

> They had their own TV and radio programmes, their mosques and their temples, their shops and cinema and social centres. More importantly, they had thrown up leaders and spokesmen who could talk to and worked with the state. They had remained parallel in terms of culture, they had merged in terms of class. [Sivanandan, 1982: 121]

According to Sivanandan, unlike the Afro-Caribbeans, the Asian middle classes (including doctors) formed a successful alliance with their white counterparts. This current situation explains the prominence of Asian health in the DHSS individual projects. It may also have influenced the campaign's strategy towards racism. How?

The AMBC linkworkers' training syllabus examined problems which are largely to do with cross-cultural communication (naming systems; medical terminology in Asian languages, and so on). The AMBC staff strongly held the view that, were health workers to acquire more information about Asian diets and cultures generally, derogatory attitudes towards Asian patients would melt away. This position is reminiscent of an earlier DHSS initiative on teaching materials for Asians.[27] In both cases, ethnocentricity is seen as a product of individuals' ignorance. At a theoretical level, English and other ethnic identities are thought to derive from a 'two-way reactive process' which is created by the ever-changing relations between the dominant white cultural system and Black and Asian subcultures (Kahn, 1982). Remove 'cultural barriers' – a favourite term among the campaign staff – and racist practices will be removed too.

This hope is certainly realistic in many cases. For instance, although language interpretation removes 'the language barrier', it falls short of assisting those health professionals who fail to understand their patients' commonsense views on health. According to the director of the campaign: 'This makes the assessment of their needs problematic from the start. The health visitors who are confronted with such a problem should get the assistance of linkworkers.'[28]

The culturalist approach has, however, been criticized for being oblivious to the growing research evidence of structural racism in the NHS.[29] According to Lawrence (1982), the cultural model reduces the positions of Asians and Afro-Caribbeans to those of any populations living in Britain who are not of English descent. By focusing mostly on cultural determinants of oppression like personal prejudice, this position fails to examine critically how covert, institutional racism also produces a 'racist patriarchal ideology based on common sense ideas of Asian sexuality/femininity' (Parmar, 1982: 258); see, for instance, the stereotyping of Asian female patients. As the AMBC reflects a cultural understanding of racism, how does this affect its response to racial politics in health?

The campaign's strategy on racism has altered dramatically over the last two years. In their first talks with health professionals on the aims and scope of the campaign, trainers were instructed not to use the word 'racism' for fear of alienating them irrevocably.[30] Asked in February 1985 to explain her position on racism in the services, the director of the campaign thought that to address health professionals on racism would be counterproductive: 'There would be a backlash from them and it would do nothing to improve the delivery of service.'

The initial campaign strategy assumed that racism was not, then, on the agenda for a public debate. But a gradual change of course appeared. While a discussion of 'racism in the NHS' occupied a short session in the training syllabus of the first linkworkers, it was given more time when the linkworkers were trained in the second year. Briefing to health professionals highlighted racist and other bad practices. In October 1986, the campaign further acknowledged that racism in the NHS was a public issue, when it organized a conference on racism in the NHS for the linkworkers and their managers which the Tory Minister of Health, Edwina Currie, attended at the end of the day.

Had there been a radical reversal of policy on the linkworkers' role? Yes and no. While the linkworkers were not initially trained to identify racial prejudice, they were now encouraged to do so and health authorities were urged to send more staff on race awareness training programmes.

This development came, in part, out of the testimonies by the campaign staff and the linkworkers that personal racism was rife in the areas where they were working and, in part, out of external pressures on the authorities. In some districts, local groups attempted to mobilize political forces against the health authority for running a 'racist' campaign. They criticized its deficit model of health inequalities, which blames Asian cultures and languages for the failure of the services to deliver suitable care. In a letter to the chair of a local steering committee in May 1986, a group of local Asian organizations stated:

> All you have done is to locate and separate our 'cultural difficulties' and 'communication problems' as the cause of your concern, and it logically follows that it's the 'fault' of Asian mothers for the high perinatal rates. Implicit to it is the distorted, invidious, racist logic that the 'victim' is the 'cause'.

Accusations of the campaign being racist and sexist merge here. Like most health education initiatives whose strategies are modelled solely on a behavioural approach to health promotion, the campaign is certainly not free from elements of a victim-blaming ideology (Russell, 1982). Thus, it is targeted at *all* Asian women, irrespective of their birthplace and social position. The burden of change is placed on them as they are urged to accept medical instructions largely uncritically. However, this is only part of the story. The campaign is gradually challenging not only personal racism by giving a voice to Asian women as Black users of the NHS – through, for instance, its training videos for health workers and accompanying materials – but also structural racism in service provision – by pointing out, for example, inadequate interpreters' facilities, inadequate Asian food or a lack of relevant health education materials.

In spite of these developments, the campaign remains within the perspective of cultural pluralism. There has been no dramatic U-turn in policy. The AMBC does not take on board the material implications for health status of racial and class disadvantages (the effects of poverty on mothers' nutrition, for example). In brief, on the issue of racism, the AMBC staff remain cautious, probably as a result of the campaign's patronage by the DHSS:

> DHSS moves very slowly and equal opportunities policies take years and years to implement. One should push for them and there are groups who should do it. But meanwhile, somebody has to look after these women who face language problems and bad service.[31]

Here the director of the campaign raises a question which creates a fundamental division between reformists and radicals: should ethnic minorities struggle for reforms which alleviate some of the effects of discrimination *now* or push for long-term, structural change? Clearly determined by its position *vis-à-vis* the DHSS and the health professions, the AMBC strategy is to follow the first option and not the second.

However, unlike the overtly racist ideology of containment which lay behind the 'port medicine' of the 1960s, the political impulse behind the campaign belongs to a liberal, reformist perspective on race relations. The agents of change are seen to be, primarily, individuals with good will (white and Asian) and not collective forces – hence, possibly, the paternalistic view expressed by the Junior Minister of Health at the AMBC conference mentioned earlier, that it was up to the linkworkers who are after all 'powerful ladies' (*sic!*) to combat racism in the NHS successfully . . . after having a word with the chairman of the health authority!

This position lends the campaign a certain democratic appeal – something can be done *now* by women in saris – but one of the effects is to camouflage its political struggle against racism. The campaign is thus engaged in a consensus-making process which constitutes Asian families as a 'special client group' (together with such other groups as mentally handicapped or the disabled). This strategy aims to gain the active support of health professionals without changing existing priorities in policies and to avoid the risk of antagonizing those health workers who would object to any form of positive discrimination in favour of ethnic minorities. For instance, in a speech to the Health Visitors Association which introduced the AMBC in 1985, John Patten (Parliamentary Under-Secretary of State at the DHSS) went to great lengths to emphasize that recognizing the needs of ethnic minorities does not imply any positive discrimination:

> It is not a question of picking out certain groups *for priority treatment, for especially favoured treatment*, but . . . equal treatment does not necessarily mean treating everyone in exactly the same way. I would pick out the special needs of certain ethnic groups, or the members of

ethnic groups, as being no different in style from special treatment for, let us say, the disabled or the elderly suffering, as they might do, from Alzheimer's disease, or any other particular group . . . . *Those needs just happen to be ethnic. It would be neither here nor there if they were not ethnic.* It is a special group that needs special treatment and that is what the NHS has set out to try to provide, reflecting local conditions. [Patten, 1985: 9, emphasis added]

This oversimplification is rather absurd! If race is 'neither here nor there' why constitute 'ethnic minorities' as a 'special group'? Why are there not already more interpreters' facilities supported by mainstream funding? Where does the need to reassure health professionals that the NHS does not set out to provide 'priority treatment' come from, if not from the fact that the racial locations in the health care system of patients and providers of care does matter in most complex ways?

Patten, like the campaign, addresses institutional racism indirectly, and in spite of claims to the contrary, it is individuals who are expected to change – not so much policies. Yet, when stigmatization of Black patients arises, this is a practice which is not due only to individuals' beliefs and values on race. It is the outcome of at least two distinct sets of political processes. The first is experienced by all such clients, that is, the ideological impact which is derived from the health services' power to define the pathologies of specific groups without always engaging in a dialogue with them (and their carers) about their self-assessed needs. The second is formed by racist practices within and outside the services which cannot be remedied through definitions and redefinitions of individuals' needs alone. In order to undermine the cumulative effects of these processes, a reallocation of power to ethnic minorities in the decision-making structures of the NHS is necessary. It is on this crucial aspect of racial politics in the maternity services that the campaign, because of its pluralist rationale, remains silent.

Conclusion

The cultural approach in no way entails any fundamental change in the structural position of ethnic minorities *vis-à-vis* the NHS. The analysis of the campaign rationale has, hopefully, made this clear. However, it would be wrong to conceive the campaign as mere tokenism or, worse, a racist initiative. Such views would underestimate its significance in the contemporary context of race and health care.

To locate the campaign in its socio-historical context is not to deny its pioneering work. The campaign is a 'new' venture so far as it brings together all the themes discussed. This is not an easy task at a time when district authorities and health professionals are not all enamoured with the government's current financial stringencies and managerial policies. Some may see the scheme as another example of direct funding by the government which increases its control over the allocation of scarce resources in the delivery of services. (Glennerster, 1985)

By and large, the AMBC does not break totally fresh ground. It follows the Stop Rickets Campaign, from which it inherited much of its design and management structure. It is also rooted in medical debates on how to measure obstetric risks and what these mean for antenatal care and health education. It relates to community-based health projects which have been inspired by the health consumers' revolt against 'high tech' obstetrics and depersonalized hospital care. The campaign is also in the liberal tradition of the DHSS interventions in policy-making for ethnic minorities. This tradition tends to substitute legitimation of piecemeal reforms for account-ability, and accommodation of marginal groups for egalitarian partnership. The political significance of the campaign lies in the need for the welfare state to create a consensus, mostly among health professionals, on how the health authorities should respond to the demands of ethnic minorities. Pluralist strategies are put forward on the assumption that multiracial care will naturally emerge once communication needs have been fulfilled. This type of reform may be radical enough to undermine personal racism. Asian linkworkers claim that often many initial difficulties – staff attitudes towards themselves and Asian patients – are improving. Precisely how this strategy will affect institutional racism remains obscure. What is clear is that the campaign was not designed to tackle it.

What is new is not the campaign's rationale but the scale of its intervention in the politics of health consumerism and health and race. Some of the controversies which surround the campaign have been its identification with these wider debates. They have in common a crucial problem: the difficulty of establishing priorities as to 'whose needs' and 'which needs' should be met. For example, should improvements in obstetrics and paediatrics be decided mostly upon doctors' interpretations of perinatal and neonatal rates as suggested by the Short Report? Should health authorities continue to employ low-status workers to help mothers and other groups like the Asian elderly or Asian victims of coronary heart disease? Would such schemes undermine English ethnocentricity and related aspects of racism in the NHS, or would equal opportunities policies achieve this Herculean task more effectively?

Any answers to these questions have a profoundly political nature because skills which are exercised to improve health generate subtle but real power relations between the health professionals and their subjects. This is particularly the case if these subjects – women, children and (one must add) Blacks – are already ascribed to subordinate positions by wider social relations. Although in our perceptions of our bodies, of health and of medical practices, we are all subject to long-established forms of medical power (Foucault, 1976), we are not always passive consumers of that power (Stacey, 1976). Movements of resistance are born out of antagonistic relations, as between women health activists and the maternity services, or Asian pressure groups and health authorities. This objective and unstable reality explains the conflicting responses to the campaign initiatives found among Asian community leaders. One of these commented on their ambivalence:

> The Campaign has been credited to our account and if tomorrow another issue comes up people will say: 'if they (the Asians) are not able to show much benefit, why should we waste more money for these people?' But we would like proper consultation so that we can advise the Authorities whether we are benefiting or not.

In the absence of a coherent, detailed and comprehensive DHSS strategy to promote a democratic health-care system, piecemeal reforms like the AMBC are most likely to improve interpersonal communication between Black patients and staff, as well as specific aspects of service provision. One should not, therefore, under-estimate such achievements. It would certainly justify the employment of linkworkers on a permanent basis. However, in the long run the progressive impact of such initiatives will be gauged not just by fluctuations in mortality rates and the delivery of a more sensitive service but by the type and scale of participation in both the allocation of resources and assessment of services which ethnic minorities will gradually demand from health authorities. Contrary to appearances, political change (if any) may be easier to assess than counts of infant death.

Notes

1 This chapter uses the term Asian to refer to people who share cultures derived from the Indian subcontinent. Some may prefer to be called Asian, others 'Black' or 'members of ethnic minorities'. All of these terms are used here.

2 In 1982–3, the Centre for Ethnic Minorities Health Studies carried out a survey of initiatives in maternity care for Black and ethnic minority users by the NHS, local authorities or the voluntary sector: 46 projects were identified and only 5 of these were initiated by health authorities. See Maternity Alliance (1985).

3 Letter to District Administrator from the campaign, September 1984.

4 Ibid.

5 This chapter is based on an evaluation of the AMBC project conducted at the Centre for Mass Communication Research, University of Leicester.

6 The perinatal mortality rate is the number of stillbirths and deaths in the first week of life per 1000 live and stillbirths.

7 Personal racism refers to the conscious or unconscious prejudice and discriminatory attitudes held by individuals towards Blacks. It is related to institutional racism. The latter is created by the overt or covert structural processes found in organizations which discriminate against ethnic minorities.

8 See, for instance, 'Campaign to Lower Asian Baby Deaths', *The Times*, 13 September 1984.

9 Their intervention is discussed in greater detail in the next section.

10 For a large survey of trends in low birthweights, see Stewart *et al.* (1981).

11 For a discussion of the ethnic question in national birth statistics, see OPCS (1980).

12 For a review of the studies on work and mental health, see Garcia and Elbourne (1984).

13 These issues are discussed in Runnymede Trust/Radical Statistics Group (1980); PEP (1977); Brown (1984); and Townsend and Davidson (1982).

14 For a comprehensive review of the literature on inequality and the health service in the 1970s, see Cartwright and O'Brien (1976).

15 The consumers' revolt is not a homogeneous movement, but differences in emphasis cannot be explored in this brief survey.

16 See, for example, Hall *et al.* (1980); and Reid and McIllwaine (1980).

17 For discussion of the origins and aims of the community health movement, see Somerville (1984).

18 See, for example, Homans (1980); Greater London Council Ethnic Minorities Unit (1985); and Larbie (1985).

19 Handout on health advocates from Haringey Community Health Council, 1984.

20 Such schemes have been modelled on health advocacy projects working in American hospitals.

21 Tape-recorded interview, 6 September 1985.

22 See, for example, Brent Community Health Council (1981), and Johnson (1984).

23 See, for example, Wandsworth and East Merton Health District (1979); Mayer (1983); Brent Community Health Council (1981); and Rathwell (1985).

24 See, for example, Torkington (1983); Wilson (1983); Larbie (1985); and Donovan (1986).

25 This was a DHSS project established in conjunction with the National Extension College and the King's Fund Project. Teaching packs and books to assist the learning of NHS staff have since been produced. See Henley (1979).

26 Apart from the Stop Rickets Campaign and the AMBC, the other DHSS-sponsored project is based at the National Extension College. See Note 25.

27 See Note 25.

28 Tape-recorded interview, 4 February 1985.

29 See, for example, Parmar (1982); Lawrence (1982); and Homans (1980).

30 Personal interviews with trainers, 1985–6.

31 Tape-recorded interview, 6 September 1985.

References

Brent Community Health Council (1981) *Black People and the Health Service*. London: Brent Community Health Council.

Brown, C. (1984) *Black and White Britain: Third PSI Survey*. London: Heinemann.

Cartwright, A. and O'Brien, M. (1976) 'Social Class Variations in Health Care and in the Nature of General Practitioner Consultations', in M. Stacey (ed.) *The Sociology of the National Health Service*. Sociological Review Monograph, no. 22, University of Keele.

Clarke, M. and Clayton, D.G. (1983) 'Quality of Obstetric Care Provided for Asian Immigrants in Leicestershire', *British Medical Journal*, 286 (19 Feb.): 621–3.

Clarkson, M.G. (1982) *Archives of Disease in Childhood* (57): 867.

Commission for Racial Equality (1983) *Ethnic Minority Hospital Staff*. London: Commission for Racial Equality.

Department of the Environment (1981) *Census Indicators of Urban Deprivation*. London: HMSO.

Donovan, J. (1983) 'Black People's Health: A Different Way Forward', *Radical Community Medicine*, Winter: 20–9.

Donovan, J. (1986) *We Don't Buy Sickness, It Just Comes: Health, Illness and Health Care in the Lives of Black People in London*. Aldershot: Gower.

Dowling, S. (1983) *Health for a Change: The Provision of Preventative Health Care in Pregnancy and Early Childhood*. London: Child Poverty Action Group/National Extension College.

Doyal, L. (n.d.) *Unhealthy Lives: Being a Woman in London*. A report commissioned by Greater London Council, Industry and Employment Branch. Available from the Women's Studies Unit, Polytechnic of North London.

Foucault, M. (1976) *The Birth of the Clinic*. London: Tavistock.

Garcia, J. and Elbourne, D. (1984) 'Future Research on Work in Pregnancy', in G. Chamberlain (ed.) *Pregnant Women at Work*. Basingstoke: Royal Society of Medicine/Macmillan.

Gillie, D.R.N., Lealman, G.T., Lumb, K.M. and Congdon, P. (1984) 'Analysis of Ethnic Influence on Stillbirth and Infant Mortality in Bradford 1975–1981'. *Journal of Epidemiology and Community Health*, 38: 214–17.

Glennerster, H. (1985) *Paying for Welfare*. Oxford: Blackwell.

Greater London Council Ethnic Minorities Unit (1985) *Ethnic Minorities and the National Health Service in London*. London: Greater London Council.

Hall, M., Chng, P.K. and MacGillivray, I. (1980) 'Is Routine Antenatal Care Worthwhile?' *The Lancet*, 12 July: 72–80.

Henley, A. (1979) *Asian Patients in Hospital and at Home*. London: King Edward's Hospital Fund for London.

HMSO (1965) *White Paper on Commonwealth Immigration*. London: HMSO.

HMSO (1980) *Perinatal and Neonatal Mortality: Second Report of the Social Services Committee*. House of Commons Paper 663–1 (Session 1979–80). London: HMSO (The Short Report).

HMSO (1986) *Perinatal and Neonatal Mortality Report: Follow up. Third Report from the Social Services Committee*. London: HMSO.

Homans, H. (1980) 'Pregnant in Britain: A Sociological Approach to Asian and British Women's Experiences'. PhD thesis, University of Warwick.

Johnson, M.R.D. (1984) 'Ethnic Minorities and Health', *Journal of the Royal College of Physicians of London*, 18: 228–30.

Kahn, V.S. (1982) 'The Role of Cultural Dominance in Structuring the Experience of Ethnic Minorities', in C. Husband (ed.) *Race in Britain: Continuity and Change*. London: Hutchinson.

Larbie, J. (1985) *Black Women and the Maternity Services: A Survey of Thirty Years of Afro-Caribbean Women's Experiences and Perceptions of Pregnancy and Childbirth*. London: Training in Health and Race.

Lawrence, E. (1982) 'In the Abundance of Water the Fool is Thirsty: Sociology and Black "Pathology" ', in Centre for Contemporary Cultural Studies, *The Empire Strikes Back: Race and Racism in 70s Britain*. London: Hutchinson.

London Association of Community Relations Councils (1985) *In a Critical Condition: A Survey of Equal Opportunities in London's Health Authorities*. London: London Association of Community Relations Councils.

London Health Planning Consortium (1981) *Primary Health Care in Inner London: Report of a Study Group*. London: London Health Planning Consortium.

Lumb, K.M., Congdon, P.J. and Lealman, G.T. (1981) 'A Comparative Review of Asian and British-born Maternity Patients in Bradford, 1974–1978', *Journal of Epidemiology and Community Health*, 35: 106–9.

MacFarlane, A. and Mugford, M. (1984) *Birth Counts: Statistics of Pregnancy and Childbirth*. London: HMSO.

McNaught, A. (1985) *Race and Health Care in the United Kingdom*. London: Health Education Council, Occasional Paper no. 2.

Maternity Alliance (1985) *Multi-racial Initiatives in Maternity Care – a Directory of Projects for Black and Ethnic Women*. London: Maternity Alliance.

Mayer, L. (1983) *A Pregnant Pause? Communication between Women whose First Language is not English, and Antenatal Clinics in Paddington and North Kensington*. London: Paddington and North Kensington Community Health Council.

Oakley, A. (1984) *The Captured Womb: A History of the Medical Care of Pregnant Women*. Oxford: Blackwell.

Office of Population and Census Statistics (OPCS) (1980) *OPCS Monitor*, CEN 80/2. London: OPCS.

Office of Population and Census Statistics (OPCS) (1982) *Mortality Statistics: Perinatal and Infant*. Series DH3 no. 9. London: OPCS.

Parmar, P. (1982) 'Gender, Race and Class: Asian Women in Resistance', in Centre for Contemporary Cultural Studies, *The Empire Strikes Back: Race and Racism in 70s Britain*. London: Hutchinson.

Patten, J. (1985) Opening address to Conference on 'Ethnic Minorities: Between Two Cultures' at the National Association for Maternal and Child Welfare, 26 June. Annual Conference Report.

Pearson, M. (1986) 'Racist Notions of Ethnicity and Culture in Health Education', in S. Rodmell and A. Watt (eds) *The Politics of Health Education: Raising the Issues*. London: Routledge & Kegan Paul.

Political and Economic Planning (PEP) (1977) *Racial Disadvantage in Britain*. Harmondsworth: Penguin.

Rathwell, T. (ed.) (1985) *Health, Race and Ethnicity*. London: Croom Helm.

Reid, M. and McIllwaine, G.M. (1980) 'Consumer Opinion of a Hospital Antenatal Clinic', *Social Science and Medicine*, 14A: 363–8.

Rosenthal, H. (1983) 'Neighbourhood Health Projects – Some New Approaches to Health and Community Work in Parts of the United Kingdom', *Community Development Journal*, 18(2): 120–31.

Runnymede Trust/Radical Statistics Group (1980) *Britain's Black Population*. London: Heinemann Educational Books.

Russell, J. (1982) 'Perinatal Mortality: the Current Debate', *Sociology of Health and Illness*, 4(3), November.

Save The Children Fund (1983) *The Stop the Rickets Campaign*. London: Save the Children Fund.

Shelham, H. and Quick, A. (1982) *The Rickets Report: Why Do British Asians Get Rickets?* London: Haringey Community Health Council.

Sivanandan, A. (1982) *A Different Hunger*. London: Pluto Press.

Somerville, G. (1984) *Community Development in Health: Addressing the Confusions*. London: London Community Health Resource/King's Fund Centre.

Stacey, M. (1976) 'The Health Service Consumer: A Sociological Misconception', in M. Stacey (ed.), *The Sociology of the N.H.S.* Sociological Review Monograph no. 22, University of Keele.

Stewart, A.L., Reynolds, E.O.R. and Lipscomb, A.P. (1981) 'Outcome for Infants of VLBW: Survey of World Literature', *The Lancet*, 9 May: 1038–41.

Terry, P.B., Condie, R.G. and Settatree, R.S. (1980) 'Analysis of Ethnic Differences in Perinatal Statistics', *British Medical Journal*, 281, 13 November.

Torkington, P. (1983) 'The Racist and Sexist Delivery of the National Health Service – the Experience of Black Women', *Spare Rib*, 138.

Townsend, P. and Davidson, N. (1982) *Inequalities in Health: The Black Report*. Harmondsworth: Penguin.

Wandsworth and East Merton Health District (1979) *Ethnic Minorities and the Health Service: Report of the Working Party on the Provision of Health Services to Ethnic Minorities living in the Wandsworth and East Merton District*. London: Wandsworth and East Merton Health District (teaching).

Whitehead, M. (1987) *The Health Divide: Inequalities in Health in the 1980s*. London: Health Education Council.

Wilson, M. (1983) 'Networking for Health', *Health and Social Services Journal*, 12 May.

Winkler, F. (1984) *Multi-Ethnic Health Workers Project*. London: City and Hackney Community Health Council.

III
RESTRUCTURING THE
WELFARE STATE

As this book's introduction points out, the decade of the 1980s has been widely interpreted as a watershed for the British welfare state. At its most straightforward this was expressed in the view that the Conservative government elected in 1979 and led by Margaret Thatcher represented a break with the underlying principles of the welfare state constructed after 1945. According to this interpretation, before the middle 1970s there was a broad consensus on welfare organized around notions of universalism and state intervention to achieve greater equality and provide forms of social support. After this time, the consensus began to break up, undermined by economic failure which meant that the costs of welfare provision could not be sustained. At the same time challenges to the old system increased, as individuals and groups complained about the bureaucratic means of delivery and the ways in which in practice it continued to reinforce inequality. The welfare state was in crisis.

If the welfare state was built around the programme of social democracy represented by Keynes and Beveridge, then the changes introduced by the Conservative governments of the 1980s seemed to be the practical expression of the ideas of the 'New Right'. The 'New Right' appeared to have a programme which resolved the crisis of the welfare state by stressing the importance of the market and the necessity for economic renewal. This programme was often summarized in a slogan which called for the 'rolling back' of the state. Its supporters criticized those who favoured an extensive role for the state in economy or society, arguing that the British welfare state contained the seeds of its own failure within it.

This is essentially the view expressed by Johnson in the first chapter of this section. He identifies a political crisis in the 1970s generated by the coming together of relative economic decline and a popular expectation of continuing material improvement. He is particularly critical of what he calls the providential view of government – that is the view that the government can be relied on to provide economic growth and material well-being, alongside an extensive framework of social services. On this interpretation, the post-1945 welfare state sponsored a move away from self-help and voluntary activity, towards a reliance on the state for support. The political process encouraged politicians and governments to make promises which they then could not deliver. In turn, argues Johnson, this began to weaken the authority of political institutions.

He is especially critical of the role of the trade unions which, he suggests, misused their power to win concessions without considering their impact on the economy. He argues that the unions represented major obstacles to the introduction of political changes which had become necessary by the end of the 1970s. For Johnson, the Thatcher governments made such changes possible for the first time. He stresses Margaret Thatcher's populism; her ability to appeal to 'ordinary people' over the heads of political elites. The key elements he identifies in the new world of the 1980s are a shift to support for the market; a move away from a view of government as 'universal provider'; and a move towards traditional institutions outside the state (including the family and voluntary organizations). The limits of the state are stressed. But he also concludes that many of the features of the welfare state survive, and that the changes are cautious, rather than revolutionary.

One of the central points stressed by Johnson is the need to give a greater role to the market. He particularly emphasizes its importance for economic growth, but, in the following chapter, Barry takes matters further to point to the market as a wider principle for the organization of social life. He rejects models of the market which start from notions of perfect competition and equilibrium, both because they can never be found in reality, and because their absence may as a result be used to justify state involvement. Instead, he stresses the messiness of market processes as a means of encouraging prosperity and ultimately increasing social benefits. He says that the market should be seen as an evolutionary process, in which co-ordination is an unintended consequence of individual decisions by entrepreneurs. He contrasts the effectiveness of the price mechanism with what he sees as the ineffectiveness of state intervention.

Barry favours a gradualist approach to the reintroduction of market principles in British society. He uses the example of the privatization of nationalized industries, and suggests a modest process of change. In practice rather more was privatized in the late 1980s than he expected or predicted in this chapter. Barry's commitment to market mechanisms also leaves him with some doubts about the value of supporting large commercial monopolies, although he still feels the market can deal better with them than the state can. He emphasizes the need to encourage the growth of small firms and in this context he justifies the setting up of enterprise zones, although in practice their operation has tended to encourage more rather than less state intervention.

The key point about the welfare state underlying Barry's arguments is the view that state officials do not always act for the public good. On the contrary, their position within the state makes such a result less rather than more likely. Unlike entrepreneurs within the market, rational action by individual bureaucrats will tend (not deliberately but nonetheless surely) to reduce social welfare. Since bureaucratic success is measured in terms of budgets managed and staff supervised, bureaucratic management will tend to encourage a growth of budgets and staff, without necessarily improving welfare. Alliances will be made with particular groups which tend to support the position of those allocating resources (and building professional empires). Barry also argues that a great deal of welfare spending creates unemployment, in particular spending on benefits and subsidized housing, because it makes low-paid employment unattractive. As a result he concludes that only narrowly defined public goods – such as the maintenance of a legal system – should be provided by the state. The state should not generally intervene, since left to its own devices the market itself will be an equalizing force.

The 'New Right' could be caricatured as simply concerned with the market, even if the case is as subtly argued as it is by Barry. But it was a more complex phenomenon, combining arguments from a range of sources to produce a political position appealing powerfully to different elements of popular consciousness – allowing Johnson to conclude that Thatcher's appeal struck a chord with the ideas of ordinary people. As well as identifying an economic and political crisis, a moral crisis was also identified. Davies puts this view most strongly. He argues that the rising crime rate, the breakdown in family life, and of what he calls civility are symptoms of a wider erosion of a belief in moral rules. He charts the symptoms of demoralization. According to Davies one of the problems is that the acts of individuals are always explained in terms that minimize individual responsibility. He criticizes notions of moral relativism according to which the main concern is to ensure that a person's desires are never to be thwarted. He forcefully rejects the arguments of those who say there is no real problem and blames the continuing influence of 'progressive' ideas associated with the high period of consensus in the 1960s.

In addition he points to the ways in which public policy has effectively endorsed these attitudes. The post-1945 welfare state, he argues, provided a basis on which the denial of individual responsibility was effectively encouraged, as it replaced other forms of social organization, including family, church and voluntary organizations. Here, too, there are echoes of Johnson's arguments and his concerns about the erosion of self-help. Davies laments the move to large-scale, collective intervention through the state and the transfer of power to professionals which is implied by it. He expresses concern about the end of family life and parental authority, arguing that stability is needed for the maintenance of an effective moral code. He points to the successes of the Victorian era, based on voluntary activity alongside the confidence of liberal commercial society and stresses that there was a decline in the crime rate throughout the period. He concludes that this means new state policies will not solve problems, but that a process of cultural renewal is required. One element in achieving this would, he says, be to move social policy away from the paternalism which he feels is dominant: cash benefits should be provided to allow the poor and disadvantaged to make their own choices about how to spend them. Social workers should become 'enablers' rather than providers.

If there were strong arguments from the Right, what of the response from the Left? To what extent were they able to or did they seek to defend the welfare state with which they were so clearly identified? These questions are taken up in the next two chapters. In the first of these, Gamble starts by setting out the main features of the old consensus before going on to survey the responses to new challenges from within it. He stresses that similar pressures existed in other western countries, in the wake of readjustments within the world economic system in the course of the 1970s. Like Johnson he notes that the authority of government was reduced because what it could achieve was also reduced. The position of national governments within an international system, itself facing economic problems, significantly restricted their room for manoeuvre. This problem was perhaps particularly sharp in the UK, but it was not unique to the UK (as Johnson's arguments tend to imply). Unlike Johnson, Gamble argues that the notion of overpowerful trade unions is mistaken and suggests that the attack on trade unions was part of a more general attack on the post-war consensus. He argues that the old consensus began to fall apart both because it could no longer deliver in economic terms, and also because it had lost its will to preserve the foundations of social order and public authority.

Although there are similarities between the explanations offered by Left and Right because each stresses underlying economic problems, the policy responses proposed are quite different. As we have seen, the Right argued for a shift towards the market and for a moral crusade. The Left sought instead to develop what came to be called an Alternative Economic Strategy. The failures of Labour governments in the late 1970s and their reluctance to implement the main features of the strategy, encouraged a campaign within the

Labour Party in the early 1980s which was intended to limit the freedom of its leaders to act outside agreed party policy. One consequence was the splitting of the party with the birth of the Social Democratic Party. Throughout the 1980s Labour remained fragmented and unable seriously to challenge the Thatcher governments. Its attention continued instead to be directed to resolving its own internal crisis. Towards the middle of the decade it was already becoming clear, as Gamble notes, that the party (under the leadership of Neil Kinnock) was beginning to move back to the centre in a search for electoral support, but to a centre whose boundaries had effectively been determined by the policies of Thatcher governments.

Thatcherism appeared to have won, with electoral victories in 1979, 1983 and 1987. But did it offer the basis of a new consensus? Gamble is sceptical. He argues that matters are less straightforward than such a conclusion would suggest. In particular, he notes that levels of public expenditure on welfare were not cut significantly in the first half of the 1980s, and suggests that, despite all the rhetoric on both sides, in the NHS and education sectors major changes have been slow in coming. Despite the hopes expressed by Davies, it looks as if moral disorder (however measured) has continued and probably increased. In retrospect, Gamble argues that the Thatcher decade looks more like a transitional phase than a new era. He suggests that the apparent power of Thatcherism was exaggerated by fragmentation on the Left. He sees the 1980s as a continuation of a longer tradition rather than a break with it, merely reinforcing an existing bias against intervention in industry and finance, compared with many other European countries.

From Gamble's perspective, the issues raised by the breakdown of the post-war consensus have still not been resolved. And the position of the Left remains uncertain. Like the 'New Right', however, Gamble stresses the need to resolve economic problems as the basis for a wider welfare settlement. Unlike them his arguments for reindustrialization stress that the market cannot solve all the problems, and they point to a continued role for the state. He does not call for a return to the past but for the development of a new set of arrangements. One attempt to see more clearly what these might be was represented in moves towards local or municipal socialism in the early 1980s, which are discussed by Green.

The importance of these local experiments lies not so much in their impact or the extent to which they spread more widely, but in the evidence they provide about possible alternatives to the policies which dominated in the 1980s. The high point of local socialism was short-lived and its success was predicated on wider political change (including the return of a Labour government) which did not take place, but the experience helps to illustrate the extent to which the new ground rules on welfare remained highly contested. Green starts by noting the social and political changes which made the rise of local socialism possible. A key feature of this was the desire to challenge not only the approach of the newly elected Thatcher government, but also to break with the political assumptions of Labour governments in the 1970s. The local leaders saw part of their task to be the provision of an alternative to the methods of the past. They were concerned to show what was possible in practice as well as presenting a political critique. Green identifies two key features of their programme: first the development of local economic planning and secondly moves to reshape the ways in which welfare was delivered. The first implied a continued commitment to economic intervention (in contrast to the policies of the market) and the second encouraged a focus on decentralization and grassroots democracy. But he also shows some of the problems the councils faced in successfully implementing the new policies.

The end of the new municipal socialism as a serious challenge to the centre came in conflicts over local taxation and levels of spending. Since the Left authorities retained a commitment to spending on welfare at local level – they started out with opposition to cuts – they soon came into direct conflict with a central government committed to restricting state spending. And in effect the defeat of the campaigns over rate-capping also meant the end of the experiment – or at any rate a shift to more carefully modulated forms of opposition and the search for other forms of ally at local level. In the case of Sheffield – from which Green draws many of his examples – there was a move away from the language of radical interventionism at the start of the decade towards a partnership with local business at its end. Gamble's discussion of the moves towards the centre within the Labour Party at national level also found reflection at local level, as Left councils began to recognize that they would have to survive in a more hostile environment.

The debates between the two sides are important, but neither seemed to pay much attention to those consuming welfare or defined as 'clients' of the welfare state. In his chapter, Seabrook develops a bleak vision of the welfare state in the 1980s by coming at the issue from a rather different angle. He tries to look at the welfare state from below, from the perspective of those receiving benefit of various sorts. For them it is the continuity of that state in shaping their lives which is most important, rather than any changes in the 1980s. His analysis is rather fatalistic. His welfare 'consumers' are demoralized – victims rather than actors in their own right. He stresses their passivity and acquiescence, despite the daily problems they face. Seabrook's conclusions are equally fatalistic. He suggests that the moves towards market methods and materialism have undermined necessary forms of collectivism within working-class communities. In direct contrast to the arguments of Davies, he argues that there should be a move away from monetized to demonetized transactions, so that the exclusion of the poor from what money can buy no longer dominates their lives.

The critique of post-war welfare state developed by Williams in the following chapter is also rather different from those of Gamble or Green, although like them it can be located on the Left. She draws on arguments from feminist and anti-racist approaches. Like Seabrook, her arguments suggest that it is the continuity of the welfare state, rather than any sharp break, which is most important. Unlike him, however, she points to the ways in which the experience of the welfare state is likely to vary for different groups in the population – Black and white, men and women, working class and middle class. Equally important, she explores the ways in which these groups play different roles *within* the welfare state. Williams' analysis stresses the role played by Black men, Black women and white women in reducing the costs of social expenditure; she explores their role in the process of social reproduction, and in the ways in which they are differentially affected by the welfare state as a system of social control. She is highly critical of those who fail to take account of race and gender in their analysis of welfare.

Her political message is different, too. Williams points to some of the ways in which the affected groups develop defensive strategies and begin to develop new political initiatives. In her picture, the consumers or recipients of welfare are not passive victims, but active participants with their own potential for political action. She concludes forcefully by developing political alternatives based around the provision of welfare itself, rather than the economic issues raised by Johnson and Gamble. She does not accept the political primacy of the economy, but points to the importance of community-based struggles and campaigns about the control of welfare, challenging notions of dependency and undermining the power of professional bureaucracies. Superficially, Williams' arguments about the need to develop independently and in conflict with the state may appear consistent with those of Johnson – she too stresses self-help and 'voluntary' activity – but, of course, her conclusions imply rather different forms of political struggle.

The experience of the welfare state in the 1980s was less clear-cut than it seemed to many commentators at the time. In part this may simply be because that state is not monolithic. Even as some parts of it become weaker, others may increase in importance. As Hills (1990) points out, overall the various elements of the welfare state survived reasonably well through the 1980s (Hills ed., 1990). Expenditure was maintained, although it may not have increased in line with need, and some parts of the system survived better than others – cuts in spending on public sector housing provide the most obvious example of an area which suffered. In the 1990s the welfare state remains a contested arena. Proposals for the introduction of bureaucratically managed forms of market within the welfare state are likely to generate new pressures, and the tensions between attempts to reduce spending and provide services are likely to continue (see Le Grand, 1990). Those groups currently excluded from the welfare state's decision-making structures are still likely to be excluded, but the campaigns and conflicts identified by Williams will also help to shape the experience and politics of welfare in the future. The overall context within which they take place, however, is likely to remain one of austerity, rather than expansion based on the identification of need.

References

Hills, J. (ed.) (1990) *The State of Welfare. The Welfare State in Britain since 1974.* Oxford: Clarendon Press.

Le Grand, J. (1990) 'The State of Welfare', in J. Hills (ed.) (1990) pp. 338–60.

12
The break-up of consensus: competitive politics in a declining economy

Nevil Johnson

Government and the economy

The 1970s were marked by uncertainty, disillusionment and a sharpening of social and political conflicts. Consensus was eroded at many points. The Keynesian view of the economic responsibilities of government and of the appropriate instruments of economic policy became increasingly discredited; the size and functions of the public sector were called into question; doubts were more frequently expressed about whether the welfare state in the form in which it had been built up during the post-war period could be sustained; coercive and sometimes violent behaviour on the part of various groups became commonplace; and doubts began to be expressed whether British political institutions were any longer able to cope effectively with the demands imposed upon them.

There is obviously no single 'correct' explanation of why the consensus which most people had perceived in the years after 1945 began to break down during the 1970s. The arguments to be used here will, however, put particular emphasis on the interaction between economic conditions and certain political ideas and practices. It will be argued that a declining economy reflected a failure to face up to the need for more rapid adaptation to the changes in the international economy. Yet whilst there was great resistance to change in the society, it was widely believed that the government had a comprehensive responsibility for economic and social well-being. Consequently, the claims made on government tended to grow, the more so as declining resources sharpened the competition for benefits. The outcome of such pressures was accelerating inflation which governments found they were more or less unable to restrain by traditional means: in particular the power of trade unions was too much for them. In such conditions the task of governing became harder, the obstacles to success more intractable. Moreover, the weakness of governments was compounded by the constraints of competitive politics: they could not keep their promises and the two major parties steadily lost public respect. So it became common to talk about 'crisis' when referring to the condition of Britain in the 1970s and to argue that the cumulative failure to cope with a wide range of problems was calling into question the familiar methods of government.

It is necessary to begin with a few comments on the economy. Britain had for a long time achieved only a modest rate of return on its use of resources. This deficiency was tolerable when the relative performance of other countries was not significantly better. But in the early 1960s it became clear that more and more countries were securing a higher return on the resources they deployed. This meant that the British economy was in relative decline, a process which continued despite notable windfalls such as North Sea gas and oil. Failure to keep up with the Joneses abroad might not, however, have mattered too much. What was more serious was the growing gap, clearly visible in the 1970s, between the rate of growth of the economy and the expectations of material benefits of all kinds on the part of the population. As this gap widened, inflation was inevitably fuelled.

The perception that economic performance was inadequate became widespread even before 1970 and was then sharpened by accession to the European Community in 1973 and the first oil crisis. The response of governments, regardless of party, was to pursue economic policies of an interventionist kind. This turned out to be true even of the Heath government which within two years gave up most of the neo-liberal commitments with which it came to office in 1970. In this preference for interventionist policies, politicians remained faithful to Keynesian doctrines about the macro-economic role of government which had been dominant since the Second World War, and had hardly been modified at all by the passing gestures towards market principles made by Conservative governments after 1951 and again after 1970. There was a pervasive faith in the ability of transient politicians and permanent bureaucrats to steer the economy and to hold to a course guaranteeing full employment and a steady rise in individual and collective prosperity (Brittan, 1964, 1969, 1971). This was of itself enough to put governments into an exposed position should they regularly fail to deliver the goods. But there were other influences at work which encouraged an even more exaggerated view of the office of government, so much so that it is not unreasonable to refer to the providential view of government. Two of these influences were of particular importance. One was popular support for a welfare state and the manner in which that idea was understood. The other was the character of British political institutions and of the underlying assumptions on which they worked. A few remarks on both these factors will be made.

Welfare as a government responsibility

The welfare state as constructed during and after the Second World War expressed the culmination of a long tradition of social reformism directed to the equalization of opportunities and the protection of wage-earners against the more acute risks of poverty, unemployment, sickness and old age. What was achieved between 1944 and 1948 was ambitious in scale and coverage, at any rate in relation to the welfare provisions of many other countries in the West at the time. Its outstanding structural characteristic was that central government assumed the major responsibility for the maintenance of the whole pattern of social services constituting the 'welfare state'. Pensions, non-contributory social benefits and the bulk of the health services were brought directly into the sphere of state control and provision. Other services like subsidized housing and public education, though provided by local authorities, came to depend primarily on central financial allocations and policy oversight. To a quite remarkable extent Britain, which prided itself on an anti-state and pro-individualist tradition, opted for state or public monopolies in the provision of welfare services in their various forms. As a result the welfare state was perceived primarily in terms of what the central government was expected to do. In the absence of any abstract or legalist conception of the state in Britain, all this was inescapable: the government had not only to manage the economy, it had also to look after the welfare state. Not surprisingly this became a powerful component in that drift towards acceptance of the providential view of government which reached its apogee in the 1970s (Johnson, 1977). Fewer and fewer people were willing to think in terms of providing and acting for themselves and this applied both to individuals and to associations or organized groups. Instead they looked to the government: faced with a problem the automatic response tended to be that the 'government' could and should do something about it.

The welfare component in this dominant view of the role of government then gained sharper emphasis during the later 1960s and on into the 1970s as a result of ideological shifts in the Labour Party. In the conception of the welfare state set out by Beveridge in his famous report (1942) there was, alongside a firm belief in the enlightened power of government, a strong element of self-help and individual responsibility. The notion of equal opportunities qualified the egalitarian thrust of the report. This was reflected in the reforms of the 1945–51 period which were characterized more by a desire to equalize opportunities than by the pursuit of equality as a condition of life. Attitudes changed in the 1960s and there was increasing support on the left of the party spectrum for an egalitarian standpoint. What this seemed to mean was that public policy should in appropriate spheres seek to establish conditions of substantive equality, and furthermore be prepared to inhibit or counteract those actions of individuals or collective agents that might result in distributions of benefits held to be unequal. The comprehensive reorganization of schools was, for example, originally advocated and pursued chiefly for the sake of improving and equalizing chances; gradually, however, it came to be seen from the egalitarian standpoint, a policy recommended for the equalization of the conditions of education that it promised. The significance of this shift in the justification for welfare state policies lies chiefly in the impact it had on argument and conflict within the society, especially during the 1970s. It fuelled the politics of envy, it widened differences between parties, and it encouraged a degree of rigidity and obduracy in the pursuit of purely sectional claims which was a major source of the undermining of governments which took place in the 1970s.

The institutions of political competition and their impact

So far it has been argued that prevailing notions of how the government should manage the economy and sustain the welfare state contributed substantially to the acceptance of a providential conception of the role of government. The traditional political institutions also tended to work in the same direction. Modern parliamentary government in Britain took shape as party government in and through Parliament. There were (and are) two basic components of this. One is that any government in possession of a majority enjoys, or can properly claim to enjoy, the virtually unlimited authority of the Crown in Parliament. This is an old notion, deeply embedded in the evolution of English institutions. It contains too a popular or democratic element, the idea of the ruler supported and authorized by the consent of the people. The other component is the competition of parties embodied in the interplay of two dominant competitors. The electorate has a clear choice: it can determine which of two parties shall form the government. And by virtue of that choice the successful party then claims a 'mandate' to use the extensive powers of the Crown in Parliament to carry out whatever policies it has proposed to the electorate or deems necessary in the public interest.

For a long time British political institutions successfully accommodated the application of these principles governing the structure of political life. There were supplementary checks and controls built into British institutions, and for a while after 1945 two-party competition really did appear to encourage parties to seek the centre ground and to pursue moderate policies. Not unreasonably it was widely held that majority party government through Parliament was a sophisticated achievement, resulting in effective governmental action, responsive behaviour by public authorities, and the maintenance of a broad consensus on the ends of political action in society (Morrison, 1954; McKenzie, 1955; Beer, 1965). But by the 1970s the gilt showed signs of coming off the gingerbread. The rather grand claims made on behalf of the Crown in Parliament no longer secured immediate acquiescence in the society, and indeed were often derided. More serious, party competition had intensified to such a degree during the 1960s that it began to threaten the authority of those who at any particular election secured a parliamentary majority. Increasingly, politicians failed to discern that the more sharply they denied any regard for the public good to their rivals, the more likely it became that their own claim to a 'mandate' or to act in the public interest would be dismissed as sectarian humbug. Thus it was that in the 1970s the style of political life in Britain came to be characterized as 'adversary politics': power was sought in adversarial competition and decisions were reached through adversarial argument. Yet at the same time many people were beginning to suspect that such a sterile process was itself destructive of authority (Finer, 1975; Johnson, 1977).

This style of politics, grafted onto an institutional tradition allowing wide discretion to governments, supported an exaggerated and unrealistic idea of what a government could and should do. To achieve success in the competition, parties tended to promise more and more, and indeed it became a virtue on the part of a government to be engaged continuously in the production of legislation. Both Harold Wilson and Edward Heath clearly exemplified this peculiar notion of the office of government. Yet at the same time governments were finding that their own authority was being eroded by the conditions of adversary politics and that their capacity to fulfil the promises they had made was declining. That in turn weakened their standing and contributed to a marked erosion of support for the two major parties in the electorate (Särlvik and Crewe, 1983).

In summary, the 1970s were characterized by the tensions arising from the attempt to maintain under adversarial conventions a providential view of government in a society beset by deep-seated and long-term economic problems. It was also a society strongly attached to an idea of the welfare state which relied heavily on the effectiveness of the central political authorities. To put the matter in over-simplified terms: the people expected too much of governments and, at the same time, appeared to endorse practices which made it virtually certain that any government would lack the authority to act.

Governments in check: some examples

The sapping of governmental authority was apparent in the frequency with which governments in the 1970s were humiliated and frustrated. Often this was brought about by forces and interests external to them, but sometimes through their own obstinacy in pursuing misguided policies. Such humiliation and failure will be illustrated by quoting three examples.

The first is Edward Heath's defeat at the hands of the National Union of Mineworkers in 1973–4. After successfully forcing the government in 1972 into a highly inflationary wage settlement, the NUM mounted a second challenge in late 1973. Faced also with other serious problems such as the first oil crisis, the government (or at the very least its leader) concluded that in the face of such a threat to its authority by the NUM, it had no alternative but to appeal to the electorate. No doubt some electors were not unaware of the extent to which since 1972 the government had abandoned its earlier market-oriented policies in favour of a thoroughly providential view of its own role and capacities. What difference, therefore, was there on these fundamental matters between the Conservative and Labour parties? Be that as it may, the electorate dithered in early 1974, depriving Heath of his majority, but failing to confer a majority on anybody else. By this action the voters unwittingly strengthened the position of organized interests like the NUM: the divine right of trade unions appeared to have been confirmed.

The second example is derived from the attempt of the Wilson and Callaghan governments to secure the co-operation of the trade unions. The Wilson government was formed in March 1974, and re-established after gaining a very small majority in the October 1974 election. The Labour Party could then govern only on terms acceptable to the trade unions. The cardinal issue was wage demands. The unions rejected the statutory policies applied by the Heath government and insisted that any incomes policy must be 'voluntary'. Faced with a dangerous escalation of the rate of inflation to something near 25 percent in 1975, they were prepared to offer – and the Wilson government to accept – the 'social contract'. Essentially this was an ill-defined agreement – more like an informal arrangement in fact – under which the unions traded wage restraint for policy concessions on many matters which they regarded as important, such as the repeal of industrial relations legislation disapproved of by them, abandonment of statutory controls on wage increases, and the application of measures of price control or restraint. For a short time the agreement undoubtedly helped to slow down the rate of wage inflation, though perhaps more effective in the struggle against inflation were the conditions imposed by the International Monetary Fund in 1976 on the loan which the British government had requested. These included a serious undertaking to control the rate of growth of public expenditure. But quite quickly prolongation of the 'social contract' became difficult. The unions were not able to deliver for long what had been promised, and in any case most of them rejected any responsibility for general economic stabilization. The outcome was the collapse of the contract and a succession of damaging strikes and industrial stoppages in the winter of 1978–9 which served to demonstrate how hollow had been the claims made for the social contract. In reality it had not strengthened the government, nor had it been an exercise in governing by consensus: instead it had merely demonstrated that abdication of responsibility which necessarily follows from a readiness to subject the decisions of government to the consent of particular vested interests in the society.

A third example, but of a different kind, is provided by the attempt to enact schemes for devolution in Scotland and Wales between 1974 and 1979. This illustrates the capacity of a government to act misguidedly and to compound its own difficulties, not least of which was the fact that it had no sure majority in the House of Commons and by early 1977 had to enter into an arrangement with the Liberals in order to survive at all. The pursuit of devolution has to be set in the broad context of the passion for institutional engineering and change which gripped Britain from about 1966 onwards (Johnson, 1976). This attitude cut right across party lines, and indeed in many respects Edward Heath was a more committed rationalizer of institutions than Harold Wilson. However, it was the latter who in 1969 set up a Royal Commission on the constitution charged with a study of devolution, being moved to do so chiefly by exaggerated fears for the retention of the Labour majority in Scotland (Kilbrandon, 1973). Some years later, returning to office after the fall of Edward Heath, Wilson decided that an attempt should be made to legislate for devolution, an effort that was to absorb much of three years of parliamentary time, provoke serious disputes within the Labour Party, and finally result in hopelessly inadequate schemes for devolution which in March 1979 failed to secure the requisite endorsement by popular vote in Scotland and Wales. Immediately afterwards Callaghan's government fell on a no-confidence motion arising out of this failure. Whatever might be the case for or against devolution, there can be no doubt that the attempt to put it into effect by the Wilson and Callaghan governments represented an extraordinary miscalculation: the episode was seen by many as an irrelevant distraction and as bearing testimony to the foolishness of politicians and their advisers.

These examples – and many others could be cited which would serve just as well – provide evidence of the weakening of governments and of their inability to live up to the claims made on their behalf. If such a condition persists for long, the authority of the institutions on which government rests is called into question. This began to happen during the 1970s and as the decade wore on there were many signs suggesting that customary practices and institutions no longer commanded as much respect and confidence in society as before. Much of the argument for constitutional reform and safeguards, emanating chiefly from Conservative circles, reflected this growing anxiety about the stability of British political institutions and the feeling that some kind of constitutional renewal was needed (Scarman, 1975; Hailsham, 1978).

Trade union power

Attention has been drawn in the preceding section to the most powerful sources of obstruction facing governments during the 1970s, namely trade unions. We now have to consider more closely whether the 1970s were marked by a peculiar and unusual extension of trade union power bearing directly on the discretion of governments. It may be that insofar as there was a political crisis it was very largely the result of the excessive intervention of the unions in public affairs. The problem of the unions and their political role must, however, be looked at in conjunction with two further issues. One is the extent to which the unions (or some of them) came to dominate the Labour Party during the 1970s; the other is the relevance or otherwise of the notion of corporatism to an understanding of the evolution of the 1970s. If corporatism is a term which can usefully be employed, then it appears to entail recognition of the importance of organized economic interests other than trade unions in the political organization of the society. To this extent corporatism would qualify any special emphasis on the role of the unions as a source of checks on the ability of governments to govern.

Somewhat ironically the 1970s opened with a serious attempt to modernize labour law and to provide a comprehensive legal framework for trade union activity. This was the Industrial Relations Act 1971, a measure bitterly opposed by the unions and a source of sharp conflict in the courts and elsewhere between them and the Heath government. In retrospect it can be seen that the Act came too early and was too rigorous in conception and aims. The public had already had some experience in the 1960s of growing intransigence on the part of unions, of their tendency to persist in unreasonable sectional demands, and in 1969 of their success in forcing the then Labour government to withdraw proposals for the reform of industrial relations law contained in its White Paper, *In Place of Strife*. Nevertheless, with over half of the working population unionized there was still a considerable fund of sympathy for trade unions and a readiness to accept that reform of them should come by persuasion and voluntary action rather than by legal enactment. Consequently, there was no widespread public reaction against the unions for their campaign against the 1971 Act. But later the unions' readiness to reinforce their privileges and to exact even further concessions from weak governments after 1974 began to contribute substantially to that popular hostility towards them on which the Thatcher government was to build so successfully.

It is a commonplace of British social development in the twentieth century that trade unions gradually acquired a position of great latent strength. This was due in the first place to a steady growth in membership which continued into the 1970s, the peak being achieved in 1979. More significant still was the fact that the unions had gained protection from a patchwork of legal immunities and were thus able to develop substantially according to their own internal dynamics rather than within a framework of conditions externally determined. Particularly important was their freedom from contractual liability for damage resulting from industrial action on their part, notably strikes. Yet whilst trade unions remained highly autonomous bodies, collectively they had achieved extensive official recognition by the time of the Second World War, and this was maintained and developed further thereafter. The outcome by the 1960s was a trade union movement enjoying substantial influence and prestige in public life, but consisting of highly independent and separate unions able to press their claims with few external constraints to remind them of the consequences of such action. Moreover, the tendency towards oligarchy and the rule of the functionary had in some unions become quite clear, whilst paradoxically there were at the same time numerous examples of the growing impatience of the ordinary members with recognized dispute procedures and their readiness to resort instantly to disruptive action.

Notwithstanding some variations within the trade union movement, it is clear that by the 1970s the unions had become the most insistent source of direct pressure in the country on both public authorities and private employers. They could act quickly and unpredictably; in some industries and services their action threatened immediate and widespread social dislocation; they rarely had to count the cost of their conduct; and they could clothe many of their demands in the rhetoric of social justice and fair treatment. The statistics of days lost through strike action and the record of poor productivity during the later 1960s and after testify, inter alia, to the serious negative impact on the economy of trade union activity.

Nevertheless, the effects of trade union power and its misuse might have been less serious but for two special conditions. One was the widespread belief that the government should be ready to assist directly in the settlement of industrial disputes – perhaps one of the more bizarre consequences of the providential notion of governmental responsibility. The other was the fact that the trade unions in Britain were an integral part of the wider Labour movement: they were linked to one of the two dominant parties in the political system, and this party was to a large extent dependent on their support. This circumstance greatly accentuated the damaging effects of the adversarial relationship in British party competition. It meant that the unions regarded one party as peculiarly 'theirs', remained persistently antagonistic towards the other major party, and had come to believe that periods of Labour rule should be used to nullify the effects of any policies by the Conservatives of which they disapproved. In this way the dynamic of two-party competition was rendered more negative and harmful in its impact on public policy and expectations than might otherwise have been the case.

It might be objected that these comments exaggerate the influence of the unions within the Labour Party and fail to do justice to the extent to which other organized interests also had a direct impact on government action. On the first point, it is true that traditionally the parliamentary leadership of the Labour Party had a wide discretion in deciding what policies to pursue and that the positive contributions of the TUC to policy-making were modest. During the later 1960s, however, individual unions and the TUC as the collective voice of the union movement began to claim something very near to a veto on policies affecting union interests. The Parliamentary Labour Party began to encounter the displeasure and opposition of trade union interests more often than in previous years. After 1974 this exposure of the party to imperative demands from its trade union wing became even more intense, culminating after the electoral defeat of 1979 in the constitutional changes of 1981 which gave the unions a weighted vote in the election of the party leader.

The more insistent role of the unions as a pressure group within the Labour Party stemmed in part simply from circumstances: as inflation rose more steeply after 1972, so the unions became more anxious and more determined to have their pound of flesh, regardless of the consequences in the later 1970s even for a government they claimed to support. But equally important was the growing radicalism within the party and several unions (notably some of those in the public sector) which in the early 1970s established mutually reinforcing pressures in favour of subordinating party leadership and policy to the requirements of a more rigid ideological statement of Labour Party aims. The party and the unions were launched on that course which right down to 1983 and after was to widen the gap between their views and those of a large section of the electorate previously sympathetic to the party.

The corporatist arguments and its limits
An explanation of the evolution of the 1970s in terms of corporatism would qualify substantially any account identifying trade union power as a primary cause of instability and tension. The corporatist thesis holds, broadly speaking, that the successful management of a capitalist economy now depends on the co-ordinated co-operation of the institutions of government (or more often, that mysterious actor, the state), the trade unions as organizations representing employees, and the network of employer organizations representing corporate business interests. It is government, or the state, which is expected to ensure the kind of co-ordinated action envisaged in such an analysis. It is further assumed that a large proportion of the capital assets in the economy is privately owned and controlled, and that market conditions largely govern the production and exchange of goods and services (Cawson and Ballard, 1984).

The difficulty about the corporatist thesis when put in such broad terms is that it is not very informative: it simply describes familiar structural features of most Western industrial societies such as the fact that governments certainly influence the conditions under which the economy evolves, employers' organizations, along with other professional bodies, express in various ways the point of view of industry and business considered as some kind of unity, and trade unions claim to represent the interests of a large segment of the working population. It is on this basis that a model of 'tripartism' – management of the economy by the joint action of the government, industry and unions – was constructed in the early 1970s. And certainly many of the organizational devices set up during this period, and especially when the Heath government was in office, did reflect a belief that the best way to handle economic and social policy-making was through linking the government with representatives of the recognized 'peak associations' of business and the trade unions.

Corporatism so defined was, however, shaky and uncertain in operation.

Moreover, any attempt to give more precision to the terms and quantities in the corporatist thesis runs into insoluble difficulties. As used during the 1970s the corporatist analysis grossly exaggerated the 'unity' of the employer and employee organizations, and their capacity to secure compliance from their members. What is more, it took little account of the dynamic aspects of social change which, even in what looked like a rigid social structure, were nevertheless at work undermining the claim that somehow or other the CBI was identifiable with 'British industry' and the TUC with 'industrial workers'. Above all, it was always implausible to assume that the representatives of capital and labour operated on something like equal terms. By the 1970s trade unions and their members knew well enough that they could more or less with impunity inflict inconvenience and loss on employers as well as undermine the standing of governments. Neither the representatives of industrial ownership and management nor the political authorities themselves had coercive weapons of this kind at their disposal: financial and material concessions appeared to them to be virtually the only way of meeting trade union threats.

Finally, as just indicated, corporatism in the British context totally lacked that element of effective state direction which belonged to the historical development of the concept and was attributed to it even in the 1970s by some of its British exponents (Pahl and Winkler, 1976). Despite the persistent efforts of successive British governments to convey the appearance of 'managing' the economy and of actively securing the co-operation of the dominant interest groups in it, it remained quite clear that no government could secure sustained compliance with its wishes and policy preferences. There was much passing deference but no readiness to accept the government as the agent of effective planning and direction. From the National Plan of 1965 through the statutory incomes policy of the Heath government to the disintegration of the social contract, repeated proof was offered that a directive role in the economy for the political authorities was in Britain both unworkable and unacceptable. The corporatist emperor had no clothes on, and it was the trade unions who first made this abundantly clear.

Social inertia and political obstruction: summary

The 1970s were a decade during which the political system became blocked: its capacity to facilitate decisions and ensure that they were carried out became severely restricted (Beer, 1982). This occurred in part because British society, which was pluralist in structure and yet often aggressively individualist in outlook, remained on the whole peculiarly resistant to many of the changes which were needed if the economy was to adapt even moderately well to new conditions in the world at large. Admittedly, there were exceptions to this hostility to change, for example in the exploitation of energy resources in the North Sea. But broadly, the society was at all levels opposed to new forms of social co-operation which might also entail some sacrifice of vested interests. Inevitably, such conditions increased the pressure on governments struggling to deal with problems which they at least knew were real.

However, it was far more than just the weight of inertia in society that reduced the capacity of governments to act. They were generally exposed as well to the active hostility of major interests threatened by changes in the structure of the economy and the organization of work. It was here that the trade unions became the major source of obstruction and social conflict. They had in Britain become peculiarly powerful, embedded in the society, yet detached from real responsibility for its well-being. Given the uncertainties of democratic majority rule and the volatility of public opinion, trade unions were able to present a formidable threat to any elected government.

In addition, the political methods and institutional structures under which Britain was governed tended to exacerbate what were already serious problems – competition, adversarial debate, the rotation of parties in office; these conditions served to raise the stakes and to increase the dangers of political blockage.

Finally, superimposed on all these influences arising from the state of the economy, the structure of British society and the institutions through which the country was governed, was the idea of providential government. To say in the conditions just summarized that the national government should accept a comprehensive responsibility for the well-being of all was to invite total frustration at some stage. This occurred during the 1970s when it became manifest that governments simply could not work the wonders expected of them: the incoherence of the providential idea of government in a free society was clearly demonstrated. As soon as a large part of the electorate had grasped this lesson, the time for a real change of direction had come.

The end of the 'crisis' of the 1970s:
the Thatcher era and its effects

During the 1970s some had predicted shipwreck, many had called for far-reaching political or, more precisely, constitutional reform. Yet shipwreck, whether in the form of economic collapse or social upheaval, did not occur. Instead there was a shift of opinion and mood just sufficient to yield a modest parliamentary majority at the 1979 general election for a Conservative government committed, as in the manner of its predecessor of 1970, to the reassertion of market principles. The accession to power of Margaret Thatcher was, however, to turn out to be far more than a mere swing of the pendulum in the two-party competition. Instead it brought far-reaching policy innovation combined with genuine conservatism in relation to institutions and political methods. By gradually redefining its role, the government regained its capacity to govern.

How is the sharp and somewhat surprising change from the conditions of the 1970s to be characterized and explained? At the level of mood and method three factors appear to have been of importance. The first was a growing realization that the retreat into illusion and make-believe characteristic of the 1970s had to stop. The British people had shown tolerance and patience in the face of the abuse of trade union power, the incompetence and weakness of industrial management in many sectors, and the failure of governments to formulate and pursue consistent and coherent policies. By the end of the 1970s there was a widespread feeling that many things had to change, though possibly little agreement on exactly what policies should be pursued. The position was mildly reminiscent of that in France at the fall of the Fourth Republic: like General de Gaulle, Thatcher could bank on a widespread willingness to accept new initiatives, though it is also doubtful whether her mandate to pursue them would have been renewed so decisively in 1983 but for the fortuitous impact on public opinion in 1982 of the conflict over the Falkland Islands. An important component of this change of mood was the reaction against trade unions. They had overplayed their hand, especially in 1978–9, exhausting the public's patience and, more importantly, the patience of many of their own members.

The second factor was recognition of this change of mood by the new government, and the readiness of its leader to appeal to populist sentiments. More than any Prime Minister since Lloyd George, Thatcher was to prove herself an outsider. Her political intuition convinced her that only with the backing of popular sympathy and support could her government put through some of the radical measures which she in particular desired to see in operation. Consequently, trade union legislation, for example, was carefully devised to cater for the claims of ordinary union members: returning the unions to them became the slogan. The sale of council houses was expressed in terms of tenants' rights; later, the sale of nationalized enterprises was also to be presented as offering the people a stake in national assets. More widely, Thatcher has, to an unusual degree, been ready to voice the opinions and prejudices of ordinary people and to assert that public policy should respect them. To the intense irritation of the intellectual classes she has shown little respect for the opinions of many of those who, by avocation, claim 'to know better'. Whatever may be the longer-term effects of this populism, there is no doubt that it has on many occasions strengthened Thatcher's position inside her own party and more generally in the country. It has made it easier for her to press on reluctant colleagues policies to which she and her keener supporters were committed.

A third factor contributing to the acceptance of radical changes in policy and in the scope of the government's responsibilities is to be found in the reaffirmation of faith in the traditional political methods and institutions.

This was in tune with that conservatism in respect of the political practices of the society which is so deeply rooted in Britain, and with the reaction against the powers of government as such which took place by the end of the 1970s. There is very little reason to believe that many people in Britain either understand or welcome constitutional innovation and the reshaping of institutions. They remain sceptical of large theories and prefer the familiar to that which is new and untried. Like Thatcher they tend to believe that personal qualities rather than organization or grand principles are decisive in getting things done. Whether such a belief is in general well-founded or not is unimportant. What matters is that it is widely held and thus established a certain degree of sympathy and support for the emphasis which Thatcher gave to acting decisively in and through the traditional institutions.

Turning briefly to substantive policy changes, the base-lines of economic policy have been decisively moved towards market principles, and control of the money supply has figured prominently in the Government's approach. Whilst it is probably still too early to reach firm conclusions about the extent to which this neo-liberal type of economic policy will turn out to be irreversible, it seems unlikely that a full-blooded version of Keynesian demand management could not be restored, not least because such methods gain no support in any major economy in the free world. This does not mean, however, that governments no longer have a great deal to do in the shaping of economic policy, but it does mean that their role is more narrowly defined and of a different nature from what was generally accepted in Britain after 1945. The government is no longer seen as the 'Universal Provider', a beneficent power charged with putting into effect a rational plan for the achievement of general well-being. Instead, the inherent limitations of government in a free society have been emphasized and its purposes redefined in terms of setting the framework within which individuals and social organizations must take decisions for themselves. In this way a weighty plank has been knocked out of the theory of providential government.

In the sphere of social policy there have on the whole been fewer radical changes than in economic policy. The underlying principles on which the Thatcher governments have acted point towards a substantial reshaping of the welfare state, reductions in its cost, and revision of the terms on which a wide range of social services are provided. But in the event social policy in the broadest sense has since 1979 been marked by some hesitation and uncertainty. Consequently the welfare state in its traditional form survives for the most part. Changes of detail have been made, more may follow in respect of pension provisions, and there have been serious attempts to contain and even reduce expenditure in some sectors of social provision. This caution reflects awareness of the strength of public sympathy for many of the familiar features of the welfare state in Britain, notably the National Health Service. But it also indicates some realization of the dangers of rising social tensions in the wake of economic policies which have accepted high unemployment as part of the price to be paid for structural adaptation in the economy and the achievement of higher levels of efficiency.

The changes effected since 1979 have been directed to the revival of a market economy. Yet, as is well known, the policies pursued in recent years have been slow to produce convincing evidence of succes. There have been important changes in the conditions under which the British economy operates and many signs of greater realism in the assessment of what is needed for commercial success. Nevertheless, the negative consequences have been obvious: unemployment levels have reached 13 percent and there has been a continuing decline in manufacturing industry. Whilst it is perfectly conceivable that the policies pursued since 1979 will eventually produce the desired results, it has become clear that they cannot do so quickly. The road to economic revival is long and stony, not least because the backlog of neglect has been so great and the impact of world recession so pervasive.

These conditions have, not surprisingly, prompted the parties in opposition, which since 1981 comprise both the Labour Party and the Liberal-Social Democrat Alliance, to advocate economic policies which point once again towards higher levels of public spending and more government intervention. Admittedly, all the parties in opposition now show far more caution in threatening a wholesale reversal of the policies pursued by their rivals than was customary in the 1970s or proposed by the Labour Party in its disastrous 1983 election campaign. Nevertheless, there remains some prospect of an attempt being made at some stage to change the general direction of public policy set since 1979. On this account alone it is premature to speak of the consolidation of a new consensus reflecting the experience and aims of the Thatcher years. That will become possible, if at all, only after such an attempt to modify its conclusions has been made and then abandoned.

If we cannot at present assess with confidence the enduring impact of Thatcher's conduct of government, nor discern exactly how much of what has been done since 1979 will become part of the received wisdom of the next twenty years or so, there can be no doubt about the extent to which what has been done represents a remarkably consistent reaction against the thinking, the practices and mood of the 1970s. That decade became for many Conservatives one of confusion of purposes, weakness and defeat. It was also one in which government appeared to have over-reached itself and, in so doing, to have lost its claim to authority. Hence, what has been tried since 1979 has been radical in respect of measures and policies, and especially in relation to the economy, yet restorationist in respect of political values and institutional practices. There has been a reaction against the passion of the 1970s for institutional reform and organizational improvement. Except in relation to the organization and powers of local authorities, Thatcher's governments have eschewed institutional engineering and constitutional innovation: the pre-1979 interest shown in constitutional reform quickly evaporated after the responsibilities of government had been taken up.

Yet despite the return to traditional ideas of how to govern, Thatcher has in style and manner been an unconventional politician, disturbing and controversial in the impact she has made. Her conduct of public affairs has demonstrated how hard it is to provide strong leadership under the British political system except in a manner which generates tensions and sharpens opposition. She has been conservative in her endorsement of the formal conditions of British political life and government, but assertive and radical in her use of the powers they confer. This leaves it uncertain whether the institutions really have that degree of vitality which since 1979 they appear to have regained. An imperious performer can usually achieve some success, even when surrounded by stage-props which are faded and worn out. In advance of the event we have no means of telling how the British political system as a mode of handling public affairs will react to the eventual departure of Margaret Thatcher. Many of her policies are likely to survive, but some of the weaknesses in the constitutional framework revealed in the 1970s may once again become apparent.

References

Beer, S. H. (1965) *Modern British Politics*. London: Faber (2nd edn, 1969).

Beer, S. H. (1982) *Britain Against Itself*. London: Faber.

Beveridge, W. (1942) *Social Insurance and Allied Services* (Cmnd 6404). London: HMSO.

Brittan, S. (1964) *The Treasury under the Tories, 1951–64*. Harmondsworth: Penguin.

Brittan, S. (1969) *Steering the Economy: the Role of the Treasury*. London: Secker & Warburg.

Brittan, S. (1971) *Steering the Economy: the British Experiment*. Freeport, NY: Liberty Press (rev. edn, Harmondsworth: Penguin).

Cawson, A. C. and Ballard, J. (1984) *A Bibliography of Corporatism (in Britain)*. Florence: European University Institute.

Department of Employment and Productivity (1969) *In Place of Strife: A Policy for Industrial Relations* (Cmnd 3888). London: HMSO.

Finer, S. E. (ed.) (1975) *Adversary Politics and Electoral Reform*. London: Wigram.

Hailsham, Lord (1978) *The Dilemma of Democracy: Diagnosis and Prescription*. London: Collins.

Johnson, N. (1976) 'Recent Administrative Reform in Britain', in Leemans, A. F. (ed.) *Management of Change in Government*. The Hague: Nijhoff.

Johnson, N. (1977) *In Search of the Constitution: Reflections on State and Society in Britain*. Oxford: Pergamon.

Kilbrandon, Lord (Chair) (1973) *Report of the Royal Commission on the Constitution* (Cmnd 5460). London: HMSO.

McKenzie, R. (1958) *British Political Parties*. London: Heinemann (2nd edn, 1964).

Morrison, H. (1954) *Government and Parliament: a Survey from the Inside*. London: Oxford University Press.

Pahl, R. E. and Winkler, J. T. (1976) 'Corporatism in Britain', *The Times* (26 March).

Särlvik, B. and Crewe, I. (1983) *Decade of Dealignment*. Cambridge: Cambridge University Press.

Scarman, Lord (1975) *English Law: the New Dimension*. London: Hamlyn, Stevens & Sons.

13
Understanding the market

Norman Barry

One of the most striking features of the development of social science during the last decade has been the re-establishment of the intellectual respectability of the decentralized market exchange system as a social institution. There has been a growing recognition of both the efficiency and freedom-enhancing properties of market society. Many socialists now admit that planned, centralized economies have performed very badly in both these respects and are now anxious to incorporate at least some features of the market in their blueprints (redprints?) for the future. As I shall show below, there is a neglected tradition in socialist thought which has always been favourable to the market.

What is noticeable about the contemporary appeal of the market is just how wide it is. In Britain the Social Democratic Party, the Liberals, and even some sections of the Labour Party, in addition to the 'Thatcherite' wing of the Conservative Party, all express (qualified) confidence in market processes; and abroad, from Western democracies to Communist China, there is renewed faith in the decentralized exchange mechanism. If the market were a person, it would be a highly promiscuous one indeed. What then, lies behind the increased demands for 'privatization', a reduced role for the public sector and the 'rolling back of the state' that are heard from a wide variety of political sources in the contemporary world?

Perhaps the matter may be clarified by identifying three possible ways of organizing a society for the production of *wanted* goods and services: altruism, central command and the market. Altruism presupposes that individuals, without either the incentives of personal gain or fear of punishment, will satisfy the wants of others in a system of generalized reciprocity. It is now generally agreed that this places impossible burdens on a fragile human nature and on human knowledge. In a large society, even if people were uncommonly well-disposed towards each other, how could they *know* what others' wants were? In fact, altruism is only conceivable in very small communities where there is a broad agreement about ends and purposes. This leaves only central command and individual decision-making as serious alternatives. The critique of central command will emerge from a consideration of the market.

A market form of organization assumes that, from a *given* distribution of property rights and claims to natural resources (about which there can, of course, be much dispute) a predictable order will emerge from individual decisions. The market order is powered primarily by the price mechanism – which is no more than an indicator of the *scarcity* of resources in a community. Thus if there is a spontaneous demand for a commodity, or factor of production (labour, land or capital), its price will rise and therefore a signal is put out which brings forth extra supplies of the wanted good or factor of production. Without the guidance of price nobody would know what to do, and without the incentive to act, via profit, nothing would be produced.

What follows from this is that a decentralized exchange system, conducted within a general system of law (crime, contract and tort, etc.), requires very little in the way of centralized direction and control. A market is in essence a self-regulating, self-correcting system in which supply and demand and profit and loss are said to allocate resources more efficiently, and therefore 'solve' the perennial 'economic problem' of scarcity, better than any known alternative. Each participant in the process has to know only those economic facts that affect him personally since the market's signals, in F. A. von Hayek's words, 'enable individual producers to watch merely the movements of a few pointers, as an engineer might watch the hands of a few dials, in order to adjust their activities to changes of which they may never know more than is reflected in the prices movement' (Hayek, 1948: 87).

This is a simple idea which tells us little about the structure of an advanced capitalist economy. But it is a very important concept because it shows how, in principle, the activities of disparate and decentralized individuals may be co-ordinated as if, in Adam Smith's memorable phrase, by an 'Invisible Hand'. For the price system is constantly reflecting those changes in tastes, technology and availability of resources that characterize a complex society. Of course, it does not reflect these instantaneously, but its reactions to changes in these data are quicker than those of humanly devised institutions.

It would be inaccurate to describe all this as laissez-faire, a much abused term: a better phrase is Smith's 'the system of natural liberty'. By this he meant that through people's natural tendency to 'truck, barter and exchange' a movement to equilibrium operates, that is, a situation in which the *interdependent* parts of an economy cannot be rearranged to bring about an improved allocation of resources. In *The Wealth of Nations* (1776) he wrote: 'No regulation of commerce can increase the quantity of industry in any part of society beyond what its capital can maintain. It can only divert a part of it into a direction which it might otherwise not have gone' (Smith, 1976: 453). Smith's implicit welfare judgement here is that governments are inevitably inferior to decentralized individuals in the production of wanted goods and services: 'I have never known much good done by those who affected to trade for the public good' (Smith, 1976: 453). He said this not merely to doubt the automatic benevolence of governors (although he certainly did) but also to stress the fact that public beneficence always emerges as the *unintended consequence* of private, self-regarding action.

Unfortunately, as economic theory developed, the virtues of the market as a social institution were neglected. Instead of emphasizing the practical advantages of the private property-free exchange system in generating prosperity, economists began to construct abstract, mathematical models of an ideal co-ordination of economic activities that had nothing to do with the real world of messy, imperfect, but still socially useful, markets. Economics became obsessively concerned with 'equilibrium' theory.

By equilibrium market economists mean the state of perfect co-ordination of economic action in which the price structure reveals no further possibility of improvement. In equilibrium every factor of production is paid its marginal product (the income just sufficient to keep it operating efficiently), there are no price discrepancies that reveal an opportunity for entrepreneurial profit, and no one person (i.e. a monopolist) can influence price (every transactor has to accept the prices of goods and services dictated by an impersonal market). This is what is meant by 'perfect competition': it is, in fact, a state of such exquisite adjustment that no further competition is required (for a critique, see Barry, 1985).

However, real-world market economies rarely resemble this ideal. There are industries in which certain producers, through the control of vital resources, can reduce output and raise prices so as to secure monopoly profits. There are always price discrepancies which can be exploited by alert entrepreneurs who buy and sell commodities for profit ('arbitrage') without, apparently, adding anything to production. Above all, there are things called 'public goods', such as defence, clean air, law and order and so on which, because they are consumed by everybody and cannot be priced by the market, are seriously under-supplied (if supplied at all) by voluntary exchanges.

All these facts, it is claimed by equilibrium theorists, justify considerable state intervention to correct market failure. This consists of taxation to eliminate wasteful profits, regulation of economic activity, nationalization and the public delivery of vital services. Note here that the psychological assumptions that underpin this approach are identical to those used by more overt defenders of capitalism. Individual wants are assumed to be autonomously generated and not dictated by profit-hungry producers and wily advertisers, and transactors are treated as atomized, egoistic utility-maximizers. It is argued by interventionists of the equilibrium school that spontaneously developing markets are simply incapable of delivering the goods. It is interesting to note that the socialist ethical critique of the market as a source of alienation and a destroyer of human autonomy and sociability came *after* persistent attempts to improve on the efficiency of real-world markets by central planning had failed.

In the equilibrium model of a market system there is no *necessary* role for private property. All that is asserted is that, given knowledge of consumer tastes, and information about the efficiency of the factors of production (land, labour and capital), an array of goods and services can be generated more effectively by intervention than by leaving real-world markets, characterized by monopoly and other imperfections, alone. The only income differentials are those required to draw the factors of production into their most efficient uses.

It is but a small step from all this to propose a fully fledged socialist economy, based on consumer choice but without the characteristics of traditional capitalist economies ('profit', private property, capital markets, etc.). This was the 'market socialist' model of, amongst others, Oscar Lange and Abba Lerner (see Lippincott, 1938). To summarize a complex and sophisticated argument, market socialism envisages a conventional market (determined by supply and demand) for consumer goods, and for the reward to labour factors. There would be no private owners earning profits but only managers of state enterprises receiving salaries. Investment decisions would be taken according to rules of efficiency derived ultimately from the equilibrium theory of the perfectly competitive market.

It is from a critique of this whole approach that the modern theory of the market derives and, with it, a defence of private property, entrepreneurship and 'capitalism'. What was wrong with the equilibrium approach was that it neglected certain social features of the market stressed by Adam Smith and his successors.

In practice, markets are necessarily imperfect: an existing set of prices will never mirror some perfect co-ordination of economic activity. It is 'rivalrous' competition between economic agents (not perfect competition as described in equilibrium theory) that gradually pushes the system towards that co-ordination, although it will be constantly pulled away by some further change in the data. In this, the *entrepreneur* plays a key role, for it is his alertness to some price discrepancy, some difference between factor cost and product price (which constitutes profit), that brings about the co-ordination. Of course, the entrepreneur does not intend the co-ordination of the whole market, that is the unintended outcome of the actions of innumerable decentralized transactors. It should be noted that it is *not* the possession of property or resources that characterizes entrepreneurship: it is simply a mental sensitivity to some price differential that can be exploited. It follows from this that in a real-world market economy there will always be 'profits' to be earned, payments made over and above the income paid to a factor of production, as long as human society remains as it is.

The best way to describe a competitive market system is in terms of an evolutionary process (see Alchian, 1977) rather than as a static equilibrium. The development of a capitalist economy does resemble a kind of 'survival of the fittest' – of firms, not individuals. Competition does weed out inefficient firms (therefore loss is as much a part of the market as is profit) and resources are continually being reallocated to the general benefit of the community as a whole. Indeed, firms 'mutate' in unpredictable ways in response to ever-changing circumstances. But what ensures 'order' in what would otherwise be chaos is the price mechanism itself which is constantly signalling information to producers and consumers.

In the light of these considerations the presence of monopoly and other market imperfections is not as alarming as equilibrium theorists have supposed. To start with, the likelihood of a pure monopoly emerging *spontaneously* from an evolutionary market process is somewhat remote. Historically, almost all cases of monopoly are created by government intervention: the granting of exclusive rights of production to privileged individuals and groups. Where examples of monopoly and quasi-monopoly do appear to have emerged naturally it should not be assumed automatically that competition has ceased. As long as access to the activity in question is *open*, a monopolist is under some constraint: if prices are raised too highly, competitors will be encouraged to come into the business.

Again the 'welfare loss' due to monopoly may be overstated. Using the perfect competition–general equilibrium model of society, where all prices are 'correct', it is easy to show the existence of monopoly prices in the real world. But this is a purely static view. In dynamic economies certain activities may be so risky that only the prospects of quasi-monopoly profits will be sufficient to induce people into the enterprises. If such monopoly gains were to be taxed away the good might not be produced at all: a considerable welfare loss indeed. Furthermore, we must not forget that monopoly gains are more often that not a reward for superior alertness. Finally, and most important, it is the case that in a free, open and evolving market monopoly profits are always precarious – subject to constant threats from predatory competitors.

Government intervention in the economy, when it has fallen short of socialist planning, cannot be said to have been successful. Britain perhaps more than any other Western democracy has experimented with piecemeal interventions in the market process, but with little discernible economic benefit. However, rather than list examples of nationalization and other corrective measures designed to remedy alleged faults in economic adjustment it might be more profitable to consider the general reasons why, in the opinion of market theorists, such actions are likely to be counter-productive. We should keep in mind the model of a market as an evolutionary process that is changing and developing in unpredictable ways. The question is: which of the two correcting mechanisms, the government or the price system, is the most efficacious? The main point is that a central organ will not have the *knowledge* to make improvements on the decentralized market, but there is another equally important consideration. This is the tendency for government to intervene to support industries which are being naturally weeded out by the competitive process: in this respect government action is necessarily anti-progressive. In the words of a respected authority in this field, government, in its industrial policy, has a genius for 'picking losers' (see Burton, 1983). In British post-war industrial history, government has consistently intervened in transport, energy, car and aircraft manufacturing and so on against the lessons of the market.

No doubt such action is motivated by good intentions and the fear that significant pockets of unemployment will emerge if a particular industry or firm is eliminated by evolutionary processes. But the fear is usually groundless: for it is never the case that when a firm goes into liquidation its assets are completely written off and *all* of its employees put out of work. Its plant and equipment will be bought up by entrepreneurs and re-allocated to more efficient uses as determined by the impersonal market. Many of its former workers will be re-hired in new enterprises. Furthermore, although there must always be frictional unemployment in an evolving market economy, experience shows that it guarantees full employment in the long run better than piecemeal intervention.

In the post-war period in Western democracies the role of the state has increased without approaching the range of economic controls exercised in a full-blooded planned economy. Nationalization is only one of the instruments of control; others include planning legislation, regulation of industry, import controls, excessive taxation and so on. The main difficulty for market theorists is to devise methods of reintroducing competitive elements into the economy without the massive disruption of plans and expectations that a sudden and wholesale introduction of laissez-faire would entail.

The most spectacular example of the gradualist approach is the policy of the privatization of state-owned enterprises; this has been pioneered by Thatcher's government and imitated to some extent in France, New Zealand and Australia. The main aims of privatization are to expose hitherto nationalized concerns to the full rigours of competition, to prevent the taxpayers being burdened with massive losses incurred by enterprises that are not allowed to go bankrupt, to end political interference with the economy and to spread more widely private share ownership. In theory, privatization should have nothing to do with the raising of money for the government so that it can reduce its borrowing and embark on tax cuts. If the government wishes permanently to reduce public spending, and therefore taxation, it can only do this by reducing public services: after all, public enterprises can only be sold *once*. Furthermore, if the point of privatization is to increase competition then there is little to be gained by selling off public assets as private monopolies.

In Britain there was increasing dissatisfaction with the 'Morrisonian' concept of the public corporation. In the post-war Labour government the model of public ownership was developed under Herbert Morrison and is typified by the coal, steel and transport industries and by electricity generation. These industries are supposed to be run as commercial enterprises subject only to overall direction and control by their sponsoring ministries. In practice they are not allowed to operate efficiently according to market principles, since the state constantly interferes with their managements. They cannot raise capital on the open market, they have to fit into government's 'national' economic plans (especially in relation to prices and incomes policies) and since they operate as quasi-monopolies there can be no genuine test of their efficiency. Furthermore, the trade unions are more powerful in them since the threat of redundancy is less immediate in the public than in the private sector. By the late 1970s in Britain the traditional public corporations had accumulated vast deficits, largely because their organizational structure made it impossible for them to adapt to the incessant change that characterizes a market system.

None of these traditional state-directed activities has been privatized. Instead, the Conservative government has sold off public assets at the 'luxury' end of the market – British Telecom and British Gas being spectacular examples. The suspicion must be that the prime aim of the privatization programme is not to increase competition but to raise money. This suspicion is compounded by the fact that the major profitable public assets have been sold off as *private* monopolies. This obviously makes them much more attractive to private buyers. It is clear, for example, that the gas industry is not a natural monopoly, that is, a singly supplied service emerging spontaneously from the market, such as the telephone system. The British Gas Corporation could have been broken up into small units, and the new companies made to compete for the favours of the gas consumer. There is no reason why gas production and the network system (the transmission of gas) should all be in the same hands. By the same logic, national airlines should not be sold off with a state-decreed control over the most profitable routes (as will happen in the case of British Airways). Genuine competition between private airlines would allow a completely free market for all routes with no state involvement at all.

Even though a private monopoly *appears* to be little better than a public one, the fact that it is private may give it some advantages for the consumer. If it is operating inefficiently then the fear of a take-over may spur the management into giving better service. However, this is most unlikely to be a threat to huge concerns such as British Gas. Ironically, the wide spread of ownership may actually be a disadvantage since the dispersed shareholders are difficult to organize to put pressure on the management to act more efficiently.

A thriving competitive market economy depends very much on small business: most new jobs in the United States and Britain are created in firms of less than twenty employees. However, the regulatory activity of the modern state impinges adversely on small business. The local rate burden and planning legislation is a much greater deterrent to the 'birth-rate' of new enterprises than is often realized. Large firms are less affected by such state impediments but they are often insurmountable burdens to small entrepreneurs.

The origin of the concept of the 'Enterprise Zone' lies in the recognition that government regulation is a serious inhibition to creativity in the market. An Enterprise Zone is a part of a large urban area (usually a derelict segment) which is freed from local planning laws that empower the local authority to prevent business expansion, and relieved of the local tax burden, so as to provide an environment more conducive to entrepreneur-ship (see Butler, 1980). Such schemes have been embodied in legislation in both the United States and Britain. It is perhaps too early to say whether they have been successful: one objection is that they tend to attract existing businesses into the privileged area rather than foster the creation of new enterprises. Nevertheless, the existence of the concept attests to the fact that it is the state itself, rather than any defect in the market, that stands in the way of economic progress. The extreme market theorist would, of course, maintain that the whole country should be made into an Enter-prise Zone, since it is the state that coagulates the market.

The movement towards a free and more competitive economy necessitates a sceptical attitude towards the state. The market theorist doubts that officials, elected or appointed, are motivated to act for the public good. He assumes that they are no less immune to self-interest than familiar market transactors. Elected politicians are likely to provide policies favourable to politically significant interest groups while officials are motivated by non-pecuniary forms of aggrandisement, such as expansions of the size of their bureaus. The difficulty with a market society is that its benefits tend to be long-term and thinly spread while the advantages of political action, such as a state subsidy or an exemption from competi-tion, are immediate to special interest groups. However, the sum of such privileges is damaging to the competitive market economy as a whole. This has been the experience of Western mixed economies over the past thirty years.

My discussion so far has been exclusively about what is called micro-economics: the behaviour of individuals and firms in decentralized exchange relationships. There is, however, another branch of economics, developed largely in the twentieth century, which has to do with the behaviour of large-scale aggregates, the money supply, the level of unemployment, the level of investment and so on. This is, of course, macro-economics. What gave great impetus to the rise of macro-economics was the experience of mass unemployment in the 1930s (to some extent repeated in the 1980s) which the tools of conventional political economy *appeared* to be unable to explain. The publication in 1936 of Keynes's *The General Theory of*

Employment, Interest and Money, a book which located the causes of unemployment not in defects in the micro structure of a market economy but in a malfunctioning of the whole system, namely a deficiency in effective demand, constituted a revolution in economic science.

However, traditional market economists have always claimed that unemployment can be explained by some malfunctioning of the price system itself. Thus labour must, in a free market, be analysed in the same terms as any other good or factor: if the price of it is too high then less of it will be bought. Historically, market economists have blamed trade unions for causing unemployment: by using their monopoly powers (granted by statute) they are able to keep the price of labour above its market clearing price, hence rewarding their own members at the cost of reducing employment for others, who would be prepared to work for less than the wage rate prescribed by unions. A large part of the market economist's political programme is aimed at eliminating the legal privileges of trade unions: immunity from tort actions in industrial disputes, the easy establishment of 'closed shops', and tolerant picketing laws. They would also stress that such privileges are much more dangerous in public sector employment since there the threat of bankruptcy does not operate to restrain the actions of unions.

It is not, however, trade unions alone that constitute impediments to the fluid operation of the labour market; in fact, many market economists think their disruptive influence has been exaggerated. Of equal significance has been the myriad of welfare benefits (and other statist interventions in the market) that have severely restricted the mobility of labour. If the difference between unemployment pay (and other welfare benefits) and the potential wage is not very great then, naturally, incentives to work are reduced. To the market economist this entails no moral judgement: in such circumstances those who choose unemployment are responding quite rationally to a market signal. Of equal significance is the establishment of minimum wage laws (especially in the United States) for these render unemployable those workers whose marginal productivity does not equal the legal minimum wage.

Of very great importance in Britain is housing policy, for misguided interventions in the housing market have reduced the incentives for the unemployed to move to places where work is available. The occupation of cheap (i.e. below market rent) public housing constitutes a kind of 'property right' which people will have to surrender if they move to an area where there is employment: there is no guarantee that they will find equivalent housing to go with the jobs. The housing shortage is compounded by rent control and security of tenure in the private-rented sector: those legislative enactments have had a drastic effect on the supply of rented property, since landlords will sell their properties rather than let them at low rents.

It is facts such as these that constitute what market economists call the 'natural rate of unemployment'. This is that rate of unemployment caused by the structural imperfections in the market mentioned above. It is a phenomenon that is virtually ignored by Keynesian economists, who see virtually all unemployment as the result of a deficiency of demand in a market economy. But the liberal economist argues that, since unemployment is the result of impediments to the smooth operation of the market rather than demand deficiency, any attempt to get unemployment below the 'natural rate' by government deficits or simple money creation will have no effect on production and employment but will raise prices all round (i.e. cause inflation). The experience of post-war Britain, and France between 1981 and 1983, indicates that the attempt to raise employment by boosting demand results in never-ending inflation with little long-term effect on employment.

This leads me to the most important feature of market theory in the realm of 'macro-economics': the necessity for monetary stability for the efficacy of a decentralized exchange system. In traditional economic theory it was argued that the money good (normally gold) would emerge spontaneously in a market system. In fact, as long as governments were constrained by the Gold Standard from excessive money creation, inflation was held at bay. The twentieth century, however, has seen the removal of all constraints, including the Gold Standard and the system of fixed exchange rates between currencies, and the handing over of *discretionary* power to governments in monetary matters. Hence, the major claim of market theorists is that monetary profligacy is inevitable unless this discretionary power of the state is removed.

There is one important area which I have not yet touched on: the 'legitimate' role of the public sector in a market economy. Apart from a minority of extremists (called 'anarcho-capitalists') all classical liberal market economists accept that certain goods and services have to be supplied by the state. These are known as public goods. They are 'non-rival' in consumption and 'non-excludable'. If a good is 'non-rival' it means that once supplied it is available for everyone (unlike a private good); and if it is non-excludable it means that it is impossible to exclude from consumption those who have not paid for it. The classic public goods are clean air, defence and a general system of law. Because of these features a spontaneous market will either under-supply, or not supply at all, public goods. It should be noted that these do not include a wide variety of activities pursued by contemporary governments, such as housing, health, education, welfare and pensions. In the opinion of market economists the removal of competition from these areas causes inefficiency and often inequality.

Despite its association in the popular mind with capitalism and inequality, the market is in many ways a 'neutral' social institution that can be used for a variety of ends and purposes. It is not necessarily opposed to equality. In fact, it is argued by classical liberals that this goal could be pursued more effectively through the market than by the extension of public services. A reallocation of property rights (perhaps through inheritance and land taxes) could produce some equality while maintaining the liberty of the market.

There is one feature of the market whose egalitarian implications have been almost completely neglected by socialists. This is the fact that competition itself is a persistent equalizing force. I have already shown that in general equilibrium theory the returns to the factors of production are just sufficient to ensure their continued operation in the productive process: inequality is therefore only required as a necessary incentive for social efficiency and 'supra-normal' profits are absent. Although a market *process* does require such profits, it must be remembered that these are constantly being whittled away by rivalrous competition. It follows from this that the best way to achieve more equality would be to subject more human activities to competition. In fact, the market economist argues that the state itself, by granting monopoly privileges to groups, and exemptions from the competitive process, does more to increase social inequality than do the activities of market transactors.

The market at the moment appears to be on the threshold of a new era of intellectual popularity. This is not merely the result of changes in fashion that inevitably occur in the social sciences but has perhaps more to do with the observed failures of alternative social and economic arrangements. The one thing that will impede its further progress is misunderstanding about its operation and nature. It is not necessarily the ideology of 'capitalists' and 'business interests'; as Adam Smith pointed out, these are the most adroit evaders of its rigours. A properly understood market process is not just a generator of economic welfare, it is also a protection for liberty and an efficient method for the realization of many desirable social goals.

References

Alchian, A. A. (1977) 'Uncertainty, Evolution and Economic Theory', pp. 15–35 in Alchian, A. A. *Economic Forces at Work*. Indianapolis, IN: Liberty Press.

Barry, N. P. (1985) 'In Defence of the Invisible Hand', *The Cato Journal* 5: 135–48.

Burton, J. (1983) *Picking Losers...?* London: Institute of Economic Affairs.

Butler, S. (1980) *Enterprise Zones: Pioneering in the Inner City*. Washington, DC: The Heritage Foundation.

Hayek, F. A. (1948) *Individualism and Economic Order*. London: Routledge & Kegan Paul.

Keynes, J. M. (1963) *The General Theory of Unemployment, Interest and Money*. London: Macmillan (first published in 1936).

Lippincott, B. (1938) *On the Economic Theory of Socialism*. Minnesota: University of Minnesota Press.

Smith, A. (1979) *An Enquiry into the Nature and Causes of the Wealth of Nations*, edited by R. H. Campbell and A. S. Skinner. Oxford: Clarendon Press (first published in 1776).

14
Towards the remoralization of society

Stephen Davies

Today British society is in a state of moral crisis. Over the last forty years or so it has become progressively demoralized. This crisis of demoralization has many symptoms, the most dramatic being the remorseless increase in levels of criminal and delinquent behaviour; others include the apparent breakdown of stable family life and the general decline of civility. To use the terminology of 'crisis' is to imply that a process of change or social transformation, taking place over a long period, has reached a critical stage where some kind of resolution of the stresses and tensions involved has become inevitable. What that resolution may be is quite another matter.

Any observer of contemporary Britain is faced with a truly colossal array of information obtained from a bewildering variety of sources. There are the statistics derived from both official and private publications, the more apparently subjective evidence of surveys and polls, the unquantified and subjective data provided by journalistic accounts and the direct knowledge gained by the personal experience of oneself and one's acquaintances. One task of social scientists is to assess and interpret all of this information. What does it tell us about the state, condition and nature of the entity called British society in the 1980s? This obviously involves making judgements as to the relative value and validity of the different types of information available. It must also involve an element of interpretation and judgement. The naive positivist or empiricist approach which claims to be neutral as between different value judgements and concerned simply with establishing 'the facts' is useless here. The precise meaning or interpretation given to a particular datum such as the number of divorces depends upon the theoretical model employed by the observer. A social analysis which will be of any use and will contribute to our understanding of where we are must have four main features:

1 It must present a model or theory which explains, integrates and interprets large numbers of brute facts.

2 It will of necessity be prescriptive as well as descriptive – a social analysis will lead to conclusions as to the proper or effective course for public policy.

3 It will be normative insofar as it will raise moral and philosophical issues and must adopt clear positions on these. Thus meaningful and useful social analysis must contain, for example, notions of the nature of the good life, the good society, the nature and causes of human action and the differentiation of public and private.

4 Finally, any effective analysis must be historically aware. All human

institutions and activities have a history and can only be properly understood in a historical context.

To summarize, the work of social scientists is not only descriptive but diagnostic in the strict sense of simultaneously explaining and prescribing. Social policy can only take place within the context of an agreed model or explanation of the state and condition of contemporary society. Thus interpretations of data feed directly into active social policy.

The main thesis being put here is that many features of contemporary British life, and much of the information available to us, are explicable only in terms of a threatened or actual process of demoralization. This has reached a stage in parts of Britain where the very existence and idea of a moral community is at risk. The notion of demoralization does not refer to such obvious matters as the rate of crime, the disregard of sexual and other taboos or levels of single parenthood. It means rather that the very idea of morality and of a moral code or rule which governs relations between individuals is in doubt. Matters such as rising delinquency are symptomatic of this erosion of the belief that there are or should be moral rules of any kind. In particular there has been a falling away from the belief that people as individuals have rights or claims which should be respected in all relations, public or private.

The main premisses on which this thesis is based are these:

1 Human beings have free will and the capacity to make choices and decisions. Indeed, life consists of the process of choice.

2 The essence of this is the use of reason and will. By virtue of their capacity for free will humans are therefore responsible beings and can be held accountable for their actions. (Clearly this does not apply in cases where the capacity of reason is undeveloped or absent, as in children or imbeciles.)

3 This accountability is what makes humans moral creatures and enables us to make judgements of right and wrong. If people lack free will in some important respect then questions of praise or censure, right and wrong, are irrelevant when applied to human action.

4 Individuals have certain rights which in one sense constitute a claim against one's fellows. The most important of these are those to life, property and security of person (Rothbard, 1981). Social intercourse between people and groups should be based upon the observance of these rights and claims – indeed if this does not happen then in a very real sense a civil society cannot be said to exist.

5 A violation of rights is a moral wrong. A truly virtuous society is one in which rights are generally observed and respected and people are free to act rather than being subject to coercion, being held responsible for their actions. This leads to the creation of a moral community where, although there may be a plurality of views on particular matters such as sexual mores, there is a consensus that people be held responsible for their actions and that social interactions should respect the rights of others thus making theft, acts of violence and so on generally reprehensible (Buchanan, 1985).

6 Conversely, a social order in which responsibility is denied and rights limited will erode virtuous behaviour until it is faced with a stark choice between moral chaos and the attempt to enforce virtue by force. This is self-defeating because if people are 'forced to be good' their status as responsible beings is further denied and the moral value of a coerced act is inherently dubious.

7 Obviously free will is exercised not in a vacuum but in a particular social and material context. This can give a proclivity to one type of choice and hence action rather than another. Crime and anti-social behaviour are the consequence of the breakdown of a moral community which leads to changes in people's subjective perception of themselves and their position vis-à-vis other individuals.

8 The most important means whereby a moral community is promoted and upheld is through a range of institutions which both enable and encourage people to act in one way rather than another. The state is the least important of these. Families and households, voluntary associations, churches, educational institutions, patterns of work and everyday living are far more significant.

9 Finally, levels of delinquent and immoral behaviour are historically variable: there is not a simple constant level.

What then is the evidence for this thesis of demoralization? To put it another way what are the phenomena which are explained by this thesis and why does it explain them better than other, alternative models? The phenomena called in aid and the evidence adduced are varied but all point in one direction. First, and most dramatic, is the seemingly constant rise in the level of crime. The statistics of crimes reported to the police in England and Wales show a rise from 1200 per 100,000 of population to almost 6000 between 1960 and 1980 (Kinsey, 1986). For some offences such as burglary and theft the increases are even more dramatic. Since 1979 recorded crime per 100,000 has risen by no less than 40 percent. Such figures are open to criticism on the grounds that they only tell us about those crimes which have reached the attention of the law enforcement authorities: the 'dark figure' of unreported crime is not shown. This means that quite large increases in apparent levels of crime may only reflect a higher level of reporting or greater efficiency on the part of the police. Thus much of the massive apparent increase in rape and sexual abuse in the last two years can be put down to a growth in the willingness of victims to come forward. However, it is not proper to assume or argue that this model of increased reporting can explain the increases in other crimes where the special factors involved in sexual offences do not apply. In fact, the crime surveys introduced by the Thatcher government and those carried out under the auspices of local authorities in Islington and Merseyside all indicate that the increase in several areas is even more rapid than the official statistics suggest (Kinsey, 1984/5; Young and Jones, 1986; Hough and Mayhew, 1983). So, for example, the British Crime Survey showed that between 1981 and 1983 burglary rose by 20 percent per capita as opposed to the official rise of 15 percent (Hough and Mayhew, 1983). Recorded crime is only the visible tip of a very large iceberg. The percentage of crimes recorded in criminal statistics varies from 98 percent in the case of car theft, through 48 percent and 30 percent for burglary and theft from a motor vehicle to 8 percent for vandalism, 11 percent for sexual assault of all types and only 8 percent for robbery/theft from the person (Kinsey, 1986). Moreover, much of this increase in crime is concentrated in certain areas: the rise in Hackney or central Manchester is far greater than that in Surbiton. For the inhabitants of these areas the growth of crime is even worse than the aggregate figures suggest. Thus the Islington survey revealed that in the previous year 31 percent of households had had a crime committed against them (Young and Jones, 1986: 201).

The rise in crime is only one part of a more general increase in delinquent, often vicious and beastly, behaviour. Sexual and racial harassment, verbal abuse and foul language, rowdy and boorish behaviour and grossly immodest acts combine to make the lives of many people a misery. Women, the old and racial minority groups are particular sufferers. Clearly this cannot be quantified in the same way as crime because of the element of subjective evaluation: one person's gross indecency or rowdiness is another one's high spirits. Even so, all the surveys and work done of late on life in contemporary Britain point to a high and rising level of delinquent, vicious behaviour (Seabrook, 1978, 1984; Harrison, 1985: esp. 228–37). The degree of pain and suffering that can be caused is indicated by one account published in the *Guardian* where a man from Liverpool describes how many are driven almost to suicide by the treatment they receive from some of their neighbours (*Guardian*, 23 August 1986).

This in turn can be seen as an extreme expression of a more general decline in civility. In this context 'civility' means not just orthodox politeness but general respect for the feelings, sensibilities and autonomy of others; thus to eat pork in front of a devout Moslem or Jew is a gross breach of civility. More seriously, activities such as the playing of very loud music which disturbs and aggravates one's neighbours, or the use of foul language in front of older people and young children, are commonplace examples of such incivility which cause much tension, even distress. Here objective assessment of change is even more difficult but it is revealing that once again a decline in consideration and civility is one of the main complaints of respondents in surveys and journalistic accounts. One fact which all accounts note is that the great offenders for both general incivility and more serious delinquency are the young, especially young males. This is the group which is also responsible for most recorded crime. A very disturbing trend is for such anti-social behaviour to start at an ever younger age; a recent report showed that according to a survey of schoolteachers the attitudes and actions of primary school entrants have declined sharply in the last ten years (Lawrence and Steed, 1986).

As well as anti-social acts there has also been a marked increase in patterns of behaviour which, while not directly anti-social, are profoundly self-destructive and irresponsible and which can contribute to more directly delinquent lifestyles. The most prominent example is the growing use of drugs, but more serious in both scale and effect is the truly massive increase in drunkenness and alcohol abuse, particularly among teenagers. This has grave implications not only because of the personal unhappiness and economic costs but also because of the clear link between drink and crime, especially violent crime.

There are several other pieces of evidence which cannot be presented in a straightforward quantified mode but are perhaps even more important. There is increasing evidence of a decline in stable social relationships, evinced by the rapid increases in levels of divorce, illegitimacy and the number of children and young people running away from home. For obvious reasons it is exceedingly difficult to discern what is happening to personal relationships within the nation's households but it would seem that family ties and relations are becoming weaker, particularly that between father and son. This partly reflects a more general erosion of the social contact between older and younger men. It would seem that for many the family is a restrictive and resented influence which prevents self-gratification and is therefore seen as a hindrance, something to be escaped from.

This in turn reflects the most sinister feature of the contemporary scene, the domination of public and private discourse and debate by a set of interlinked and mutually reinforcing beliefs.

First is moral relativism, the great scourge of our time: the assumption that there is no right or wrong, that one act or code is as good as another with everything dependent upon the situation or the whim of the actor.

This leads directly to nihilism, perhaps the most fashionable idea of the moment amongst people of all types and conditions. Nihilism comes in two brands, one cheerful, the other despairing, but both share the common premisses that nothing matters, nothing has any real value and that virtue is impossible.

Third is the unquestioned assumption that desires and wishes should never be thwarted and that anything which prevents the realization of wants should be removed. This found classic expression during the public debate on *in vitro* fertilization where the desire of parents to have children was taken to be an unanswerable argument – how could anyone prevent the realization of such a desperate want? (I should point out that I am in favour of both *in vitro* fertilization and surrogate motherhood but for other, better reasons.)

However, the most influential and pernicious of all these notions is the denial of personal responsibility. It is one of the great commonplaces of modern times that we are not truly free, that we live in a system of concealed domination and manipulation so that our acts are not our own (Minogue, 1985). The capacity of humans to make choices of their own free will is systematically denied in much modern thought. Actions are explained instead in terms of biology, economic status, environment, uncontrollable psychology and many other factors, seldom in terms of responsible choice. This notion is found on both 'Left' and 'Right', the former explaining crime by pointing to the deprived background of the criminal, the latter blaming drug use on malevolent pushers and ignoring the choice of the users who are seen as helpless puppets.

Fifthly, the notion of identity and character as the product of a series of willed choices is denied. Character and identity are thought to come from outside the individual, being socially determined, and the whole idea of identity becomes problematic.

Finally, one can call in aid several cultural phenomena, notably the cult of violence and aggression which finds expression in films such as *Rambo* and the profoundly anti-social values expressed by the 'youth culture' which represent a working-out in concrete and overt form of the five ideas spelt out above. The diagnosis put here is that all of this forms and is caused by a moral crisis.

What though of other, alternative theories and how can we judge between them and the one put forward here? Are social science models incommensurable paradigms with the decision as to the one you support a matter of political sympathy or personal taste? Actually a model can be judged on several criteria. These are: internal logic and consistency – does it contain major contradictions or anomalies?; its success in explaining the known data – are there any data which it cannot account for?; it may generate predictions which can then be tested by empirical research; and it may generate specific conclusions for public policy which can then be tested in practice.

There are several alternative models but these can be classified under four main heads. Firstly, there are several which either deny that any problem exists or else seek to minimize its extent. One argument is that there are not enough statistically sound data to prove the existence of a true problem of crime and delinquency. The available statistics are held to show only that the legal system is working in a particular way, concentrating upon certain types of case rather than others. By this argument the present state of affairs is neither grave nor historically unusual. This kind of model is flawed in three ways: it overlooks the varying experience of different geographical areas and social groups – there may not be an objective crisis in Surrey while there is in Merseyside; it ignores the overwhelming evidence of the crime surveys that crime and delinquent behaviour are actually more common and rising more rapidly than the statistics indicate; while historically aware, the historical evidence is misinterpreted (see below).

More sophisticated is the popular argument that the present concern with crime and order is a 'moral panic', designed to legitimate an increase in the power of the state and particularly the police (Hall et al., 1978). In this model crime and delinquency serve the interests of a dominant class by legitimating repression at a time of capitalist crisis, by promoting mutual suspicion and weakening solidarity among the subordinate classes and by isolating the most economically exploited members of society as a labelled 'underclass' of incorrigible delinquents while ignoring the crimes and wrongs of the powerful (Box, 1984). Some of these points are shrewd and well taken. The growth in the numbers and powers of the police will on the evidence have little effect on levels of anti-social behaviour and probably does derive primarily from fears for public order: the notion of a 'criminal class' does not stand up to analysis, whether of today or any other historical period (Beier, 1985; Hall et al., 1978). However, because a rising level of delinquency may have the effect of strengthening support for a strong state, it does not then follow that the rise is imaginary or invented. The panic promoting coverage of certain types of crime by the popular press does not mean that there is no problem, only that it is being presented in a misleading way. This type of model also falls foul of the evidence which undermines the first type and has recently been sharply criticized from the 'Left' by the 'Left Realist' school of criminology (Young, 1981; Matthews and Young, 1986: 21–5; Lea and Young, 1984: 11–49; Rafter, 1986).

The third main 'no problem' model is one which portrays delinquent behaviour as simply activity which challenges the dominant ideology, hence anti-hegemonic, with the perpetrators labelled by the use of the criminal law. This model has several crucial faults. Even its advocates hesitate to describe some crimes such as rape as simply anti-hegemonic. More generally, as Rafter points out, such theories ignore the demonstrable fact that while there may be divergent views within society as to the rights and wrongs of, for example, drug-taking, there is a very wide agreement found in every recorded society that acts directly harmful to the person such as theft or assault are wrong and punishable (Rafter, 1986: 11). The ideological challenge model also has trouble explaining why most delinquents are not part of deviant subculture but often highly conventional members of the 'dominant culture'. What all of the 'no problem' theories overlook is that the main sufferers from the rising tide of delinquency are the poor, disadvantaged and weak. To assert that their problems are imaginary or 'got up' by the ruling class is both factually inaccurate and offensive.

Secondly, there are theories which admit the existence of a social problem of delinquency but explain it by reference to environmental factors rather than the choices of the actors. The most popular accounts for the growth of anti-social behaviour by reference to the economic conditions of modern economies, especially the historically high levels of unemployment. Many of the arguments on both sides of this particular debate are weak. It is easy to show that there is a close correlation between the rise of crime and the increase of unemployment. However, that by itself is not enough to demonstrate a causal connection: if the two are both increasing at the same time there will be a correlation whether they are connected or not (Bottomley and Pease, 1986: 137–40). The common counter-argument that because high unemployment did not lead to high crime levels in the 1930s it cannot be responsible for the high levels of today is also logically faulty. The experience of unemployment may be crucially different today as compared to fifty years ago so that its effect may be different. More to the point, the present rising curve of delinquency was well under way before the world economy slipped into recession in 1973. The flaws in this model are more basic. If criminal and anti-social acts are a consequence of the level of unemployment then one would expect people directly affected by it to be more likely to engage in such acts; this is not the case. This model also has problems with the motiveless and vicious nature of many delinquent acts: if they are a response to an economic situation then why are they so futile by any standard of rational conduct? In particular why should sexual offences increase as a result of a change in levels of economic activity? These questions can only be answered within the terms of the model by adopting a determinist notion of human action which makes economic factors account for almost all choices and renders acts such as rape unblameworthy: how can one criticize somebody for acts which derive from the way they are affected by economic forces over which they have no control?

A slightly different argument explains high rates of crime as the inevitable consequence of modernity. This is easily refuted. It is historically inaccurate: modernity has co-existed with falling rates of recorded crime (Gatrell, 1980). In the contemporary world there are societies such as Switzerland and Japan which are undoubtedly modern but have stable or falling rates of crime (Clinard, 1978).

Another argument which has gained currency recently lays stress upon the physical environment and especially the type and pattern of housing (Coleman, 1985). The empirical evidence here is very impressive, with Coleman's study showing a clear correlation between types of anti-social behaviour and particular forms of housing such as deck access. However this again does not explain the totality of delinquent behaviour, nor does it explain why people have responded to particular features of the new urban environment by acting in one way rather than another. Why should the dark, dank tunnels of many estates be used mainly by potential or actual thieves? In other words this theory again lacks an adequate model of human motivation and action.

One model which is not lacking in that regard is the one best described as 'populist conservative'. The main feature of this theory is a pessimistic picture of human nature. Humans, especially men, are naturally sinful and prone to wicked acts. They need to be restrained by force or the fear of punishment. Social institutions exist to tame the natural anti-social instincts of men. Delinquency is thus a historically inevitable fact; increases in its incidence are due primarily to the demise of socializing influences and a diminished likelihood of effective punishment (Van Den Haag, 1975). This model has strong elements, for example the stress upon socialization, but the emphasis on punishment overlooks the clear evidence that there is no clear correlation between patterns of punishment and levels of delinquency: Britain today has higher levels of crime than other comparable countries yet the pattern of punishment is more severe and the likelihood of detection similar.

All of these models share certain features. They are all, except for the conservative, concerned with aggregates and skirt around the question of why individual people act in the way they do. Apart from the conservative they all have trouble with the marked gender variation in delinquency and with crimes such as rape or sexual harassment. None is sufficiently historically aware. They all have problems with features of many delinquent acts such as their frequently impulsive and petty, even pointless nature. Not enough stress is put on the relations between individuals which form the 'sharp end' of crime and delinquency – the methodology is generally collectivist rather than individualist. All except the conservative tend to ignore the wider range of phenomena which go along with more serious delinquency.

The model of demoralization argues that crime, delinquency and the other phenomena listed above are all part of one dynamic process. As the idea of respect for other people's rights has declined and the very notion of a moral code has been eroded so the consciousness and ways of thinking of individuals are altered. Their actions and decisions are based upon premises which lead often to anti-social acts; this can lead to a vicious circle of demoralization where each breach of the general principle of responsibility and regard for others leads to further breaches. This model explains a wide range of phenomena, not simply overt crime. What, though, has brought about this situation? It is always hard in social science to distinguish between effects and causes; to take one part of a phenomenon and present it as the cause of the rest is often misleading or worse. Sometimes there is an initial event or happening which then sets a self-sustaining process in train. The demoralization of Britain can be ascribed to some things which are peculiar to this country, others which are found in most industrialized nations, whether capitalist or socialist (in recent years accounts of delinquency have become a major concern of the Soviet press); it is the countries with low and stable or declining levels of delinquency such as Switzerland and Japan which are exceptional.

A central place must be given to the hegemony of the body of ideas set out earlier. This is both part and cause of the crisis. These ideas took a long time to achieve their current pre-eminence in thought and debate for although they first appeared in the 1880s it was not until the 1930s that they came to dominate intellectual debate and only in the early 1960s did they achieve the status of 'common sense'. Changes in the patterns of thought and belief of a given society can affect the actions and behaviour of individuals quite dramatically, as the impact of religion on a recipient culture demonstrates. The more dominant one set of beliefs becomes the more true it appears to be as ever-increasing numbers of people act on the basis of these notions of irresponsibility and self-gratification but from small beginnings they have come to dominate every area of intellectual life – the idea that history or literary studies, for example, should contain an essential element of moral judgement is hardly considered. The source of these ideas is problematics; some would see them as a response to the breakdown of the Newtonian cosmology with its associated 'mechanical' world view (Johnson, 1983), while others present them as a response to the cataclysmic political events of the years since 1914. Yet others identify the beliefs but argue that they are part and parcel of an advanced economy or of some complex psycho-historical process (Bell, 1976; Lasch, 1979). This debate is relevant insofar as it has implications for any attempt to undermine the hegemonic status of this body of belief; if they are a response to the demands of a particular type of economy, as Bell argues, then logically the economy must change if the ideas are to be affected. If the ideas are thought to have an autonomous status then intellectual argument and debate may be sufficient of themselves.

Beside the influence of ideas and beliefs is the effect of economic and social policy. The policies followed in both of these areas over the last forty years or longer have worked to insidiously undermine crucial notions of responsibility and respect for others. The main aim of public policy in both areas has frequently been to protect individuals and groups from the consequences of their actions. This undermines any idea of responsibility. The practice of economic intervention and a great deal of social policy have undercut the idea that people as individuals have rights which should be respected since the operative theory has been that the needs of others supersede those rights. Paradoxically, the insistence upon rights in the sense of entitlements when applied to social policy has again eroded the concept of responsibility. These, however, are intellectual effects. More important in matters of policy is the impact which social and economic policy has had on the pattern of everyday life. Since the early 1920s the effect of public policy has been to undermine any sort of self-determining activity such as mutual aid or collective self-help. In the previous century most people were involved in an array of voluntary organizations which met the needs of most for education, leisure, assistance or simple conviviality. The common response to any social problem, personal or collective, was mutuality and co-operation. This tradition apparently died after the First World War and today is much diminished, though there is some evidence of a revival. Since that time the whole emphasis of public policy has been upon large-scale, collective solutions to social problems using the apparatus of the state. This amounts to a radical change in the experience of the majority of people from a situation where the response to any problem was to act on one's own responsibility to one where the assumption is that any difficulty is a public problem and should be dealt with by a paternalistic state. This amounts for many to a removal of practical responsibility for and control over one's own life. Against this one can point to the record number of charities and voluntary organizations. However, many of the largest are professionalized with little or no direct relationship between the members/donors and the recipients, while a charity is in any case a different type of animal from a mutual aid association. Again many voluntary bodies partake more of the nature of pressure groups and see their main role as being advocates for an interest in the public policy arena. Even so there has been a revival of true mutual aid in recent years and this is a welcome development, but it has a very long way to go.

Social and economic policy has had other effects which have diminished the role and importance of personal responsibility. In particular it has in practice led to a great transfer of power to professionals. The most obvious case are social workers but perhaps the most harmful example of this process has been the change in the relationship between public and police. Since the turn of the century the entire thrust of public order policy has been to enhance the role and importance of the police while reducing that of the public. The protection of the rights of others is now thought of as a matter which concerns primarily the police, not the public at large. Since all the evidence shows that it is the public which is mainly responsible for upholding order and that public co-operation is essential if any policy strategy is to be effective this has had disastrous consequences (Kinsey, 1986).

Perhaps the most visible effect of public policy which has contributed to the demoralization is the state and nature of public housing stock. The physical structure and layout of many post-war estates have exacerbated the problems of delinquency and anti-social behaviour by making personal contacts in some ways more tenuous and by providing the opportunity for anti-social acts on a massive scale. Significantly, the crucial error appears to have been the creation of many large public spaces which no one was or felt responsible for and which have become derelict, a no man's land of violence, graffiti and vandalism (Coleman, 1985).

The blurring of cause and effect can be seen in the case of a large part of the cultural production of our times. This both reflects a moral vacuum and reinforces it, feeding back into both popular and elite attitudes and beliefs. There are certainly autonomous influences which have played a major part in aggravating this, particularly television and the psychological impact of the nuclear arms race. In the instance of television, the problem is not the content or bias of the programme but rather the nature of the medium itself, which appears to promote passivity and lack of engagement as well as other undesirable qualities such as difficulty in concentrating. However these are broadly exacerbatory influences rather than original causes.

Finally, there is the decline, already alluded to, of socializing and moralizing institutions. Human beings are free to act and to choose, hence responsible, but the way they act reflects the way their character and identity have formed as well as their presumptions. During the formation of character the institutional and social context within which it takes place has great influence. A person brought up in an environment which emphasizes clear rules and respect for others is probably going to act and develop differently to one raised in an environment of anomie[1] and irresponsibility. The most important factors seem to be the following: growing up in a stable household, at least in the earlier years of life; contact with adult members of society, especially during adolescence, which encourages integration into adult society; the existence within the home and life-sphere of a clear system of values; the opportunity to have responsibility and to take part in activities which promote civility and co-operation as well as personal responsibility (Murray, 1984). One should stress that the precise composition of the household or of the system of values is secondary; what matters is that these exist. Thus a single-parent household can be stable, more so than one with serious family divisions. The crucial matter is the reason for its being a single-parent household and the way it functions. However, it is of course much more difficult to meet some of the above criteria when a single parent but it can be done. There is a high correlation in the United States between single parenthood and delinquency (Murray, 1984) but these are both the product of a demoralized culture rather than one being the cause. The question of contact with adults is particularly important. As indicated earlier, young men are far more likely to be delinquent than women of a similar age. Setting aside the argument that girls are nice while boys are male barbarians/animals, the crucial difference appears to be that young men have far less contact with mature older men than girls have with older women. This makes the dominant influence the peer group which, given other factors, is a profoundly anti-social one (Morgan, 1978). The decline of moralizing agencies creates a vicious circle – as one generation succeeds another so the moralizing agencies are weakened to an ever greater degree.

Before examining the prescriptive element, what of the historical context? Some would have it that the current state of affairs is merely a reversion to a historical norm. In this way of thinking it is the low rates of crime and delinquency recorded between about 1920 and 1960 which are aberrant (Pearson, 1983; Middleton, 1986). However, this overlooks several facts. Most notably it ignores the historical pattern of crime, delinquency and anti-social behaviour recorded in Britain over the last 150 years. This shows a prolonged decline from the middle of the last century up to about 1900 followed by a long period of stability then a sharp rise. In other words, since the Industrial Revolution levels of crime and delinquency have been static or declining as often as rising. The definitive work in this area is that of Gatrell, which shows quite clearly the scale and extent of the fall (Gatrell, 1980; Gatrell and Hadden, 1972). Trials for all indictable crime fell from 288 per 100,000 to 164 between the 1860s and the late 1890s while for violent crime the decline was even steeper (Gatrell, 1980: 280–92). The fall in crime was even steeper than these suggest for the increasing efficiency of the police led to a higher rate of detection which for some time counterbalanced the real decline.

What can explain this dramatic change? The obvious answer is that it reflected the impact of the New Police following the County and Borough Police Act of 1853 and the deterrent effect of the new penal regime adopted after the Prison Act of 1877. However, as Gatrell points out, the evidence does not support this for the pattern of conviction and sentencing did not change markedly (Gatrell, 1980: 293–301) so that there is no evidence for any deterrent effect. Again there is no demonstrable correlation between police activity and levels of crime: in Manchester the fall in recorded crime began after the peak of police activity and during the period when the local police were plagued by corruption so flagrant that the Home Office was obliged to suspend the authority and impose a new Chief Constable (Davies, 1985; Jones, 1982). A similar pattern is found elsewhere. The decline in crime began at roughly the same time all over England and Wales regardless of the nature and level of policing in any particular locality and continued until just before 1900. Moreover there is abundant evidence of a more general decline in anti-social behaviour. The acute problems of drunkenness and social breakdown commented on by observers of the 1830s and 1840s had declined till by the late 1890s they were confined to a relatively small section of society. All the observers of the later period commented on the increased sobriety and respectability of the mass of the people in late Victorian England. What had happened between 1840 and 1900 was a great process of moral reform; the contrast at every level between the state of affairs in 1900 and 1910 is so sharp as not to require comment. Gradually Victorian society had developed mechanisms which minimized anti-social behaviour and controlled it when it did occur.

This change had come about not as a result of direct political action but through the combined effects of voluntary action and the development of a liberal commercial society which by its workings encouraged the upholding by most people of a code of personal responsibility and respect for others. The process of reform had begun long before the decline in anti-social behaviour showed itself – there would seem to have been a one-generational delay in its effects being felt. What does the historical evidence and the diagnosis presented earlier indicate about the proper response to the problems of today?

The prescription which derives from the diagnosis is sweeping and has some surprising elements. In general, if anti-social acts are the outcome of the decline in the notion of morality and particularly the belief that others rights should be respected, then the crucial need is to reconstruct these ideas. What is needed is a cultural/moral reform like that achieved between 1840 and 1900. This implies some measures/strategies which will not yield results for a long time and others which will have a more immediate palliative effect. In the short term changes in state policy are important but the longer term requires social or private action. Indeed in the longer term the role of state action in the process of remoralization should be peripheral rather than central.

1 The reform and physical reconstruction of a large part of the housing stock is clearly an urgent matter. This will be expensive but the immediate results, as experiments in London have shown, can be dramatic. The cost can be reduced by resort to self-build/rebuild schemes which have the additional advantage of making people once again responsible for their environment.

2 The entire pattern and strategy of policing needs to be rethought to involve the public and re-emphasize the general responsibility to uphold the law and respect others. This could mean going beyond neighbourhood watch schemes and reviving old institutions such as Associations for the Prosecution of Felons, as well as private prosecutions and more local control of the police.

3 In penal policy there is a need firstly for clear and certain penalties for wrongdoing, implying far less independence for magistrates and secondly for penalties which emphasize the personal responsibility of the delinquent for their act and towards their victim. This implies a major move towards a restitutive system of penalties as opposed to a retributive one (Barnett and Hagel, 1977: 331–83).

4 The criminal law should be reformed so as to emphasize the nature of crime and delinquency as breaches of individuals' rights to life, property and security of person. This implies firstly that most of the offences now covered by criminal law should be reclassified as civil wrongs (torts) since they do not involve such a breach but are rather acts of nuisance or else breaches of regulations of one kind or another. The criminal law should be reserved for acts which are offences against the rights set out above, so marking them out clearly as peculiarly reprehensible. Secondly, this implies that victimless crimes should be abolished since no person's rights

have been infringed. This may seem strange in the context of an argument for remoralization – surely acts such as drug-taking and prostitution are among the main targets for any process of remoralization? Indeed so, but the crucial question again is that of responsibility. Where people engage in voluntary acts which harm themselves they must bear the responsibility for those actions and their effects. Any reform must be voluntary since, as said earlier, a coerced act cannot be moral except in the cases of children and mental incompetents. The state can act as an agency of remoralization via the criminal law only where individuals' rights have been violated. Elsewhere, as in the cases of drunkenness and drug use, the process must be voluntary and carried out by other means than through the state. This would have the additional benefit of making people such as drug users more demonstrably responsible for their own acts and condition which on the evidence of alcoholism is the only hope for them anyway.

5 There need to be radical changes in social policy away from a paternalistic or protective model to one which emphasizes choice and personal responsibility. The state should not provide services or goods directly; it should be an enabler, not a provider. This would mean major changes in social security and a general move to cash payments rather than free services with individuals left responsible for the disposal of the cash (Davies, 1986). Some may argue that welfare payments should be made in the form of vouchers rather than cash on the grounds that otherwise one could not ensure that money would be spent on the things for which it was intended. Such a policy, however, would undercut the fundamental idea of enhancing responsibility and control over one's own actions. Inevitably some people will act irresponsibly but the solution is not to take responsibility away from them – this will only increase their irresponsibility – but to ensure that they face the consequences of their actions. The underlying assumption behind the idea of using vouchers is that there exists a class of irremediably irresponsible people who must be guarded and regulated by a paternalistic elite. If this is so, then any idea of moralization would be impossible.

6 There should be changes in the practice and theory of social work with a move back towards the ideas put forward in the last century by the Charity Organisation Society, moving away from the notion of the social worker as a 'protector', responsible for looking after a client who is incapable of judging what is in their own best interest. The social worker should rather be an 'enabler' or 'assistant' who helps self-motivated action on the part of the client but no more. Such ideas are already widespread in social work but need to become more dominant in practice. (For the COS and its ideas see Mowat, 1961.)

7 The government should seek, perhaps through financial incentives, to encourage the formation of stable households and to better integrate young men into society. The critical factor here is obviously youth employment

which implies steps to remove the various regulations which inhibit the entry of young men into the labour market, most notably minimum wage rules (this has been done to a great extent by the removal of young people from the coverage of Wages Councils) and qualification regulations.

8 In the longer term there must be firstly a revival of private action and mutual aid to give more people a greater degree of control over and responsibility for their own lives. This could be encouraged by the state but must ultimately depend upon private action.

9 There needs to be a non-state-led campaign of moral reform, carried out by private and voluntary organizations and dependent upon personal action. The model to adopt is that presented by self-help groups such as Alcoholics Anonymous or the Temperance movement of the last century which stress the personal responsibility and morally accountable nature of the individual.

10 Lastly – what will probably take longest – there must be change in the climate of opinion and belief. This requires action from everybody but particularly from schools, churches, writers and journalists and academics. This will be the slowest to have effect but the impact will be the most profound and long-lasting.

Faced with the crisis of the early nineteenth century our ancestors were able to moralize their society with a consequent reduction in all sorts of anti-social activity. In our own time that achievement has been progressively undermined with disastrous consequences for all of us but especially the weak and disadvantaged. The social crisis affecting much of Britain today is at root a moral crisis. Social policy must be directed mainly to solving that crisis and remoralization should be its prime aim in every area.

Note

1 Anomie is a concept first formulated by the nineteenth-century French sociologist Emile Durkheim and means literally lack of rules or norms. It is used to mean a condition where there are no clear rules of conduct or interaction leading to a perceived lack of purpose and meaning in peoples' lives.

References

Barnett, R. E. and Hagel, J. (eds) (1977) *Assessing the Criminal: Restitution, Retribution and the Legal Process.* Cambridge, MA: Ballinger.

Beier, A. L. (1985) *Masterless Men: the Vagrancy Problem in England, 1560–1640.* London: Methuen.

Bell, D. (1976) *The Cultural Contradictions of Capitalism.* New York: Basic.

Bottomley, K. and Pease, K. (1986) *Crime and Punishment: Interpreting the Data.* Milton Keynes: Open University Press.

Box, S. (1984) *Power, Crime and Mystification.* London: Tavistock.

Buchanan, J. M. (1985) *Liberty, Market and State.* Brighton: Harvester.

Clinard, M. B. (1978) *Cities with Little Crime: The Case of Switzerland.* Cambridge: Cambridge University Press.

Coleman, A. (1985) *Utopia on Trial*. London: Allen & Unwin.

Davies, S. (1985) 'Classes and Police in Manchester, 1829–1880', in Kidd, A. J. and Roberts, K. W. (eds) *City, Class and Culture: Studies of Cultural Production and Social Policy in Victorian Manchester*. Manchester: Manchester University Press.

Davies, S. (1986) *Beveridge Revisited: New Foundations for Tomorrow's Welfare*. London: Centre for Policy Studies.

Gatrell, V. A. C. (1980) 'The Decline of Theft and Violence in Victorian and Edwardian England', pp. 238–370 in Gatrell, V. A. C., Lenman, B. and Parker, G. (eds) *Crime and the Law: the Social History of Crime in Western Europe since 1500*. London: Europa.

Gatrell, V. A. C. and Hadden, T. B. (1972) 'Nineteenth-Century Criminal Statistics and Their Interpretation', in Wrigley, E. A. (ed.) *Nineteenth Century Society*. Cambridge: Cambridge University Press.

Hall, S., Critcher, C., Jefferson, T., Clarke, J., Roberts, B., (1978) *Policing the Crisis: Mugging, the State and Law and Order*. London: Macmillan.

Harrison, P. (1985) *Inside the Inner City: Life Under the.Cutting Edge*. Harmondsworth: Penguin (rev. edn).

Hough, M. and Mayhew, P. (1983) *The British Crime Survey: First Report*. London: HMSO.

Hough, M. and Mayhew, P. (1985) *Taking Account of Crime*. London: HMSO.

Johnson, P. (1983) *A History of the Modern World*. London: Weidenfeld & Nicolson.

Jones, D. (1982) *Crime, Protest, Community and Police in Nineteenth Century Britain*. London: Routledge & Kegan Paul.

Kinsey, R. (1984/5) *Merseyside Crime and Police Surveys 1984/5*. Merseyside County Council.

Kinsey, R. (1986) 'Crime in the City', *Marxism Today* (May): 6–10.

Lasch, C. (1979) *The Culture of Narcissism: American Life in an Age of Diminishing Expectations*. New York: Norton.

Lawrence, J. and Steed, D. (1986) 'Primary School Perceptions of Disruptive Behaviour', *Educational Studies*, 12(3): 147–58.

Lea, J. and Young, J. (1984) *What is to be Done about Law and Order?* Harmondsworth: Penguin.

Matthews, R. and Young, J. (eds) (1986) *Confronting Crime*. London: Sage.

Middleton, P. (1986) 'For "Victorian" Read "Georgian"', *Encounter* 67(2): 5–9.

Minogue, K. (1985) *Alien Powers: the Pure Theory of Ideology*. London: Weidenfeld & Nicolson.

Morgan, P. (1978) *Delinquent Fantasies*. London: Temple Smith.

Mowat, C. L. (1961) *The Charity Organisation Society, 1869–1913: its Ideas and Work*. London: Methuen.

Murray, C. (1984) *Losing Ground: American Social Policy 1950–1980*. New York: Basic.

Pearson, G. (1983) *Hooligan: a History of Respectable Fears*. London: Macmillan.

Rafter, N. H. (1986) 'Left out by the Left', *Socialist Review* 89: 7–24.

Rothbard, M. (1981) *The Ethics of Liberty*. New York: Random House.

Seabrook, J. (1978) *What Went Wrong?* London: Gollancz.

Seabrook, J. (1984) *The Idea of Neighbourhood*. London: Pluto.

Van Den Haag, E. (1975) *Punishing Criminals*. New York: Basic.

Young, J. (1981) 'Thinking Seriously about Crime: Some Models of Criminology', in Fitzgerald, M., McLennan, G. and Pawson, J. (eds) *Crime and Society: Readings in History and Theory*. London: Routledge & Kegan Paul/Open University Press.

Young, J. and Jones, T. (1986) *The Islington Crime Survey: Crime, Victimization and Policing in Inner-City London*. Aldershot: Gower.

15
The weakening of social democracy
Andrew Gamble

Was there a consensus?

The 1970s were a time of political turmoil, marked by a prolonged recession in the world economy, a deep-seated crisis of state authority, a sharp polarization between the political parties and the revival of ideology. It was the decade when the post-war consensus disintegrated, when social democracy was plunged into disarray, and when Thatcherism began its ascent. 1979 has been seen as a watershed election, marking the decisive break between the era inaugurated by the Attlee government after 1945 and the new politics of Thatcher.

This was certainly the perspective of many of the participants. The supporters of Margaret Thatcher openly scorned consensus politics and talked about a return to a politics of principle and conviction. Many of their opponents saw themselves as the defenders of the consensus policies of the 1950s. On the Left the collapse of consensus was welcomed as providing a new political space for radical politics.

There is, however, a wide gap between rhetoric and reality. In order to establish how much the post-war consensus came under challenge and how innovative and radical Thatcherism has been, it is first necessary to explore exactly what this consensus was.

Belief in the existence of a new consensus crystallized during the 1950s and 1960s. The success of the British political system in providing political continuity and social stability was frequently ascribed to the 'political settlement' of 1945. What had been 'settled' were the claims of the labour movement for an extension of citizenship rights.

The post-war consensus can be viewed on three levels. It expressed first of all a major political shift. The formation of the Coalition government followed by the election of the first majority Labour government in 1945 marked the break-up of the political pattern of the 1920s and 1930s. Labour won more than 40 percent of the vote and decisively shattered the dominant party system which the Conservatives had succeeded in establishing. A new two-party system emerged in which both parties enjoyed almost equal and very stable support.

Secondly, the consensus involved a major policy shift. The implementation of the reconstruction programme extended the role of the state and created new citizenship rights. The income maintenance proposals of the Beveridge Report, the full employment techniques recommended by Keynes, the new National Health Service and improved educational provision – all these added up to a sustained attempt to reduce inequality through public action.

Thirdly, the consensus involved a shift of power between labour and capital. Acceptance of Labour as the alternative party of government gave a new role and importance to the unions. The need to integrate the trade unions as an organized interest in the process of economic policy-making was considered essential by Labour and was increasingly accepted as necessary by the Conservatives. The Industrial Charter of 1947 was a sign of how far some of the New Conservatives were prepared to go in envisaging a partnership between state and unions.

The Conservatives' willingness to administer rather than dismantle the welfare state helped ensure the consolidation of the new policy regime in the 1950s. The Conservative election victories meant that there was no prospect of further measures of socialization. The line had been held. But the Conservative leadership had no desire to undo the reforms of the 1940s. They accepted them as a necessary and desirable evolution. There was less positive endorsement from Conservative partisans in the constituencies and the media. But majority opinion within both parties came to see the post-war arrangements and the post-war policy regime as an acceptable compromise. Relatively few partisans on either side enthused about the outcome, but it proved durable.

In foreign policy the consensus between the party leaderships went rather deeper. The continuation of the wartime alliance with the United States, the commitment to Nato, and the acceptance of American leadership of a new Western political, military and economic order overshadowed domestic politics and helped to promote co-operation between the political parties.

The priority given to Britain's relationship with the United States was a central part of the post-war consensus. The ideological war against Communism helped discredit the idea of socialism both among voters and within the Labour Party itself. Conservative leaders speedily recognized the importance of achieving a united front of democratic forces in support of the main lines of post-war foreign policy. Their eagerness that Labour should participate made them more ready to accept compromises on domestic policy.

These twin pillars – Nato and collective welfare – were the heart of the post-war accommodation between Left and Right in Britain. But the compromise that was achieved was ultimately shattered, in part because of the very priorities which had been accepted in the 1950s.

The commitment to the Atlantic Alliance meant an attempt to rebuild an international economic order, multilateral trade and convertible currencies. Displaced from the leading role in this world economy, Britain still retained aspirations to a world role and the trappings of a world power. This involved a defence policy that was very costly and increasingly out of line with Britain's economic status. It also involved re-establishing sterling as an international currency, and giving priority once again to the development of the financial sector rather than to domestic manufacturing (Blank, 1977).

The consequences of the international orientation of British policy were reinforced by the manner in which the domestic policy consensus had been achieved. Welfare programmes had been greatly extended, trade union rights had been secured, but there had been no transformation of relations between government and industry sufficient to ensure a programme of continual innovation and modernization to keep British industry competitive in the reorganized world market. Apart from the nationalization measures, which were confined to the public utilities, British industry was left to reorganize itself.

The British economy was not strong enough nor productive enough to fund both its welfare programmes and the level of overseas military spending and investment which the maintenance of a world role for Britain demanded. The period of Conservative government between 1951 and 1964 was not only a period of consensus but also a period of painful adjustment to decline.

A modernization programme had become a pressing necessity by the end of the 1950s because of the mounting evidence that the British economy was failing to perform as well as its main rivals. The urge to copy the best 'modern' practices from other countries became irresistible. This inaugurated a new phase in post-war politics. The drift and inertia of the 1950s were replaced by a host of programmes designed to remedy British deficiencies. But they remained recognizably within the bounds of the post-war consensus.

There was bitter dispute over whether or not Britain should join the EEC, but the Atlantic Alliance and Britain's participation within the open world trading order were not questioned. The commitments to full employment and to the existing range of welfare programmes were also upheld.

The main emphasis of the modernization was to find ways to improve the performance of the British economy. The aim was to ensure that expanded public services could be afforded, while living standards continued to rise. Growth without inflation was the watchword and, to make it possible, public responsibilities were further extended, most notably in the successive attempts to devise an incomes policy. Major new spending programmes on health, education, housing and transport were launched, and many new public agencies were set up.

The durability of the consensus between the two parties was shown in the elections in 1964 and 1966. There were no basic disagreements over the goals of policy. Both parties offered themselves as the best agency for modernizing the economy and British society. Labour inherited and developed many of the initiatives of the Conservative government.

The breakdown of consensus

What, then, caused the consensus to fall apart? Why was the continuity of policy in the 1950s and 1960s succeeded by a resurgence of ideology and a polarization of opinion in the 1970s? Four arguments predominate. The first focuses on the changes in the political parties themselves – the rise of ideological politics, a 'New Left' and a 'New Right'. Ideological partisans, it is claimed, were successful in winning control of their respective parties, and then, aided by the vagaries of the British electoral system, were able to win government office and begin implementing their extreme policies. Consensus was destroyed by adversary politics. The parties vacated the centre ground which the bulk of the electorate still occupied (Finer, 1975).

A second argument is that the parties only vacated the centre ground under pressure from changes in the electorate. The weakening of the attachment between voters and political parties meant that the parties had a dwindling base on which they could rely. The increasing volatility of the electorate destroyed the stability on which the two-party system of the post-war years had depended.

The rise of nationalist parties, the periodic surges in support for the Liberals, the growth of pressure groups and social movements outside the bounds of conventional party politics, and the rise of new social divisions important in shaping electoral choices, substantially changed the agenda of British politics and forced the two major parties to adopt new populist strategies to recapture their lost support (Dunleavy and Husbands, 1985).

A third argument locates the trigger for ideological polarization and electoral volatility in the failure of the modernization programmes of the 1960s to remedy the causes of decline. This caused deep disillusion in the electorate as well as giving ammunition to the critics of the party leaderships. The existing policy regime was severely discredited by the dramatic worsening of performance on unemployment, inflation, economic growth and the balance of trade. Industrial militancy grew, public expenditure seemed to be out of control and incomes policies to be unworkable. Any policy regime requires occasional success to remain viable. There was little around in the 1970s (Glyn and Harrison, 1980).

The fourth argument goes beyond the particular problems and experiences of the British political system. It focuses on the major shift that took place in relationships between states and economies in the world system in the 1970s. The weakening of the economic position of the United States, the collapse of the system that fixed exchange rates in 1971/2, the explosion of commodity prices, the ending of the long boom and the advent of the first generalized recession in the world economy since the end of the war brought into being a new politics.

Keynesianism gave way to monetarism because of the change from fixed to floating exchange rates. A new mechanism for ensuring reasonable financial discipline became essential. The scope for national economic management had been drastically curtailed by the growing integration and interdependence of the world economy. Far-reaching changes in the international division of labour and the introduction of major new technologies implied major adjustments in all states within the world system (Brett, 1985).

All these explanations as to why consensus has weakened point to a deep-seated crisis of state authority in the 1970s. This crisis was not confined to a single country but was a common experience throughout the Western states, although there were many important local variations. Some commentators spoke of government being 'overloaded', of the expectations of voters about what government could do being 'excessive', of the public interest being subordinated to the interests of pressure groups. The identity of the villains varied according to the ideological perspective. But there was some agreement on the main structural shifts that had rendered government impotent, much less agreement on the remedies for it.

The most important cause of the crisis of authority was recognition of the severe constraints that now existed on any exercise of national sovereignty. So interdependent had the world economy become, so integrated its financial circuits and so powerful its main agents of accumulation – the multinational companies – that the scope for independent national economic policies had diminished.

Recognition of this painful reality reduced the authority of governments because it reduced the expectations of what they could achieve. International forces beyond the control of national governments appeared to dictate national policy. The pressures for greater dependence appeared much more powerful than the pressures for greater autonomy. The changes in the world system in the 1970s imposed major new burdens and problems on national government, obliging them to seek strategies of adjustment to limit damage to their own societies and to take steps to make their economies more competitive.

The end of the long boom was a profound psychological and political shock which did more than anything to invalidate the political calculations that had underlain the post-war consensus. All governments were forced to accept a changed role for their economies within the world system and to refashion their domestic policies. The discrediting of Keynesianism meant national economic management policies aimed at stabilizing demand were replaced by the sound money policies which won the confidence of the increasingly powerful financial markets. National Keynesianism required either fixed exchange rates or currency blocs. In the absence of either, only the adoption of monetarism throughout the international capitalist economy could ensure reasonable currency stability.

This had major consequences. As a result of the slowdown in growth the funding of the existing public sector became critical. The fiscal crisis of the state – the tendency of expenditure to outrun revenue – became a problem for all states, and the politics of the budget moved centre stage, as huge battles erupted over the size and content of the major spending programmes. Pressure mounted to find ways to reduce and control spending, as well as to restructure it in the longer term.

The impact of recession upon employment meant that many traditional sectors of industry were suddenly faced with extinction, and unemployment began to soar. Major debates developed as to what kinds of intervention by government were effective and what its objectives should be. The attention of all policy-makers and politicians became focused on the supply side and on the changes that were needed in institutions to promote adjustment and economic survival. Trade unions, the civil service, enterprises, education and local government all became targets for reconstruction.

The difficulty of devising national policies to cope with these changes was related to the wider crisis of state authority, the problem of making them legitimate. Reliance on the authority of the popular mandate which a party could claim by winning an election had become increasingly empty with the centralization of power in executives and party leaderships, and the weakening of legislatures and political parties. Governments increasingly sought to make their policies legitimate through involving organized interests in policy-making. This elevation of the producer groups to the status of 'governing institutions' injected a corporate bias into the process of policy-making and led to many experiments with corporatist institutions and tripartite bodies (Middlemas, 1980).

By involving all major interests in the formulation and implementation of policy, governments hoped to secure better management of the economy through consensus. Relying on the mechanism of party alone could not secure this, since no party could command even majority electoral support for its programme. Corporatist structures were also found wanting. The TUC and the CBI were unable to deliver their members' support on all issues, and the state seemed increasingly weak because its authority appeared compromised.

Many commentators used the evident impasse of British politics in the 1970s to paint lurid pictures of the power of the trade unions. New Right analysts argued that governments were incapable of acting decisively because they were trapped in a web of special interests.

The thesis of overmighty trade unions was wide of the mark. The movement was almost entirely defensive in its orientation. The power of capital was always much greater (Leys, 1983). The inability of the trade unions to prevent the return to mass unemployment in the 1970s under a Labour government showed where real power lay.

The attack on the power of the trade unions was a crucial step in a much broader assault on the post-war consensus. Trade union power was linked to overmanning, strikes, inefficiency, waste and low productivity, but also to collective welfare, full employment and a large and expanding public sector.

For Conservatives on the New Right the attack on trade unions was not just a question of economic efficiency. They believed that the social democratic state, the creature and protector of trade union power, had gradually undermined institutions such as the family and schools essential to the maintenance of social order.

Enlarging the sphere of public responsibility and extending individual rights through progressive social legislation in turn encouraged the growth of radical social movements pressing for further reforms. The attack on patriarchal authority and the campaign to transform gender relationships by the women's movements was paralleled by attacks on other forms of authority, particularly in educational institutions.

Greater freedom and diversity in life-styles, and greater assertiveness of some minorities, led to fears that a tide of permissiveness was sweeping the country, challenging all established authority. The threat to labour discipline from the wave of unofficial strikes became linked with other fears such as the threat to public order posed by the rise in crime and vandalism, the threat to social and national cohesiveness posed by the counter-culture and by black immigration, and the threat to family stability posed by collective welfare and the spread of a permissive sexual morality (Hall, 1978).

The crisis of state authority in the 1970s gravely weakened the old political consensus. Social democracy appeared to be failing not only in its ability to deliver continuing economic prosperity, but also in its will to preserve the foundations of social order and public authority.

The fragmentation of the Left

In the 1970s a new politics was forced on all political parties by the changing context of national policy-making. The attempt to think through and develop new programmes and new constituencies of support brought a major revival of ideological debate within and between the parties.

On the Left there was a strong reaction to the failures of the Labour government between 1966 and 1970. The revisionism which had dominated the party since the 1950s was discredited. Trade union resistance towards incomes policies and to government attempts to impose a legal framework for industrial relations grew. Interest revived in public ownership as a means of shifting power between classes and in particular in counteracting new forms of capitalist power such as multinational companies. Redistribution of income through fiscal and welfare programmes was considered no longer sufficient. The redistribution of wealth and the control of property once again became central to the socialist project.

This revival of class politics received an enormous boost from the resistance that was organized to the policies of the Heath government. The campaign against the Industrial Relations Act provoked a running battle between the unions and the courts. The closure of Upper Clyde Shipbuilders in 1971 sparked a work-in and a long struggle by the workforce and the local community for the right to work (Foster and Woolfson, 1986). The battle against pay norms in the public sector saw defeats but also some major victories in particular by the miners in 1972 and 1974.

The revival of the Left in the Labour Party was strongly associated with the struggle of the unions against corporatism. On the Right, corporatism was often treated as a synonym for trade union power but the Left also rejected corporatism, regarding it as a means of subordinating the interests of the working class to the interest of private capital through the organizations of the workers themselves (Panitch, 1980).

When the world economy plunged into recession in the 1970s the Labour Party already had an influential left-wing analysis of the shortcomings of social democracy and corporatism, and had adopted a radical domestic programme. The dislocation of the world economy was treated as a major new crisis of capitalism comparable to the crisis of the 1930s. The Left argued strongly against any retreat to traditional social democratic policies. Only a radical programme could solve the problems of the British economy and extend support for the Labour Party.

There were many versions of the alternative economic strategy in the 1970s but what they shared was a rejection of the foreign economic policy priorities of the post-war consensus. This meant abandoning the political and defence commitments at the heart of the Atlantic Alliance and challenging the way in which the British economy was integrated into the world economy. The British economy could only be rebuilt and the gains of social democracy extended if the influence of the dominant sector of British capital – the City and British multinationals – over national economic policy were confronted and overcome (Benn, 1980).

The 1974 Labour government was armed with a radical programme, very little of which it attempted to carry out. Its domestic support was narrow and the financial and political pressures on it were intense. As the world economic crisis unfolded, laying bare the accumulated weaknesses of the British economy, the government sought desperately to manage the crisis. It abandoned all its radical proposals, and launched some major new corporatist initiatives to provide the legitimacy which its parliamentary and popular support could not deliver.

The rejection of any alternative economic strategy culminated in the Labour Cabinet's acceptance of the IMF conditions for credits to support sterling in 1976. Coupled with the 'voluntary' incomes policy, the abandonment of an interventionist industrial strategy and the increasingly severe public expenditure cuts, the Labour government was accused by the Left of betraying once again the programme on which it had been elected (Coates, 1980).

This gave enormous impetus to the campaign for changing the Labour Party's constitution. The aim was to make the Leader and the MPs more accountable to Labour activists and to make conference decisions binding. The Campaign for Labour Party Democracy wanted to ensure that any future Labour government would try to implement radical change instead of postponing it.

The gulf between the party conference, in which the Left was increasingly dominant (Minkin, 1980), and the parliamentary party and the Labour leadership had become very wide by the end of the 1970s. The Left finally succeeded in the aftermath of the electoral defeat in 1979 in pushing through two of the three major constitutional reforms it sought – a mandatory reselection process for MPs and an electoral college broader than the parliamentary party to elect the party leader.

This was the trigger for a major split in the party, with a number of MPs under the leadership of David Owen and Shirley Williams breaking away to form the SDP. They justified the split on ideological grounds; the differences between social democrats and democratic socialists had become too large.

Many social democrats remained within the Labour party, however, and the Left failed to win complete dominance in the party even after the SDP had departed. The narrow failure of Tony Benn to oust Denis Healey from the Deputy Leadership in 1981 was the high point of the Left influence. The crushing electoral defeat in 1983 was followed by the election of Neil Kinnock. The old coalition of Left forces in the party fell apart and the parliamentary leadership began gradually to re-establish strong central direction of the party.

Labour renewed its commitment to an alternative programme in 1981–3. The gulf between the two major parties appeared wider than at any time since the war, particularly because Labour was rejecting so much of the post-war consensus on foreign and defence policy. But the ability and the commitment of the Labour leadership to carry through a radical programme was always very doubtful, and under Kinnock the Labour Party moved back towards the centre. The area where its approach remained radical was defence. Commitment to a non-nuclear defence policy struck at one of the key pillars of the world role and the international orientation of policy which, by sacrificing the domestic economy, had contributed so much to the relative economic decline.

The resurgence of the Right

The failure of the Left in the 1970s left the way open for a successful challenge to the consensus from the Right. In the Conservative Party the rejection of consensus politics by an important section of the party led to the election of a government in 1979 committed to the implementation of a radical programme. Unlike the alternative economic strategy the social market strategy of the Thatcherites did receive a trial.

Thatcherism is a contradictory and complex phenomenon which was always much more than the particular style of one political leader. The election of Thatcher as Leader of the Conservatives in 1975 created the political space in which many of the radical ideas of the New Right for dealing with Britain's economic, political and social problems could begin to influence policy. Thatcher herself encouraged the challenging of certain assumptions which had underlain government policy, both Conservative and Labour, since 1945 (Hall and Jacques, 1983).

But radical though it was in some areas, in others Thatcherism signified endorsement and indeed reinforcement of the central priorities of post-war policy. In domestic policy Thatcherism was strongly identified from the first with the new monetarist policy regime and with the rejection of Keynesianism. Stable prices became the chief objective and this meant giving unemployment and growth a lower priority. Thatcherites argued that only if inflation was overcome could unemployment be brought down and the rate of growth increased. Making a monetarist policy credible required a strong attack on public expenditure and the removal of obstacles to free markets.

Public spending cuts existed long before Thatcherism. What the Thatcherites did was to argue that cuts were not only necessary but desirable. Far from public expenditure being regarded as benign it was now regarded with suspicion. Questioning the need for public spending programmes brought a flood of proposals for privatization of publicly owned enterprises, private health insurance, the abolition of the State Earnings Related Pension Scheme, education vouchers, student loans and many more.

Even more significant, however, was the policy towards the unions. The Conservatives were aware that they had to show they could handle the unions if they were to restore their credibility as a party of government. The strategy that was adopted was to introduce industrial relations legislation step by step and with provisions which would make it hard for unions to challenge the government directly.

The huge rise in unemployment in 1979–81 and the dismantling of most corporatist structures brought a major weakening in the unions' position. They lost much of their direct access to government and many of their legal privileges were stripped away. Strikes in the private sector declined to negligible proportions and in the public sector the Government chose its time and the ground for fighting major battles over pay and employment.

Its most severe test came in the 1984 miners' strike. The breaking of the power of the NUM, which had been one of the strongest unions in the 1970s, was evidence of how the Government had gained the upper hand in its struggle with organized labour. This allowed it to override or ignore opposition to the way in which the economy was being restructured.

A new consensus?
The electoral triumphs of the Conservatives in 1979 and 1983, the disarray of the opposition parties, and the growing acceptance of many of the radical ideas of the New Right seemed to confirm that the election of Thatcher in 1979 was the watershed in British politics and the beginning of the new consensus which the Thatcherites proclaimed.

Such claims are only partially true. As with radical governments elsewhere, the Thatcher experiment has been disappointing for its strongest supporters. Public expenditure and taxation have been restructured but not reduced. A very large income transfer towards the upper income groups has been engineered with a corresponding significant increase in poverty. There has been an enormous shake-out of labour but few signs of the permanent increase in productivity needed to improve competitiveness. Crime has continued to soar, and moral and social disorder have not been checked.

The Thatcher government succeeded in reducing the influence of the trade unions and tried to give much greater power within enterprises to management. But it proved very cautious in its handling of health, education and collective security. The proposals for a 'New Beveridge' were not very radical and revised almost as soon as they were published.

The Thatcher government avoided a frontal assault on social democracy, preferring to encourage the growth of private provision in health and education while restricting resources in the public sector. This policy had most success in housing. The tax concessions given to home ownership had created the climate where a direct assault on the principle of collective provision was possible. The sale of council houses reinforced this pattern. But there were few parallels elsewhere. The attempt to spread share ownership more widely had only limited success. Many industries were privatized and the upper income groups further enriched, but the share-owning democracy remained as far off as it had ever been.

The scope of the privatization programme did greatly reduce the size of the public enterprise sector but, in part because of the enterprises chosen, there were few noticeable effects on economic performance. The programme highlighted how much the real heart of social democracy was not nationalization but the citizenship rights enshrined in the programmes of collective welfare.

The post-war consensus proved durable because it was the expression of shifts in party strength, a change in policy regime, and an altered balance of power between labour and capital. If the new Thatcherite consensus is analysed in the same terms it looks more like a transitional phase than the decisive founding of a new era.

The principal development in party politics during the Thatcher years was the fragmentation of the Left. This concealed the relative weakness of Conservative electoral support. Popular majorities were not secured for many of the central objectives of Thatcherism (Jowell and Airey, 1985). The revival of Labour Party support after 1983 and the continuing strength of third parties, particularly the Alliance, meant that a new dominant party system was unlikely.

This would not have mattered if the other parties had fully accepted the new policy priorities of the Thatcher government, as the Conservatives had accepted those of the post-war Labour government. But many of these new priorities were fiercely contested even within the Cabinet. On some minor issues, such as council house sales, the Conservatives won new ground, but many central issues of policy remained in contention, and a chasm opened up on defence.

The most important change that has taken place is capital's increased power over labour, although the scope of this on the shop floor has been disputed (Batstone and Gourlay, 1986). Like so much else, it was already under way before the Thatcher government took office. The changes in the world division of labour and the impact of recession destroyed the viability of a policy regime geared to full employment and growth, and exposed organized and unorganized workers to strong attacks on rights, jobs and pay.

The reduction in the industrial power and political influence of the unions did not bring about the economic renaissance that was expected, partly because what made it possible was the rapid contraction of manufacturing industry. The power of the financial and rentier sector was confirmed and enhanced. The division of the economy into a prosperous southern heartland and a decaying periphery in the inner cities and the old industrial regions became ever more pronounced. Although unwilling to launch a frontal assault on the welfare programmes of post-war social democracy the Thatcher government did much to undermine them by reinforcing the non-interventionist bias of British policy towards industry and finance.

During the Thatcher years politics became more open, and the two-party system suffered serious damage. All parties claimed to reject centralism and proclaimed the virtues of populism and local and individual initiatives. But the conversions were never total. While the Conservatives sought to 'free' the economy they also wanted the state to be strong – to uphold and police the institutions necessary for a market order. This explained why Conservatives were to be found rolling the state back in some areas but vigorously rolling it forward in others (Gamble, 1987).

In the Labour Party a major impact was made by the new urban Left and the new social movements. Pressure to extend political, legal and social rights to all citizens gave rise to a much broader politics than traditional Labourism. The party rediscovered some of its own anti-statist and anti-centralist traditions. Local initiatives on employment and transport, and popular control of welfare services, came to the fore.

The problem for the Left was how to combine decentralization of power and resources to local authorities and regions with a national programme for the reconstruction of the economy. In thinking through the constitutional implications of decentralization the Alliance parties were ahead of Labour. The Labour leadership still clung to the centralist model of single-party control which the post-war consensus and the two-party system had fostered, though there were signs of movement.

A precondition for any viable programme of economic reconstruction is a major constitutional reform. One aim of this would be to devolve effective powers to elected regional authorities and to destroy the centralized Westminster state which the Conservatives have dominated for so long. This metropolitan power has served the interests of the international sectors of the economy and protected industries, such as defence and agriculture, and successfully resisted all attempts to redirect it.

Conclusion

For all the turmoil of the 1970s and the Thatcher years the problem of British economic decline remained unresolved. The ravages of Thatcherism left parts of the economy more exposed than ever before. A continuation of Thatcherite policies would mean further polarization and impoverishment. The Thatcher government had hoped by reversing decline to create the basis for a new one-nation politics. But in practice both its friends and its critics agreed that it had failed: its critics because the project itself was impossible; its friends because the government did not push through the radical measures needed to make the experiment succeed.

The breakdown of the consensus in the 1970s had still not been resolved by the mid-1980s. The impasse of British politics and the depressed sectors of the British economy had been deepened by the attempted cures of Thatcherism. The kind of one-nation politics practised by both Conservatives and Labour in the past increasingly lacked either economic viability or electoral necessity.

The Conservatives showed that shrewd attention to the interests of their electoral base and the dominant bloc of rentier, financial and commercial interests concentrated in the South meant they could afford to ignore the claims of the old industrial heartlands, the inner cities, Scotland and Northern Ireland. The logic of the policy on which the Thatcher government had embarked was a steady strengthening of the repressive arm of the state to improve policing and surveillance of the dependent and the marginalized, while furthering the internationalization of all other parts of the economy.

The destruction of the old manufacturing base of the economy, the erosion of public services, and the rundown of the infrastructure have now gone so far that alternatives to Thatcherite policies often lack credibility. There may be no national programme that can now bridge the interests of the international sector and the rest of the national economy. Given the pressures that can be exerted by international financial markets this may mean that any attempt to restore prosperity to the national economy will be sabotaged.

Shifting the emphasis of British economic policy to industrial reconstruction is now an immense task. But it is one which any party that seeks to remain national and democratic will be forced to attempt. The alternative is to see the further erosion of democracy through the growth of a strong and repressive central state, and the emergence of radical separatist movements in the depressed regions.

References

Batstone, E. and Gourlay, S. (1986) *Unions, Employment and Innovation*. Oxford: Blackwell.

Benn, T. (1980) *Arguments for Socialism*. Harmondsworth: Penguin.

Blank, S. (1977) 'Britain: The Politics of Foreign Economic Policy', *International Organisation* 31(4).

Brett, E. A. (1985) *The World Economy Since the War*. London: Macmillan.

Coates, D. (1980) *Labour in Power*. London: Longman.

Dunleavy, P. and Husbands, C. (1985) *British Democracy at the Crossroads*. London: Allen & Unwin.

Finer, S. E. (ed.) (1975) *Adversary Politics and Electoral Reform*. London: Wigram.

Foster, J. and Woolfson, C. (1986) *The Politics of the UCS Work-in*. London: Lawrence & Wishart.

Gamble, A. (1987) *The Free Economy and the Strong State*. London: Pluto.

Glyn, A. and Harrison, J. (1980) *The British Economic Disaster*. London: Pluto.

Hall, S. *et al.* (1978) *Policing the Crisis*. London: Macmillan.

Hall, S. and Jacques, M. (eds) (1983) *The Politics of Thatcherism*. London: Lawrence & Wishart.

Jowell, R. and Airey, C. (1985) *British Social Attitudes: the 1985 Report*. Aldershot: Gower.

Leys, C. (1983) *Politics in Britain*. London: Heinemann.

Middlemas, K. (1980) *Politics in an Industrial Society: the Experience of the British System Since 1911*. London: Deutsch.

Minkin, L. (1980) *The Labour Party Conference: a Study in Intra-Party Democracy*. Manchester: Manchester University Press.

Panitch, L. (1980) 'Recent Theorisations of Corporatism', *British Journal of Sociology* 31: 159–87.

16
The new municipal socialism

Geoff Green

In a brief period from the elections in 1979 to the ratecapping defeats of 1985 and the dissolution of the Greater London Council and metropolitan counties in 1986, a new municipal socialism flowered in a few British cities. Despite Labour's national defeat in the 1979 general election, simultaneous local authority elections saw Labour victories in a number of urban areas, reviving the possibility of advancing socialism locally in a cold climate.

Labour's electoral history has been reassuring on the narrow but essential condition of maintaining strong bases in certain towns and cities and in the industrial counties in periods of parliamentary opposition. For much of the 1930s Labour controlled Sheffield, Glasgow, Derby, Hull, Norwich and Stoke, half the London Boroughs and London County Council, and twenty industrial towns in South Wales and the North. These councils' struggle to implement progressive policies in a hostile economic climate laid the foundations for the physical and social reconstruction of our cities by the post-war Labour government, and, because of the consensual strength of these ideas, by its successors also. During thirteen years of Conservative government, predominantly Labour councils implemented the great transformation of housing, education and welfare services.

In the later, less certain, periods of Labour government, council allies bore the brunt of cuts in public expenditure and the party was pushed back into its early interwar heartlands: between 1968 and 1970 it retained only four London boroughs, three industrial counties, and the city of Stoke-on-Trent; in the next trough of 1977–8 it also retained Sheffield, Hull, Norwich, Manchester, Salford, Newcastle and fourteen of the thirty-two London boroughs. In 1979, taking this longer view of swing and counter-swing, District Labour Parties might have been expected to consolidate and expand their limited local bases in at least the majority of years to the next general election. In fact, this symmetry was upset when part of the social democratic wing of the Labour Party broke away in 1981 to form the Social Democratic Party. Thereafter in most prosperous towns and counties, especially in the South of England, the Alliance displaced Labour as the main opposition party to the Conservatives, and in 1985 became the biggest or second party on nearly half the shire county councils. In the industrial conurbations and cities the pattern was quite different. The Alliance gained some suburban Conservative wards, but Labour often brushed aside Liberals from seats in poor inner-city districts gained earlier by grassroots community politics. The new political geography divided the opposition and strengthened Labour's grip in its traditional areas. It did not mean a return to the old Labourism, however. Instead these old heartlands generated a new radicalism.

16.1 The roots of the new municipal socialism

The new municipal socialism was not created in a dozen places by the new municipal governors – the councillors – in eclectic combination, but rather by the local Labour movement which put them there: it had specifically nominated them in Labour Party branches, ratified their candidature in District Labour Party meetings and campaigned for their election on an agreed manifesto. Municipal socialism in the 1980s grew out of local socialism in the 1970s. And local socialism had its most vigorous roots in towns and cities undergoing great structural change, shaped by great economic and social forces and in turn shaping a political response.

Extensive slum clearance and redevelopment had a profound impact on the pattern of city life in the 1970s; a high-powered municipal machine destroyed and rebuilt whole districts. By 1975 the poor and dispossessed – by unemployment and by racial and sexual discrimination – no longer characteristically rented old terraced houses from private landlords, but occupied instead the new high-rise and system-built flats which replaced them. These were new ghettos in the making, slums from a municipal drawing-board. Their tenants soon reacted, not so much to rent levels (from which they were protected by rebates or social security) but against the physical form of the new council housing. Through acts of sabotage and vandalism to the lifts and walkways of this brutal environment, the tenants challenged the municipal machine and the city bosses who had failed to deliver decent homes.

New tenant activists, often women, helped to radicalize local Labour parties on this issue, but an even greater influence was exercised by a new generation of owner-occupiers in older districts untouched by the bulldozer. They were educated away from home in a period of liberal higher education and they chose to live in the Victorian suburbs of their adopted city. They smartened up their houses and, to secure their investment as well as help their neighbours, fought and won the conservation and planning battles against an older Labour vision of a new municipal Jerusalem. They were called either community activists or the 'new gentry' (according to the balance of altruism and self-interest). Then the radicals among them joined later settlers to become the 'new urban Left'. Often this group had jobs in an expanding public sector. But they substituted the politics of neighbourhood for the traditional politics of workplace. They joined local branches of the Labour Party and helped give voice to their neighbours' problems – talking the language of 'multiple deprivation' in the inner city. They resisted the racism of many older members (and alienated them) during the tense period of National Front activity during 1976 and 1977. Though often outmanoeuvred by the less rule-bound campaigning of various revolutionary socialist groups, their determination did encourage later recruitment of black neighbours into the party, helping to supplant a vestigial white working-class culture with a 'rainbow coalition' of minority groups.

The economy of British cities also changed dramatically during this period. A long property boom had transformed the central business districts with office blocks and helped switch the balance of local employment away from manufacturing to service industry. The financial crash which so dramatically heralded the 1974–6 recession left tangible reminders in empty offices and abandoned building sites. These were eventually developed in the next economic upturn, but not so the factories and workshops upon whose prosperity the big cities had been built. The recession exposed (as the 1980–2 downturn was to do even more clearly) a longer-term structural weakness which general prosperity had masked. When factory gates closed they often closed for good.

Ultimately the driving forces for industrial change would only be managed at the national and international level. Their impact, however, was dramatically local. Each round of closures and redundancies undercut a succession of staple industries in the old manufacturing cities: shipbuilding in Glasgow and Newcastle, docks and dock-related processing in London and Liverpool, steel in Sheffield, cars in Birmingham and Coventry. Britain's old regional problem, legacy of the great inter-war depression, had become an inner-city problem, most visible landscape of a second slump. Such structural changes had two profound effects on local trade unionism and hence on the composition of city Labour parties. First, public sector unions grew larger than those organized in manufacturing industry, and their activists came to dominate local Trades Councils. Secondly, within the industrial sector, bargaining power shifted from the shop floor organizations built up plant by plant around pay and conditions, to combines which matched the scope of multinational employers to switch investment and jobs between their factories. They were supported by a new generation of committed researchers working for city-based trade union resource units and intellectually federated in organizations like the Conference of Socialist Economists and the Manchester Engineering Research Group.

16.2 The rise of a Labour New Left

Many activists joined local Labour parties in the four years bisected by the 1979 general election. They came to occupy centre stage from both wings: shop stewards and union militants on the one hand, from community groups and the women's movement, on the other. Some came direct to the Labour Party through simple conviction, others via revolutionary socialist groups to begin a long and determined march through the institutions of local government. All were united in opposition to the Labour government's corporatist economic strategy and to the cutbacks in public services forced upon local councils. All were joined in opposition to the right-wing Labour MPs who most clearly supported the government, and, in local branches, to the councillors and trade union officials who most eagerly implemented government policy. The sense of betrayal of the Callaghan years intensified the movement for accountability of government to party nationally (culminating between 1980 and 1982 in bitter conference divisions), a movement which had exact parallels locally. The party had created district parties in 1974 to separate local government issues from the industrial militancy and communist influence of Trades and Labour Councils. Within five years a new radical coalition, outflanking the declining Communist Party, argued that these local parties should assert their constitutional right to make council policy and to select a panel of council candidates. These were to be the two key procedural conditions of municipal socialism.

In many cities the New Left progressively displaced in branches, districts and on councils a traditional hierarchy dominated by right-wing trade union officials and by long-established councillors often dispensing patronage, sometimes corruptly – the 'municipal mafia' as they were called in Birmingham. The advance was uneven. The New Left remained a minority in most places – for example, in Birmingham and Newcastle, in the cities of West Yorkshire and the towns of South Yorkshire. Where they did gain control of the council they invariably dominated the local party first, but the time lag varied between one and five years. In some places like Sheffield it was impossible to pinpoint, as the old guard was gradually eclipsed and incorporated rather than defeated, though the election of a radical administration in 1980 was a clear finale.

In other places the battle lines were firmly drawn. In Southwark control by the New Left of the borough party, amid recriminations in 1981, brought control of the council in the all-out elections in 1982. In Manchester domination of the party by 1980 was not sufficient to avoid the hostile Labour Group expelling councillors sympathetic to the New Left in a series of well-publicized confrontations; it took another four years before the New Left gained control of the council. In Liverpool the Left dominated the party by 1978 and began to revitalize the rump of Labour councillors who had escaped Liberal inroads, but it was not until 1983 that a succession of yearly electoral advances brought in a radical Militant administration. The Greater London Labour Party was also dominated by the Left after its election defeat in 1977, but it took another three years of careful planning, primarily through *London Labour Briefing*, to ensure victory in the 1981 Greater London Council (GLC) elections. However long it took, there were by 1984 a dozen places identified with the new municipal socialism: a constellation of the six London boroughs of Hackney, Haringey, Islington, Camden, Greenwich and Southwark, which returned a mixture of New Left and older Left administrations in the 1982 elections; marginal Lambeth; the GLC and Inner London Education Authority, Liverpool, Sheffield and Manchester. There were also shooting stars in the firmament: Walsall and Lothian between 1980 and 1982, Stirling, Thamesdown and Basildon – 'Moscow down the Thames' according to Patrick Jenkin, the government minister in charge of local government during the critical period of confrontation.

The newly elected Labour groups set out to control the local state rather than to administer local government. They would use it politically as a focus for opposition, releasing resources for experiment and reform. They would demonstrate socialism at work and prefigure the institutions of a broader socialist society. But it would only be achieved against all the historical precedents. Though few councillors had read the theoretical reformulations of the state by marxist intellectuals, these ideas filtered down in pamphlets and conversational second-hand. And they all pointed in the same direction – the local state as an agent of central government and handmaiden of capital, whichever political party was nominally in control and however radical its intent.

So, from the beginning, New Left councillors were ambivalent about their chances of success. Many doubts were soon engulfed by a great tide of council business which left little time for thought. Others rationalized their ambivalence in the formal contradictions allowed by socialist analysis. The local state was not subordinated to the centre and to the capitalist institutions of the British economy in an immutable monolith. The picture was closer to a can of worms than a carefully constructed temple. There were tensions and conflict, opportunities and resources within this dominant system. It could be challenged internally and, maybe, in the end, transformed. Influential books like *In and Against the State* and *Beyond the Fragments* gave some practical guidance on how to relate personal to political struggle.

The new municipal administrations advanced neither a revolutionary nor a parliamentary road to socialism, occupying instead a minor constitutional crossroads in between. Writing in *London Labour Briefing* after his GLC election victory in 1981, Ken Livingstone saw County Hall as a 'campaigning base to bring down the Conservative government'. *Labour Herald*, launched three months later in September 1981 (edited by Ken Livingstone, Ted Knight, Leader of Lambeth Council, and Matthew Warburton, Lambeth's Housing chair), consistently argued for council resistance to central government. There followed a series of confrontations over enforced council house sales, cheap public transport and government curbs on council spending. Though many local people were drawn into these political campaigns, the issues were resolved by the legal argument and counterargument of a handful of lawyers. Until 1985, councillors were not prepared to step over the shrinking constitutional boundaries of local government and act illegally out of principle as in pre-war Poplar. Instead they sought to protect vulnerable local communities (as their predecessors had conventionally done) against a government determined to reduce services – providing the 'dented shield' of Neil Kinnock's speech to the Labour Party Local Government Conference in 1985.

What does distinguish this early period is an attempt to improve as well as to defend council services; to revitalize traditional Labour welfare upon socialist principles of equality rather than patronage; to open up new areas of municipal enterprise in the local economy. This was the message of the local manifestos and not so different from the agenda of Herbert Morrison, the inter-war leader of first Hackney, then the London County Council. His avowedly constitutional aim was to 'create an efficient machine for high moral purpose' which would draw people to socialism by showing what could be achieved locally. Hilary Wainwright, a member of the GLC's Economic Policy Group, called the new municipal socialism of the 1980s 'propaganda by example'; 'an administration which might prefigure a wider socialist society', argued David Blunkett and Geoff Green in *Building from the Bottom: the Sheffield Experience*.

16.3 Local economic planning

The massive rise in unemployment from 1.5 million to 3 million between 1980 and 1983 put local economic issues high on the agenda of all Labour councils. Economic units and departments multiplied. Most were mutations of economic development agencies characteristic of the previous decade, giving loans and grants to encourage industrial firms, providing land, property and infrastructure. Radical economic policies which characterize the new municipal socialism did not extend much beyond a small core group of the Greater London Council, Sheffield City Council and the West Midlands County Council. From time to time even they slipped pragmatically into the wider group. A problem from the beginning was that their more demanding definition of success – nothing less than the reorganization of their local economies to serve the social needs of their people – could not be achieved without parallel structural changes nationally and internationally. There were two question marks, the first over the relative autonomy of local economies. Local evidence of decline was there for all to see in the devastated industrial landscape, but did the nexus of economic forces behind it amount to a 'local economy' and was it susceptible to local intervention? Hence the second question, of the balance of economic power between local and national state. The London Labour Party's manifesto presented to the council as a *Minority Party Report* in March 1981 says:

It would be easier to create this public sector impetus for economic recovery if we had a government that believed in economic planning, investment by the public sector, and institutions like a strong National Enterprise Board. But in the absence of such a government, the case is no less important. And considerable progress can be made by an imaginative and determined use of the GLC's existing powers and resources. [Greater London Council, 1981]

The sentiment 'we cannot wait for the return of a Labour government' was taken a step further by David Blunkett writing as Sheffield's new leader in the same period: 'Waiting for the next Labour government to change the world, to legislate for democratic control and the economic millenium simply will not do. Not only cannot Parliamentary action miraculously change the world, but nor should it' (Blunkett, 1981). The theme was central to Sheffield District Labour Party's manifesto adopted by the City Council two years later.

An alternative strategy which brings together these three – unmet needs, physical and technical capacity, and people's right to work – naturally requires co-ordination at a national level by a future Labour Government. But such a plan cannot be devised in Westminster or Whitehall by politicians and civil servants; such a plan must be based on the skills, knowledge and initiative of ordinary working people if it is going to meet their needs. A socialist authority like Sheffield will have a crucial role to play in making such a plan come to life for the benefit of Sheffield people. [Sheffield District Labour Party, 1983]

The segmented circle and its outer ring in Figure 1 represent the deployment of labour in a city economy. The segments show the balance between public and private sector, the unemployed and the unwaged labour of domestic work. The paradigm underpins the London Industrial Strategy (LIS) promised in the manifesto and published in 1985 as the most coherent expression of a socialist economic strategy for local state intervention. The aim was to shift the boundaries by squeezing unemployment and expanding the public sector, radically restructuring economic relations in all segments to give labour more control over its work and social priorities for its product. The strategy challenged the post-war Keynesian consensus which separated 'private enterprise to run economic production, from the state which looked after the distribution of income: the one efficient, the other fair'. Instead, economic means and social needs would be brought together again by planning the production of goods and services. At a critical period in the fortunes of the Labour Party nationally here was a local experiment which could help to build a credible alternative to the new Conservative economics of the market place.

Throughout the 1970s the left wing of the Labour Party nationally had argued for the alternative economic strategy (AES) of a centrally planned economy with state control over multinational companies who owed no allegiance to a British electorate. Municipal socialists embarked on a programme of popular economic planning to turn these ideas into projects

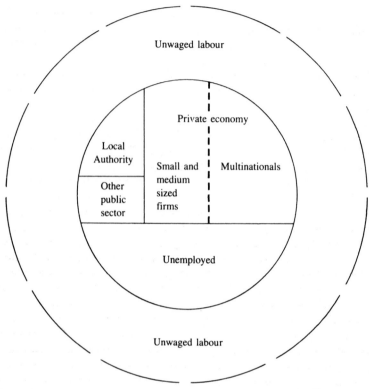

Figure 1

which struck a chord with the experience of local workers and with potential users of their product. Labour councils had a long tradition of supporting local workforces on strike or facing redundancy. The GLC's Popular Planning Unit and Sheffield's Employment Department, both operational by 1982, aimed to broaden narrowly defensive campaigns by helping to produce alternative industrial sector or company plans, providing research, new technological expertise and publicity resources. For example, in Sheffield an initial success was transforming a bankrupt machine tool company into a workers' co-operative to produce dehumidifier machines to ease council tenants' problems with damp flats. Sheffield's 'Electrify for Steel' Campaign brought together steel-producing unions facing over-capacity in the industry and railway unions pushing for electrification of the network which would use millions of tons of steel.

Success invariably depended on new investment. Directors and managers could often be persuaded to the negotiating table, but soon left again if local councils could not raise funds to back up their plans. As the GLC Labour Party manifesto said in 1981, 'Only a large-scale investment programme aimed at key sectors of London's industry will rescue the capital's manufacturing economy from almost total annihilation. The public sector will have to take an active role in such a strategy.' And, according to the LIS, the Greater London Enterprise Board was to be 'the instrument of that active role in the private economy'. There were similar moves in Sheffield. The District Labour Party's 1983 manifesto proposed to investigate how the Council might 'redirect private or public investment back into local industries to arrest the decline and regenerate the local economy'. But District Councils like Sheffield did not even have sufficient capital available to spend putting their own houses and schools in order, so major manufacturing investment was left to the metropolitan county councils. Their wider rating base allowed them to raise many more millions for investment (£38 million a year for the GLC) and they also controlled huge employee pensions funds. Five major Enterprise Boards were set up in 1982 and 1983 by the GLC, West Midlands, Lancashire, West Yorkshire and Merseyside County Councils, essentially to invest these funds to secure local industry and so save or create unionized jobs and improve the local authority's rating base. The provincial emphasis was on filling an investment gap (identified by the Wilson *Committee to Review the Functioning of Financial Institutions*) between conservative fund-holders prepared only to invest in property or second-hand shares, and manufacturing industry desparately needing an injection of capital to underwrite new production.

The public economy segment of the paradigm was the second target. In the early 1980s it accounted for a third of waged employment in London, and slightly more in Sheffield because of its nationalized steel industry. This sector can be split into five smaller segments, each graduated according to the degree of local democracy, measured by the extent of council influence. Over the remote bureaucracies of public corporations and nationalized industries at one end of the spectrum there is none. Next, the branches of central government like Social Security and the Manpower Services Commission offices do depend marginally upon co-operation from the local authority. Labour councils could not transform these, but might, at least, negotiate minor reforms such as improved training and job creation. In the middle of the spectrum, the block of councillors on local health authorities could exert some formal influence on the way National Health Services were run, and throughout the 1980s their aim was to extend or at least defend jobs within the service against government pressure to contract them out to the private sector. However, because Labour was in a minority to Conservative government appointees for most of the period, their opposition was largely ineffective. In contrast Labour did have effective control of public transport in the metropolitan counties following the 1981 elections, and their aim, indeed the achievement of the 'Socialist Republic of South Yorkshire', was to run a cheap, efficient and extensive public transport service.

For local authorities themselves, at the democratic end of the spectrum, the twin economic objectives were expansion and reform. At the beginning the ideal was not essentially a local version of Keynesian reflation (with public sector demand creating private sector jobs), though such arguments were to become important, rather an extension of democratic control over local production processes. Municipal enterprise, by cutting out profit, was cheaper than private enterprise and, since it could be planned to meet need rather than depend on the vagaries of the market, was potentially more efficient. This had been the message of *Six Years of Labour Rule in Sheffield: 1926–1931* (Sheffield District Labour Party, 1932) which had inspired the new municipal socialists in Sheffield. Since that time, of course, local authorities had lost many productive functions such as gas, electricity and water. The 1980s saw the attempt to advance again into the private economy, to integrate vertically by taking over production to meet the Council's social responsibilities. Printing and laundries are old examples, recording studios new; always the biggest is the construction and repair of council houses, roads and sewers by direct labour organizations. Reforms were necessary, however; socialist principles had to be translated into a service attractive to both workers and users. Industrial relations thus became a top priority: no-redundancy policies, the elimination of low pay and bonus systems which failed to guarantee basic wages above the poverty line, equal opportunities for women and ethnic minorities, equal status for manual and white-collar workers.

It is difficult to gauge how successfully all these alternative programmes were implemented in the following years. Evidence is fragmented in myriad council reports and summarized selectively for propaganda purposes. But the big picture is clear. Between 1981 and 1986 the sector boundaries in each city economy shifted against the socialist paradigm. Unemployment rose substantially; the public economy contracted; the private economy expanded by taking over public services. Industrial restructuring went further and faster than most councils anticipated. If their priority was manufacturing industry, then they found this rapidly declining into a smaller and subordinate part of an economy dominated by financial and consumer services. In consequence the increase in unemployment was greater in old manufacturing districts, the inner city and the North, the very areas which elected Labour councils in order to stem the tide. With hindsight, industrial decline was irreversible and predictable even before the 1979 general election. But few socialists could have anticipated the success of two Conservative governments in shrinking the boundaries of the public economy. Nationalized industries and public corporations were sold outright or (the case with steel) merged with private sector partners. As last bastions of resistance, Labour councils can claim to have slowed down the government's programme of rolling back state frontiers in health and transport. Even so, all Health Authorities were obliged to contract out some ancillary services to private firms; local public transport was removed from local democratic control and part of it put into the hands of private operators.

Local authorities were themselves subjected to a battery of legislation and administrative fiat to force the reduction in their workforces – by general financial restrictions but also by a series of measures designed to privatize a range of services, most especially construction. Despite these changes Labour councils have held on to most of their traditional work-forces. Many have made only minor cuts; most radical authorities have expanded at the margin and absorbed in addition former metropolitan county council employees made redundant by abolition. So, in declining city economies, their segment has increased relative to the private economy. With the closure of major manufacturing plants they have often become by far the biggest local employer. This represents a small victory for good employment practice since many have led the private sector in promoting equal opportunities and providing security.

Exceptionally, reformed direct labour organizations have expanded their share of a declining provincial construction industry and private competitors have been obliged by the terms of local authority building contracts to adopt good employment policies themselves, particularly about health and safety and training apprentices. Otherwise the balance of evidence is that even Sheffield's employment programme (maybe the closest to municipal socialism since the abolition of the GLC and the metropolitan counties) has, in a desperate search for capital investment from the government and financial institutions, entered a more pragmatic and traditional partnership with the private sector, providing infrastructure, land and property (not least a science park), grants or loans, and promo-tional material, in much the same way as their conventional predecessors. Any grand design for restructuring the private economy in the interests of labour has had to be abandoned until the return of a Labour government.

16.4 Reforming the welfare state

The second half of the agenda for municipal socialists was the reform of the welfare state. A large part of it is administered by local authorities: a triad of education, housing and personal social services together with smaller services such as recreation and environmental health. Such social provision is the essence of the contemporary local state, accounting for over 90 percent of aggregate expenditure and materially overshadowing any economic initiatives. It was the primary target for reduction in the 1979 Conservative election campaign and by two subsequent Conservative governments. The criticisms struck a chord in everyday experience: a 'nanny state'; inefficient, remote and paternalistic bureaucracies; badly designed and ill-maintained council houses; tenants with little control over their environment; prospective tenants as supplicants; authoritarian old people's homes; rude dustmen; interfering and incompetent social workers; quite apart from profligate expenditure on the undeserving poor or subsidies to better-off council tenants. Conservative legislation built upon this discord: first, and most successfully, extending the right of council tenants to buy their houses at a discount, and for remaining tenants to have their rights spelt out in a charter; subsequently, espousing the policy of 'community care' for sick and elderly people which shifted responsibility from the state back to the family; and going on to consider 'social market' packages of health care or education to be paid for privately or with subsidized vouchers.

The response of most progressive councils was to build equally upon widespread but often latent public support for the welfare state, characteristically to reform and improve services rather than merely to defend them. Walsall's early but short-lived experiment (*Walsall's Haul to Democracy*, 1982) in radical decentralization of housing services to thirty-one neighbourhood offices aimed to encourage mass participation, even local control. In the event it proved a high point in grassroots democracy. The aim of the dozen or so councils who subsequently went local, and of those still waiting in the wings with a manifesto commitment, has been to improve the management of the welfare state and local government, and by implication the bases of the Labour Party, during the long period of parliamentary opposition. David Blunkett put it explicitly in the 1983 report, *Campaigning for Local Freedom*, which helped establish the Local Government Campaign Unit:

> Local government is the only place where currently Labour Party representatives are seen to be making decisions about the lives and well-being of ordinary people. Therefore bad experiences from Labour Authorities increase Thatcher's credibility, while positive and innovatory experiences, along with efficient and sensitive local services, help to rebuild the vitality and electoral success of the Party generally. The revival of the Party and its organizational re-invigoration go hand in hand with saving local government. This essentially means looking at the way in which local government provides services so that not only the quality but the method of delivery, the nature of participation and accountability, play their part in increasing the commitment of individuals and groups to the collective ethos. [Blunkett, 1983]

He distinguishes a distributional defence of 'a public sector which helps the poor and dispossessed' (which would be shared by social democrats) from the intrinsic value of collective public provision. And it is this more radical collectivist vision of municipal socialism which has been so difficult to reconcile with individual user choice and responsibility. Maybe the problem lies at the heart of the relative failure by most authorities to make much progress with decentralization. Certainly it has led some to separate out what they see as a liberal confusion between participatory democracy and service delivery. So, for Sheffield's Housing Committee, individual tenant choices can be more effectively made because of technical proficiency in carrying out repairs and because a relatively authoritarian management structure codifies and clarifies procedures for allocating resources and allocating tenancies. Local democracy is exercised separately through a plethora of consultative committees meeting regularly about isssues of collective concern and feeding a stream of recommendations to formally constituted area committees. In theory there is no room for old style patronage, staff discretion is limited and well defined; prejudice and racism are outlawed by enforced codes of practice. The discipline can be hard on council workers – radical as well as reactionary – and in 1984 and 1985 caused a wave of strikes by white-collar employees of most radical councils.

Tenant complaints still dominate councillors' surgeries in the big cities and towns with a high proportion of council houses. The primary cause is now financial. Choice depends not only on efficient management and community participation, but also on the resources to back them up. Capital investment is vital. In the past it provided new council houses which gave slum-dwellers hope and laid the foundation of the old municipal socialism. In the 1980s it was essential to the success of new municipal socialism when all the physical defects of an earlier expansion crowded in on each other – the wall-tie failures and outside WCs of early cottage estates, roof-spread in the shoddily built homes of the post-war Macmillan period, grave structural and environmental problems in the tower blocks and system-built estates of the 1960s and 1970s. Yet between 1979 and 1986 the Conservative government effectively halved capital investment in public sector housing. 'Capital capping', as Sheffield's finance chairman called it, received less publicity than ratecapping and certainly did not lead to the same intensely political struggle and clear defeat. But councils' enforced backstage manoeuvres to secure investment funds by asset sales, creative accounting and partnership deals with the private sector, just as surely undermined the economic principles of local state socialism. When tenants of the crumbling council estates of Labour controlled Knowsley and Greenwich turned their backs on the party in key parliamentary by-elections in 1986 and 1987, they could see over the water, down the river, Mersey or Thames, in office blocks and garden festivals, the tangible signs of massive capital investment by the private sector. The Parliamentary Labour Party clearly failed to make the economic connexion between private affluence and public squalor.

'A plebeian under the patronage of a patrician' is how the Oxford English Dictionary defines a client. Although the term is largely confined to social work staff, for many councillors it summed up the attitude of council officials to their electors. It was also identified with traditional Labour welfarism. All the early radical manifestos express a determination to overturn it by providing services with people rather than for them. And in the following years, attitudes were successfully changed. But again powerful economic and financial pressures subverted these gains. High unemployment doubled, then trebled, the number of city-dwellers living in poverty. Labour cities suffered most. Even in Sheffield, with unemployment just above the national average in the mid 1980s, half the households were drawing means-tested state benefits and on some council estates it was three-quarters. Much of this welfare is administered by local authorities. The biggest component, housing benefit, was transferred across from the Department of Health and Social Security in 1983. For many more people in the 1980s, in Labour rather than more prosperous Conservative-controlled districts, and, most especially, in those cities run by municipal socialists, their most frequent contact with the town hall is queueing for welfare.

The problem of welfarism was magnified by the Conservative government's selective help to the poor. The market, they argued, should take care of most needs. Councils should cater for a residuum. Social services and housing especially should shrink. Certainly they should not be sustained by central government grants. Jaguar cars parked outside council houses, rich elderly widows with bus passes and free home helps, gave the policy populist appeal. Labour councils countered with equally powerful memories of humiliating means tests which were an integral part of selectivity. Radical councils revived the alternative socialist principle of universal public provision to eliminate the root cause of poverty. Sheffield's City Council's *Good Health for All* (1987) restates the case.

Patterns of health inequality across our cities [are] related to class and caused by the environment. Illness and premature death are not primarily a problem of individual neglect or immorality, nor remedied by individualized medical attention. Instead the causes are common, part of the structure of our society. Our remedy is collective, planned and public. [Sheffield City Council, 1987]

Council housing again exemplifies the conflict of ideas. Much of the earlier stock was built for the respectable working classes. Though slum clearance introduced poorer tenants, by the 1960s the average council household was still a family with a skilled manual worker in employment. In the years following the 1980 Housing Act, the Government accelerated the change to a residual welfare tenure by forcing councils to sell the best 12 percent (750 000) to the most affluent and by switching Exchequer subsidy from council housing in general to housing benefits for the poor. Most Labour councils offered limited resistance after failing to stop sales in 1981. It was easier to raise rents rather than cut services to balance their books if housing benefit automatically covered the majority of tenants. In short it was financially attractive to provide for the impoverished, and, indeed, radical housing pressure groups argued even greater priority for those in social need over the claims of average working-class applicants on the waiting list. Only a handful of radical councils – Sheffield and Liverpool are good examples – held on to universal provision. The cause was lost on the Parliamentary Labour Party whose shadow spokespeople had by 1980 dropped their opposition to sales, and all but abandoned a principled defence of council housing.

16.5 The battle over rates

Socialist programmes which are freely or cheaply available to all the population rather than the selected poor require high levels of public expenditure. Their success between 1981 and 1985 put pressure on the budgets of most radical administrations and became a target for government criticism and action. Extra spending was needed just to stand still, let alone improve these services. Factory closures had diminished the rating base of city councils and therefore their ability to raise local revenue. Against these pressures the government's declared intention was to cut back on local authority expenditure:

> Thus in May 1979 the incoming government inherited a seemingly inexorable long-term growth in current expenditure and manpower. They considered it essential to reverse the trend. The public sector – including both central and local government – had grown too large and was imposing too heavy a burden on the wealth creating private sector. [Department of the Environment, 1983]

During the Conservative government's first period in office their instrument was the Rate Support Grant (their annual financial contribution to local authority services) as defined by the 1980 Land and Planning Act and the 1982 Local Government Act. The big change was not to increase grant in line with expenditure but rather to decrease it dramatically once a specified target had been overrun. In order to penalize a limited group of 'high-spending' Labour authorities without squeezing Conservative authorities which were raising expenditure from a traditionally low base, and without setting arbitrary targets, the government were obliged constantly to revise their formulae, using seven variations in the period to 1984. They did successfully reduce their contribution to local authority expenditure from 61 percent in 1978–79 (it had been 66 percent in the first years of the previous Labour government) down to 53 percent in 1983/84. They were less successful in reducing local authorities' overall level of expenditure. Radical administrations compensated for loss of government grant by increasing charges for their services (primarily council house rents) or their revenue from ratepayers. Both were unpopular. Increased charges reduced take-up of the very services socialists wanted to extend, and alienated those council tenants whose rents were not automatically covered by social security. Rate increases hit hard not just local commerce and industry, which complained loudly with some effect on local opinion, but also those ordinary working-class households not poor enough to be subsidized by rate rebates. The period was characterized by an intense propaganda battle between local authorities and the government over the value of local public expenditure and an attempt to pin on the other, blame for the rate increase. Electoral success in 1982 and 1983 seemed to vindicate local socialists.

In 1983 the Conservative government sought a fresh mandate to limit rate increases by a group of about twenty local authorities. Their strategy was first to abolish the five metropolitan councils and the GLC because '. . . they have come to be seen by the public as remote, expensive, wasteful in manpower and contribute disproportionately to the problems of over-spending' (Conservative Party, 1983a). Secondly, 'We shall legislate to curb excessive and irresponsible rate increases by high spending councils and to provide a general scheme of limitation on rate increases for all local authorities to be used if necessary' (Conservative Party, 1983b). Immediately after the general election the target list of fifteen high spenders and the threatened counties – all Labour-controlled – met to plan resistance. The two-year period of confrontation before they were defeated in the summer of 1985 falls into two parts: first, the campaign to prevent ratecapping legislation which lasted until the Royal Assent in June 1984, then the year-long struggle not to comply with the new laws.

In the first period the campaign had two faces. On the one hand, radical councils successively mobilized active support for their jobs and services within their local communities. Many activists shared the view of many miners who went on strike in the spring of 1984, that extra-parliamentary action, in the form of massive popular resistance could defeat the recently elected government. On the other hand, the national co-ordinating groups set up by the radical councils, the Association of London Authorities in July 1983 and the Local Government Campaign Unit the following November, regarded sympathetic Conservative parliamentarians as the primary agents for defeating the legislation. The covert campaign was essentially 'soft' lobbying of Conservative 'wets' and lords – those who had defeated similar constitutional proposals two years earlier. The issue was constitutional – the future of local democracy rather than the value of public jobs and services. David Blunkett summarized the relation between the two strategies:

> Public pressure is essential but can only be seen as raising the temperature and providing a backcloth to real influence and lobbying on those in the House of Commons or House of Lords. . .
>
> Whilst campaigning at local level is critical in underpinning support and ensuring that community groups, tenants, voluntary and charitable organizations, trade unionists and political organizations are committed at local level, it may well be that these are more use in building bricks for withstanding future action once legislation is passed rather than in helping to stop the legislation. [Blunkett, 1983]

In the end, neither popular support nor low-key lobbying was ultimately successful. The government's White Paper, *Rates*, was published in August 1983, introduced as a Bill into the House of Commons in December, passed its Second Reading with only forty Conservatives abstaining or dissenting, and passed through the House of Lords in June 1984 (when amendments were rejected by majorities of 15 and 18) by 235 to 153 votes. The campaign had won popular support for its theme of local democracy – town hall not Whitehall – but lost the first battle.

The new municipal socialists entered the final confrontation optimistically. As Stewart Lansley reflected, the political climate was unusually favourable to defiance; Liverpool Council appeared to have forced substantial concessions by delaying setting of a rate.

> The miners' strike was at its peak. The government was heavily on the defensive over the abolition of the GLC and metropolitan counties and had been forced to concede direct elections to the Inner London Education Authority. Most important of all the ambiguity over the legality of not making a rate created a strategy which could be all things to all men and women in the struggle, at least in the short run. [Lansley, 1985]

Differently interpreted, without hindsight, the aim was to develop a strategy which reconciled unity of purpose with the different financial circumstances and political complexions of individual authorities. The government had isolated eighteen local authorities for ratecapping in July 1984. The Conservative councils soon conceded. The aim of the group of sixteen Labour councils was to prevent further subdivision and isolation. The general assumption was: 'If enough local authorities resist government imposed spending levels and refuse to implement this Rate Act and the abolition proposals for the metropolitan councils and the GLC, it will be impossible for the government to make them work and they will be forced to retreat' (Statement by the Sheffield District Labour Party and Labour Group, 30 June 1984). The campaign was co-ordinated primarily by the management group of the LGCU, expanded from the leadership of the original target group to any Labour authority at risk. Since the whole strategy hinged upon a common line, it took on a form of executive responsibility.

The target authorities quickly resolved not to comply with the law either by cutting services or by 'creative accountancy', for that would pave the way for more oppressive measures in future years. Neither would they mount the barricades immediately, openly and illegally defying the government, for that would alienate a minority in each Labour group who would vote with the opposition to defeat the purpose. Instead they resolved on a middle strategy of non-compliance which crystallized by December 1984 into a tactic of not setting a rate. This would bring all constituent members into confrontation with the government on the same day in March 1985. There was a fatal flaw, as Stewart Lansley argued. Success depended on unity and in turn legality or at least legal ambiguity. It became increasingly clear in the new year that this meant negotiating as reasonable men and women around the new constitutional frontier. The first problem was squaring this with an aggressive populist campaign against the government. A far greater problem was that at the very beginning of the campaign the most important point of agreement was that no member authority would negotiate with the government using the specific derogation procedures in the Act, for that gave the government even greater powers of intervention over individual budgets. There were moves to negotiate collectively in the new year and eventually such a meeting with the Secretary of State for the Environment took place on 4 February 1985. But by then much of the legal room for manoeuvre had been closed off by the strict parliamentary timetable set out in the Act. In the face of an uncompromising government the only legal (and realistic) option, since most Labour groups were divided, was to defer setting the rate for as long as it did not cost the authority too much in lost income. The illegal alternative was a modern version of Poplarism,[1] supported by the majority of local activists, and, indeed, by a substantial minority of the ordinary residents in the affected communities, according, at least, to a contemporary opinion poll in Sheffield. That local coalition, it was argued, could create such disruption that the government would be forced to intervene with substantial concessions. In the event, every council voted to set a rate. In a string of individual defeats stretching from 7 March to 3 July, when Lambeth finally conceded, they bowed to the law, just as in the previous months striking miners had returned to pit after pit.

16.6 Postscript

The defeat on ratecapping coupled with the abolition of the metropolitan counties and the GLC brought almost to an end the experiment in municipal socialism. Politically they brought in their wake bitterness and division within the New Left coalition which had set a distinctive course away from traditional Labour welfarism. Financially they had the effect of limiting resources available for social provision. Most importantly abolition brought to a close the most advanced economic, cultural and public transport programme. The consequence, certainly since the end of the GLC in March 1986, has been retrenchment, both materially and ideologically. Cuts in services and jobs were always inevitable in defeat unless there were great advances in organizing the local state and planning efficient socialist programmes within a limited budget. And even then Fabian planning of this kind without the political accountability which comes from a confident local labour movement is always likely to be subverted by the capitalist forms of corporate management so roundly condemned by the New Left in the 1970s. Ideologically the new municipal socialism has lost much of its radicalism. The relentless pressures of managing the local state in a hostile political and economic environment have caused weariness or exodus into oblivion or parliament. The coalition is breaking up. The most that is being achieved at a local level is consolidating advances already made. As a testing ground for a future Labour government, then, municipal socialism has not been a great success. For if the essence of municipal socialism is the extension of collective social provision rather than selective Labour welfarism, an economy geared directly to social needs rather than the market, then the national Labour Party's programme has largely passed it by.

Notes

1 Poplarism: a locally-based Labour radicalism of the 1920s, whose main feature was to challenge existing rules on the level and distribution of outdoor relief under the Poor Law. Although originally associated with the Poor Law Guardians of Poplar between 1919 and 1925, who have since attained heroic status within labour movement mythology, the label was applied at the time by their opponents to all Labour-controlled authorities held to be carrying out wasteful expenditure on the poor. Labour's more respectable municipal leaders (such as Herbert Morrison) did their best to distance themselves from the trend.

References

Blunkett, D. (1981) *Alternative Economic Policies: a Socialist Local Government Response*. Discussion paper presented to the Association of Metropolitan Authorities.

Blunkett, D. (1983) *Campaigning for Local Freedom*. Unpublished report.

Blunkett, D. and Green, G. (1983) *Building from the Bottom: the Sheffield Experience*, Tract 491. London: Fabian Society.

Conservative Party (1983a) *Candidates' Briefing Notes*. London: Research Department, Conservative Party Central Office.

Conservative Party (1983b) *Election Manifesto*. London: Conservative Party Central Office.

Department of the Environment (1983) *Rates: Proposals for Rate Limitation and Reform of the Rating System* (Cmnd 9008). London: HMSO.

Department of Trade and Industry (1980) *Committee to Review the Functioning of the Financial Institutions*, Report and Appendices, Sir Harold Wilson (Chair) (Cmnd 7937). London: HMSO.

Greater London Council (1981) *Minority Party Report: a Socialist Policy for the GLC*. London: London Labour Party.

Greater London Council (1985) *The London Industrial Strategy*. London.

Lansley, S. (1985) 'The Phoney War', *New Socialist* 29 (August).

London Edinburgh Weekend Return Group (1979) *In and Against the State*. London: Pluto Press.

Rowbotham, S., Segal, L. and Wainwright, H. (1979) *Beyond the Fragments*. London: Merlin Press.

Sheffield City Council (1987) *Good Health for All: the Sheffield Plan*. Sheffield.

Sheffield District Labour Party (1932) *Six Years of Labour Rule in Sheffield: 1926–1932* (reprinted 1982).

Sheffield District Labour Party (1983) *Manifesto*. Sheffield.

Walsall Metropolitan Borough Council (1982) *Walsall's Haul to Democracy*. Walsall.

17
Living on welfare

Jeremy Seabrook

In describing the lives of those who depend for their subsistence on the welfare state, it is important not to reduce them to the sum of their income. There are vast resources, reservoirs of inventiveness in even the most deprived. To say this is not in any way to proclaim the virtues of poverty; but the hidden economy, especially the work of women, has the effect of mitigating what would otherwise be an unendurable experience. The poor are almost universally represented as victims; and while it is true that they remain excluded from the ever-extending spread of market transactions in the lives of the majority of people, their resilience is seldom celebrated, even though their survival depends upon it.

Freda's mother died early in 1986 in her East London flat. Although the cause of death was officially pneumonia, she actually died of self-neglect and malnutrition. The photographs which Freda took of her during the fortnight she spent with her daughter show her gaunt, emaciated. 'We didn't want her to go back. She hated that flat. My brother said he'd been applying to the council for a transfer for years, but they said they had no record of any application. Either they lost the forms, or he never sent them.'

Her mother was 77. She had worked in the clothing industry in the East End, both as a young woman, and as a widow while her children were still at school. She knew she was born to labour – machining, child-rearing, keeping the dingy flat clean in the Buildings where they lived.

Freda also worked as a machinist when she left school, but before her third child was born she was deserted by her husband. ('Deserting', she says, 'is about the only thing he was any good at. He deserted from the army, he done a bunk from his Mum, he cleared off on us.') He has never seen his youngest daughter, who is now 17. Since then, Freda has been on benefit. There have been occasional attempts to increase the family income – work in a Bingo hall, making soft toys, machining at home; but these were both ill-paid and insecure. So that the neighbours would not write anonymously to Social Security, she muffled the sound of the machine while she worked at night by placing cushions and padded bags round the doors and windows.

Freda now lives in a new town, although her estate was built just after the war. The house is small, but is in a terrace of about eight, bounded by the wire fencing of a school playing-field. This means there is no traffic in the street, the aspect is open and there is a reasonably sized garden. Freda keeps the radio on all day, Radio Caroline: this is the only way to prevent the neighbours from hearing every word she and her family say, and the only defence they have against the sounds from next door. 'At night it's bad. You can hear her calling him a filthy bastard and he's calling her a filthy cunt. Next morning you see them walking down the street arm in arm, nobody but us knows what's been going on between them. I'd rather not know; you have no choice.' In order to shut the neighbours out, they have replaced the garden fence with some sheets of corrugated metal.

Recently, Freda threw out her copy of the painting of the Crying Boy: there had been much discussion, in the *Sun* and elsewhere, about whether this picture brought bad luck. Certainly, Freda has had her share. She thought that if she threw it into the builder's skip at the bottom of the road, her luck might change.

For one thing, her elder daughter, still only 19, left home to get married two years ago. Michelle always felt that Lissa, younger by 18 months, was her mother's favourite. The man she left home for treated her badly, gives her a good hiding when he feels like it. 'As long as he's tinkering with his Cortina, has a drink and his smokes, and a bit of sex when he needs it, he's all right. Otherwise, she gets it.' Last year, Michelle left her twin babies anonymously with a Social Services Department in North West England. There was a brief mention of it on TV news: she had left a note saying that she couldn't cope and that her name was Michelle. Somebody saw it and told Freda. 'How do you think it makes you feel, to hear what's happening to your family through the television? I couldn't believe it. She was never brought up like that. They're beautiful kids.' She shows the photogaphs of two healthy babies in white Babygro suits. 'They've already moved them from one foster-home; her children got jealous, so she couldn't keep them. I'd have them. The social worker came down, there isn't enough room here. I suppose they want somewhere they can get a better start in life. It broke my heart, going up there to see them. I wanted to take them away with me. I can't understand it. It's not Michelle, it's him. He's got a power over her. She can't keep away from him. He was in a car accident. He's supposed to have had head injuries. It might be that that's made him funny. I've only heard from her once in the last eight months.'

Lissa left school last year. She has just finished a year's YTS placement, as typist and receptionist with a timber firm in the town. She has taken her Pitman's courses, and proudly shows her certificates – typing, Intermediate First Class, Office Skills, Communication Skills. She is an exuberant and engaging young woman; wears a long beige dress, short blonde-tinted hair, swept back, pale lilac eye-shadow and lip gloss. She has been applying for jobs every day: she would like to work as a receptionist or switch-board operator. She has been practising her accent. She is keeping up her typing speeds on the machine in her bedroom, typing pages of the romances she reads. Since her sister left home, Lissa feels the pressure more strongly that she must be 'the good one of the family'. She has bought many of the little ornaments and knick-knacks with which the shelves and walls are crowded – little brass bells, glass animals, pieces of china in transparent plastic containers, a black velvet hanging with a poem in gold thread on 'A Father's Love'. The books belong chiefly to Lissa – *Readers' Digest*, Barbara Cartland novels, a medical book and an encyclopedia.

Edward, the oldest of Freda's children, is now 22. He went to a Special School, and now goes to Training Centre, where he helps in the canteen, serving tea and taking the money. He is a large good-natured young man, wearing a new track-suit, dark grey with a broad yellow band down the side. He is on disability benefit. A few years ago, he was run over. I remind him that when I visited him in hospital, he said proudly, 'I got killed by a car.' Edward is trying to grow a beard, but it is very slow – a fringe of dark hair around his chin. Every Friday night, he goes to a pub in the town centre to watch the strippers. He says, 'There's a white girl and a black girl. I like the white girl best. She takes everything off. Then I have 2½ pints of lager, then I come home and go to sleep.' When he was younger, Edward was badly bullied by the other children on the estate in Hackney. He was suspected of being sexually interested in younger children, but it was simply that his backwardness made them his natural companions; it was hard for Freda to explain this to the neighbours. Edward started fires, and once burned out the bedroom in the flat.

Since Freda met Colin seven years ago, her life is more settled. 'You can't keep on running for ever,' she says, falling easily into the language of her favourite Country and Western songs, which speak to her in a way that contemporary British culture does not. 'You're only running from yourself.' She met Colin in the street. He was a sweeper for the Borough Council. He invited her to meet him in the pub. 'I went to see him, didn't I, and of course, I went in the Saloon and he was sitting in the Bar. I felt a right fool. Next time I saw him, I said "What happened to you? I was there. Anyway, if you want to see me, you'll have to come round my house." And he did.' Colin suffers from asthma, and when he left his job, he had to go on long-term invalidity benefit. He has a severe stutter, although it only affects him now when he meets strangers. Freda says it helps him to have the radio on; if there's background noise he doesn't stutter at all.

They have an allotment about a quarter of a mile from the house. They grow all their vegetables – potatoes, carrots, onions, beans and cabbage, and there is still room for raspberries and blackcurrants. This year they planted two Victoria plum trees. 'In summer we're both quite happy to spend the whole day there.' Freda has learned many older survival skills from an earlier tradition of poverty. She knows about cheap cuts of meat, stuffing breast of lamb, ox-tail and offal, and she has made many of the children's clothes. She insists that her mother did not teach her these things. 'It's common sense. If you know you're never going to have much money, you might as well get on with it, make the best of it you can.'

Freda is a very tenacious woman, and much of her life has been dedicated to keeping the children with her, even in the most adverse circumstances. She made a disastrous second marriage to someone who, she says, 'was a Mummy's boy. He went back to her in the end. He liked the idea of a ready-made family, but couldn't get on with the people in it.' He had threatened her, hit the children. For two years they scarcely spoke to each other. On the day he left, he had the gas and electricity cut off. I remember visiting her at that time: cold flat, with a solitary candle in a milk bottle. Her husband had removed the lock from the door and written in lipstick on the looking-glass: 'Goodbye Freda I still love you ha-ha.' It had taken her a year to get rid of him and to gain possession of the flat. After the fire, she had been taken in by a friend who had five children of her own. The friendship very soon soured, and she was ordered to leave. I met her that day too, walking with the three children through the sleet; a draggled despairing group on a bleak steel-grey night. They were carrying their few belongings in a cardboard carton that said 'Sell your eggs in rotation', and two torn polythene bags – a few clothes, some bedcovers and children's toys. They were placed in a bed-and-breakfast hotel in Islington. It was, behind the facade, a squalid place. The room which Freda shared with the three children was infested with mice; there were holes in the wainscot, and all the food had to be hung up in bags. She was expected to be out of the hotel beween the hours of ten and five. This showed her at her most resourceful: she telephoned the newspapers. The *Morning Star* and the *Evening Standard* wrote a feature about her plight; the *Guardian* published her picture. Freda had the gift of being able to mobilize people on her behalf – doctors, social workers, psychiatrists, officials, teachers, friends, neighbours. At one time, she says proudly, she had thirty people working for her. She even joined the National Front at one time, and had the telephone number of a self-appointed vigilante called Sundance, whom she was to summon if she had any trouble. It didn't last long. 'They were rubbish,' was her verdict.

Although she feels guilty about her mother's death ('I keep thinking of her in that flat on her own, I can see it happening to me'), Freda is happier now than she has ever been. Edward will never be really independent and Michelle is a lost cause. Lissa will have to look after her. 'I don't worry about what I can't have. I walk into town, two miles each way, every day; take the dog. Go up the allotment. Colin does a bit of gardening for people, it makes an extra quid or two. We stay at home in the evening. What you haven't got, you have to learn to do without.'

William and Sharon are 22 and 25. Sharon has two children from a previous marriage, Alice 6 and Mary 4. Their own child, Stephanie, is 2. Stephanie has never seen electric light in her own home. All she knows is the single butane flare which lights one corner of the living room and the candles which light them to bed and to the lavatory in the yard. Bedtime for the three little girls is a time of shadows and fears added to those known to most young children: the flickering candlelight dances in the draught, and the empty stairwell echoes. Nightmares and bed-wetting only add to the burden of being poor.

William hasn't worked for wages for three years. Before that he was in a hotel, waiting; later he worked as a warehouseman. He has worked voluntarily in a geriatric hospital, but gave it up, because the sadness and dereliction of the people 'gets to you in the end'. He doesn't want to be accused of being a scrounger, and feels he ought to 'earn' the £75 which he and his family live on.

There has been a long story of conflict with the Electricity Board about unpaid bills. For one thing, Sharon lived in the house for three years with her first husband before William moved in, and there was a substantial debt carried over from that period. William has calculated that if he has to pay the whole debt off before reconnection at the present rate of paying off the debt, it will be eighteen years before the lights are turned on again.

Such tangles of despair and confusion with the public utilities are common enough; but William is convinced that he is being punished: a warning to others. And it is true that in the shell of community in which his family lives – the short-life housing in the streets with boarded-up shops and empty factories on the corners – this is their only function, to terrify everybody else into conformity. They are known as 'the family without electricity', as though they were lacking some essential human attribute. They illustrate precisely the meaning of 'deprivation', that euphemism that actually reveals more than it hides: deprivation means that something has been taken away or withheld. It is a more nakedly social product than poverty.

Sharon says that nobody in the neighbourhood ever mentions it, but people are watching. When she goes into the local shops, conversation ceases. Other people's children are not allowed by their parents to come and play in the house. William has managed to fit up an old black and white television set: he runs it from a lorry battery. Periodically, someone calls from the Electricity Board to make sure they are not tapping the mains supply illegally. William and Sharon wonder how other poor families manage. 'They must go without all sorts of things for the sake of the electricity – food, clothes, who knows?' They wonder if there are people whose children go to bed hungry for the sake of maintaining light and TV; if so, they do not understand why this should be considered more virtuous than their priorities of good food and warm clothing.

That the children should suffer is of course merely an unfortunate by-product of the example that is being made of their parents. And as far as William is concerned, he has plenty of time to get used to his status as victim. He always felt, as a child, that he was blamed for whatever went wrong in the family, was unloved and scapegoated. He left home and went in the army; but was discharged, officially for 'homosexual offences', but he claims, it was because of his shyness and inability to mix. After this, he neglected himself, drank a lot and became demoralized. 'I used to wear a leather jacket with studs and ELVIS LIVES painted on it. I went around with a gang of lads. We did a break-in and got caught. I tried to kill myself with a carving knife; it pierced my stomach and came out the other side.'

It was while he was in this condition that he met Sharon, whose husband was working at the probation hostel where William was living. Sharon smiles deprecatingly as he says this, but she accepts the tribute and knows it is true, when he says, 'If it hadn't been for her, I'd be in prison or in my grave.' Sometimes, he still feels the old resentment and anger; his feeling about the way he was treated as a child has a direct bearing on the rage he feels about being poor and unemployed. 'When I get like that, I could easily go out and nick something. If she encouraged me, I'd go out and do it.' But Sharon tells him that if he does, she won't be there when he gets back. William was only 19 when they married. He loves all the children, and his delight in Stephanie is very touching: she marches round the room in one red wellington and one blue, offering everyone a salt and vinegar crisp.

The house is poor. The glass in the front door is broken, and in its place is a square of hardboard. On it, someone has written Merry Xmas in white paint. Downstairs there is a single room: the floorboards are covered with strips of old carpet, the pattern almost worn away. A series of battered cupboards, sideboards, kitchen cabinets stand round the edge of the room – other people's rejects or picked up for a pound at the second-hand shop. There is a three-piece suite, cut moquette, grey with red braid, that is about thirty years old. If you touch it vigorously, clouds of dust rise. The plaster is coming away from the walls; the wallpaper stained and faded by damp. Over the chimney breast there is a darker paper, and here William and Sharon have pasted pictures of the children, a few old Christmas and Mother's Day cards: a little island of comfort and reassurance colonized out of the surrounding bleakness.

Living poor in 1986 means that a packet of biscuits is a luxury. It means living on mince ('God knows what it's made of, you find bits of hair and what feels like toenails in it'), and by the end of the fortnight, a meal of soup and bread or potatoes in gravy. It means buying food in the supermarket when the Eat-By date has expired, and buying dented tins cheaply – when the labels have come off, says Sharon, you don't know what's in them till they're opened. 'You don't know if you're having spaghetti rings or Creamed Rice, it makes life a bit more exciting.' Living poor means using old newspaper instead of toilet paper; using a 30p tin of condensed milk and dilute to make three pints instead of fresh milk. It means queueing up at church jumble sales; mending the broken window with sellotape and cardboard. It means reading by candlelight. It means buying twenty loaves a fortnight, and never being able to afford cheese.

Late in the afternoon Stephanie drops a glass she has picked up from the table: a thin tumbler with a red-painted rim. It shatters on the worn carpet. William picks up the biggest pieces, then takes the yard brush and vigorously sweeps the strips of carpet. The dust rises; specks of glass lodge in the worn pile. He tries to pick up every piece, but it is impossible to see them in the gathering darkness.

The sadness of evening is always intensified by their inability to dispel the shadows. For William and Sharon every evening is the same. When the children have gone to bed, they might watch the flickering TV, but the picture is very hazy. Sharon prefers the radio – a small tinny object with failing batteries and held together with two pieces of Elastoplast. Most evenings Sharon does some washing. She has to boil the kettle on the gas stove six or seven times to get enough hot water, until the house is full of steam. Then it all has to be passed through the old-fashioned mangle that stands in the yard, ornate metal base, big grey rollers; all the buttons have to be removed and then sewn on again, because they would be crushed. Occasionally, they play cards. William has a cigarette, Sharon reads a Mills and Boon story.

They don't talk about the future. Even the strength of their relationship, this moment of stability in their lives, seems fragile and threatened. They feel stranded. Not many people visit. 'What have we got to offer them?'

Perhaps because of the overwhelming nature of his personal experience, William has little sense of social injustice. If he is out of work, it is his own fault, even though he concedes there are no jobs to be found. 'Nobody owes me a living,' he says. 'It's up to me to get a job. If I can't, well I'm over 21, nobody else is responsible for me, are they?' He says he is grateful for the money from Social Security; on the occasions when the giro has been delayed in the post, he borrows £5 from his Nan. In the election of 1983, they voted SDP, and even had a poster in the window. 'It was a waste of time. I don't know why we bothered. I shan't vote next time.' It isn't that he is particularly disenchanted with the SDP; rather it is that he feels there ought to have been some pay-off for voting at all; and clearly, there wasn't.

The children put on their coats against the cold, because they use the gas fire very sparingly: a few minutes at a time only when the cold becomes unbearable. Then they all crouch round, extending their hands towards the blue and orange flame. The candlelight dances on the thin curtains which move in the constant draught. The butane lamp hisses. In the back yard, an old teddy bear has been left out in the rain; and his saturated body looks as if it is bleeding onto the grey garden slates.

As you leave, the street is brighter than the interior. What strikes you most forcefully about the lives of Sharon and William is the importance of the other side of the rewards-and-incentives argument, the fact that its power would be considerably diminished without the obverse – the deterrent force of poverty. The Poor Law may have ceased to exist, but the law for the poor is unchanged; it is that they must suffer. They do not have a strong feeling that their plight is socially remediable. Indeed, it seems as though they do not see being poor as a social problem at all, but as a personal one. Certainly, they do not think of themselves as living in a particular social and economic system. For them, society is given: as though it were a phenomenon of nature.

A few weeks later, after payment of a small portion of the arrears, the electricity was turned on again. Within three months, they were rehoused, a new town-house with three bedrooms. But after that, everything seemed to go wrong. It seemed that the darkness had mercifully concealed a great deal about their lives. They split up when Sharon was seven months pregnant. William decided that he was too young to settle down, that he had had too little enjoyment in life. He wanted to 'hang loose' for a while, to live a little. Sharon was left alone with three children and the new baby, in a strange neighbourhood, at the far end of the bus route.

Marie has gone into hiding. In her long experience of dealing with the caring agencies of the state, she has learned that the only way to get attention is by means of creating high drama that the authorities cannot ignore. Violence, danger, self-damage, children at risk – there is an increasingly competitive clamour for attention. Anything less will not be considered sufficiently urgent for action.

It's actually a good place to hide: shielded from the busy road on the edge of the city, you go down about twenty steps and find a fortress-like low-rise building from the late seventies, a hexagon, with cobbled courtyards and beds of silver-green conifers and pyrocanthus. Marie's flat is secure, with an extra Chubb lock which she keeps closed whether she is out or at home.

Marie is here temporarily, having abandoned her flat and gone to a women's refuge some twenty miles from where she was living. Her husband, Greg, had left her only a few months after their marriage. She had always known it wouldn't work. 'I tried to talk him out of it, but he didn't want to know. He thought getting married makes people love each other; getting married is the surest way of finding out you don't.'

It wasn't Greg who had beaten her up; he is not a violent man. Within a few weeks of being married, he spent a month in gaol for breach of parole, and within four weeks of release he had left home. He had returned, saying he wanted to start again, and Marie, who is a placid, good-natured woman ('They can see me a mile away,' she says deprecatingly about herself), agreed to try once more.

Six weeks later, there had been a row, and he left home for good. To make matters worse, he went to live with Marie's best mate, Tina, and her boyfriend, who lived on the same estate, no more than 300 yards away. One weekend, Marie's parents had come to stay, to cheer her up and help with the three children. Her father had parked his Reliant Robin three-wheeler outside the flat. On the Saturday morning the car had gone. Scouring the estate for it, Marie had called at Tina's, and found the garage door open with Ted working on her father's car. She challenged Tina, and asked her if she knew her father's car had been nicked by Greg. Tina said it was news to her, and promised to make sure that Greg would return it straight away.

Later in the afternoon, Marie went to get some ice-cream for the children. She saw her father's car parked outside the shop, driven by a stranger. This woman said she had just bought it. She had paid £100 cash. She was told that it was stolen: Marie's father produced the papers. The woman went to the police.

Tina believed that Marie had told the police that the car had been in her garage and that Greg had taken it. For Tina, the idea that her mate had grassed on her was too much: she had a few drinks and worked herself up into a state of fury and indignation. In fact, the police had called on Marie, and asked to see Greg; she had told them she didn't know where he was. All she said was, 'If you find him, keep him away from me or it's me you'll be arresting for murder.' The policeman replied, 'That's all right, it isn't a crime to kill a Taylor' (Greg's surname). As soon as the police left, Tina arrived. As Marie opened the door, she had rushed at her, beating and bruising her, breaking her nose, tearing out some hair and blacking both eyes. Marie's father tried to intervene, was no match for Tina's rage.

Marie rang the women's refuge where she had retreated earlier when a boyfriend had given her a good hiding. There was no room, but she was told to try the refuge in the next city. Her father drove her there in the car which he had repossessed. 'I was the only woman there who'd been beaten up by another woman,' says Marie. 'They thought I must be a lesbian.'

After a few days, she was temporarily rehoused in her present flat. The two younger children are with their father, who has just remarried, and Marie is here with her 10-year-old, Stephanie. After the shock and the extremes of emotion, Marie says she now feels empty. She finds herself confiding in Stephanie, telling her things that she knows no 10-year-old ought hear. 'But I can't help it. Stephanie says she's never going to get

married. I just don't know how to get through the days.' In the same block
Marie has started a friendship with a man in his fifties, who has brought
up two boys on his own. His wife left him ten years ago, and he determined
not to let the children go into care, because he himself had been brought
up in a Dr Barnardo's home, where his memories are of being always cold
and hungry, over-punished and under-loved. He urges Marie not to let
the two younger children stay with their father, but to keep the family
together. He is now semi-retired, and does a part-time job driving a lorry.
'The curse of my life now is loneliness. My youngest is now 15, he's
got his own life. The older boy has left home. It hurts when they grow
away from you, but I'd rather lose them this way, through their choice,
rather than through mine. People thought I was mad, a bloke on his own
bringing up kids. But I wouldn't want any kids to go through what I did.'

Marie's secret dread, and what tempts her to leave the younger two
with their father, is that she finds it increasingly hard to cope with the
three of them together. Her first husband is now working on a Community
Programme scheme; he can give them the firm hand she feels she lacks.
'With me, they just run wild.' Stephanie is difficult enough; she goes into
long sulks, sits under the table and will not speak for hours at a time.
She is teased at school because she wears jumble-sale clothes; today she
has gone to school in a pair of plastic sling-back shoes with the heels sawn
off. The other children have called her gipsy and flea-bag.

It has required great strength for Marie not to return to the flat, and
not to signal to her friends where she is. 'I always get in with the wrong
people.' She wonders what has happened to the flat. 'There's nothing in
it I care about. I don't want to see it again. They tried to put pressure
on me to go back, because the flat is in a joint tenancy with Greg, but
now I've been told that they will rehouse me here, so I won't have to
go back. I want to start a new life. I'm thinking of changing my name.
I don't want to be reminded of anything in my past. There's only one
trouble. Where the kids are with my first husband, they've got a lodger;
and he's an old flame of Tina's. Tina's old flames, there's enough of them
to start a forest fire, they're everywhere.'

The Social Services have been good to her here; and she is getting more
from the DHSS than she received in her former home, £37 a week plus
Child Allowance. She has a big box of Meredith and Drew's broken
biscuits which she got on the market for £2. In the kitchen there are two
meat pies in silver foil ready for the evening meal. She can buy frozen
chops and ox-tail and bacon from the butcher's for £5 to last the week.
It costs 62p for her and 31p for Stephanie to go into town.

'I'm finished with men,' she says. She reflects on her relationship with
her father, which had never been particularly happy. 'He always preferred
my brother. He never took any notice of my girls; it wasn't until Kevin
was born that he noticed I had any kids at all.'

We go over the bridge to meet Stephanie out of school; eighty-six steps, past the cement works that has coated all the trees and pavements with a film of grey dust; over the busy main road, and then a pathway bordered with trees, where Marie says dirty men are always lying in wait for the children. The graffiti on the bridge say 'Karen is a Slag, Jason and Kelly shagged here', 'Women Don't Want Equality – They Just Want Your Jobs'.

Many people have observed the relative apathy or quiescence of the poor in recent years, in spite of the inner-city riots. At the same time, there has been an increase in crime and violence, combined with a decreasing level of political activity and protest. What seems to have happened is that the images and symbols of wealth are so pervasive and insistent that the rich are not so much objects of resentment as models of aspiration and hope. If there are more crimes, greater violence, a more ready breakdown of relationships, much of this is contained within the poor communities themselves, with relatively little effect on the mainstream of social life. Some of the poor have learned to play the system, as though it were a kind of refined roulette wheel; others have set out, often parodying the values of enterprise and initiative of the dominant culture, to get, by fair means or foul, the money without which a decent life is not possible; but the vast majority accept the curtailed and diminished possibilities that being 'on benefit' implies. It is not, on the whole, public disorder and protest that characterize the lives of the poorest, but their acceptance of the often imperfect structures of caring, it is their patience and endurance, their extraordinary longanimity; which all suggest how little has changed beneath the constantly shifting surface of things.

* * *

There is now a significant core of people in Britain who have grown into adult life as dependents of the welfare state. They have come through childhood on what was National Assistance, later Supplementary Benefit, into adult unemployment, and have now brought up their children in similar circumstances. The conditions in which many such people live are familiar, not only to social workers, but to any viewer of those TV documentaries of which they are so often the subject: the hard-to-let estates with the barricaded shops, the rank grass and half-wild dogs, the broken windows and burgled meters, the jumble-sale clothes and Social Services Department furniture, second-hand cookers and foam mattresses; 'existing, not living', as they will tell you.

There is something both upsetting and disturbing about dependency upon the caring agencies of the state (the dwindling benign effects of which are so frequently counteracted now by its multiplying agencies of control). This is not to suggest that there is anything morally bracing about leaving the poor to fend for themselves, to make their own accommodation with unemployment, disablement and death: this will merely fill the towns and cities with beggars, as any visitor to the cities of the South is immediately aware. It isn't even that the labyrinthine and sometimes impenetrable workings of the welfare system itself are the source of the wrong (although they are no help either), or even their not particularly well rewarded and often resentful custodians and administrators.

What makes life on welfare so cruel – and it is a different kind of cruelty from that in societies where there is no welfare provision at all – is the context in which that system of relief has to operate. For dependency on welfare is only another aspect, a more intensive version of a wider and more institutionalized dependency that pervades all the rich industrial societies; and that is the ever-extending and more total dependency upon money and what it will buy. It is not welfare, but the growing, indeed, it sometimes seems, boundless power of money and our increasing reliance upon it that is the true cause of the loss of autonomy and independence in people. This is what more and more constrains human – as opposed to entrepreneurial – initiative, stifles creativity, directs great areas of activity through the severe filter of the markets. The spoiling, the degrading and exclusion of the freely given, the spontaneously offered, the mutually exchanged service, the monetizing of all the things that human beings have always provided for each other without cost, leads to a slow shrinking of that realm of social intercourse not subject to market and commoditized relationships.

It is a commonplace in the critique of conventional economics that this measures only the cash transactions of the official market economy: all private sector production, employment, consumption, investment and savings; all state and local government expenditure and income. That this is supported by a cash-based 'underground' economy is also recognized. But all this, in turn, rests upon the non-monetized 'counter-economy' as Hazel Henderson (1986) calls it, which subsidizes the GNP sector with unpaid labour, do-it-yourself, bartering, social, family and community structures, unpaid household work, parenting, voluntary work, sharing, mutual aid, caring for the majority of the old and sick, home-based production for use, subsistence agriculture. All of this, of course, is sustained by the natural resource base, which absorbs so many of the external costs of the official economy as well as many of those of the counter-economy.

What we have lived through in the West has been the accelerating passage of non-monetized activity into the formal economy. Being on welfare illuminates the extent to which the poor have also been penetrated by this dominant process (and market penetration is precisely what the ugly jargon suggests, a form of violation). For them, the last penny is accounted for before it even reaches their hands. The sense of impotence in the presence of money all used up in advance is what makes of welfare so shaming and unfree an experience. The poor, more than anyone else, feel the limitations of lives in which all human abilities are in the process of being superseded by the supreme ability – the ability to pay. Such processes can occur only in societies in which a majority of the people have access to a rising disposable income; enhanced purchasing power masks the decay of other, human powers and possibilities. While the rich seek out more and more ingenious things to spend their money on, the poor are increasingly stranded, excluded, set apart; and this process is experienced by them as both arbitrary and violent.

One of the reasons why so many young people leave school able neither to deal with the institutions of the society that shelters them, nor to respond to its most elementary demands is because their understanding has been not aroused, but smothered by that superior knowledge that money can buy, and without which, as they will readily tell anyone who asks, you can do nothing; as though money itself were the key to all human activity. Buying and selling have long since ceased to be simple negotiations over daily necessities: they have become the locus where action, invention and creativity are extinguished. The decay of human possibilities is written into the very structure of the market economy. This perhaps helps to explain the increase in crime and violence as society gets richer, a development which has puzzled so many commentators and observers. Far from being 'mindless', it has a precise cause, and is a response, not merely to an absence of material things, but to more violent underlying processes of expropriation and loss.

As we become more dependent upon money, we feel more disempowered, and thus more prey to terror at the thought of any change or diminution of what we have. Our much-cherished 'standard of living' is a kind of life-support system, which in fact indicates very little about the *level* at which we live, but everything about the *way* in which we live. Faith in the rising income attaches us securely to a marketplace which suggests to us, prompts, inspires us even, in the spending of our money. In other words, the marketplace becomes the focus of all hope of increase and enlargement in our lives.

No policy for improving the condition of the poor can be effective if it ignores the wider context. Such a policy would need to look at ways, not of deepening our subordination to the cash economy, but of seeking to release us, where possible, from it. It would propose a process of reclamation of all that we can freely offer each other without the mediation of money; would seek to regain as many freely exchanged services and commodities as may be; it would consider reducing the marketplace to a minimal role in our lives, not allowing it free passage into deeper and deeper places in both heart and imagination.

The projection onto welfare of a major disabling influence on people's lives has gone unchallenged, and for an obvious reason. Because the alternative to the market economy appears so bleak – that, state planning of those clumsy mechanisms that fail the people in Socialist countries which are so crude and cumbrous – this does not mean that the market economy is therefore perfection and beyond critical scrutiny. Yet this is what has happened. The inadequacies of existing alternatives make the market system the object of a taboo. Indeed, it is proclaimed as the surest guarantor of our liberties; it is celebrated as the finest ornament of Western civilization.

Beyond a certain level, the extension of market transactions into human lives becomes damaging, corrosive, destructive. Because there is no limit to the needs, satisfactions and consolations which can be turned over to the markets, no individual can ever possess enough money to achieve them all. When everything is for sale, we want everything; and yet we still want for so many things. Security, sufficiency, mutuality remain elusive, for they are not to be found in the realm of monetary satisfactions. Commodity substitution for our deepest yearnings is a profanation of our humanity; and this is what the poor, of both North and South, are trying to say to us.

Reference

Henderson, H. (1986) in Ekins, P. (ed.) *The Living Economy.* London: Routledge & Kegan Paul.

18
The welfare state as part of a racially structured and patriarchal capitalism

Fiona Williams

18.1 Introduction

In this chapter I shall present an analysis of the role that Black men and women and white women play in the welfare state as workers, unpaid and paid, as consumers and as people involved in struggles over welfare. Gough's model of the welfare state suggests that the welfare state, in fulfilling the function of social reproduction, serves also to maintain conditions favourable to capital accumulation as well as the maintenance of social harmony. However, none of this process is straightforward or cut and dried. Since it is difficult clearly to separate these functions (for example, the containment and control of disaffected groups – legitimation/repression – may be partially carried out by the education system which also fulfils the function of social reproduction), this chapter highlights particular and significant elements of these areas in relation to 'race' and gender. We examine these in three sections: first, the role that Black workers and Black and white women have played in maintaining lower social expenditure; secondly, social reproduction in terms of the reproduction of sexual and racial divisions of labour and in terms of the maintenance (and non-maintenance) of the non-working population; thirdly, forms of social control in relation to 'race' and gender – Black pathology, containment and incorporation, internal controls and maintenance of female dependency and subordination. Finally we look at the issues raised by the struggles of women and Black people against oppression and their implications for welfare strategy. As will be clear from the following accounts, the dimensions of 'race', class and gender can each have a specific as well as a combined effect on the provision and experience of welfare.

18.2 The role of Black men and women workers and white women workers in maintaining lower social expenditure

The post-war expansion of the welfare state drew its workforce, skilled and unskilled, from the 'reserve army of cheap labour' – Black and white women and Black men. As well as constituting the low-paid workers in the welfare services, women, Black and white, have been the unpaid welfare workers in the home and the unpaid voluntary workers in the community. In addition to this, the British state has shown at best an ambivalence about bearing the social costs of Black immigrant workers. These five factors in different ways and at different times over the post-war period have played an important role in keeping down the 'relatively rising costs' of welfare provision. By attempting to keep down the costs of welfare, the state hopes to stave off possible conflict between capital and labour whom it would otherwise have to approach to foot the bill.

Welfare services are labour intensive and provide far less opportunity than manufacturing industry for the use of automation as a way of offsetting rising costs. Black and immigrant workers are one section who play an important role, particularly in the health service, of limiting these rising costs. The study of Doyal, Hunt and Mellor (1981) shows clearly how, since the 1950s, the NHS has been dependent on overseas workers, both as contract labour and settlers, from the Caribbean, India, Ireland and Malaysia, at all levels of skills, though they tend to be concentrated in the lower grades and many of them are women. One third of the doctors and 20 percent of student nurses working in Britain in 1981 were born overseas. In the London hospital in the Doyal study, 84 percent of domestics and 82 percent of catering workers were from abroad. Further, in spite of immigration controls, the NHS has continued to recruit skilled overseas workers and until recently, by a number of anomalies, unskilled labour. Since there are limits to the scope of rationalization of labour in such a heavily labour-intensive sector as the health service compared with private industry, the availability of cheap labour has been particularly crucial in keeping costs down. On the other hand, where rationalization and deskilling *have* taken place, this has been made possible by the use of overseas nurses, concentrated in SEN training and less prestigious areas like the psychiatric and geriatric services. A further point related to the question of social costs being borne by the immigrant's country of origin is that many of the doctors and nurses have had their training paid for by their own – far poorer – countries and the children of many of those women on contract labour are being cared for and educated in their own countries. In other words 'the need to reproduce labour power effectively while at the same time keeping down the costs of reproduction to capital as a whole . . . helps to explain the need for migrant labour both historically and today' (Doyal *et al.*, 1981: 68).

The issue of social costs of immigrant workers was an important debate in the late 1940s as the government looked for new sources of labour. The failure of the post-war government to acknowledge the social costs of the new immigrants, to make necessary adjustments in the provision of welfare, can be understood in terms of the priorities given to other issues in the debate about how to meet labour shortages. One of these issues was how to dispose of labour once it was no longer needed and the other was the effect upon the host population if the immigrants were to stay longer. The 1949 Royal Commission on Population emphasized that immigrants should be 'of good human stock and were not prevented by their religion or race from intermarrying with the host population and becoming merged in it' (quoted by Booth in Dummett, 1986: 117). In both these terms Europeans from Holland, Greece, Italy and Eire were not seen as posing great problems – they could enter the country on temporary work permits and thus return when no longer required, or if they stayed they would 'merge in'. Black immigrants, however, as Commonwealth subjects had rights of settlement and also were seen to be bearers of radically different – and inferior – cultures. In other words, they were seen even before their arrival as a 'problem'. However, at the same time, as Joshi and Carter (1984) point out, Commonwealth workers were cheaper than aliens because they were British citizens, and as such were deemed to have come 'individually and on their own initiative' and so there was no need to make welfare provision for them. There was thus *no intention* to provide for them, and when Black immigrants *did* use welfare services they were seen as scroungers. The juxtaposition of these two features is pinpointed by Jacobs when he says: 'black workers were acceptable as cleaners, porters, kitchen staff, even nurses and doctors, but never wholeheartedly, as patients. They could build council houses but were not expected to live in them' (Jacobs, 1985: 13).

As it was, immigrants came from Europe, particularly Eire, and the Commonwealth, pushed by economic necessity as well as pulled by Britain's demands for labour. Yet the notion of an immigrant 'problem' was applied much more to the presence of Black immigrants, especially after manifestations of white racism like the Notting Hill riots of 1958 (although this is not to deny that forms of racism were and are still experienced by the Irish, the Italians, the Greeks, Jewish refugees and existing Chinese and Polish communities). The response of post-war governments was to bring the rights of Black Commonwealth immigrants more in line with the lesser rights of aliens, but in a way that would not break up the Commonwealth.

The introduction of the first set of immigration controls, the 1962 Commonwealth Immigrants Act, which marked the beginnings of the selective admission of immigrants in terms of their skills, as well as the gradual erosion of their settlement rights, led to concern in academic and political circles about the *numbers* of immigrants and the costs to the country, and one of the main arguments *in defence* of the presence of immigrants was their cheap labour and their minimal social costs. The Conservative Home Secretary, R.A. Butler, in 1961, argued 'our hospitals . . . would be in difficulties were it not for the services of immigrant workers' and *The Times* wrote that 'Britain's essential services could not carry on without immigrant labour' (both quoted in Cohen, 1985: 90). The appeasement of white racism and the need for cheap labour in the welfare and public services were therefore not without their contradictions. Nor were they without their challenges. Needless to say, Black workers had no time for this patronizing attitude: in the health service strikes against the pay freeze in 1972 and later against low wages and cutbacks in 1982–3, Black women ancillary workers were a major force (see Bryan *et al.*, 1985: 45–50).

A further dimension in this issue is the role that women's work in general plays in the welfare state. The state is the largest employer of women workers and most of these women work in the welfare services of health, education and the social services. Women constitute 75 percent of the manual labour force in local authority employment (Coyle, 1985). At the professional level this has a long history, a history of class and gender divisions. At the beginning of this century this work was an important route for economic independence for middle-class unmarried women. At the same time, gender inequalities, male domination and the sexual division of labour were often reproduced in this work. Women could be nurses but not doctors; teachers, but not wives and mothers as well (the marriage bar was not removed until 1950; David, 1980). However, these women found themselves, as teachers, health visitors or social workers, directing their working-class sisters into marriage and motherhood, and once there, supervising them. The post-war expansion of the welfare state reveals this first process more markedly. Whilst women have provided the socialized forms of care they have done so consistently in the lower-paid grades of the welfare state. What highlights the particularly exploitive nature of women's work is not simply that in many cases employers use the cleaning, cooking and caring skills that women have developed in their homes and label it as low paid *unskilled* work, but also that so much of this work is *part-time* and therefore low paid (Beechey and Perkins, 1987). This is particularly true of cleaning and catering, home helping, clerical and secretarial work, but it is also the case that professionally qualified staff – teachers and nurses especially –

are employed as part-timers, which has no comparison in the manufacturing sector. Part of the reason for this lies in management's need for flexibility – for example, where residential care has to be maintained day and night, or where peak times have to be covered – like crossing patrol wardens outside schools. However, to a large extent it is because much of this work is seen as *women's* work engaging *women's* skills and, in the absence of social provisions for women workers, it has been constructed as part-time therefore low paid to fit in with domestic commitments. Men's work in equivalent areas, such as the work of ambulance men and hospital porters, also requires full-time cover but is organized as full-time shift work. In the 1980s the trend has been to make more women's work in the welfare services part-time or temporary; for example, school catering workers now receive no money during school holidays. Furthermore the part-time nature of much of this work has meant that its privatization has been that much easier to manage – for example, the contracting out of hospital cleaning (Coyle, 1985). In other words, women's vulnerable position in relation to the labour market, combined with the skills they offer by virtue of the sexual division of labour in the home, has provided the welfare state with the opportunity to limit its costs. Again it would be wrong to assume that women have been passive victims in this process. The major growth in post-war trade unionism has been in the public sector – NUPE, for example, where women are about 70 percent of the membership (but only 10 percent of the full-time officials), and significant struggles have been waged over many of these issues (see *Feminist Review*, 1986). However, at the same time some of these issues are marked by their failure to attract support from the bulk of the male trade union movement (see Coyle, 1985).

In addition to this, women provide much of society's welfare as unpaid workers in the home, caring for the young, the sick, the elderly, as well as their entirely able-bodied husbands. This is reinforced by social security legislation and the ideology of the social work, education and health services. The fact that present trends by the Conservative government are to reduce the costs of welfare by transferring institutionalized care back into the 'community' testifies to the savings women continuously provide. 'Community care', as has relentlessly been explained by social policy writers, means care by the family, and that means women (Finch and Groves, 1980; Walker, 1982). In addition, when reports and reviews of 'community care' identify the formal or voluntary networks in the community (for example, Barclay, 1982) these too refer to the unpaid work of women. Women's voluntary work has a long history dating back to the Victorian philanthropy exercised by middle-class women. Changes over the last hundred years, however, suggest that women's ability to take on more unpaid labour is severely limited. Many more women combine paid work with their domestic commitments. Women comprised 41 percent of the workforce in 1982, and in 1979 52 percent of women with dependent children did paid work (Study Commission on the Family, 1983). The importance of a woman's wage to the family can be understood by the fact that the number of families living near the poverty line would increase three to four times if her wage were withdrawn (Study Commission on the Family, 1980).

Nevertheless, families, usually women, do still provide the main care for the elderly and infirm (see Ungerson, 1987). Cutbacks in welfare and the disproportionate burden these place on the poor, on women and on Black people, represent the other side of the coin of the exploitation some members of these groups suffer as workers within the welfare state.

18.3 Social reproduction

In general, the concept of social reproduction when used of the welfare state refers to its role in ensuring that labour power is produced, cared for, skilled and disciplined appropriate to the needs of capitalism. What we are concerned with here is what that means for women and Black people, as well as the extent to which this process also involves the reproduction of the social relations of patriarchal and racial domination. We look first at the involvement of the welfare state in reproducing racial and sexual divisions, and secondly at the maintenance of the non-working population.

Sexual and racial divisions of labour in welfare provision

It is clear that women play a central role in producing, caring for and nurturing members of their family or household. They also play a crucial role in mediating between their family and the services provided. It is they who take their children to the doctor, who are expected by schools to help teach their children to read, and it is *women* who often provide the services themselves. The state then plays a major role in assuming a sexual division of labour in which women do these activities, and in defining and supervising the way they are carried out. The education system provides a good example of all these different operations. In the past, education policymakers made clear divisions between the curriculum for boys and that for girls according to their assumed destinies. Some of this is now contested within and outside education, but a labour market structured on class, 'race' and gender lines still persists and influences the destinies of young women. Girls still tend to 'choose' arts and social science subjects, teachers allow boys to dominate in the classroom and playground, women or Black people are not represented in the teaching presentation of history, for example, and girls emerge with fewer qualifications, a situation compounded by 'race' and class. Girls not only learn that there are limited opportunities for them in paid employment, and that they will have domestic duties but that they should be subordinate to men (Stanworth, 1981). Some of these lessons are apparent to them in the organization of school life where women work as teachers mainly on the lower grades and in certain subjects, or with pastoral roles, or as cooks and cleaners and caretakers' wives, often as part-timers, whereas men run schools, are full-time science and maths teachers or caretakers. Furthermore, it is mothers, as parents, who are deemed to bear the responsibility for their child's achievement or otherwise at school, for, it is presumed by schools that mothers are the ones who prepare their children for school by helping them to read and write, by dressing them and generally negotiating the passage of their child's education career. All these different operations are also shot through with class differences, so that it is working-class girls whose destinies are most limited and their mothers who receive most blame.

Of course these differences are shot through with 'race' too. The idea of the Black child and her/his family or culture as an educational 'problem' is a theme that runs through much educational thinking and official policy even though it has moved from assimilation, integration, dispersal and multiculturalism. Brah comments that the 'deficit model' of the aspirations, abilities and cultures of Asian and Afro-Caribbean children persists in educational thinking in spite of official policy having traversed the assimilation, integration and multicultural models (Brah and Deem, 1986). Young Blacks who dream of a better future are deemed to have 'unrealistic aspirations', and Asian girls are denied career opportunities because of assumptions about Asian culture and the 'passive' role of women therein. None of this is helped by the fact that only 2 percent of teachers are Black, and that a study by the Commission for Racial Equality in 1986 found that the main reason for Black teachers leaving the profession was the racism of their pupils and colleagues.

The MSC's youth training programmes, juggling between the conflicting ideologies of equal access, 'special needs' and social control and containment, also reinforce existing racial (and gender) inequalities and structures as young Black people are filtered into the lower-status Mode B schemes (Solomos, 1985; De Sousa, 1987).

Rex has also pointed out how the 1977 White Paper on Inner City Policy made racist assumptions about the occupational destinations of those living in the inner cities. It argued in effect that as the inner cities were revived and new industries developed, the present resident (mainly Black) would be unsuitable because of their lack of skills. The assumption is that Black people and their children can only work at unskilled levels (Rex, 1984).

The welfare services themselves also reproduce racial divisions, with Black women in particular occupying the lowest-grade positions. Hazel Carby (1982) makes the observation here that the employment of Black women as carers and cleaners in the health service is not so much an extension of their caring role but of their *servant* role in imperialist social relations.

A final example of racial divisions in welfare is council housing (see Jacobs, 1985). Jacobs describes the post-war relationship between council housing and 'race' as 'the British road to apartheid'. Qualifications of residency, the blaming of Black people for inner-city problems, racist allocation procedures, fears of a white backlash, dispersal (the spreading of Black tenants in white areas to avoid ghettoization), punishment and deterrence of Black homeless families have all contributed to a segregated system which furthers racial divisions:

> By locking the black working class in council ghettos, the state aims to perpetuate, through the generations, the immigrant status of the black community. The purpose is to ensure, without need of further immigration, that black Britain continually replenishes capital's reserve army of labour. Largely unopposed by the Labour movement it has been effortlessly achieved under the cloak of a caring welfare state in the name of socialist housing. [Jacobs, 1985: 25]

At a local level the policies for equal opportunities in local authorities and anti-sexist and anti-racist strategies in schools, colleges and social services represent an important initiative in attempting to raise these issues to be fought.

Maintenance of the non-working white population, but limitation and control of the Black

Part of the welfare state's role in social reproduction as identified by Gough (1979) is the maintenance of the non-working population – the elderly, the young, the unemployed. Once again the shifting relationship between the state, the family and women is crucial here in defining *the need* and *the source* of maintenance, and in particular in defining women as dependants of their husbands. Women cohabiting with their husband or male partner are deemed to be dependent upon him in social security legislation. Moves to equality in this area have merely given the woman the right to claim and make him her dependant. Similarly, a long-term unemployed spouse is deemed his/her partner's dependant. Basically the system works on the basis of a single family wage rather than the reality where both partners work but where, because of domestic commitments and low wages, the woman's wage is usually less, though still of vital importance in maintaining the family above the poverty line. The married man's tax allowance, an additional allowance granted to working men in recognition of their wife's dependent housekeeping status, further reinforces the notion of the dependent housekeeping wife, and also discriminates against women earners. It is quite difficult for a woman unless she is above 21, never married and childless, to be regarded as an independent person in social security provisions. For example, if a woman with children makes claims for social security, efforts will be made to establish her 'liable relative' – the man responsible for maintaining her and her children (see Land, 1983). (Women are not the only people affected in this way. With the growth of youth unemployment, recent trends in social security eligibility have shifted the financial and housing responsibility for young people away from the state and back to the family.) The issue of divorce also raises starkly the question of women's limited opportunity for economic independence through the wage system and the reluctance of either husband or the state to accept responsibility. Where and when the state does accept financial responsibility for maintaining a woman (and her children), then she will be thrown on to the poverty line of social security subsistence level. For some women this poverty is often preferable to an oppressive marriage in which she has little control over her access to money: what Hilary Graham calls 'the two dimensions of lone motherhood: their absolute poverty and their relative power' (Graham, 1987). For other women, like older women living alone whose major source of income is social security benefits, the poverty they endure in old age is merely a cruel intensification of their financial dependence and/or low pay during their lives (Peace, 1986). Though changes in pensions were made in 1978 which improve women's access to occupational schemes and acknowledge their 'non-working' years at home, ultimately women's access to a decent living in old age 'reflects the changes of the labour-market and the marriage-market' (Groves, 1983: 60). The final main point to be made here is that when women are not in receipt of a living wage then maintenance by a man is a risky and uncertain business and maintenance by the state almost inevitably means poverty. Women are a major group in poverty by virtue of either low state subsistence or inequality and financial dependency in marriage.

When we turn to the question of the maintenance of the Black non-working population the 'race' dimension shifts the issue into different perspective. We have noted up to now the way the state reinforces women's mothering role but for Black women the emphasis has not been so much on the 'endowment' of motherhood and the maintenance of dependants, but on the *restriction* of motherhood and *limitation* and *control* of dependants. This is illustrated in two ways: immigration control and reproductive policies. Paul Gordon (1985) cites many examples of instances where normal rights afforded dependants through social security are denied to Black people, or where their having made claims renders them guilty of 'scrounging'. The Home Office ordered Nasreen Akhtar to be deported following the break-up of her marriage. Her having claimed supplementary benefit was cited as evidence of her intention to remain dependent on social security for as long as she could. The order was eventually overturned by the Immigration Appeal Tribunal (see Gordon, 1984). More generally, the concern about 'numbers' surrounding the 1962 and 1971 Commonwealth Immigration Acts, was about *'dependents'*, wives, children and grandparents, and the shift that the immigration laws mark from citizen to migrant worker is precisely about the denial of benefits to those dependants and therefore about their limitation. Refusal of admission to many immigrants is on the basis of dependants having to prove they have no recourse to public funds and can be maintained by a relative or friend already resident. (This does not apply to Commonwealth citizens with right to abode, or to pre-1973 settlers.) Gordon also points out that although the 1977 Child Benefit Act was hailed as progressive for the way it transferred money for children from fathers to mothers, it also had the effect of withdrawing financial support for children living abroad but with a parent working here, as child tax allowances could be claimed in this instance but child benefits cannot. The 'Sole Responsibility' rule of the 1971 Act also makes it difficult for single parents to bring their children into the country unless they have themselves solely main-tained and *visited* them (Bryan *et al.*, 1985: 157). The non-maintenance of Black dependants is reinforced further by the assumption that Asian cultures, in particular, are self-supporting and have no need for public provision. This underlies the lack of provision for elderly Black people. Yet, in one study 26 percent of the Black elderly interviewed had no family in Britain (Bhalla and Blakemore, 1981).

This concern with 'numbers' has also centred around the fertility of Black families. A crop of studies in the 1960s was directed at future estimates of the numbers of Black children, given the rate of fertility of Black families. Such concerns are heavily influenced by eugenicist ideas, and racist ideas about Black sexuality. It is not surprising therefore that the rights of Black mothers to fertility are not always taken for granted as Black women's campaigns over the use of the long-lasting contraceptive injection Depo-Provera, abortion and sterilization have shown (Bryan *et al.*, 1985: 103–4). In general then, as mothers, Black women's experience is not the same as that of white mothers.

> Black women, as mothers, encounter other state agencies such as the DHSS, schools and so on in a very particular way: they may be asked to produce their passports before being considered eligible for benefit, or before their children are allowed to be enrolled in schools. [Bhavnani and Coulson, 1986: 84]

18.4 Social control
The modification of behaviour, attitudes and practices towards work and family is a well-acknowledged historical role of all aspects of the welfare state. It has particular resonance with the poor, the residuum, the undeserving (Piven and Cloward, 1972). But it intersects with 'race' and gender in a number of very particular ways. We look first at three ways in which social control is implemented and the racist justifications of that implementation: Black cultural pathology; Black people as a 'danger'; and internal controls – the use of welfare agencies to police immigration controls.

Black cultural pathology
The characterization of individuals, families or communities being to blame for their deprivation because of their way of life, their culture, has long been part of commonsense ideas in social work, education and health care. But deeply embedded notions of cultural and racial superiority, absorbed and reworked through different modes of racial domination, gave rise in the post-war period to specific and often contradictory ideas of the deficiencies of Afro-Caribbean and Asian families and cultures. They are particularly persistent in education, social work and health care. Hazel Carby points out that Black children are seen to fail at school either because their Asian mothers are too passive and withdrawn and stay in the home, or because their Afro-Caribbean mothers are too assertive and go out to work (Carby, 1982). Illnesses, such as rickets, are seen as resulting from unsuitable diets rather than the need for a policy for vitamin D to be put into chappati flour or ghee. The problems of adolescents are translated in terms of their parents' maladaptive child-care practices. The Black Health Workers and

Patients Group points out that 40 percent of all Black people in NHS beds are psychiatric patients, and that 'multiculturalism' has affected psychiatric diagnosis in such a way as to reinforce racism: ' "the hysteric" young Asian women in dread of arranged marriage . . . the vicious and violent Afro-Caribbean male youth, perhaps already implicated in the social psychosis of Rasta' (1983: 32). This last example points to another variation in social control: potential danger and the need for containment.

Danger, containment and incorporation
The presentation of the presence of Black people as a cultural threat, a danger to the 'British way of life' has been a recurrent political and popular obsession since the 1920s. When riots happen these are given as evidence of the failure of Black people to adjust to British democracy. The theme has a long history and has been played on anti-Irish and anti-Semitic variations. The theme also has a variety of key signatures: not just the threat to 'culture' and 'democracy' but also to 'morality' and to 'health'. These latter two were also part of the moral panic of Black immigration in the 1950s and early 1960s. A Birmingham newspaper in 1956 carried the story of two white girls aged 15 and 16 found at night in the house of 'coloured men' who were recommended to be put into care for being in 'moral danger' (Joshi and Carter, 1984). In Bradford in 1961 a smallpox scare in the Pakistani community gave scope to scaremongering about the health risks that Black immigrants carried (see Gordon, 1983). At the same time little was done to resolve the overcrowding that Black families suffered. Lambeth Council, for example, decided it could not enforce the Public Health Act because it would have been forced to place Black families in council housing (Jacobs, 1985: 20). During the 1960s the moral and cultural threat shifted to a 'material threat' that Black people posed in terms of jobs and housing. In the 1970s and 1980s the two themes became forcibly intertwined.

Hall *et al.* (1978), Gilroy (1982) and Solomos (1985), have all shown how policies on law and order, youth and unemployment have been constructed upon the image of Black youth in the 'urban ghetto' as a potential danger, in terms of increased crime and political instability. This has emerged particularly since the 1970s and the economic crisis and the identification of Black unemployed youth as part of the 'enemy within'. It is not only through law and order that containment policies are practised. In 1980 the ILEA provided £1.6 million for disruptive units in schools. Increasingly, evidence and suspicion mounted that disproportionate numbers of

Black children were being sent to them (as with the earlier incidence of ESN classes and schools), such that Black parents in Haringey demanded that the provision be stopped (Carby, 1982: 205). According to the Black Health Workers and Patients Group (1983), Section 136 of the 1959 Mental Health Act which empowers the police to remove to a place of safety someone thought to be dangerous to themselves or others, is three or four times more likely to be used on Black people than white. Further, Black people are more likely to be offered drug or ECT treatment than therapy (Mama, 1984). Bryan *et al.* (1985) also claim that attitudes of cultural pathology and lack of access to housing and child-care facilities lead to the likelihood of Black children being taken into care in the event of homelessness, or domestic violence. Indeed, as Jacobs (1985) points out, in the event of allocation, Black tenants are more likely to find themselves on more heavily controlled and policed estates. The 1981 riots crystallized the rationalization of such policies for the Right. But it should also be noted that the threat of political instability had also led to the voicing of a different approach – most notably by Lord Scarman. His line is away from the tough law and order approach to one of consensus through community consultation as well as the injection of money into deprived areas. This has been criticized as soft social control and incorporation by many:

> Increasingly the effect of state funds on our community has been to neutralize its militancy; political mobilization has come to be seen as a salaried activity . . . accountable not to the Black community but to the State which pays them. Their brief, however unwitting, is to keep the lid on the cauldron, and their existence is seen as proof of the government's 'concern' to soften the effects of its own institutionalized racism. [Bryan *et al.*, 1985: 179]

Others argue that such policies at least expose the contradictions, and create openings and opportunities for anti-racist struggle and debate (Hall, 1982). More recently a new twist in the idea of Black people as a 'threat' has emerged. This is the New Right emphasis on the danger to British cultural values.

Internal controls
A third form of control adopted by the welfare state is that of policing the immigration control laws, which has already been described as having an important historical dimension. Gordon (1985) has documented the way medical techniques have been used as an administrative form of immigration control. Until a public outcry in 1979 doctors were used by immigration authorities to

make 'virginity checks' on women from the Asian subcontinent entering Britain to marry their fiancés. In addition, until 1982 children entering Britain were turned away if they were not the age claimed, and the age was determined by the potentially harmful use of X-rays. Mental ill-health can also be grounds for refusal of entry, and the Home Secretary has the power to repatriate an alien receiving treatment for mental illness. In addition to these uses of medical techniques, medical care has been used as a method of immigration control. In 1979 a DHSS circular, 'Gatecrashers', asked area health authorities in London to ensure that people 'not ordinarily resident' in Britain did not get free NHS treatment. In Leicester in 1976 nearly 200 women attending an antenatal clinic were asked to show their passports. In 1982 the government introduced 'charging' for overseas visitors. The effect of this is to encourage the questioning of right to free access of anyone who 'appears' to be foreign (Gordon, 1983).

The other aspect is the increased liaison between the welfare services and the administration of immigration control. Housing departments have liaised with the Home Office over the eligibility of people applying to be housed. Checking a passport is not uncommon nor is the evasion of responsibility to house homeless persons. An investigation by the Commission of Racial Equality, for example, found that the London Boroughs of Barnet and Kensington and Chelsea were refusing to house permanently work permit holders even though these workers were within their rights to be housed (Gordon, 1985: 88). In social security and further education too administrators have been required to act on behalf of the immigration authorities by checking immigration status or by refusing access to services on the assumption that the client was not eligible. Such liaison has been made easier with the introduction of computerized information systems. However, the combined effects of these control processes is, first, to flout principles of confidentiality, secondly, to deny provision to bona fide immigrants like fiancées, work permit holders, students and others awaiting permission to stay on, or even subject them to deportation if they do 'have recourse to public funds', thirdly, to deter *all* Black people from claiming their rightful benefits, and legitimize and institutionalize racist practices in the provision of welfare, as well as, finally, criminalizing an area of activity – misuse of welfare provision by immigrants – the extent of which is neither particularly significant nor proved. What is most disturbing is the rootedness of these controls in the welfare state; as Cohen comments, 'welfarism is intimately linked to immigration control and cannot be understood other than as a construct of the basest nationalism' (1985: 92).

Social control, women and welfare
It is clear that the welfare state operates in ways that maintain the financial dependence of women in the home, their subordination to male authority in the home and at work, and to define, limit and constrain women's sexuality, their mothering, their reproductive powers and their access to an independent income. At the same time two qualifications have to be made. The first is that this process operates differently according to class and 'race', and the second is that this process is neither monotonous nor monolithic but both contradictory and contested. There are times when the welfare state has, for example, sought to make provisions for women with children to enter paid work, during the war for example, although this provision was ill co-ordinated (see Riley, 1983). If we take health care as an example, we can see evidence of many of these different points: 'Health policy reflects and helps to maintain gender divisions that characterise society as a whole. In this sense medicine is a form of social control: a way of putting women in their place – wherever that place ought to be' (Oakley, 1983).

Women constitute 75 percent of the health service workforce yet very few of them occupy positions of power and status. Approximately 10 percent of hospital medical staff are women, and 10 percent of consultants are women (DHSS, quoted in Oakley, 1983: 120). Women also use the health service more often than men. This is, amongst other things, because of their caring role and the fact they have children. Yet doctors' prescriptions for and treatments of women are significantly different from those for men. According to one survey, doctors classified their most troublesome patients as 'female', 'inadequate', not employed and working class with vague symptoms of psychiatric illness that were difficult to diagnose and treat (study by Stimpson, quoted in Oakley, 1983: 105). Doctors are also more likely to diagnose women's health problems as neurotic or psychiatric requiring drug therapy or psychiatric treatment. Often the acknowledged aim of such treatment is to help the patient adapt to her housewifely, motherly duties. As an extreme example, Diane Hudson (1987) shows that a leucotomy (surgical removal of part of the brain) is twice as likely to be performed on a woman than a man presenting with depressive illness. Health policy and practice also identifies mothers as protectors of their family's health: exercising responsibility, self-sacrifice and good example. Such an analysis detracts from the social causes of ill-health as well as from the differential access women have to doctors and hospitals where transport, time and geographical area play an important part. In terms of women's own health, class differentials have widened over the years. Women who are married to semi-skilled and unskilled workers are 70 percent more likely than women married to professionals and managers to die prematurely (1986 Office of Population Census and Statistics, quoted in Doyal, 1987). Women from the lowest social class group are also three times more likely than those in the highest group to suffer chronic illness (Doyal, 1987: 176).

The particular area where doctors increasingly exercise control over women's lives is in reproductive technology. Access to most forms of contraception, sterilization, abortion and infertility services is via the medical profession. Thus doctors' perceptions of acceptable female behaviour are extremely important in determining women's ability to have their needs met. Women wanting abortions may have to suffer the indignity of being considered inadequate or promiscuous, or both. At the same time doctors may make their own decisions about patients who require sterilizations or more secure but dangerous forms of contraception which are based on pathological and racist views of Black and working-class families (Rakusen, 1981). The development of services for infertility further exemplifies these points. The provision of infertility services is patchy and, in common with other forms of provision, services are better in the more affluent parts of the country. However, 40 percent of district health authorities have no special provision. This means that time and money are necessary if patients wish to have consultations out of their area. On top of that, treatment is rarely entirely free; for example, for artificial insemination patients have to pay a £10–15 insemination fee (Doyal, 1987: 179). Most *in vitro* fertilization is carried out privately with total costs ranging from £2000 to £2500 with no guarantee of success (Doyal, 1987: 81). The availability therefore of such services to poorer women is limited. There is also sufficient evidence to suggest that some of the causes of infertility are, in common with much ill-health, more common amongst the poorer sections of society.

What further characterizes the operation of infertility services is the ideology of appropriate motherhood. As Lesley Doyal points out, a major contradiction exists between the idea that *all* women's ultimate ambition is to become a mother, and the practice of accepting only *some* women as suitable for infertility treatment: 'the allegedly biological maternal instinct is assumed to affect only those heterosexual women who are married or enjoying a "stable and happy relationship with a man" ' (1987: 182). Indeed the 1985 Warnock Report on human fertilization and embryology stated: 'We believe that as a general rule, it is better for children to be born into a two-parent family, with both father and mother, although we recognise that it is impossible to predict with any certainty how lasting such a relationship will be' (pp. 11–12, quoted in Stanworth, 1987: 24). This attitude discriminates against lesbian and single heterosexual women, but a case in October 1987 of a woman turned down for *in vitro* fertilization (IVF) treatment on the grounds that she had once been a prostitute, even though she now fulfilled the criteria of heterosexual coupledom, shows that the administration of such a service can be both discriminatory and punishing.

The lessons women have learned from this apply to other areas of welfare: women need to be able to have the technology and the freedom to have children as well as the technology and the freedom not to have children. To be able to have these, women, as practitioners and clients, should play a major part in the decision-making of such services, with a recognition of the differential nature of women's experiences, whether fertile or infertile, Black or white, middle class or working class, heterosexual or lesbian, old or young. Those services themselves should be set in the context of a health service which provides a preventive approach to the social and environmental as well as physical causes of ill-health. Such a challenge does exist and the implications of this and other struggles are detailed in the next section.

18.5 The implications for welfare analysis and strategy of struggles against Black oppression and women's oppression

> For [women] going into politics is a gesture of defiance, however timid, against their domestication, although they usually bring with them their experience of domestic responsibility. This is true whether we are talking of the Labour Party women's sections, the contemporary women's liberation movement or campaigns on issues which have been traditionally politicised by women – health housing and children. [Campbell, 1984: 191–2]

> In the light of our experiences of racism in the field of health it is little wonder that Black women regard the State's surveillance of our lives through the combined Health and Social Services with growing distrust. Increasingly alienated from potentially beneficial provisions, we have been among the first to question the overall power of the Welfare State to record, control and intervene in our lives. [Bryan *et al.*, 1985: 110]

The struggles by Black women and white women and the struggles by Black men and women, singly and together, are of extreme importance to welfare strategy. First they point to the importance of struggles in the *community*, often left out of account in mainstream and political economy writings, where the issues are precisely those about welfare provisions – housing, health, children, older people, poverty. Secondly, because of this they represent a major challenge to the narrow reformist, economist and nationalist concerns of the labour movement, organized in the workplace. Thirdly, these struggles highlight in its most stark way a major contradiction, a need for the provisions of welfare – decent housing, health and child-care facilities – violated by the reality of welfare services that have controlled and divided and rendered its users subordinate and dependent. Out of this contradiction has come a critique of bureaucracy, of professionalism, of hierarchy and most importantly the demand for *control* of welfare provision. The objectives of women's struggles have been to link the demands about home life to the demands about worklife, indeed the very process of such struggles requires continual negotiation between the demands of private family life and the need to enter public political life. At the same time, the roots of much Black political consciousness lie in struggles against slavery and colonialism and international forms of exploitation, and potentially challenge the nationalist confines of welfare capitalism. These issues are now examined in greater detail.

Women's struggles for family allowances, for the right to determine their fertility, for legal and financial independence, for financial recognition of their caring skills, for the right to define their own sexuality, for freedom from violent and oppressive relationships, all challenge the form, the nature and the objectives of welfare policy. They do this, first, by challenging the taken-for-granted areas of family life – the financial, emotional and physical relationships in the family. In particular they are able to challenge the notion of *dependency* and of *caring* by unlocking them from their assumed biological master – the fact that women bear children. Women's biology, as developments in reproductive technologies show, is a constantly changing phenomenon, yet it is not this which determines women's oppression, but rather the social conditions and social relations under which that biology exists. In more general terms, women demand that that area known as reproduction become central to political demands for change, that questions of who cares, how and when, are central to any economic reorganization of society; secondly, they demand that the bureaucratic and professionally controlled relations of welfare have to be replaced by non-hierarchal, non-sexist and non-racist egalitarian relationships. Finally, women's struggles have also highlighted the need to link the often conflicting needs for women in the here and now (an adequate benefit for carers, for example) with the long-term needs for women (to break free of the assumption that women are the carers, for example).

Campaigns directed at social security legislation or the low rates of child benefit highlight the dependent status of women in the family and the insecurity and inequality of this. By challenging this assumption of dependency it can be argued that women have paved the way to question other conditions of dependency which are often taken as fixed. That is to say, women have questioned their own dependency and in so doing have challenged, not simply the assumption of financial dependency, but of physical and psychic dependency which are assumed to give rise to financial dependency, Old age, disability, mental handicap and not least childhood are all forms of dependency which have been challenged recently, All have pointed to an important issue for future welfare strategy: the need to disentangle dependency that is socially constructed by being denied access to an independent income through work and/or benefit, from emotional and physical needs. At present, state provision often serves not to remove dependency but simply to restructure and reinforce the boundaries of dependency, Present changes in employment benefit for young people lengthen the time for which they are financially dependent on their parents; compulsory retirement policies structure old age; the present push for 'community care' will, without the massive necessary funding for community-based provision, increase the dependency of the elderly, disabled people, the mentally ill and mentally handicapped upon female relatives who are expected to care for them, and further render these women more dependent upon the wage of a male partner. This issue of dependency is doubly significant for women, for it is in caring for the elderly or frail or sick or young that they themselves are rendered financially dependent. It is this perspective of a shared problem between the dependency of women and those for whom they care which is important to emphasize, otherwise, there is a danger of a polarization taking place between the needs of 'carers' and the 'cared for' (see Croft, 1986).

The issue of 'caring' – who does it and why – is central to welfare strategy and women's lives. The emphasis of its being unpaid and exploitive work carried out within the isolation of the home has been countered by some feminists keen to assert women's pride in their skills. This view celebrates women's special nature which emerges from their caring role as bearers of a nurturing and supportive, collective culture. The difficulty with this is that it can serve to lock women back into their 'special nature', away from the public world of production and power. It is possible to understand women's caring role in materialist terms, that is, as the way patriarchal capitalism reproduces its labour power and maintains its non-working population, and at the same time recognize the importance of this caring experience for women's sense of the need to change the world. Ann Ferguson and Nancy Folbre explain it like this:

> The social relations of our nurturance work account on the one hand for our oppression (sacrificing our own interests for those of men and children), and on the other hand for our potential strength as bearers of a radical culture: we support an ethic of sharing, co-operation and collective involvement that stands in clear opposition to an ethic based on individualism, competition and private profit. [1981: 329]

In this way, it is possible to acknowledge caring as part of 'women-centred values' without returning to a biological essentialism, and further, to see within these values important aspects which form the basis of an alternative model to the present bureaucratic, professionalized, authoritarian relations of welfare today.

What is interesting about many women's struggles is that the process of struggling has been as significant as the aims of those struggles. Fighting for rights at the political level in trade unions, or political parties, involves fighting for them at the personal level too. ' "The first hurdle you have to get over is your husband", said a Midlands hospital worker in her forties with a family and a husband, who, like all of these women, had to negotiate her right to become a shop steward during the hospital workers' dispute' (Campbell, 1984: 193–4). This necessity to combine personal struggle with political struggle has given rise to two significant general features. The first is the attempt to organize in ways which are themselves anti-sexist, anti-hierarchal, anti-racist and anti-bureaucratic. The Women's Health Movement, for example, has struggled for forms of health care where women are not treated as passive, and where their domestic role, maternal intentions, marital status, their 'race' and sexual orientation, are neither abused nor assumed. This has also entailed the attempt to demystify and share with others medical knowledge, or the setting up of self-help groups, as well as challenging hierarchical forms of organization between the workers in welfare services, and most particularly in the relationship between the users and providers of the service. Another example is the establishment of women's refuges for women subjected to domestic violence. Many of these refuges, though certainly not all, have aspired to organize themselves in a collective and non-hierarchical way where decision-making is shared between residents, paid staff and volunteers, where residents themselves play a major part in counselling and supporting other women who have been victims of male violence in the home. The attempt in both these cases is to struggle against unjust features of this society in ways which prefigure a new and better society (Rose, 1985). This attempt at 'prefigurative politics' is not just a feature of feminist women's organizations but reflects an aspect of many working-class community groups run by women, like tenants' associations or action groups, who would not necessarily call themselves feminists: an attempt to inject politics with the essence of shared and collective living rather than with formality, bureaucracy and hierarchy.

The second general important point which emerges from the nature of women's struggles is that, in so far as these struggles are often situated in the community rather than the workplace and are battling over questions of reproduction and not just production, they begin to break down the distinction set by state and the labour movement alike. This is the distinction between work and home, where work is what men do, where they get paid and where they struggle against capitalism, and where home is where women's unpaid caring work is rewarded by men's pay, and improved by virtue of men's struggles. The idea that reproduction and production are seen as interdependent forms of equal importance and not separate forms in which the organization of reproduction follows in the wake of production has important implications for welfare analysis and welfare strategy. It means that the future of employment cannot be considered separately from the future of welfare. But more than that it means that the central questions of both are: who is dependent on whom and who cares for whom? Any integrated social and economic policy has to provide an answer to these questions in ways that recognize the diversity of needs and of household forms and in ways that do not oppress, exploit or assume the rights of others to do so.

Many struggles in the Black communities over, for example, high suspension rates amongst Black children in schools, over SUS – the disproportionate numbers of Black youths arrested for being a suspected person – over the need for the NHS to recognize sickle-cell anaemia, over trans-racial child care, over homelessness, and over deportation, have often involved mainly, though not exclusively Black *women*. Such campaigns point to an experience where the welfare state, in setting women up, puts them down as well. They point to the differences in the ways in which the state oppresses different women. Where that process has involved racism it has been particularly controlling, subordinating, blaming and punishing. These struggles range from workplace to community, they address questions of culture, and of human need. Where women's struggles have demanded a reassessment of the relationship between production and reproduction, Black struggles raise a further dimension: the relationship between welfare policies, the state and the *international division of labour*. It is this internationalism – of connecting to the oppression and exploitation in the Third

World, to the global division between North and South – which perhaps raises the greatest challenge to socialism in general, to welfare strategy in particular.

How are these issues of community struggle, human need, culture, the state and internationalism raised by Black and anti-racist welfare struggles?

Struggles at Grunwick, Imperial Typewriters and Chix linked workplace to community, for it was from the Black communities that financial and organizational support was forthcoming when the trade unions and welfare agencies failed. The organizations of Black parents against suspensions, harassment and even, in the case of Manchester Burnage High School, murder, are important welfare struggles which, while they focus on *specific* racial aspects, also challenge central issues concerning form and control in state provision. A different example of the link between community and workplace is provided by Paul Gilroy's suggestion that there was a 'continuity of protest which links the 1981 riots with the Health Service strike that followed them' (1987a: 37). Gilroy also suggests that in the political activity of Black Britain class antagonisms are felt as community antagonisms. It is in and through the community that struggles over state services, over cultural identity and for political autonomy or self-management take place.

> Each of these features can be found in the recent history of Britain's black communities: struggle over the services provided by the state, particularly the quality of educational opportunities for black children have been intense . . . and the demands of community organisations have repeatedly focused on the need to gain a degree of control over the processes which shape day to day experience. Local campaigns for police accountability, prompted by concern about the organisation and role of the force in inner-city areas, perfectly illustrate the . . . last category.
> [Gilroy 1987a: 230]

In some cases experience of racism in the statutory services has led to the setting up of self-managed supplementary provision outside the state, like Saturday schools. These have operated in some Black communities as a reaction to schools' classifying Black children as 'educationally subnormal' but also to teach about Black history and cultures. In challenging not simply the question of access to welfare, but the entire basis of welfare and the form of its provision, such struggles are about the politics of need – challenging the state's, the administrators' and agencies' definition of need: if your access to health care is determined by the need for a doctor or nurse who speaks your own language, then this becomes not a 'special' but a basic need. At the same time this issue of the assertion of cultural identity is a difficult one to negotiate, particularly in view of the emergence of a right-wing redefinition of cultural difference which masks a racial superiority. What is necessary is to understand culture in materialist terms, that is to say, as the means by which oppressed groups struggle to retain solidarity against the material and ideological forces which oppress them. For example, Avtah Brah's of the need for anti-racist schooling presents a nine-point strategy that involves reclaiming *culture* as 'an oppositional force which stands in a complex relationship with the material conditions of society' (Brah and Deem, 1986: 76). This extends far beyond multiculturalism and is important, for just as within the women's movement claims to 'women's special nature' run the risk of biological essentialism, so too do claims to cultural identity have to be able to counter the sort of cultural essentialist thinking which acknowledges the importance of culture but also claims a hierarchy of cultures and justifies racial domination. The materialist view of culture is exemplified nicely by Paul Gilroy in the following way: 'In our multicultural schools the sound of steel pan may evoke Caribbean ethnicity, tradition and authenticity yet they originate in the oil drums of the Standard Oil Company rather than the mysterious knowledge of ancient African griots' (1987b: 12).

After the riots of 1981 several local authorities began to introduce equal opportunities policies not only for Black people but for women and, in some areas, for the disabled and homosexuals and lesbians. Such policies include positive action in employment and training (for example, provision of training schemes for Black or women workers in areas where they are under-represented); monitoring of, for example, housing allocations, or employment; reviewing appointment procedures; creating anti-racist and anti-sexist strategies in teaching or social work practice; and creating forms of consultation with women's groups or Black groups in the community. In many ways these policies have been an important source of legitimation of Black people's and women's struggles. They have created a framework and sets of tangible objectives around which women and Black people can organize, and they have created the opportunity for an acknowledgement and unveiling of different processes of racism and sexism operating within institutional settings, rather than simply by individuals. In some cases, particularly within the GLC, these policies have created the opportunity to influence the local state into less bureaucratic and formalized procedures, to 'prefigure' good practice, to get local authorities and trade unions to centralize 'social' issues, and provide blueprints for other organizations to follow. The fact that the Conservative government dissolved the GLC and the metropolitan counties in

1986 and has since begun to put into action its own inner-city initiative shows in a negative way some of the success such local authorities had in effecting, with community support and involvement, equal opportunities policies. At the same time, there are some aspects which inhibit the full effectiveness of such policies: first, they operate within the constraints of national economic policy – high unemployment and a restructuring of employment which render Black people and women badly off. Secondly, such policies have been seen as an attempt by the local state to incorporate the leadership of the Black communities and to create a layer of 'femocrats' to disarm grassroots activities by women and Blacks. Thirdly, in relation to Black professionals, social services management, for example, may consider Black social workers more effective at social control of the Black population than white social workers and use equal opportunities policies to achieve such effectiveness. Fourthly, the operation of employer-led anti-racist training is sometimes counterproductive amongst white employees, who see it as management telling them what to do. In fact, the successful implementation of anti-racist and anti-sexist strategies requires the involvement of white and Black people, female and male, and in schools, for example, parents and children, in the articulation and operation of policies. What these observations point to is the need for a significant transfer of power and decision-making to women and Black people in the community, and accountability to them, as well as the need for organizations of the white working class to pursue equal opportunities policies and anti-racist and anti-sexist strategies. As far as trade unions are concerned, some local authority trade unions do operate their own equal opportunities policies on behalf of their members at work as well as within their organizations. Clearly the second strategy, particularly in creating policies to get women and Black people into positions of responsibility at all levels of union activity, is vital to ensure the effectiveness of equal opportunities by employers. A final aspect of these strategies is the danger of limiting the problems faced by women and Black people to national if not local policies, especially given the fact that many of Black women's and men's struggles have been informed by an internationalist consciousness.

We look finally at the challenge these struggles present to imperialist and nationalist ideology and practice. Many of those who came from Asia and Africa in the inter-war and early post-war years and became involved in trade unions or in community campaigns had long experience of anti-colonial struggle. For example, Udham Singh was a skilled electrician, an active trade unionist and delegate on his local trades council, and founder in 1938 of the first Indian Workers' Association. In 1940 he was hanged for shooting Sir Michael O'Dwyer, who had been Lieutenant-Governor of the Punjab and in 1919 had been in charge of the forces responsible for massacring unarmed peasants and workers at Amritsar (Sivanandan, 1982: 3). This internationalist consciousness has been explained by Gilroy in the following way:

> The need to develop international dialogues and means of organisation which can connect loyalty and immediacy across the international division of labour is perhaps more readily apparent to black populations who have recent experience of migration as well as acute memories of slavery and international indenture. [1987a: 68]

The appeals to national strength, national unity and national identity have long underpinned the argument for welfare provision. The New Right's racism has colonized with particular strength the appeal to cultural nationalism, and used this to argue for a restructuring of welfare and an acceptance of inequalities. Demands which are able to counter the ideological and material effects of this nationalism are therefore very important. Struggles against immigration controls, for instance, are also struggles against the international exploitation of labour. In the late 1970s, for example, the exposure of the use of Depo-Provera, unwarranted termination and sterilization on Black women in this country made links to the use of Third World Black women as guinea-pigs in contraceptive drug trials. From Black feminists in this country has also emerged the important attempt to make links of solidarity between the female workers in the sweated industries of the West (many of them Black workers) with the female workers who work often in the same multinationals in the Third World. Swasti Mitter (1986) sees in this the possibility of a 'novel labour movement'. What further marks this novelty is that the demands of these women workers incorporate demands against imperialism and against racism as well as a restructuring of domestic work and paid work. Mitter concludes:

> the division between core male workers and peripheralized women workers in the international political economy is based precisely on the generally accepted role of women in the domestic sphere. Hence it would be futile to counteract the challenges of the global corporations until and unless there are extended social provisions for the care of the young and the elderly, and men are willing to share domestic work. [1986: 162]

It is clear from this that these internationalist perspectives have implications for welfare strategy. In addition to the priorities suggested by Mitter, the connections between access to welfare and immigration status must be cut. Welfare provision should be available to all who live in this country. Links between welfare agencies and immigration authorities should be removed. Indeed the aims, principles, systems of categorization and assessment of immigration controls should be questioned. In the immediate situation, policies which make immigrants prove they will have 'no recourse to public funds', or which create entitlement to welfare benefits according to immigrant status, or tests of residence in relation to receipt of benefits and services, or requirements to check passports before granting access to benefits or provision, should be challenged. Gordon (1985) proposes that the decriminalization of immigration – the removal of police as enforcement agents – would be an important step towards the ending of the passport checking by immigration officials that exists in the welfare services. Storey (1986) suggests there should be strict guidelines on confidentiality with disciplinary sanctions taken against welfare officials who abuse or pass on information or use it for anything other than the purpose for which it was given. Local education authorities, for example, could operate a policy whereby they had no obligation to educate a child who would be staying in the country less than six months, which would then require no further investigation. Health authorities could treat all, including visitors, without charge on a 'Good Samaritan' policy. All these challenges rest on changing immigration policy. The restoration of 'no immigration controls' is feasible only as an ultimate goal achieved in co-operation with other countries of the world. This clearly would save money and bureaucracy and would allow families to be united and refugees to enter countries freely. However, in the meantime a move to a just and non-discriminatory immigration policy for Britain is probably more feasible. As a move in this direction Ann Dummett (1986), on behalf of the Action Group on Immigration and Nationality, suggests that international standards and conventions could be brought to bear on British immigration and nationality laws – for example, the rights to have family life respected and the elimination of racial discrimination are both tenets of international law on immigration and nationality. A different issue but nevertheless one which indicates the connections between welfare and international policies, is the exploitation of Third World countries through the export of inappropriate forms of welfare aid, for example drugs and medical technology which are unable to deal with and often reinforce the problems of ill-health in these countries (Doyal, 1979). The representation of this issue closer to home is the exploitation by polytechnics and universities of 'overseas students', often from the Third World, who are taught and trained – whether in science or social policy – on courses whose content bears no relation to the needs of the countries from which they have come and to which they will return. Part of an anti-racist strategy within higher education might involve addressing sensitively the needs of such students. At a broader level an internationalist perspective also demands a critical view of exhortations by policy-makers and politicians, of the Left and Right, to welfare strategies which appeal to the 'British Nation' or 'British interests' for the racism they, consciously or otherwise, generate.

Finally, this internationalist perspective forces us to reconsider on what basis welfare capitalism can progress. In the past the welfare state has represented – at some expense to women and considerable neglect of Black and other immigrants – an accommodation of capital's and labour's interests to guarantee social reproduction. But as Hilary Rose points out, 'even this view of the welfare state being about the gains of the male working class and the sacrifice of women – a history of partial progress at best – is precluded by the new forms of industrialisation' (Rose, 1986: 87).

These new forms of industrialization are the ones described by Mitter and Sivanandan earlier – the movement of capital and production to some Third World economies, high unemployment in Britain, with a labour market increasingly divided between a highly skilled, high-waged, mainly white male sector and a low-waged/ part-time/unemployed sector of women, unskilled men, young people and Black people, men and women, young and unskilled. In other words some acknowledgement is required, as Rose puts it, of 'the international dimensions of the crisis, in which production work is being moved out of the old societies, throwing into question the extent of the state's commitment to guarantee social reproduction' and secondly of 'the centrality of women within the crisis both within the deindustrialising and the industrialising societies' (1986: 92).

This chapter has examined some of the main aspects in the relationship of 'race' and gender to welfare provision today in terms of the roles women and Black people play as providers of welfare, paid and unpaid, as claimants, patients, clients, tenants, parents and schoolchildren, and as people struggling, in any of these roles, over welfare issues. Such an examination has revealed a whole range of important issues: of caring – who cares for whom, why, and how – of dependency, of the relationship between home and work, of immigration controls on Black people, of the way the economic, political and cultural relations between the global North and South worlds are played out within the British welfare system, of the struggles to create forms of non-sexist and non-racist welfare practice which enhance ordinary people's control over the form and nature of welfare provision, of the importance of recognizing the specific needs that arise from sex differences or diversities in culture, but without returning to a biological or cultural essentialism. I hope too I have begun to show that these are important areas for the study of welfare, but also areas that give rise to issues, demands and strategies which all those who are part of the institutions of welfare can (or will continue to) press for.

References

Barclay, P. (1982) *Social Workers: Their Role and Tasks*. London: Bedford Square Press.

Beechey, V. and Perkins, T. (1987) *A Matter of Hours: Women, Part-time Work and the Labour Market*. Cambridge: Polity Press.

Bhalla, A. and Blakemore, K. (1981) *Elders of the Ethnic Minority Groups*. London: All Faiths for One Race.

Bhavnani, K. and Coulson, M. (1986) 'Transforming Socialist-feminism: the Challenge of Racism', *Feminist Review*, 23.

Black Health Workers and Patients Group (1983) 'Psychiatry and the Corporate State', *Race and Class*, 21.

Brah, A. and Deem, R. (1986) 'Towards Anti-sexist and Anti-racist Schooling', *Critical Social Policy*, 16.

Brannen, J. and Wilson, G. (eds) (1987) *Give and Take in Families: Studies in Resource Distribution*. London: Allen & Unwin.

Bryan, B., Dadzie, S. and Scafe, S. (1985) *The Heart of the Race: Black Women's Lives in Britain*. London: Virago.

CCCS (Centre for Contemporary Cultural Studies) (1982) *The Empire Strikes Back*. London: Hutchinson.

Campbell, B. (1984) *Wigan Pier Revisited*. London: Virago.

Carby, H. (1982) 'Schooling in Babylon', in CCCS (1982).

Cohen, S. (1985) 'Anti-Semitism, Immigration Controls and the Welfare State', *Critical Social Policy*, 13.

Commission for Racial Equality (CRE) (1986) *Survey on Teaching*. London: CRE.

Coyle, A. (1985) 'Going Private: the Implications of Privatization for Women's Work', *Feminist Review*, 21.

Croft, S. (1986) 'Women, Caring and the Recasting of Need: a Feminist Reappraisal', *Critical Social Policy*, 16.

David, M. (1980) *The State, the Family and Education*. London: Routledge & Kegan Paul.

De Sousa, E. (1987) 'Racism and the YTS', *Critical Social Policy*, 20.

Doyal, L. (1979) *The Political Economy of Health*. London: Pluto.

Doyal, L. (1987) 'Infertility – a Life Sentence? Women and the National Health Service', in Stanworth (1987).

Doyal, L., Hunt, G. and Mellor, J. (1981) 'Your Life in Their Hands: Migrant Workers in the National Health Service', *Critical Social Policy*, 1(2).

Dummett, A. (ed.) (1986) *Towards a Just Immigration Policy*. London: The Cobden Trust.

Feminist Review (ed.) (1986) *Waged Work: a Reader*. London: Virago.

Ferguson, A. and Folbre, N. (1981) 'The Unhappy Marriage of Patriarchy and Capitalism', in Sargent (ed.).

Finch, J. and Groves, D. (1980) 'Community Care and the Family: a Case for Equal Opportunities', *Journal of Social Policy*, 9(4).

Gilroy, P. (1982) 'Steppin' out of Babylon – Race, Class and Autonomy', in CCCS (1982).

Gilroy, P. (1987a) *There Ain't No Black in the Union Jack*. London: Hutchinson.

Gilroy, P. (1987b) *Problems in Anti-Racist Strategy*. London: Runnymede Trust.

Gordon, P. (1983) 'Medicine, Racism and Immigration Control', *Critical Social Policy*, 7.

Gordon, P. (1984) *Deportations and Removals*. London: Runnymede Trust.

Gordon, P. (1985) *Policing Immigration, Britain's Internal Control*. London: Pluto.

Gough, I. (1979) *The Political Economy of the Welfare State*. London: Macmillan.

Graham, H. (1987) 'Being Poor: Perceptions and Coping Strategies of Lone Mothers', in Brannen and Wilson (1987).

Groves, D. (1983) 'Members and Survivors: Women and Retirement – Pensions Legislation', in Lewis (1983).

Hall, S. (1982) The lessons of Lord Scarman. *Critical Social Policy*, 2(2).

Hall, S., Critcher, C., Jefferson, T., Clarke, J. and Roberts, B. (1978) *Policing the Crisis: Mugging, the State and Law and Order*. London: Macmillan.

Hamner, J. and Maynard, M. (eds) (1987) *Women, Violence and Social Control*. London: Macmillan.

Hudson, D. (1987) 'You Can't Commit Violence against an Object: Women, Psychiatry and Psych-surgery', in Hamner and Maynard (1987).

Jacobs, S. (1985) 'Race, Empire and the Welfare State: Council Housing and Racism', *Critical Social Policy*, 13.

Joshi, H. and Carter, B. (1984) 'The Role of Labour in the Creation of a Racist Britain', *Race and Class*, 25(3).

Land, H. (1983) 'Who Still Cares for the Family? Recent Developments in Income Maintenance, Taxation and Family Law', in Lewis (1983).

Lewis, J. (ed.) (1983) *Women's Welfare – Women's Rights*. London: Croom Helm.

Mama, A. (1984) 'Black Women, the Economic Crisis and the British State', *Feminist Review*, 17.

Mitter, S. (1986) *Common Fate, Common Bond: Women in the Global Economy*. London: Pluto.

Oakley, A. (1983) 'Women and Health Policy', in Lewis (1983).

Owen, E. (ed.) (1986) *Comparing Welfare States and their Futures*. Aldershot: Gower.

Peace, S. (1986) 'The Forgotten Female: Social Policy and Older Women', in Phillipson and Walker (1986).

Phillipson, C. and Walker, A. (eds) (1986) *Ageing and Social Policy: a Critical Assessment*. Aldershot: Gower.

Piven, F. and Cloward, R. (1972) *Regulating the Poor: the Function of Public Welfare*. London: Tavistock.

Rakusen, J. (1981) 'Depo-Provera: the Extent of the Problem. A Case Study in the Politics of Birth Control', in Roberts (1981).

Rex, J. (1984) 'Black Marks for a White Paper', *Guardian*, 15 February.

Riley, D. (1983) *War in the Nursery: Theories of the Child and Mother*. London: Virago.

Roberts, H. (ed.) (1981) *Women, Health and Reproduction*. London: Routledge & Kegan Paul.

Rose, H. (1985) 'Women's Refuges: Creating New Forms of Welfare?' in Ungerson (1985).

Rose, H. (1986) 'Women and the Restructuring of the Welfare State', in Owen (1986).

Sargent, L. (ed.) (1981) *Women and Revolution*. London: Pluto Press.

Sivanandan, A. (1982) 'Race Awareness Training and the Degradation of Black Struggle', *Race and Class*, 26.

Solomos, J. (1985) 'Problems, but Whose Problems? The Social Construction of Black Youth Unemployment', *Journal of Social Policy*, 14(4).

Stanworth, M. (1981) *Gender and Schooling, a Study of Sexual Divisions in the Classroom*. London: Hutchinson.

Stanworth, M. (ed.) (1987) *Reproductive Technologies: Gender, Motherhood and Medicine*. Cambridge: Polity Press.

Storey, H. (1986) 'United Kingdom Immigration Controls and the Welfare State', in Dummett (1986).

Study Commission on the Family (1980) *Happy Families? A Discussion Paper on Families in Britain*. London: Study Commission on the Family.

Study Commission on the Family (1983) *Families in the Future*. London: Study Commission on the Family.

Ungerson, C. (ed.) (1985) *Women and Social Policy. A Reader*. London: Macmillan.

Ungerson, C. (1987) *Policy is Personal: Sex, Gender and Informal Care*. London: Tavistock.

Walker, A. (1982) 'The Meaning and Social Division of Community Care', in A. Walker (ed.) *Community Care: the Family, the State and Social Policy*. Oxford: Blackwell.

Warnock, M. (1985) *A Question of Life: the Warnock Report on Human Fertilization and Embryology*. Oxford: Blackwell.

IV
SOCIAL SCIENCE AND
SOCIAL PROBLEMS

Platt's chapter is a spirited defence of the value of social science in the development of social policy. Defence is needed because the social sciences (and sociology particularly) have been strongly attacked in recent years from both Right and Left on the grounds of bias. The political Right especially has blamed sociology and sociologists for biased research on issues such as the extent of poverty and whether health inequalities have widened between social classes. The Right has come to view sociology as a left-wing subject which seeks to lay the blame · for social problems on governments rather than on individuals and which does so by using jargon as a way of driving out common sense or 'what everybody knows'. It was not always so, and Platt comments on the comparatively recent identification of sociology with left-wing opinion. She attacks the hostile charges of political bias and of excessive jargon and argues for the continued importance of the social sciences in helping to develop a basis for the state's intervening in a rational way to alleviate poverty, ill-health, homelessness and other social problems.

The social sciences are relatively new as a university subject and as a discipline for research. Sociology in the period up to roughly the middle 1970s was largely committed to the idea of social reform based on a careful study of the facts and an evaluation of the best means to achieve desirable ends such as better health for the population generally, sustained full employment, and adequate income in old age and sickness – the bases of the welfare state. There was consensus between public and political opinion and the social science community on the objectives which society hoped to achieve and on what means should be used to do so. This consensus was first attacked from the political Left in the late 1950s and the 1960s on the grounds that it was biased in favour of 'welfare-capitalism' and the Left argued that consensus in social science research and teaching had hidden the continued poverty and inequalities of the British welfare state. The attack from the Left was soon overwhelmed by the wider debate which the New Right initiated on the problems of Britain's economic decline. The welfare state was one of the factors which the New Right blamed for Britain's lack of competitiveness and its relative decline. Public spending, including welfare spending and the costs of some parts of higher education, came under attack and sociology was quickly singled out as neither scientific nor useful in rebuilding a Britain in which the burden of the state on private initiative and 'wealth creation' had to be rolled back.

The immediate results of the political success of the New Right was a reduction of funding for social science research together with an attack on its intellectual value and independence. The Social Science Research Council was reviewed by Lord Rothschild, who was expected to recommend a shift to contract research rather than fundamental research. The model in mind was the one that industry uses in funding scientific and technological research, where the funders specify the research objectives closely and where results are expected on schedule. Lord Rothschild failed to deliver quite what the Thatcher government wanted (though the word 'science' was removed and the SSRC became the Economic and Social Research Council) but the funding for pure or fundamental research in the social sciences was markedly reduced. The ESRC is the poor relation of the Research Councils (covering Medical, Science and Engineering, Natural Environment and Agriculture and Food) which fund basic research of the sort which is too long-term or fundamental to attract industry and commerce. Most funding for social science research comes from other sources, particularly local and central government departments. The proportion now coming from just two central government departments (the Training Agency and the Department of Education and Science) eclipses the funding to the ESRC (*Economic Trends*, 1989) and in financial terms, research contracting has come to dominate basic research in the social sciences in the past ten years. Under research contracts of the type favoured by government (imitating private sector research contracts in science and engineering) the funder sets the research objectives and asks for bids to deliver the evidence. The critical and sceptical inquiry which Platt says characterizes social science research has become a minority pursuit when measured in terms of money input.

However, independent and critical social science research is far from dead. Much social research is small-scale, conducted by university and polytechnic teachers as part of their work, and here the New Right attacks on teachers in higher education has been less successful than the cutbacks in the funding of 'big' research through the ESRC or the agenda-setting of the big funders in central government departments. Halsey (1989) and Pahl and Westergaard (1989) believe that the tide has turned in the drive to reduce the importance of sociology and the number of sociologists in British higher education, and that the fear of the virtual disappearance of critical social science which was held in the early 1980s has gone. Not having to rely on sources of funding for research which dictate the issues to be investigated (and to some extent the ways in which inquiries are to be conducted) means that independent and critical research is still alive and well in Britain.

References

Economic Trends (1989) 'Research and Development in the United Kingdom in 1987', Central Statistical Office. August: 90.

Halsey, A.H. (1989) 'The Turning of the Tide', *British Journal of Sociology*, 40(3).

Pahl, R. and Westergaard, J. (1989) 'The University Grants Committee's Review of Sociology', *British Journal of Sociology*, 40(3).

19

The contribution of social science

Jennifer Platt

Social science is one of the major areas of intellectual life in advanced societies, yet it seems to be especially exposed to criticism. There are oddities about the treatment of social science as compared with other areas of knowledge. Natural science is not criticized for its incomprehensible jargon; its need for special technical terms is taken for granted, and non-scientists do not expect to understand them. Politicians may suggest that sociology departments be closed down because they are of no practical use, but fail to note that by this criterion departments of literature are even stronger candidates for closure. Why is this?

Social science is exposed to particular criticism because it has a special position. It is indeed potentially useful; when it is applied to policy issues these are often contentious ones, where combatants think from pre-established positions. It is about subjects close to everyday experience, where everyone feels themselves concerned and qualified to comment. Thus it makes its claims in areas where others have their own reasons to contest them. How far can these claims be justified?

We shall approach the issue by considering the criticisms made, and the weight that can be attached to them. We shall take it for granted that the ideal of a systematic and disciplined study of social life is an attractive one, and that the issue is whether it is or can be done well enough. We shall need to bear in mind that social science is a large and varied enterprise, ranging from comparative studies of political systems to individual psychology, from detailed qualitative studies of tribal societies to computer modelling of advanced industrial economies; what is true of one part of it may well not be true of another.

Evaluations of social science – as of anything else – may be either absolute or relative. Absolute judgements assess how far it is inherently a Good or a Bad Thing, while relative judgements compare its merits with those of alternatives. Relatively speaking, the better alternative is to be preferred even if it is not very good; absolutely speaking, Good Things are chosen and Bad Things rejected. (In reality, of course, life is not as simple as this; in particular, even Good Things have costs which need to be taken into account.) On a practical matter, relative judgements are more relevant than absolute ones. The question, then, of the alternatives to social science, or the standards with which it is being compared, must be raised. Three comparisons are common, though they may not be made explicit: common sense, natural science, and perfection. Common sense is actually an alternative, since we could do without social science and use common sense instead. The other two provide standards by which actual social science may be judged inferior, but do not themselves constitute alternatives; the implied alternatives are either the improvement of social science, or once again the substitution of common sense.

The standard of perfection is a fine one to aspire towards, but nothing can be dismissed as useless because it is less than perfect; the question is whether it is at least moderately useful, and how we can do better.

Comparisons with natural science usually rest on an image of it as finding out, by conclusive methods, more and more true and undisputed facts, all of which are instantly applied to improve our standard of living. This image is often supported by reference to the work of philosophers who have written about the logic of science, even though they do not share the image. Popper, for instance, sees all knowledge as provisional, and explanatory theory, which does not simply follow from the facts, as science's central intellectual focus; he emphasizes the crucial importance to good science of searching for potential refutations of theories (Magee, 1973). Sir Keith Joseph, when Secretary of State for Education, invoked Popper's conception of science as a reason for not regarding the social sciences as really 'scientific', and so for cutting their funds. In doing so he revealed his ignorance of the many studies by social scientists (such as Collins, 1985; Gilbert and Mulkay, 1984) which show that in practice in natural science facts are disputed, evidence is often equivocal and open to rival interpretations, scientists do not accept apparent refutations of their theories, theories are in conflict. And, of course, much natural science is not immediately applicable, or is applied in ways whose advantages can be questioned.

What about the common-sense alternative? The attraction of common sense stems from a dilemma for the social scientist which has often been noted. If social-scientific findings agree with common sense, they are seen as obvious; if they do not, they are rejected. But is that rejection justified? And are 'obvious' findings worth making with all the panoply of social science? That depends on the merits of common sense. On this, let us quote a classic source, a review of the results of US Army research in the Second World War:

> 1   Better educated men showed more psychoneurotic symptoms. . .(The mental instability of the intellectual. . .has often been commented on.). . .
> 3   Southern soldiers were better able to stand the climate in the hot South Sea islands than Northern soldiers (of course, Southerners are more accustomed to hot weather).
> 4   White privates were more eager to become non-coms [NCOs] than Negroes. (The lack of ambition among Negroes is almost proverbial.). . .
> But why, since they are so obvious, is so much money and energy given to establish such findings? . . .*Every one of these statements is the direct opposite*

of what actually was found...If we have mentioned the actual results of the investigation first, the reader would have labelled these 'obvious' also. [Lazarsfeld, 1949: 380]

The more different 'obvious' positions there are, the easier it is to feel that a finding is 'only' common sense. The real problem is to show *which* common-sense position, if any, is adequate.

Common sense is likely to be inadequate because of its sources. All everyday experience is partial, and reflects the social location of the person both in the range of knowledge it confers and the perspective on it that it gives. Everyone is tempted to generalize from their own experience, but no one has good reason to do so. Another way in which everyday experience may be inappropriately generalized is when conclusions which are justified for the individual or the household are extended to larger social wholes: it is highly questionable, for instance, whether ideas about balanced budgets which work well for families have the same effects for national economies. (I remember a *Manchester Guardian* piece by Michael Frayn in which he remarked that, contrary to the item in the financial news, money still seemed to be in quite heavy demand around his neighbourhood; indeed, the milkman insisted on being paid.) Another source of common sense, paradoxically, is social science. As Keynes pointed out long ago, '...practical men, who believe themselves to be quite exempt from any intellectual influence, are usually the slaves of some defunct economist...' (Merton, 1981: 42). This points to another problem of recognition for social science, whether up to date or out of date. The more successfully it is diffused, the less likely it is to continue to be recognized as social science. Merton (1981) shows how terms like 'in-group', 'white-collar crime' and 'charisma' have become part of the general vocabulary. Originally surprising findings, like the importance of class background to educational achievement, become part of the conventional wisdom. Abrams calls this the 'Cheshire Cat problem': disappearing social science (1985: 202).

Common sense, therefore, does not provide a satisfactory alternative, since, whatever the personal conviction it inevitably carries, neither its content nor its sources are such that they will stand up to close examination. But social science is criticized on many other grounds besides its failure to agree with common sense: let us turn now to consider these criticisms.

Who makes such criticisms? Some of them are made from within social science, and pit Freudian against behaviourist, monetarist against Keynesian, positivist against interpretivist. These are not attacks on social science as such, but advocate one version of it rather than another, so we shall not be concerned with them. Our main focus will be on the criticisms made by politicians and practical men (sic), or by students or general readers. They include these assertions:

(a) It is incomprehensible and full of ugly jargon.
(b) It is too abstract.
(c) It is a soft option, not a real discipline.
(d) It is left-wing, ideological indoctrination.
(e) It has no definite conclusions, and is full of disagreements.
(f) It is irrelevant, impractical, not applicable.

What can we reply?

Jargon and incomprehensibility are relative. The outsider's jargon is the insider's indispensable technical term. When technical terms catch on with outsiders their origins are forgotten and they cease to be regarded as jargon. But it is not reasonable to expect instant understanding in a specialized field, even if it is human to do so when the field deals with one's own life. It is arguable that social science has a special need for technical terms in order to encourage the detachment, and the transcendence of common sense, which are especially hard to achieve. This does not mean that there is no unnecessary jargon, or that the jargon chosen is not ugly; it does means that particular instances need to be judged on their individual merits, and that the standard to apply is whether the usage conveys a meaning which could not be conveyed more simply.

Abstraction is one of the reasons for jargon; special terms are needed for ideas that cut across the specifics of daily experience. Social scientists vary in the level of abstraction at which they work. Some social science is extremely concrete: Burgess's *Experiencing Comprehensive Education* (1983), for instance, is full of rich historical detail about a particular school and its members. But even some very detailed and concrete studies have more abstract parts. Lacey's *Hightown Grammar* (1970), another detailed school study, describes the processes observed in a streamed grammar school as 'differentiation' and 'polarization'; Becker's (1963) studies of marijuana users and jazz musicians led to conclusions about 'deviance'. Such abstraction is necessary to go beyond the particular instance: theories of 'deviance' apply to burglars and transvestites as well as pot-smokers and jazz musicians. Whether the same theory can really account for the deviance of all these groups is an *empirical* question which can only be answered by more research. But if it can, it is a good theory: both a more impressive intellectual achievement, and of wider practical use. 'There is nothing so practical as a good theory' (Myrdal, 1958: 230). Basic research not originally aimed at practical problems may nonetheless turn out to be highly relevant to them; for example, the technique of 'conversation analysis' has been fruitfully applied to improve consultations between doctors and patients (Heath, 1986).

However, there is another sense of abstractness which does not depend on the use of abstract words. Many general theories abstract from the complexity of real situations to deal with only a few factors at a time. It is impossible to study everything at once. Social scientists cannot usually, like many natural scientists, deal with the problem by creating an artificial experimental situation. No single theory can account for all the details of an actual historical situation; there always has to be an 'other things being equal' clause, which points to further factors which will need to be taken into account in particular cases. That does not mean that there is anything wrong with the theory, any more than there is with the equivalent theories of physics. It does mean that the theory cannot on its own make plausible predictions about real cases, and some economists provide examples of the dangers of doing so. There have been areas of economic theory which assume that people have perfect knowledge about how to maximize their economic advantages, and so act purely on the basis of rational expectations, or that there are markets which operate without banks or trade unions: it is plain that these are not realistic assumptions. (See chapters by Hutchison and Morishima in Wiles and Routh [1984].) The fact that such errors can be made does not condemn abstraction as such.

Are the social sciences a soft option, lacking in real discipline? The plausibility of this suggestion may depend on which bit of the social sciences one is thinking of: it is hard to imagine anyone applying it to the technical rigours of econometrics, or the elaborate experimental design of laboratory psychology – or, for that matter, to the theorizing of Max Weber, or the tough fieldwork of anthropologists in alien settings. At the student level, the social sciences ask for philosophical self-consciousness and critical judgement rather than rote learning, as well as the continuous disciplining of theory by facts, which is not the sign of a soft option. It may be that some parts of the total range of social-scientific activity lack intellectual discipline, but others certainly do not, so the generalization is not a plausible one.

What about the disagreements among social scientists? First, some of them are not about social science, but about personal values. If two economists give different priorities to fighting unemployment and inflation, they will disagree about what should be done even if they are in perfect agreement about what causes have which effects. Secondly, some apparent disagreements arise because people are playing different roles in the intellectual division of labour, or not really working on the same problem. Thus, for instance, a psychologist explaining suicide is likely to stress individual mental states like depression which lead to the suicide; a sociologist studying the 'same' problem is likely to treat such states as merely intermediate in the chain of causation, and to stress the social characteristics of those who do and do not commit suicide and to assume that these cause depression. Such differences are not irreconcilable. Thirdly, some differences are a necessary part of intellectual progress:

perhaps part of the process of paradigm change (Kuhn, 1970), perhaps due to fresh findings having new implications for old theories, perhaps because speculation has not yet been disciplined by data. In the early 1960s it became fashionable to suggest, on the basis of rather limited evidence, that 'affluent' manual workers were becoming middle class. Once the arguments involved had been closely analysed, and data collected which were specifically planned to throw light on this issue and refuted the earlier interpretations, these suggestions were no longer made (Goldthorpe et al., 1969).

The extent to which it is impossible in social science to reach agreement has been very much exaggerated and, as Flew (1976: Ch. 2), Mann (1981) and Collins (1986: 1344) have pointed out, no one really consistently believes this in practice – indeed, if they did they would not attempt rational argument to prove the point. Lukes's (1981) argument about the contested nature of theories, and their under-determination by the data, appears to rest on the implied definition of 'theory'. He says that social theories come in packages which include moral and political positions – but cannot the strictly social-scientific theories be disengaged from those positions? Lukes himself recognizes (p. 403) that, in his example of different theories of the state, the accounts offered may be empirically equivalent, but curiously fails to conclude that, in that case, there is no real *social-scientific* dispute. Writers disagree on what level of resources should be called 'poverty' and defined as a social problem, but that is a quite different sort of disagreement from the technical ones which may arise, and do get resolved, over how to measure levels of resources. (And if they are not resolved, those disagreeing can still agree on what the underlying facts are.) The nearer a theory is to having empirical implications, the more open it is to the possibility of agreement at least at these levels; if it does not have any empirical implications, what use is it as social science? Yes, that is an evaluative judgement. It has been fashionable in recent years to stress disagreements, and to organize knowledge in terms of 'approaches'. There is no space here to go into the philosophical issues, but in practice the effect of this epistemological despair or anarchism is to discourage serious attempts to find out the way things really are. It is only by acting *as if* there were a definite reality waiting to be found out that we can establish the limits to that working assumption. I maintain, therefore, that while some disagreements may be necessary and fruitful the inherent necessity of others has been very much exaggerated.

The claim that the social sciences are ideological or indoctrinatory is in part connected with the theme of disagreement, since if differences cannot be resolved rationally choices may be made on ideological grounds. However, if social scientists inevitably disagree at least they can't all be left-wing! But the real issue is not whether social scientists are personally left-wing – there is some evidence that they are more so than members of other academic disciplines (Halsey and Trow, 1971; Ch. 15; Lipset and Ladd, 1972) – but whether their intellectual product is. There is a sense in which social science is inherently disturbing or critical, because to look for explanations of what is normally taken for granted as natural, or to show as much interest in the perspectives of underdogs as of dominant groups, runs counter to the norms of everyday behaviour (cf. Berger, 1963: Ch. 2). However, this should make social science as disturbing to left-wing as to right-wing regimes, as indeed the constraints on it in the Soviet Union suggest that it is. It is arguable that a full grasp of the complexity of society is likely to lead to perception of the extreme difficulty of bringing about intentional social change, and thus promotes 'right-wing' conclusions, even if these are reached with regret. Ignorance can be bliss – which is one of the reasons why practical people tend to object to what social scientists have to offer them as too hedged about with qualifications (cf. Shipman, 1976: 151).

Sociology, probably the discipline most often seen as left wing, has been attacked from the Left (for example, Nicolaus, 1972; Shaw, 1972) as much as from the Right (for example, Scruton, 1985, 1986a and b; Dale, 1984). But Scruton acknowledges the existence of some exceptions to his generalizations, and many of the critics from the Left are themselves sociologists and so exceptions to their own argument. Respected historians of sociology (for example Nisbet, 1968) have shown that many of its central ideas are drawn from conservative traditions of thought. Recent intellectual fashion in this country, some of it institutionalized (in the Open University as elsewhere) by recruitment of those young during the great expansion of the social sciences of the 1960s and 1970s with their preoccupations, has been left wing, but one has only to look at the much-criticized American sociology of the 1950s to see that this is not an inherent feature of sociology as such. Indeed, it has also been asserted that, since the money to fund research is only in the hands of dominant groups, empirical work inevitably reflects their interests whatever the personal views of those doing the research. This has some plausibility, although one has only to recall such work as that of Becker (1963), Willis (1977) or Young and Willmott (1957) to realize that many cases do not fit the generalization.

I conclude that those who see social science as potentially subversive of any status quo are right, but that to treat it as inherently left wing in any more specific sense is an error.

Whether being left or right wing is undesirable social-scientifically, rather than simply from a right- or left-wing position, can be questioned. If it is possible to detect a bias, that implies that it is possible to delineate an unbiased position from which the biased one deviates. If the political position enters only into the conclusions drawn for action, that leaves it possible for others with different values to draw other conclusions. If it leads to an unbalanced choice of topics or to unjustified interpretations of the evidence, these are indeed to be regretted – but they can be corrected by further research and other interpretations, and can occur for reasons (such as funding bias, stupidity) other than political bias. Moreover, it can sometimes be valuable, as Lakatos (1970) and Feyerabend (1975) have argued for the natural sciences, to persist with a certain viewpoint despite conflicting evidence. (The grounds on which they argue this are, for instance, that this will keep open the possibility of finding that the evidence conflicted only superficially, will ensure that a theory necessary to guide research is retained until a replacement has been found, and will lead to the choice of unfashionable directions and the discovery of fresh data.)

Left- (or right-) wing bias is, of course, an advantage for users interested in the implementation of left- (or right-) wing policies, and that thought may lead into our discussion of the applicability of social science. It directs attention to the fact that it takes two to tango: application involves *two* parties. If, for instance, industrialists are prepared to use social science only if it confirms their preconceptions, or politicians will draw on it only if it supports policies they plan to implement in any case, much of it will not be used – but that does not mean it is not usable. Another factor is that the characteristic styles and problems of practitioners and of social scientists differ. Social scientists lay most emphasis on the phenomena they see as the fundamental causes, while practitioners are interested in what they can do something about and do not see 'theoretical' discussions of variables they cannot manipulate as useful. Practitioners need to make *decisions now*, on the basis of whatever information they can get, while social scientists are reluctant to make clear-cut statements about complex situations requiring further research; this can lead to a preference for charlatans, whose messages are simple and unqualified. Practitioners mix mostly with practitioners, social scientists are primarily oriented towards an academic audience; both sides may thus be unaware of possible connections, or have difficulty in translating the other side's statements into their own terms. Thus division of labour creates barriers, although special efforts or the creation of intermediary roles may overcome them. (For documentation and further discussion of these points, see Abrams [1985], Bulmer [1978], Shipman (1976) and Thomas [1985].)

Despite these problems, much social science is used even by those who criticize it. Those in control of the money are prepared to pay for the kinds of social science which directly support their ends: politicians of all parties are eager consumers of poll results, and have apparently shown much interest in Atkinson's (1984) work on which features of speeches attract applause; and there is a thriving market research industry. More polemically, one might observe that when the Government goes to the trouble of changing the basis on which the unemployment statistics are compiled, or partially suppresses the Black Report (Townsend and Davidson, 1982) on class differences in health, it is paying tribute to the powerful relevance of social-scientific data. Yet governments hostile to social science, like the Thatcher government, cannot avoid drawing on a whole range of social-scientific contributions for the daily business of government. The Treasury is deeply involved in economic forecasting; the Family Expenditure Survey provides the foundations for the cost of living index; the Census provides basic information used for planning both nationally and locally . . . and so on.

However, such direct use of social-scientific material for policy is much less likely outside the sphere of official statistics. The rationalistic model by which social science provides the data on which policy-makers immediately act does not fit the realities well, but that does not mean that research does not affect policy. The recommendations made by *Family and Kinship in East London* (Young and Willmott, 1957) were not implemented, but there can be little doubt that it affected the climate of opinion by drawing attention to the way in which housing is intertwined with social relationships. Work on the distribution of income within the family (Pahl, 1984) contributes to undermining the official assumption that the family should be treated as a single economic unit. The development of methods such as the social survey, the input-output table, cost-benefit analysis or the intelligence test has made a vital contribution to research carried out for policy purposes and to the policies implemented. Consumers and pressure groups often use social-scientific data to support their cases, and policy-makers respond to their pressures. Morever, it is not only 'policy-makers' who may make practical use of research. *Where?*, a magazine on education for parents, used to quote in its advertising the finding that parental interest improved children's achievement in school. It seems very likely that some parents acted on this message. (Am I the only parent who, when choosing a secondary school for our daughter, took with me to open evenings a checklist from Rutter et al. [1979] of the characteristics of schools which make a difference?) Thus there are many ways in which social science is applied indirectly and in the longer run.

Indeed, it is clear that many aspects of social science have developed in response to social demand, even market forces. This could be taken as evidence of prostitution, but it is also evidence of utility. (The resources needed for large-scale empirical research are such that very few private individuals can, like Booth [1902–3] or Rowntree [1901], provide them themselves. Charities, pressure groups and educational bodies as well as government and industry fund research.) It has a special link with the rise of the multi-functional modern state, which needs information for many of its activities, and in particular with the democratic state, which both wishes to know and adjust to the impact of its activities on citizens and is under constant pressure to justify its actions to the opposition and to special-interest groups.

But social science cannot be accounted for only in terms of social usefulness, or distinguished so simply from other aspects of society. It is itself, like every other form of knowledge, a social product, and it is part of the self-consciousness of a self-conscious age. Horton (1971), in a fascinating paper on the similarities and differences between African traditional thought and Western science, argues that the key difference between traditional and scientifically oriented cultures is that the latter are 'open' in the sense that they have a high awareness of alternatives to the established body of theory, and that this openness is produced by special social circumstances. His arguments are as applicable to social science as to natural science. But he also points out that most lay members of the 'scientific' cultures may be no more 'open' than the African peasant. This may contribute towards the tendency for some social-scientific theories to be used as religion. Gellner (1985) suggests that this has been true of psychoanalysis, especially in America; Marxism in the USSR is clearly a state religion (Lane, 1981), and functions as a less official religion for some true believers in the West. I would not myself follow Comte, the founder of sociology, in *recommending* social science as religion, but such realities should not be ignored. Less controversial is its role in relation to values and 'philosophies of life' more generally. Not only are social facts relevant to values, even if they cannot determine them, but there is a long tradition in social science of critical discussion of society and its underlying trends, and the nature of the good society and how to achieve it. Some very distinguished 'theory' is of this nature, and makes a contribution to society quite different from that of the more 'scientific' aspects of social science. (On these topics, cf. Berger, 1963: Ch. 2.) Some ages express themselves in theology, some in literature; it can be argued that it is characteristic of our age that it expresses many of its values in the forms of social science.

Whether social science in this wider sense should be regarded as cause or as effect is ambiguous. It is probably both. Scruton (1986a) argues that some social science has had pernicious moral consequences, undermining the sense of individual responsibility by explaining instead of blaming. One may doubt that a social science likely to have such consequences could have arisen, or had such significant influence, unless other social forces were also at work. It may be no more reasonable to blame the intellectual content of social science for some of the things done in its name than it is to blame Christianity for torture and wars in its name. But social science could have such consequences even if all its conclusions were fully justified by the evidence. Should the truth therefore be suppressed? There is a real moral dilemma, which Scruton does not explore.

To impute such fundamental effects to social science is, at any rate, certainly not to undervalue its social role. Some social science may be weak, limited or misguided; it has that in common with parts of all other major human activities, including natural science. This does not prevent social science from also making major social and scientific contributions. It is such a fundamental part of the consciousness of the age that it has its ripples well beyond the boundaries of academic life, even if the conclusions of its research are seldom directly used in the formulation of policy. They could usefully make a larger contribution there, but for this to occur it is not only social science that would need to change. To say that there is no satisfactory alternative to social science sounds negative, but is really an important positive point; we cannot do without it. To think of social science only in the context of policy intervention is too narrow. Understanding and explanation are to be valued even when we understand or explain why no change is desirable, or desirable change cannot be achieved by intervention at all, or except at too great cost. The defining enterprise of social science is not intervention, even though it has much to contribute to the elucidation of social issues and the discussion of possible interventions.

References

Abrams, P. (1985) 'The Uses of British Sociology, 1831–1981', in Bulmer, M. (ed.) *Essays on the History of British Sociological Research*. Cambridge: Cambridge University Press.

Atkinson, M. (1984) *Our Masters' Voices*. London: Methuen.

Becker, H. S. (1963) *Outsiders*. New York: The Free Press.

Berger, P. L. (1963) *Invitation to Sociology*. Harmondsworth: Penguin.

Booth, C. (1902–3) *Life and Labour of the People of London*. London: Macmillan.

Bulmer, M. (ed.) (1978) *Social Policy Research*. London: Macmillan.

Burgess, R. G. (1983) *Experiencing Comprehensive Education*. London: Methuen.

Collins, H. M. (1985) *Changing Order*. London: Sage.

Collins, R. (1986) 'Is 1980s Sociology in the Doldrums?', *American Journal of Sociology* 91: 1336–55.

Dale, D. (1984) 'The Politics of Crime', *The Salisbury Review* 3(1): 13–17.

Feyerabend, P. (1975) *Against Method*. London: New Left Books.

Flew, A. (1976) *Sociology, Equality and Education*. London: Macmillan.

Gellner, E. (1985) *The Psychoanalytic Movement*. London: Granada.

Gilbert, G. N. and Mulkay, M. (1984) *Opening Pandora's Box*. Cambridge: Cambridge University Press.

Goldthorpe, J. H., Lockwood, D., Bechhofer, F. and Platt, J. (1969) *The Affluent Worker in the Class Structure*. Cambridge: Cambridge University Press.

Halsey, A. H. and Trow, M. (1971) *The British Academics*. London: Faber.

Heath, C. (1986) *The Social Organisation of Speech and Body Movement in Medical Interaction*. Cambridge: Cambridge University Press.

Horton, R. (1971) 'African Traditional Thought and Western Science', in Young, M. F. D. (ed.) *Knowledge and Control*. London: Collier-Macmillan.

Hutchison, T. W. (1984) 'Our Methodological Crisis', in Wiles and Routh (1984).

Kuhn, T. S. (1970) *The Structure of Scientific Revolutions*. Chicago, IL: University of Chicago Press.

Lacey, C. (1970) *Hightown Grammar*. Manchester: Manchester University Press.

Lakatos, I. (1970) 'Falsification and the Methodology of Scientific Research Programmes', in Lakatos, I. and Musgrove, A. (ed.) *Criticism and the Growth of Knowledge*. Cambridge: Cambridge University Press.

Lane, C. (1981) *The Rites of Rulers*. Cambridge: Cambridge University Press.

Lazarsfeld, P. F. (1949) 'The American Soldier – An Expository Review', *Public Opinion Quarterly* 13: 377–404.

Lipset, S. M. and Ladd, E. C. (1972) 'The Politics of American Sociologists', *American Journal of Sociology* 78: 67–104.

Lukes, S. (1981) 'Fact and Theory in the Social Sciences', in Potter, D. (ed.) *Society and the Social Sciences*. London: Routledge & Kegan Paul/The Open University Press.

Magee, B. (1973) *Popper*. London: Fontana.

Mann, M. (1981) 'Socio-logic', *Sociology* 15: 544–50.

Merton, R. K. (1981) 'Our Sociological Vernacular', *Columbia* (November), pp. 42–4.

Morishima, M. (1984) 'The Good and Bad Uses of Mathematics', in Wiles and Routh (1984).

Myrdal, G. (1958) *Value in Social Theory*. London: Routledge & Kegan Paul.

Nicolaus, M. (1972) 'The Professional Organisation of Sociology: A View from Below', in Blackburn, R. (ed.) *Ideology in Social Science*. London: Fontana.

Nisbet, R. A. (1968) *Tradition and Revolt*. New York: Random House.

Pahl, J. (1984) 'The Allocation of Money within the Household', in Freeman, M. (ed.) *The State, the Law and the Family*. London: Tavistock.

Rowntree, B. S. (1901) *Poverty: a Study of Town Life*. London: Macmillan.

Rutter, M., Maughan, B., Mortimore, P. and Ouston, J. (1979) *Fifteen Thousand Hours*. London: Open Books.

Scruton, R. (1985) 'Who Will Cure This Social Disease?', *The Times* (8 October).

Scruton, R. (1986a) 'Immoral Man's Survival Kit', *The Times* (25 February).

Scruton, R. (1986b) 'Sociology, Bias and Indoctrination', *Network* 35 (May): 2–3.

Shaw, M. (1972) 'The Coming Crisis of Radical Sociology', in Blackburn, R. (ed.) *Ideology in Social Science*. London: Fontana.

Shipman, M. (ed.) (1976) *The Organisation and Impact of Social Research*. London: Routledge & Kegan Paul.

Thomas, P. (1985) *The Aims and Outcomes of Social Policy Research*. London: Routledge & Kegan Paul.

Townsend, P. and Davidson, N. (eds) (1982) *The Black Report* (Report of the Department of Health and Social Security Working Group on Inequalities in Health, Sir D. Black [Chair]), Harmondsworth: Penguin.

Wiles, P. and Routh, G. (eds) (1984) *Economics in Disarray*. Oxford: Blackwell.

Willis, P. E. (1977) *Learning to Labour*. Farnborough: Saxon House.

Young, M. and Willmott, P. (1957) *Family and Kinship in East London*. London: Routledge & Kegan Paul. (See also 1986 edition for 'New introduction'.)

Index

Index compiled by Jackie McDermott

About the contributors

Norman Barry is Professor of Politics at the University of Buckingham. He has previously taught at the universities of Exeter and Queen's Belfast, and at Birmingham Polytechnic. He has written extensively in the fields of political philosophy, political economy and public policy. He is the author of *Hayek's Social and Economic Philosophy* (1979) and *An Introduction to Modern Political Theory* (1981). He has two new books scheduled for publication: *On Classical Liberalism and Libertarianism* and *The New Right*.

John Clarke is a Senior Lecturer in Social Policy at the Open University and is a member of the D211 Social Problems and Social Welfare course team. **Tom Hulley** is a part-time member of the Open University's teaching staff and a full-time carer and housewife.

Joan Cooper is Honorary Visiting Research Fellow, University of Sussex, and formerly Director, Social Work Service, DHSS, and Chair, Central Council for Education and Training in Social Work, 1984–6. She is the author of *Patterns of Family Placement, Groupwork with Elderly People in Hospital* and *The Creation of the British Personal Social Services*.

Stephen Davies is Lecturer in History at the Department of English and History, Manchester Polytechnic. He has published several articles on Scottish legal history, the history of ideas and social policy and the history of liberalism. He is currently working on a book concerned with the last of these.

Ann Davis is a qualified social worker who has worked in psychiatric hospitals and in local authority residential and field social work. She is a Lecturer in Social Work and Social Policy at Birmingham University. Her publications include *The Residential Solution* (1981) and *Women, the Family and Social Work* (1985) co-edited with Eve Brook.

John Ditch is Senior Lecturer in Social Administration and Policy at the University of Ulster at Jordanstown. He has undertaken research on such topics as Social Security, long-term unemployment and low pay. He has a special interest in the social construction of welfare, and is the author of several studies dealing with social policy in Northern Ireland.

Felicity Edholm is a social science staff tutor, working in the London Region of the Open University.

Andrew Gamble is Professor of Politics at the University of Sheffield. His publications include *The Conservative Nation* (1974) and *Britain in Decline* (second edition 1985). He is currently working on a book on the Thatcher government entitled *The Free Economy and the Strong State*.

Geoff Green is Principal Strategy Officer, Central Policy Unit, Sheffield City Council and joint author with David Blunkett of the Fabian pamphlet on municipal socialism, *Building from the Bottom: the Sheffield Experience*.

Nevil Johnson is Professorial Fellow of Nuffield College and Reader in the Comparative Study of Institutions in the University of Oxford since 1969, Honorary Editor of *Public Administration* (1967–81) and member of the Economic and Social Research Council (1981–7). His publications include *Government in the Federal Republic of Germany* (1973; second edition 1983) and *In Search of the Constitution: Reflections on State and Society in Britain* (1977).

Mary Macleod is now a Counselling Manager in a voluntary child-care agency. **Esther Saraga** is a Social Science Staff Tutor at the Open University. They worked together for ten years teaching students and workers in the voluntary and statutory sectors on child abuse at the Polytechnic of North London, where they set up the Child Abuse Studies Unit to develop a feminist approach to theory and practice on child sexual abuse.

Patrick Minford is Edward Gonner Professor of Applied Economics at the University of Liverpool, where he has been since late 1976, after spending a year as editor of the Review of the National Institute for Economic and Social Research. Prior to that he was economic adviser to HM Treasury's external division, and was with HM Treasury's Delegation in Washington, DC, during 1973 and 1974.

Jennifer Platt is Reader in Sociology at the University of Sussex. She is author of *Social Research in Bethnal Green* (1971) and

Realities of Social Research (1976), and joint author (with John H. Goldthorpe, David Lockwood and Frank Bechofer) of *The Affluent Worker: Industrial Attitudes and Behaviour, The Affluent Worker: Political Attitudes and Behaviour* and *The Affluent Worker in the Class Structure* (1968–9). Her current research is on the history of sociological research methods.

Yvette Rocheron joined the Centre for Mass Communications Research at the University of Leicester as a Research Associate in 1983. She has taught women's studies and has completed several research projects on health promotion and race relations. She has also published on AIDS and the media.

Jeremy Seabrook was born in Northampton in 1939. He worked as a teacher and a social worker from 1962 to 1975. A regular contributor to *New Society* and to the *Guardian*, he is the author of *Underprivileged* (1968), *City Close-up* (1970), *Loneliness* (1973), *Everlasting Feast* (1975), *What Went Wrong* (1978), *Mother and Son* (1979), *Unemployment* (1981), *Landscapes of Poverty* (1985) and *A World Still to Win* (with Trevor Blackwell, 1985). He has also written many radio, television and stage plays (mostly with Michael O'Neill) as well as television documentaries.

Carol Smart is Lecturer in Sociology at the University of Warwick, and formerly Director of the National Council for One-Parent Families. Her main publications include *Women, Crime and Criminology* (1976), *Women, Sexuality and Social Control* (1978) edited with Barry Smart, *The Ties that Bind* (1984), and *Women in Law* (1985) edited with Julia Brophy. She is currently writing a book on feminism and the sociology of law.

Alan Walker is Professor of Social Policy at the University of Sheffield. His publications include *Community Care* (edited, 1982), *Public Expenditure and Social Policy* (edited, 1982), *Social Planning* (1984), *Ageing and Social Policy* (edited with Chris Phillipson, 1986), plus numerous articles on social policy and related subjects.

Malcolm Wicks is the Director of the Family Policy Studies Centre and was previously Research Director and Secretary of the Study Commission on the Family. He was a Lecturer in Social Administration at Brunel University and was a Social Policy analyst in the Home Office Urban Deprivation Unit. His major publications include *Old and Cold: Hypothermia and Social Policy* (1978), and he is the co-author of *Government and Urban Poverty: Inside the*

Policy-making Process (1983). His latest book is *A Future for All: Do We Need the Welfare State?* (1987).

Fiona Williams is a Lecturer in the Department of Health and Social Welfare at the Open University. She is the author of *Social Policy: A Critical Introduction* (Polity, 1989) and co-edited with D. Atkinson *Know me as I am: An Anthology of Prose, Poetry and Art from People with Learning Difficulties* (Hodder & Stoughton, 1990). She is also a member of the editorial collective of the journal *Critical Social Policy*.